AA

ILLUSTRATED TOURING ATLAS

Produced by The Automobile Association, Fanum House, Basingstoke, Hampshire

Photographs by the AA Publications Photographic Library and the British Tourist Authority

© The Automobile Association 1983 56504

Crown Copyright Reserved. Based upon the Ordnance Survey Maps with the permission of the Controller of H M Stationery Office. The Ordnance Survey is not responsible for the accuracy of the National Grid in this production.

The contents of the publication are believed correct at the time of printing but the current position may be checked through the AA. Nevertheless the Publisher and the AA can accept no responsibility for errors or omissions or for changes in the details given.

ISBN 0 86145 128 7

Printed and bound by Graficromo S.A., Cordoba, Spain.

Cover photograph of Isabella Garden, Richmond Park, Surrey.

The Slad valley near Painswick…inspiration for Laurie Lee's novel, *Cider with Rosie*

INTRODUCTION & CONTENTS

The *Illustrated Touring Atlas* has been designed to help the motorist get the most out of travelling in Britain. A selection of the most interesting and enjoyable towns and villages which appear on each map page are described on the facing page. Important attractions are included as part of this gazetteer and many entries are illustrated with colour photographs–vividly bringing the maps to life.

This atlas can be used not only as an invaluable aid to travelling around the country, but also as a means of discovering the numerous treasures of Britain that await the motorist.

ROUTE PLANNING MAPS

If your destination is a town or village whose location you do not know, you should turn to the index section at the back of the book and find the place name you require. The name is followed by a page number and a National Grid reference. Turn to the atlas page indicated and, using the National Grid reference supplied, you can locate the place concerned.

Having located your destination in the main atlas, find the nearest large town, which also appears on the Route Planning Maps, pages IV to IX. These maps show the principal routes throughout Britain and a basic route can be planned from them. A more detailed route can then be worked out from the main atlas, taking note of the road numbers and route directions. These notes can then be used on the journey, minimising the need to stop to consult the atlas. Remember that, in general, motorways are quicker and more economical than other routes because you can maintain a more consistent speed and avoid traffic delays. If you cannot use a motorway, the primary route system should be considered. These roads are coloured green on the maps and are signposted in green on the roads.

It should be remembered that the shortest route is not necessarily the quickest, and primary routes tend to take you around towns rather than through their centres, thus avoiding delays caused by traffic lights, one way systems, etc. It is always a good idea to keep an alternative route in your mind should the road you are planning to use be the source of some delay, such as road works.

If you have a radio in your car, it is worth listening to traffic reports during the journey. Frequent bulletins are issued by national and local radio stations on road conditions, local hold-ups, etc., and these can be of great assistance to motorists in avoiding delays. This will be especially valuable if you are catching a ferry or have to keep an urgent appointment. Alteration to your route could save you from missing a boat or aeroplane. Always leave plenty of time for your journey.

On a particularly long journey allow extra time for short rest breaks. A tired driver is a hazard to himself and other road users, and the extra time spent during the journey will help ensure a safe arrival at your destination.

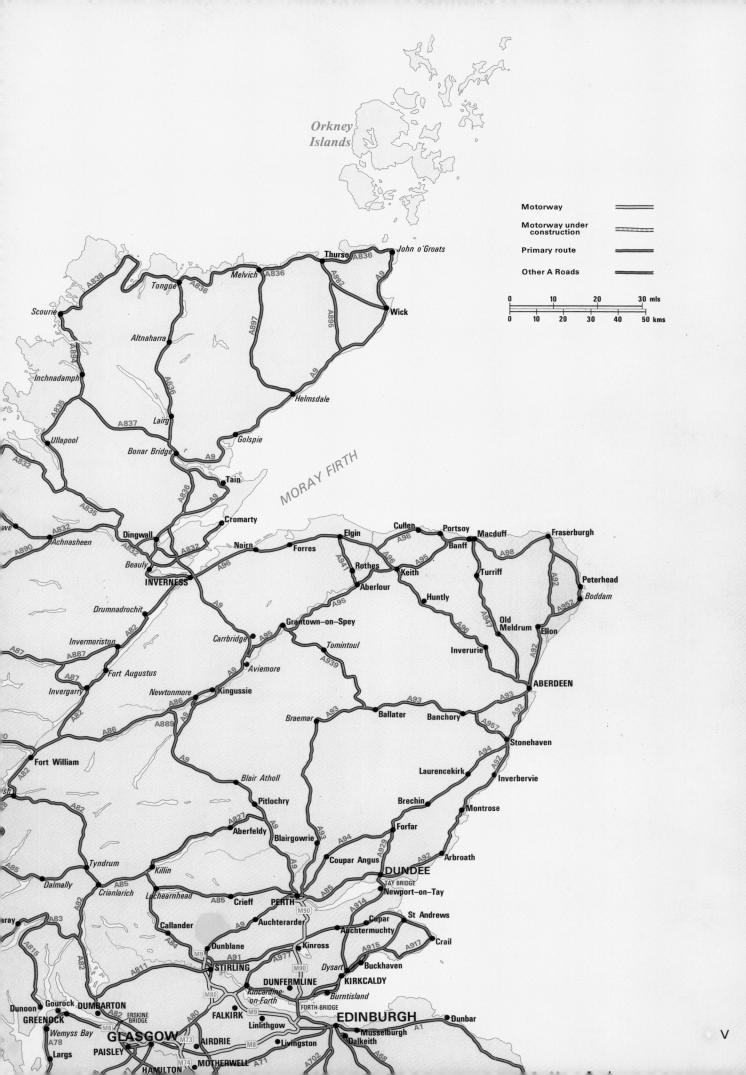

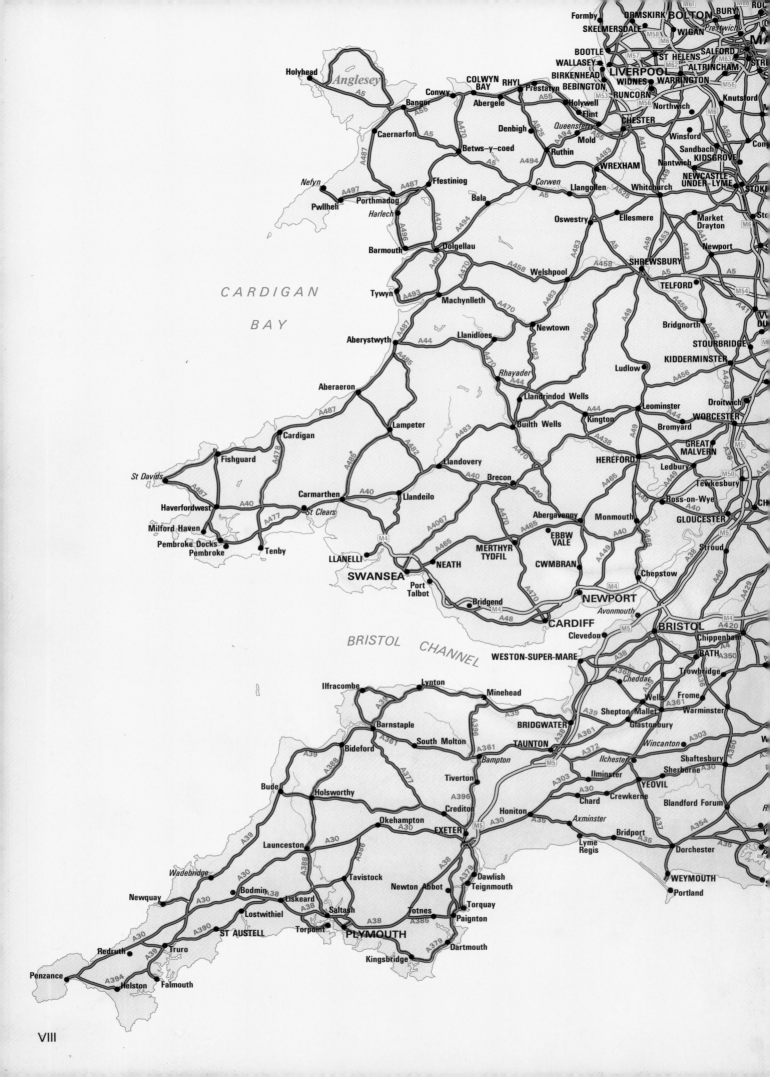

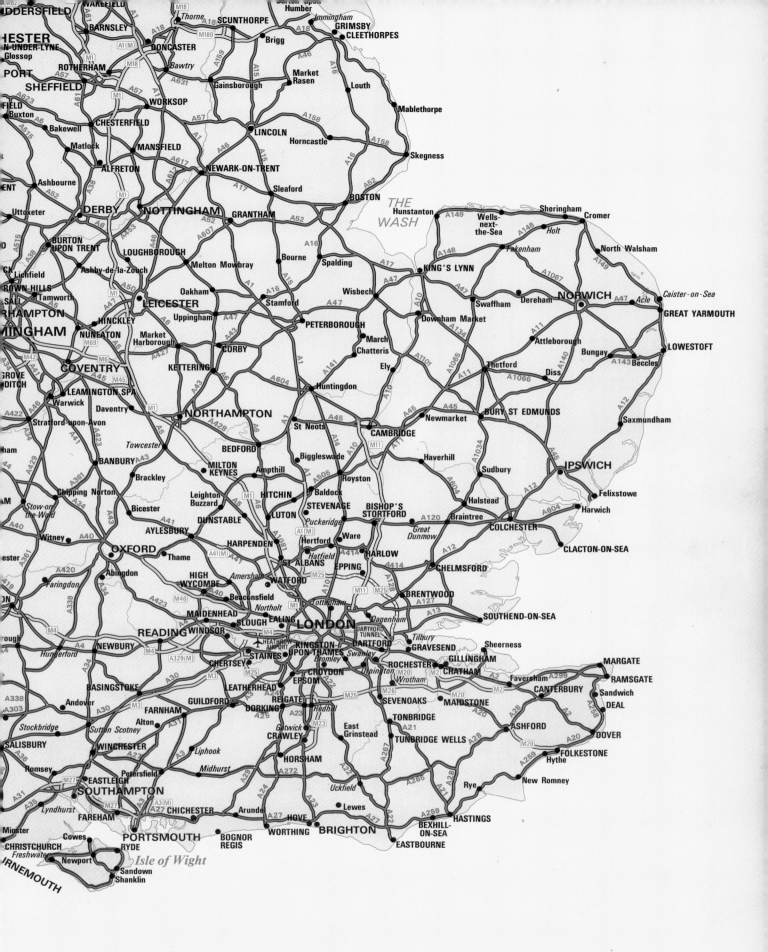

LEGEND

AUTOSTRADA	AUTOBAHN		MOTORWAY	AUTOROUTE
N. di autostrade	Autobahnnummer	M3	Motorway number	Numéro d'autoroute
Nodo stradale con e senza numeri	Anschlusstellen mit und ohne Nummern		Junctions with and without numbers	Echangeurs avec et sans numéros
Nodo stradale con entràte ed uscite limitate	Anschlusstellen mit beschränkten Auf-oder Abfahrten		Junctions with limited entries or exits	Echangeurs aux entrées ou sorties restreintes
Area di servizio	Tankstelle mit Raststätte	S	Service area	Aire de service
Autostrada e Snodo i costruzione	Im Bau befindliche Autobahn und Anschlusstelle		Motorway & Junction under construction	Autoroute et Echangeur en construction
STRADE	**STRASSEN**		**ROADS**	**ROUTES**
Rotta primaria	Hauptverbindungsstrasse	A9	Primary route	Route primaire
Altre strade A	Andere A Strasse	A129	Other A roads	Autres routes A
Strade Classe B	Strasse der Klasse B	B2137	B Roads	Routes catégorie B
Non-classificate	Nicht klassifizierte Strasse		Unclassified	Non classifiée
Corsia a due piste	Strasse mit getrennten Fahrbahnen	A7	Dual Carriageway	Double chaussée
In construzione	Im Bau befindliche Strasse		Under construction	En construction
Scozia : strade strette con aree di passaggio Scotland	Schottland: enge Strasse mit Uberholstellen		Scotland: narrow roads with passing places.	L'Écosse: Route étroite avec lieu de déplacement
SERVIZI AA DI SOCCORSO E DI INFORMAZIONI	**AA-PANNEN-UND INFORMATIONSDIENST**		**AA BREAKDOWN & INFORMATION SERVICES**	**SERVICES AA DEPANNAGE ET DE RENSEIGNEMENT**
Centro di servizio (24 ore ☎)	Dienststelle (24 Stunden ☎)	AA 24 hour	Service centre (24 hours ☎)	Station-service (24 heures ☎)
Centro di servizio (ore di lavoro normali)	Dienststelle (übliche Bürostunden)	AA	Service centre (normal office hours)	Station service (heures d'ouverture normales)
Centro di servizio autostrada	Autobahndienststelle	AA info	Motorway Information Centre	Centre-service d'autoroute
Centro di servizio strada	Strassendienststelle	AA 13	Road service centre	Centre-service de route
Centro di servizio porto	Hafendienststelle	AA	Port service centre	Centre-service de port
Telefoni AA & RAC	AA und RAC Telefonzellen	☎	AA & RAC telephones	Téléphones AA & RAC
Telefoni PTT in aree isolate	Öffentliche Telefonzellen in abgelegenen Gebieten (PO)	☎	PO telephones in isolated areas	Téléphones PTT dans endroits isolés
Area di pic-nic	Picknickplatz	PS	Picnic site	Terrain de Pique-nique
Punti di vista AA	AA-Aussichtspunkt	Bembridge Viewpoint	AA viewpoint	Points de vue AA
Inclinazione (la freccia indica in pendio)	Steigung (Pfeile weisen bergab)		Steep gradient (arrows point downhill)	Côte (la flèche est dirigée vers le bas)
Pedaggio Strada	Gebührenpflichtige Strasse	Toll	Road toll	Péage de route
Passaggio a livello	Bahnübergang	LC	Level crossing	Passage à niveau
Traghetto veicoli (Gran Bretagna)	Autofähre (Grossbritannien)	V	Vehicle ferry (Gt Britain)	Bac pour véhicules (Grande-Bretagne)
Traghetto veicoli (continentale)	Autofähre (Kontinent)	CALAIS V	Vehicle ferry (continental)	Bac pour véhicules (Continental)
Aeroporto	Flughafen	✈	Airport	Aéroport
Area urbana Villaggio	Stadtgebiet Dorf		Urban area Village	Zone urbaine Village
Confine nazionale	Nationale Grenze		National boundary	Frontière nationale
Confine di contea	Grafschaftsgrenze		County boundary	Frontière provinciale
Distanza in mille fra simboli	Entfernung zwischen Zeichen in Meilen	2	Distance in miles between symbols	Distance en milles entre symboles
A.S.M. in piedi	Ortshöhe nach Füssen	2525	Spot height in feet	Altitude en pieds anglais
Fiume e lago	Fluss und See		River and lake	Rivière et lac
Numeri di pagine di seguito	Hinweiszahlen für Anschlusskarten	13	Overlaps and numbers of continuing pages	Chiffres de guide pour cartes voisines

Scale 5 miles to 1 inch   1: 316,800

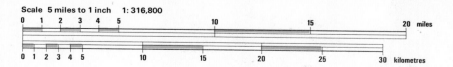

0 1 2 3 4 5 .... 10 .... 15 .... 20 miles

0 1 2 3 4 5 .... 10 .... 15 .... 20 .... 25 .... 30 kilometres

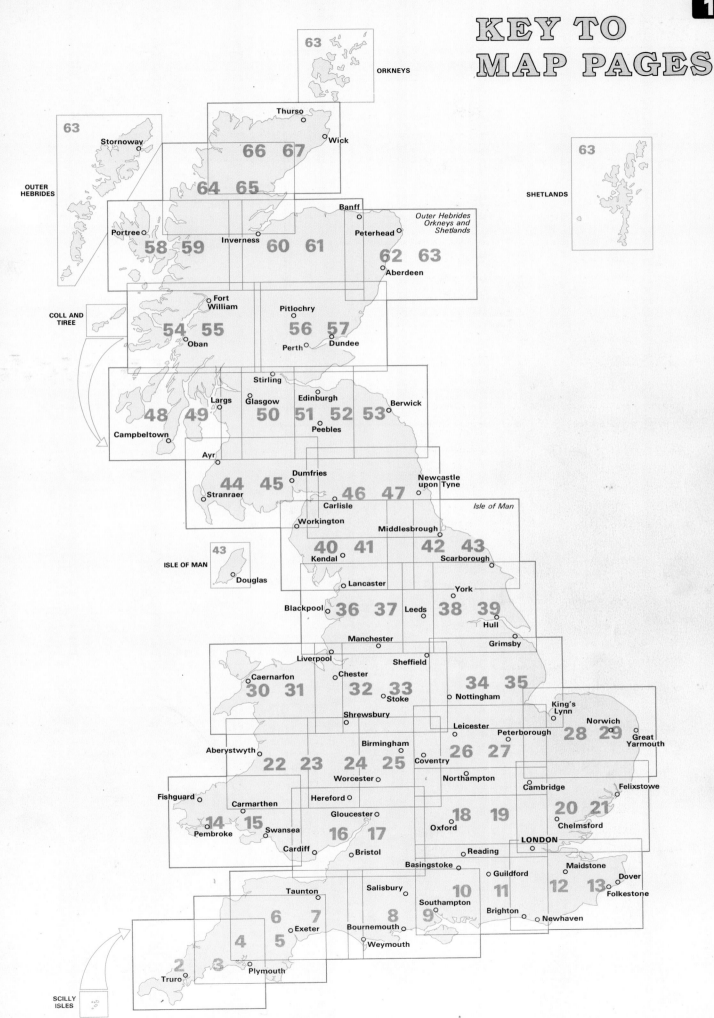

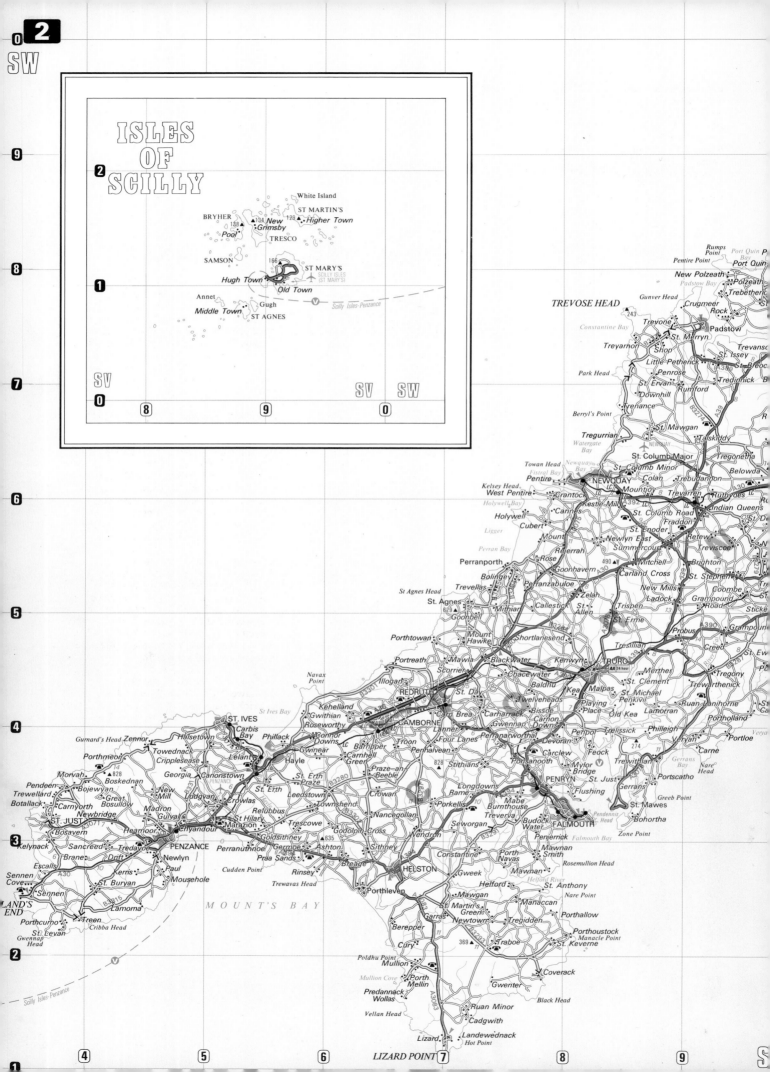

ISLES
OF
SCILLY

White Island
St Martin's
BRYHER   New   Higher Town
New Pool   Grimsby
TRESCO

SAMSON   166
ST MARY'S
Hugh Town   SCILLY ISLES
(ST MARY'S)
Old Town

Annet   Gugh
Middle Town   ST AGNES

Scilly Isles-Penzance

SV   SV   SW
0   8   9   0

Rumps
Point   Port Quin
Pentire Point   Bay
Port Quin
New Polzeath   Polzeath
Padstow Bay   Trebetherick
Gunver Head
TREVOSE HEAD   Crugmeer
Rock
Trevone   St. Merryn   Padstow
Constantine Bay   Trevanson
Treyarnon   Shop   St. Issey
Little Petherick   St. Breoc
Penrose   Tredinnick
Park Head   St. Ervan
Downhill
Trenance   Rumford
Berryl's Point
Tregurrian   St. Mawgan   Talskiddy
Watergate   Tregonetha
Bay   St. Columb Major   Belowda
Towan Head   St. Columb Minor
Fistral Bay   Colan   Trebudannon
Kelsey Head   Pentire   NEWQUAY   Mountjoy   Trevarren   Ruthvoes   Indian Queens
West Pentire   St. Columb Road
Crantock   Kestle Mill   Fraddon   St. D
Holywell Bay   Cannes
Holywell   Newlyn East   Retew
Cubert   Summercourt   Treviscoe
Ligger   Mount   Brighton
Perran Bay   Rejerrah   Mitchell   St. Stephen
Rose   Carland Cross
Perranporth   Goonhavern   New Mills
Bolingey   Coombe
Trevellas   Perranzabuloe   Zelah   Ladock   Grampound
St Agnes Head   Mithian   Callestick   St-   Trispen   Road   Sticke
St. Agnes   Goonbell   Allen   St. Erme
Porthtowan   Mount   Shortlanesend   Probus   A390
Hawke   Tresillian   Creed   Grampou
Portreath   Mawla   Blackwater   Kenwyn   TRURO   Merther   St. Ew
Navax   Scorrier   AA 24 hour   Tregony
Point   Illogan   Chacewater   Kea   St. Clement   Trewarthenick
REDRUTH   St. Day   Baldhu   Malpas   St. Michael
Kehelland   Carn Brea   Twelveheads   Penkivil   Ruan Lanihorne
St Ives Bay   Gwithian   Carharrack   Playing   Old Kea   Portholland
ST. IVES   Roseworthy   CAMBORNE   Gwennap   Bissoe   Place   Lamorran
Carbis   Connor Downs   Lanner   Carnon   Philleigh
Gurnard's Head   Zennor   Bay   Phillack   Barripper   Troon   Four Lanes   Downs   Penpol   Veryan   Portloe
Halsetown   Carnhell   Perranarworthal   Devoran   Carne
Porthmeor   Towednack   Gwinear   Green   Penhalvean   Carclew   Mylor   Trewithian   Nare
Cripplesease   Lelant   Hayle   Praze-an-   Longdowns   Ponsanooth   Bridge   St. Just   Head
Morvah   14   828   Beeble   Rame   Feock   274   Portscatho
Boskednan   Georgia   Canonstown   Stithians   828   PENRYN   Gerrans   Bay
Pendeen   Bojewyan   New   St. Erth   Crowan   Mabe   Flushing   Greeb Point
Trewellard   Great   Mill   Leedstown   Porkellis   Burnthouse   St. Mawes
Botallack   Carnyorth   Bosullow   Madron   Relubbus   Townshend   Nancegollan   Treverva   Budock   FALMOUTH   Bohortha
ST. JUST   Gulval   St. Hilary   Trescowe   Seworgan   Water   Pendennis   Zone Point
Bosavern   Heamoor   Chyandour   Marazion   Godolphin Cross   Wendron   Penjerrick   Head   Falmouth Bay
Kelynack   Sancreed   Tredavoe   PENZANCE   Perranuthnoe   Goldsithney   635   Constantine   Porth   Mawnan
Brane   Drift   Newlyn   Germoe   Ashton   Sithney   Navas   Smith   Rosemullion Head
Escalls   Paul   Praa Sands   Rinsey   Breage   HELSTON   Gweek   Mawnan   Helford River
Sennen   St. Buryan   Mousehole   Cudden Point   Porthleven   Helford   St. Anthony
Cove   Kerris   Trewavas Head   Gwendron   Nare Point
LAND'S   A30   Lamorna   Mawgan   Manaccan
END   St. Martin's   Porthallow
Porthcurno   Treen   MOUNT'S BAY   Garras   Newtown   Tregidden   Porthoustock
St. Levan   Cribba Head   Berepper   Manacle Point
Gwennap   Cury   Traboe   St. Keverne
Head   369   11
Poldhu Point
Mullion   Coverack
Mullion Cove   Porth   Gwenter
Mellin   Black Head
Predannack
Wollas
Vellan Head   Ruan Minor
Cadgwith
Lizard   Landewednack
Hot Point
LIZARD POINT

Scilly Isles-Penzance

Falmouth, *Cornwall* sw 8032
This busy port and holiday resort with good bathing and yachting facilities is renowned for its mild climate. The main street follows the River Fal from the harbour to Pendennis Head where Pendennis Castle – one of Henry VIII's coastal forts – stands. 3m SW Penjerrick Gardens have exotic displays of sub-tropical flowering trees and shrubs.

Helston, *Cornwall* sw 6527
Helston, one of Cornwall's four ancient stannary towns, is now most famous for its curious annual Furry Dance held in May. Housed in the attractive old Butter Market is a folk museum covering all aspects of local history. Cornwall Aero Park and Flambards Village, S on the A3083, are both of interest and have landscaped gardens and a boating lake.

Hugh Town,
St Mary's, Scilly Isles sv 9010
This is the largest town on these captivating islands and all ferries and boat trips leave and arrive here. An excellent museum in Church Street has exhibits mainly connected with the sea, including fascinating accounts and finds from the many local wrecks.

Marazion, *Cornwall* sw 5130
Offshore from Marazion lies the famous little granite island known as St Michael's Mount, which can be reached on foot by a causeway exposed at low tide, or by boat from Marazion. Perched on the island are a castle and a priory both founded by Edward the Confessor in the 11th century. Armour and furniture are on display inside the priory.

Newquay, *Cornwall* sw 8161
This, Cornwall's largest resort, boasts fine cliffs, sands and surfing. It first prospered in the 16th century as a centre for pilchard fishing and the Huer's Hut perched above the town recalls those less

The peaceful waters of the Carrick Roads flow past St Mawes into Falmouth Bay

commercial days. Deep-sea fishing boats may be chartered from the harbour – one of the town's most picturesque areas. Cornwall's only zoo is situated in Trenance Park where there is also a boating lake and a miniature railway. Trerice Manor, a lovely gabled Elizabethan manor house, lies 5m to the SE.

Padstow, *Cornwall* sw 9175
Intriguing lanes lead down to Padstow's attractive old fishing harbour which opens into the Camel estuary. A colourful bird garden in Fentonluna Lane breeds birds from all over the world. Every May Day a bizarre Hobby Horse festival transforms the town into a carnival.

Penzance, *Cornwall* sw 4730
Handsome Georgian buildings still standing in Chapel Street are reminders of the town's popularity in the 18th century. Note number 19, now the home of the Museum of Nautical Art and Man-O-War Display. There is another museum in Penlee Park where the local

history of the area is well illustrated. Trengwainton Gardens, about 2m inland, specialise in glorious magnolias, azaleas and rhododendrons.

Probus, *Cornwall* sw 8947
Garden lovers are well catered for in this little village. The County Demonstration Garden and Arboretum nearby has permanent displays of the many different aspects of garden layout, and beautiful Trewithen Gardens lie between Probus and Grampound on the A390. Many rare trees and shrubs are grown here and some of these varieties are on sale.

Redruth, *Cornwall* sw 6941
Redruth has always been the centre of mining in Cornwall so it is appropriate that two aspects of the old industry have been preserved nearby. One is at the Tolgus Tin Company 2m N, where the ancient practice of streaming is still carried out and the other is at Pool, where a winding engine and a pumping engine can be seen in action.

St Agnes, *Cornwall* sw 7150
In the past this was one of the chief mining towns in Cornwall and the old disused mine workings scar the surrounding countryside. On the cliff towards Chapel Porth the Wheal Coates Engine House has been restored and the mechanics of winding, pumping and mine ventilation are demonstrated. St Agnes Beacon, 628ft high, is one of the outstanding landmarks of the area.

St Ives, *Cornwall* sw 5140
Artists have, understandably, always favoured this well-known resort where tiny cottages and twisty alleys cluster round the harbour. Sculptress Barbara Hepworth lived here and her home is now a museum of her work and possessions. The Barnes Museum of Cinematography provides an interesting contrast.

St Mawes, *Cornwall* sw 8433
St Mawes faces Falmouth across the Carrick Roads and a passenger ferry plys back and forth between the two. Like Falmouth, St Mawes also has a defensive castle built by Henry VIII in the 16th century. It saw very little military action and is in a good state of repair.

Truro, *Cornwall* sw 8244
Truro, Cornwall's only cathedral city and onetime stannary town, is the county's unofficial capital. During the 18th century it rivalled even Bath as a fashionable centre and the fine Assembly Rooms and the Georgian houses in Lemon Street are a legacy from those elegant days. The Truro Museum in River Street includes a world-famous mineral collection and Japanese ivories and lacquerwork. Trelissick Garden, 4m S, overlooks the River Fal and has beautiful lawns with winding walks through dense trees and shrubs.

Fishing trips and coastal cruises are two of Cornwall's most popular attractions and those from Penzance are no exception

Bodmin, *Cornwall*   sx 0767
Bodmin's position on the edge of Bodmin
Moor, halfway between Cornwall's
southern and northern coasts, makes it
an ideal touring base. An interesting
regimental museum is appropriately
housed in the keep of the Victoria
Barracks. 4m N on the A389 stands
Pencarrow House – a charming Georgian
mansion surrounded by 35 acres of landscaped gardens. Another fine house,
Lanhydrock, lies 2½m SE.

Boscastle, *Cornwall*   sx 0990
A steep valley tumbles down to the small
harbour at Boscastle which is protected
on each side by great cliffs. Nearby, an
unusual museum of witchcraft and black
magic illustrates the past and present
customs of witches and their accessories
in the south-west of England.

Bossiney, *Cornwall*   sx 0688
A steep winding path leads from this tiny
village down to a lovely spacious sandy
beach. Half a mile away more beautiful
scenery can be enjoyed in Rocky valley.
One of the most magnificent features is
the 40 ft waterfall called St Nectan's
Kieve. Nectan was a Celtic hermit saint
said to have had an oratory here.

*Tourism has replaced Mevagissey's fishing
industry but the harbour is still its hub*

Camelford, *Cornwall*   sx 1083
Legend claims that this was once the site
of Camelot, King Arthur's romantic
kingdom, but there are many contenders
for this honour. An interesting museum
of rural life housed in The Clease includes blacksmith's and wheelwright's
tools and a gay collection of bonnets.

Delabole, *Cornwall*   sx 0683
At one time nearly all the slate for
Cornwall's houses came from the quarry
here and the huge excavations can be
seen from the old village. One quarry,
which has been worked continuously
since 1555, has a museum attached to it
where the workings of the industry are
clearly explained.

Fowey, *Cornwall*   sx 1251
Fowey, pronounced Foy, stands at the
mouth of the Fowey estuary where
numerous yachts and dinghys ride at
anchor. Overlooking the town's attractive
streets is St Catherine's Castle – a ruined
16th-century stronghold built by Henry
VIII. It was restored in 1855. Nearby
Readymoney Cove is a pleasant sandy
beach suitable for swimming.

Lostwithiel, *Cornwall*   sx 1059
During the 13th century this was the
capital of Cornwall and another of the
county's four stannary towns. Traces of
the great hall that housed the stannary
offices are still visible in Duchy House in
Quay Street. A mile to the north is
Restormel Castle which has stood in
ruins since the 16th century. Its great
circular keep has survived, however, and
there is a 13th-century chapel nearby.

Mevagissey, *Cornwall*   sx 0144
Colour-washed cottages ramble up the
steep cliff behind Mevagissey's picturesque harbour which once enjoyed
notorious fame as a smugglers' haunt.
Shark and mackerel fishing trips operate
regularly from the harbour and a folk
museum occupies an old boatbuilder's
workshop on the East Quay. Another
attraction in this pretty village is a model
railway which runs through realistic ter-
rain and has over 1,000 model trains.

St Austell, *Cornwall*   sx 0152
Great white spoil-heaps have disfigured
the moors around St Austell ever since
china clay was discovered here in 1775.
However, despite the great boom of this
industry, the town has remained unspoilt
and has a number of attractive buildings.
2m N, on the A391, the clay industry can
be seen at close quarters at the open-air
Wheal Martyn Museum. Complete clay
works from the 19th century have been
restored, including working water-
wheels and two steam locomotives, and
the whole history of the industry is
clearly illustrated.

*Fowey's church in the centre of town has one
of the highest towers in Cornwall*

Tintagel, *Cornwall*   sx 0588
One of the most interesting buildings
along Tintagel's touristy main street is
the old slate-built post office. Originally
built as a manor house, it dates from the
14th century and now belongs to the National Trust. However, it is the romantic
legends of King Arthur which have
brought fame to this popular little town.
High on the rugged cliffs of Tintagel
Head nearby cling the ruined remains
of a castle – reputedly the birthplace
of King Arthur. Views from this exhilarating eyrie take in the great slate
caverns on the other side of Tintagel
Cove, and a waterfall that rushes down
the cliff face.

Wadebridge, *Cornwall*   sw 9972
An impressive medieval bridge spans the
River Camel in the centre of this small
market town. An enterprising vicar of
Egloshayle (the village on the opposite
bank) originally built the 320 ft-long
bridge with 17 arches, but these have
since been reduced to 14. Packs of wool
are thought to have been used as a base
for the pillars.

*Tintagel Castle stands on a peninsula known as The Island which was originally joined to
the mainland . When the rock collapsed a footbridge was built to span the gap*

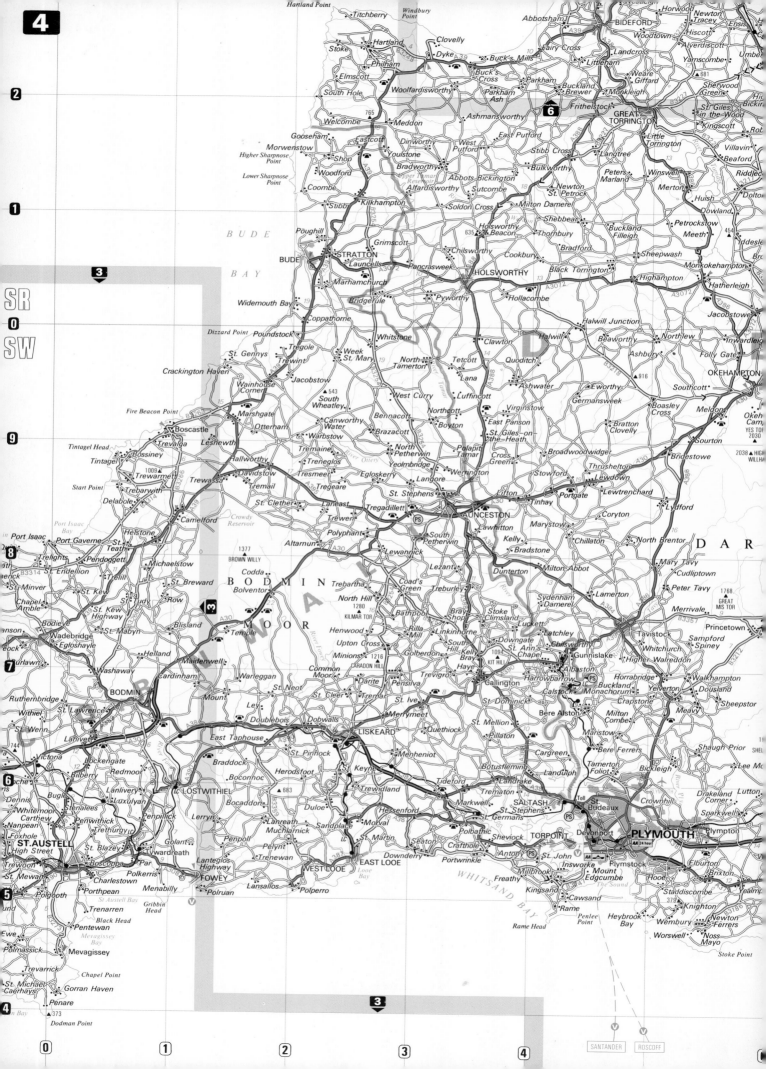

The beach at Bude

Bude, *Cornwall*   ss 2006
The huge Atlantic rollers which pound the beach at Bude provide exhilarating surfing that attracts enthusiasts of the sport from far and wide. For the less adventurous, there is more sheltered swimming at nearby Summerleaze beach where a swimming pool is naturally refilled by the sea.

Calstock, *Cornwall*   sx 4368
Market gardens surround the quiet village of Calstock on the banks of the River Tamar. 2m further along the river is Cotehele House which dates from 1485 to 1627. Beautiful formal Victorian terraces enhance the house and the grounds beyond roll down to the wooded valley where there is a manorial watermill.

Dobwalls, *Cornwall*   sx 2165
An extensive miniature railway based on the steam era of the American railroad

begins just north of the village and runs through realistic canyons, forests, tunnels and embankments. Nearby, in a large converted barn, a unique collection of work by Archibald Thorburn forms a permanent memorial exhibition to this great British painter of birds.

Great Torrington, *Devon*   ss 4919
Dartington glass is made in this hilltop market town and there are tours around the factory where glass-blowers can be seen at work. About 1m SE the Rosemoor Garden Trust specialises in ornamental trees and shrubs of great botanical interest.

Launceston, *Cornwall*   sx 3384
One of Cornwall's most attractive inland towns, Launceston was the county capital until 1838. A ruined Norman castle overlooks the town and miles of countryside can be seen from its great keep. Many Georgian houses add grace to the town's ancient streets, but the most interesting is Lawrence House in Castle Street. Now in the care of the National Trust, some of its rooms are open as a museum of local history.

Liskeard, *Cornwall*   sx 2564
Steep narrow streets characterise this busy market town that teems with life twice a week when the cattle fair takes place. A fascinating collection of mechanical musical instruments founded by Paul Corin can be seen at St Keyne Mill 2½m away.

Looe, *Cornwall*   sx 2553
This is Cornwall's chief centre for shark fishing and exciting fishing trips are available from the quay. The local marine aquarium contains various local species and the shark museum has stuffed sharks. Murrayton Monkey Sanctuary, 3m away, breeds appealing South American woolly monkeys. All the animals,

including geese, rabbits and donkeys, roam free.

Mount Edgcumbe, *Cornwall*   sx 4553
Mount Edgcumbe House, facing Plymouth across the Sound, was severely damaged during the 1941 blitz. Now restored as a Tudor mansion, the house is filled with elegant Hepplewhite furniture and its lovely gardens and grounds command extensive views of the Sound.

Okehampton, *Devon*   sx 5895
Okehampton serves the extensive farming area to the north of Dartmoor National Park. Just to the south of the town in Castle Lane are the ruined chapel, keep and hall of an 11th- to 14th-century castle destroyed by Henry VIII.

Plymouth, *Devon*   sx 4755
This popular yachting resort and important maritime city has been a naval base since the 16th century when the Pilgrim Fathers set sail to the New World. Prysten House, the city's oldest building, contains an exhibition about the *Mayflower* and a model of Plymouth as it was in 1620. Another museum relating to Plymouth's history can be seen in the Merchant's House in St Andrews Street. The City Museum and Art Gallery is also well worth a visit. Much of the city was rebuilt after the dreadful bomb damage of World War II and today it boasts one of the finest shopping complexes in Europe.

Plympton, *Devon*   sx 5356
Plympton was once an important town with a wealthy priory but now it is really a suburb of its younger neighbour, Plymouth. Tudor Saltram House, just south of the bypass, has two rooms decorated by Robert Adam. The features of the lovely garden include an 18th-century summerhouse and an orangery. Dartmoor Wildlife Park lies 3m away at Sparkwell, N of the A38.

Polperro, *Cornwall*   sx 2051
Tiny cottages crowd haphazardly down to the little harbour that has become one of the most popular in Cornwall and a great favourite with artists. A smuggling museum in Talland Street recalls the romantic trade that operated in Cornwall so profitably during the 18th century.

Torpoint, *Cornwall*   sx 4355
Torpoint, situated on the Hamoaze, is linked to Devonport across the river by a car ferry. A fine National Trust property, Antony House, stands 2m NW of the village with fine views of the Lynher estuary.

Yelverton, *Devon*   sx 5267
A beautiful array of over 800 paperweights has been collected at the Paperweight Centre at Leg-O'Mutton Corner and there are always some for sale. Famous Buckland Abbey, 3m W, was originally built by Cistercian monks in 1278. It now houses a Drake museum and the grounds feature herb gardens and a tithe barn.

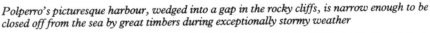
Polperro's picturesque harbour, wedged into a gap in the rocky cliffs, is narrow enough to be closed off from the sea by great timbers during exceptionally stormy weather

Ashburton, *Devon*   sx 7569
This attractive little town includes several
old gable-style houses. A museum in
West Street has unusual American and
Indian antiques and various geological
specimens.

Buckfastleigh, *Devon*   sx 7466
A great attraction to this old wool town is
the Dart Valley Railway. Originally built
in 1872 to serve the mining and farming
industries, the line now takes passengers
to Totnes and back and there is a store of
Great Western rolling stock and locomotives at Buckfastleigh. Nearby Buckfast Abbey has stood on the same site
since the 12th century and the interesting
House of Shells Museum next door
imaginatively demonstrates the use of
shells in arts and crafts.

Dartmouth, *Devon*   sx 8751
During medieval days Dartmouth was
one of the busiest ports in England and
the imposing Royal Naval College main-
tains this naval tradition. The castle, a
Tudor stronghold dating from 1481,
guards the entrance to the Dart estuary.
A small maritime and nautical museum is
housed in the half-timbered Butterwalk,
and the Newcomen Engine House is next
to it.

Drewsteignton, *Devon*   sx 7391
Sir Julius Drewe chose the outskirts of
this tiny village on which to build himself
a remarkable 'castle' where he could
retire. It stands on a spectacular crag
900 ft above the wooded gorge of the
River Teign. Sir Edwin Lutyens
designed the house and the high,
unplastered granite walls, numerous
passages and great staircase are impressively dramatic.

Exeter, *Devon*   sx 9292
Much of medieval Exeter was destroyed
in World War II but fortunately the
beautiful cathedral and the old houses
around the Close survived. In keeping
with its long maritime tradition, the city
has a large maritime museum by the quay
with over 100 historic ships. Other features not to be missed include the underground passages; Rougemont House
Museum; the Royal Albert Memorial
Museum and St Nicholas' Priory.

Kingsbridge, *Devon*   sx 7344
The estuary reaching up to Kingsbridge
provides a sheltered harbour which is
very popular with yachting enthusiasts.
William Cookworthy, pioneer of the
china clay industry, was born here and a
museum in Fore Street contains an exhibition of his history and porcelain.
Kingsbridge Miniature Railway runs
along the quay.

Newton Abbot, *Devon*   sx 8671
Wednesdays and Saturdays are the best
days to visit Newton Abbot as this is
when the large general markets are held.
Many of the most interesting houses are
centred around Courtenay Park and
Devon Square, and there is a pottery and

*Remains of Exeter's Norman castle stand in
the pleasant Rougemont Gardens*

leather factory in Forde Road where
guided tours are available. Bradley
Manor on the western outskirts is considered to be one of the finest medieval
houses in the West Country.

Paignton, *Devon*   sx 8960
Paignton, set on the huge sweep of Tor
Bay, has a great range of holiday
amenities as well as good sandy beaches.
Interesting places to visit include Kirk-
ham House – a restored 14th-century
Priests' House, and Oldway – a 19th-
century house containing replicas of
rooms in the Palace of Versailles. On the
outskirts of the resort Torbay Aircraft
Museum, Torbay and Dartmouth Railway and the Zoological and Botanical
Gardens are all well worth visiting.

Salcombe, *Devon*   sx 7338
Salcombe, at the mouth of the Kingsbridge estuary, is surrounded by beautiful cliff scenery: the 5m cliff walk from
Bolt Head to Bolt Tail is considered one
of the finest in England. At nearby
Sharpitor there is a museum of local history
surrounded by six acres of gardens.

Teignmouth, *Devon*   sx 9473
A sandy beach, a fine golfcourse overlooking the town and a sheltered
attractive harbour ensure Teignmouth's
(pronounced Tinmouth) popularity with
holidaymakers. Tropical marine and
freshwater fish and an exhibition of local
marine life can be seen at Aqualand in
The Den. A bridge and a passenger ferry
cross the estuary to Shaldon and boat
trips run up river to Newton Abbot.

Tiverton, *Devon*   ss 9512
Rich wool merchants of the 17th century
bequeathed many fine buildings to this
prosperous agricultural town. Henry I
founded a castle here in 1106 which has a
notable medieval gatehouse, a clock
museum and a Joan of Arc gallery. Near
the town hall a restored 19th-century
school has been turned into a comprehensive folk museum.

Torquay, *Devon*   sx 9164
Sub-tropical gardens and whitewashed
villas rising up behind the wide bay give
Torquay a distinctly Continental atmosphere. Among its attractions are Aqualand on Beacon Quay, which specialises
in marine fish; Babbacombe model village; Torre Abbey Mansion, and the
Natural History Society Museum where
finds from local caves and exhibits of
Devon folklife can be seen.

Totnes, *Devon*   sx 8060
Situated on the River Dart, Totnes is one
of England's oldest boroughs. The shell
keep of its ruined Norman castle is one of
the town's chief features, but there are
also several fine Elizabethan and Georgian houses. One, in Fore Street, dates
from around 1575 and has been converted into a museum of domestic bygones, toys, costumes and archaeology.
Near the quay, where steamer trips leave
for Dartmouth, a motor museum spans
50 years of motoring.

*The old court room in the 16th-century Guildhall at Totnes is still used by the town's council.
Locally minted Saxon coins are on display here among other relics of the town*

Appledore, *Devon*　ss 4630
Despite the existence of Europe's largest covered shipbuilding dock on the Tor-ridge estuary, Appledore has retained its charm made up of cobbled streets, colour-washed cottages, a quay and a sandy beach. Some of the cottages have extra large upstairs windows which used to light sail-makers' lofts. Imaginative exhibitions and displays of North Devon's maritime history are on display in Odun House, Odun Road.

So steep is Clovelly's main street that some doorways overlook nextdoor's roof

Arlington, *Devon*　ss 6140
Arlington Court is the main attraction in this tiny hamlet. Miss Rosalie Chichester (Sir Francis Chichester's aunt) bequeathed the house to the National Trust in 1949 having lived in it all her life. She was a great collector and the rooms are filled with the treasures she spent a life-time accumulating – model ships, shells, snuff-boxes, fans, porcelain etc. The stables, built in 1864, house an extensive collection of horse-drawn carriages. Shet-land ponies and Jacob sheep roam free in the park where there is also a heronry and a duck sanctuary.

Barnstaple, *Devon*　ss 5533
Barnstaple is one of the oldest boroughs in Britain and during the Middle Ages was a major port and shipbuilding centre. Much of the town's architecture is Georgian and one of the finest buildings is Queen Anne's Walk – the colonnaded Exchange by the river. Here, on the Tome Stone outside, merchants struck verbal bargains. There is a small local history museum in St Anne's Chapel which stands in the pleasant churchyard in the middle of the town. One of the prettiest shopping streets is 19th-century Butchers Row.

Bideford, *Devon*　ss 4526
During the mid 16th to mid 18th century this was North Devon's chief port and the centre of a famous ship-building industry. The tree-lined quay is still a lively part of the town and the estuary is popular with yachtsmen. An ancient and appealing feature here is the 15th-century bridge which has 24 arches, each of a different width.

Braunton, *Devon*　ss 4836
Reputed to be the largest village in England, Braunton stands on the edge of Braunton Burrows and Saunton Sands. The Burrows, 3–4 sq m of sand dunes, have been designated a National Nature Reserve and access on foot is permitted. Vast stretches of sands are revealed at low tide at Saunton.

Clovelly, *Devon*　ss 2124
Clovelly's steep cobbled main street lead-ing down to the harbour is one of the prettiest in England. Cars must be parked at the top of the hill, but donkeys may be hired to carry luggage and a Land-Rover service is available.

Combe Martin, *Devon*　ss 5846
The village rambles for about a mile down to the sea and the most distinctive building is the Pack of Cards pub. It is said to have been built by an 18th-century gambler and looks remarkably like a house made of cards. Watermouth Castle, 1½m E, is a large Gothic building which houses a variety of displays and activities to interest all the family.

Ilfracombe, *Devon*　ss 5147
When the railway arrived the hitherto quiet fishing village was transformed into a large holiday and retirement resort dominated by grand hotels and guest-houses. The harbour – an important trading centre at one time – now forms an attractive focal point to the town and trips along the coast leave from here. The conical hill by the harbour is crowned by St Nicholas Chapel, which has guided ships in since the 14th century. Chambercombe Manor, 1m E, is one of England's oldest inhabited houses, parts of which date back 800 years. A cobbled courtyard, informal gardens and a haunted room lend the manor a charm-ingly romantic air.

Lynton, *Devon*　ss 7149
Victorian architecture predominates in this pleasant little resort set up above its sister village of Lynmouth, and one Victorian eccentricity which has survived is the water-powered cliff lift. The Exmoor hills roll away behind the village and the Lyn and Exmoor Museum in St Vincent's Cottage includes a history of Exmoor, an exhibition of old local arts and crafts and models of the old Lynton to Barnstaple railway.

Porlock, *Somerset*　ss 8846
A beautiful mixture of Exmoor moor-land, cliff scenery and a peaceful valley surround this large village. Nearby Por-lock Weir is a pretty medley of cottages, pubs and a harbour, and a delightful cliff walk from here takes you to Culbone.

South Molton, *Devon*　ss 7125
Known to have existed as a Saxon settle-ment, this little town lies just south of Exmoor and serves as an agricultural centre for the region. An elegant Geor-gian square is complemented by the town's grand 18th-century Guildhall and 19th-century Assembly Rooms, all built with the profits from wool and minerals. Part of the Guildhall houses the town museum which includes a cider press and an 18th-century fire engine.

Old houses crowd along the quayside of Ilfracombe Harbour which lies between the narrow promontory of Lantern Hill and the mainland. The pier forms a small inner harbour

Abbotsbury, *Dorset* SY 5785
A huge medieval tithe barn is all that remains of the Benedictine monastery founded here during the 15th century. Just south of Abbotsbury is the famous swannery established by the monks to provide a source of food. Now there are some 500 swans and numerous other water birds tended daily by a swanherd. Another attraction in the village are the sub-tropical Abbotsbury Gardens.

Bridport, *Dorset* SY 4692
Local trade has centred on rope and net making for over 750 years and these crafts are featured in the town's museum and art gallery in South Street. Bridport's main street is lined with stalls on market day (Saturday).

Dunster, *Somerset* SS 9943
This beautiful medieval village belonged to one family – the Luttrells – for about 600 years until 1975 and as a result has remained exceptionally well preserved. The castle was originally the family seat and contains rare portraits and leather hangings. Forming a centrepiece to the village is the octagonal Yarn Market which dates from Dunster's days as an important cloth centre.

Exmouth, *Devon* SY 0080
This pleasant town, situated on the estuary of the River Exe, is Devon's oldest resort. Also one of the largest, it has all the usual seaside attractions. About 2m N, off the A376, is a strange circular house known as A La Ronde. The rooms are arranged around a 16-sided hall and there is an unusual shell gallery above. One of the largest working country life museums in Britain lies 1m SE.

Glastonbury, *Somerset* ST 4938
Legends connected with Avalon, Joseph of Arimathea and King Arthur have always been associated with Glastonbury and the conical-shaped Tor rising above the town's skyline certainly inspires romantic fancies. At one time the abbey was one of the richest and most influential in England and the majestic ruins still convey its former splendour. Most interesting is the Abbot's Kitchen, still intact, and the gatehouse where a small museum is housed. The old abbey barn now provides an appropriate setting for the Somerset Rural Life Museum.

Lyme Regis, *Dorset* SY 3492
Part of the considerable appeal of this little seaside town is its position on the hillside and the steep steps and streets leading down to the bay and the harbour. During medieval times this was a busy port and the Cobb – one of the town's most attractive areas – seems to have changed very little since those days. The area is a rich hunting ground for fossil hunters and the museum in Bridge Street includes a good collection of local finds.

Montacute, *Somerset* ST 4916
At the heart of this pretty village, built almost entirely of golden-yellow Ham stone, is one of England's finest Elizabethan mansions. Montacute House was built for Edward Phellips in 1588 and the numerous turrets, gables, balustrades, figures and windows reflect the lavish style of the period. Since acquiring the empty house in 1931 the National Trust have completely refurbished it.

Sidmouth, *Devon* SY 1287
A resort was created here during Regency times and it became one of the most exclusive in Britain. The shingle beach is backed by dramatic red cliffs and nearby Peak Hill and Salcombe Hill offer spectacular coastal views. An elegant Georgian house next to the church contains the town museum.

Taunton, *Somerset* ST 2324
Situated in the fertile plain of Taunton Vale, this prosperous agricultural town is the county capital of Somerset. There has been a castle in the town since about 710 and, altered and added to over the centuries, it now contains the Somerset County Museum. British Telecom in North Street has early machines and equipment (open by appointment).

Washford, *Somerset* ST 0441
Just outside the village of Washford are the ruins of Cleeve Abbey – a 13th-century Cistercian house with a notable gatehouse, dormitory and refectory. South of the abbey, off the B3190, is an unspoilt 14th-century manor house called Bardon Manor which is said to be haunted.

Wells, *Somerset* ST 5445
This beautiful little city nestling at the foot of the Mendip Hills has one of the finest cathedrals in the country. The west front is adorned with hundreds of statues and inside there is a unique 14th-century clock and a lovely double-branching staircase. Other ecclesiastical buildings in the medieval precinct include the Bishop's Palace, surrounded by a moat where swans ring a bell at feeding time, and Vicar's Close – a street of beautifully preserved 14th-century houses.

A high wall dating back to the 13th century surrounds the Bishop's Palace in Wells

Wookey Hole, *Somerset* ST 5347
Thousands of years ago the River Axe eroded the great complex of caves known as Wookey Hole. Between the Iron Age and the Roman occupation they were inhabited and a small museum contains many fascinating finds from these periods. The old mill at the cave entrance is used as a store for Madame Tussaud's waxworks and Lady Bangor's Fairground Collection.

Glastonbury Tor, rising out of the Somerset Plain, is crowned by the tower of 15th-century St Michael's Church. The Holy Grail – the chalice used at the Last Supper – is thought to have been buried by Joseph of Arimathea beneath Chalice Well at the foot of the Tor

Huge natural caverns have been sculpted out of the soft limestone at Wookey Hole

Bournemouth, *Dorset*　sz 0991
Six miles of sandy beaches, deep wooded ravines and sandstone cliffs, together with excellent shopping and entertainment facilities all contribute to Bournemouth's great popularity. There are three excellent museums in the town – the Russell-Cotes Art Gallery and Museum, the Rothesay Museum, which includes the British Typewriter Museum, and the Big Four Railway Museum.

Christchurch, *Dorset*　sz 1593
Until the 12th century Christchurch was called Twynham – an ancient word meaning the meeting place of two rivers – as it stands on the estuaries of the Avon and Stour. The name was changed when the great Norman priory was built. Red House Museum and Art Gallery, surrounded by rose and herb gardens, contains local history and Victoriana.

Corfe Castle, *Dorset*　sy 9681
The skyline behind this stone-built village is dominated by the striking ruins of its castle which crowns an unnaturally symmetrical hill. A tiny building below houses a museum of ancient village relics, including dinosaur footprints thought to be about 130 million years old. A road leads E to Studland and just beyond, at Shell Bay, a car ferry operates across to Bournemouth.

Dorchester, *Dorset*　sy 6990
Thomas Hardy, born 2m NE of Dorchester at Higher Bockhampton, made the town famous by featuring it in many of his novels. The Dorset County Museum includes many of Hardy's personal possessions and there is a statue of him in The Grove. The town is also famous for Judge Jeffreys' 'Bloody Assize' held at the Antelope Hotel in 1685, and the trial of the Tolpuddle Martyrs which took place in the courtroom of the Old Shire Hall. Wolfeton House, a fine medieval and Elizabethan manor house, stands on the A37 1½m to the NW.

Frome, *Somerset*　st 7747
Pronounced Froom, this old wool town has several attractive old streets leading off the busy market place, but Cheap Street, with its central water conduit, is the prettiest. About 4m SE is one of England's most popular stately homes – Longleat House. Its great attraction is the drive-through Safari Park where lions and other wild animals roam free.

Salisbury, *Wilts*　su 1429
When Old Sarum, a Norman cathedral town with a castle, was abandoned in the 13th century, Salisbury Cathedral was begun and the new city grew up around it. Many beautiful old houses flank the exceptionally large Cathedral Close, but two of the most interesting are Mompesson House, which now belongs to the National Trust, and the King's House where there is a museum relating to the city and south Wiltshire. Exhibits include finds from Old Sarum and Stonehenge.

Built by the Normans to defend a gap in the Purbeck Hills, Corfe Castle was blown up by Cromwell during the Civil War leaving these impressive ruins

Shaftesbury, *Dorset*　st 8622
Originally called Shaston, Shaftesbury began when an abbey was founded here in about 880. Although completely destroyed at the Dissolution, various relics are preserved in the local history museum on Gold Hill. This steep cobbled street commands lovely views of the Blackmore Vale.

Sherborne, *Dorset*　st 6316
Yellow-stone houses dating from the 15th-century onwards line the winding streets of this beautiful and historic town. Before the Dissolution an abbey flourished here and a museum of local history is housed in the gatehouse. Sherborne Castle is actually a 16th-century house built by Sir Walter Raleigh and the ruins of the town's 12th-century castle stand in the grounds landscaped by Capability Brown. Compton House, an Elizabethan mansion to the W, houses a unique butterfly farm and the Lullingstone Silk Farm.

Stourton, *Wilts*　st 7733
The pretty little village of Stourton stands at the edge of the famous Stourhead estate built by the Hoare family in the 18th century. Classical garden temples surround the beautiful artificial lake and the great banks of rhododendrons and azaleas provide a heady combination of colour and perfume.

Weymouth, *Dorset*　sy 6778
King George III began taking holidays here in 1789 and the town subsequently became a fashionable resort. Georgian terraces overlook the broad esplanade and narrow back streets twist around the old harbour. There is a museum in

Westham Road and a 17th-century house in Trinity Street has been refurbished with contemporary furnishings.

Wilton, *Wilts*　su 0931
Carpet-making is usually associated with Wilton and the Royal Wilton Factory is open to visitors. The town is actually one of the oldest boroughs in England and in 871 King Alfred founded an abbey where Wilton House now stands. This was designed by Inigo Jones, Holbein and James Wyatt and contains a world-famous collection of paintings, sculpture and furniture.

Wimborne Minster, *Dorset*　sz 0199
The twin-towered minster from which Wimborne gets its name stands at the centre of this old market town by the River Stour. Near the Cornmarket a model town represents Wimborne in minute detail and many items of local interest can be seen in the Priest's House in the High Street. S of the town are the Merley Bird Gardens.

Wimborne Minster's minster church of St Cuthberga encompasses nearly every style of architecture from Norman to Gothic

Beaulieu, *Hants* su 3801
Beautifully situated on the Beaulieu
River, Beaulieu is enhanced by the magnificent ruins of its Cistercian abbey. The
old abbey gatehouse has been converted
into Palace House and elsewhere in the
grounds is the famous Motor Museum,
veteran bus rides, a monorail and a
model railway. Bucklers Hard 2m S is
one of the most attractive spots in the
New Forest. Broad grass verges and
18th-century cottages flank the single
street which leads down to the quay, and
there is a good maritime museum.

Bembridge, *Isle of Wight* sz 6488
Bembridge Sailing Club is one of the best
in England and the natural harbour at the
mouth of the Eastern Yar teems with
yachts. There is a fascinating maritime
museum designed to interest the whole
family in Sherborne Street, and an 18th-
century windmill that was used up until
1913 stands off the B3390.

Carisbrooke, *Isle of Wight* sz 4888
This was the old capital of the island, and
the 'Governor' lived in Carisbrooke
Castle set up above the village on a 150ft-
high plateau. The Isle of Wight Museum
is housed in the castle, but most appealing of all is the donkey working the great
waterwheel.

*Morris Dancers at Beaulieu outside Palace House. This was rebuilt in 1872 and is now the
home of Lord Montagu – owner of the estate*

*The gatehouse of Tudor Carisbrooke Castle
was built beneath the high Norman keep*

Cowes, *Isle of Wight* sz 4995
For one week during August Cowes
teems with yachtsmen and spectators
here to enjoy one of the greatest competi-
tive events of the year – Cowes Week. A
row of brass cannons pointing out over
the Solent starts the yacht races. The town
is divided by the River Medina and on
the outskirts of East Cowes stands Os-
borne House – the former holiday retreat
of Queen Victoria and Prince Albert.

Lyndhurst, *Hants* su 2907
Set in the heart of the New Forest,
Lyndhurst is known as its 'capital'.
Queen's House, the to W of the church,
is still used as a meeting place by the
Verderers who administer the Forest.
Their Court Room, decorated with ant-
lers, can be visited.

New Alresford, *Hants* su 5832
Handsome colour-washed Georgian
houses line Alresford's wide main street,
aptly named Broad Street. A tributary of
the River Itchen skirts the town and a
pleasant walk along the towpath takes
you past the picturesque old fulling mill
(now a private residence) and bright
green watercress beds. Alresford Station
is a terminus for the Mid Hants Railway,
popularly known as the Watercress Line.

Portsmouth, *Hants* su 6501
Portsmouth has been an important naval
port for centuries and now the docks
cover some 300 acres. Most famous of all
the ships that have docked here is Nelson's flagship HMS *Victory*, now fitted
out to show conditions during the Battle
of Trafalgar. The Royal Naval Museum
is nearby. Charles Dickens was born in
the city and his house in Old Commercial
Road has been refurbished as a museum.
Southsea, which runs into Portsmouth,
has developed as a resort and the Castle
and Museum on the esplanade are of
particular interest.

Romsey, *Hants* su 3521
Romsey grew up around the abbey
founded here on the banks of the River
Test. The foundations of the abbey are
Anglo-Saxon, but most of the existing
abbey church was built during the 12th
century. Broadlands, famous as the home
of the late Earl of Mountbatten, lies off
the A31 bypass. This elegant country
home is filled with fine works of art.

Southampton, *Hants* su 4212
Southampton has been an important seaport for centuries and is particularly
famous today for its huge docks.
Although much of the city is new due to
heavy war damage, there is still much to

see of the old city. Bargate, one of the
entrances in the defensive town walls
dates back to Norman times, and its
upper floor houses the town museum.
Overlooking the old town walls and the
docks is Tudor House, a fascinating half-
timbered building housing a museum of
historical and antiquarian interest. Wool
House Maritime Museum is also worth a
visit.

Ventnor, *Isle of Wight* sz 5677
Ventnor's sheltered aspect provides a
mild climate which has earned the town
repute as a winter holiday and health
resort. A pier, a Winter Garden Pavilion
and a short esplanade have all been built
this century to cater for visitors. An
exciting smuggling museum in the
Botanic Gardens covers 700 years of this
notorious practice.

Winchester, *Hants* su 4829
Onetime capital of England, Winchester
is a charming old city with a magnificent
cathedral dating from the 11th century at
its heart. Another of the city's ancient
establishments is Winchester College –
the oldest public school in England –
founded by William of Wykeham in
1382. All that remains of Henry III's
castle is the Castle Hall where the famous
round table commemorating King
Arthur hangs. The Hospital of St Cross,
S of the city, is the oldest functioning
charitable institution in England and still
issues the wayfarers' dole.

Yarmouth, *Isle of Wight* sz 3589
Ferries from the mainland dock at Yarmouth and it is a good starting point for
exploration of the island. Henry VIII
built one of his numerous coastal defence
forts in the harbour which is now a
popular sailing centre.

Alton, *Hants*   su 7139
Brewing and cloth manufacture brought prosperity to this historic market town during the 18th and 19th centuries and many fine Georgian houses line the main street. Craft tools, dolls and toys can be seen in the Curtis Museum.

Bosham, *W Sussex*   su 8004
The quay at Bosham is a very popular yachting centre and its delightful setting attracts many artists and sightseers. Picturesque old cottages line the strand and the village green leads down to the waterfront.

Chawton, *Hants*   su 7037
A plain redbrick cottage in Chawton's pretty main street was the home of Jane Austen for the last eight years of her life. She lived there with her mother and sister and the cottage, now a museum of her life and work, has changed very little over the years.

Farnham, *Surrey*   su 8446
Elegant redbrick Georgian houses and façades predominate in this charming town, but a variety of attractive buildings of much earlier periods form its basic fabric. Partially hidden by trees at the top of Castle Street is Farnham's castle, originally dating from the 12th century but considerably altered and rebuilt over the centuries. The town's museum occupies Willmer House, where local history is well represented.

Hungerford, *Berks*   su 3368
An ancient ceremony called Hocktide takes place in Hungerford every second Tuesday after Easter. This is the day when the town's governing body of Feoffees is elected while Tuttimen and the Orange Man exchange oranges for kisses. Antique shops flourish and there is plenty for the browser to enjoy. Littlecote House lies 2m NW. This Tudor manor house has a unique collection of Cromwellian armour and an incongruous Wild West Frontier City has been created in the grounds.

Mapledurham, *Berks*   su 6776
Pretty cottages, a row of 17th-century almshouses and a 15th-century watermill form the attractive heart of this Thameside village. The mill is the last working corn and grist mill on the Thames and wholemeal flour can be purchased. Mapledurham House, set by the river, was built by Sir Michael Blount during Elizabethan times.

Newbury, *Berks*   su 4666
In the past Newbury was an important cloth town and the Cloth Hall in Wharf Street was built in the 17th century to employ the poor. Now it houses the town museum which includes prehistoric finds, Civil War relics and a camera collection. Newbury is famous today for its racecourse.

The ruins of Donnington Castle stand NW of Newbury near the River Lambourn

Petersfield, *Hants*   su 7423
Prosperity first came to this old market town through the wool trade and later it became an important coaching stop on the busy London to Portsmouth road. A towering equestrian statue of William III dominates the central square where a market is held every Wednesday. Queen Elizabeth Country Park which lies 4m S includes an Iron Age farm, countryside displays and crafts, guided walks and pony trekking.

Reading, *Berks*   su 7272
The history of Reading dates back to 871 when it was occupied by the Danes but relatively little of the old town has survived. An interesting part of the University is the Museum of English Rural Life which has a comprehensive collection of agricultural, domestic and crafts exhibits. Also of interest is the Museum and Art Gallery in Blagrave Street.

Selborne, *Hants*   su 7433
Naturalist Gilbert White brought fame to this village through his classic field study, *The Natural History of Selborne*. He was born in the vicarage in 1720 and later returned to Selborne where he lived in a fine house called The Wakes, which now houses the Oates Memorial Library and Museum and the Gilbert White Museum. Selborne Hill rises steeply behind the village and a zig-zag path weaves up through the dense beech hanger.

Sherborne St John, *Hants*   su 6155
Along a country lane NE of this pleasant village is The Vyne, one of Hampshire's most appealing country houses. It was built by William Sandys in about 1510 and later passed to the Chute family. The lovely chapel, oak gallery and magnificent staircase are just some of the fine features of the house. Informal lawns sweeping down to an artificial lake with fields beyond provide a beautiful setting.

Uppark, *W Sussex*   su 7717
Uppark, standing high up on the Sussex Downs overlooking miles of rolling fields, has one of the most beautiful settings in England. The square, redbrick mansion was built in about 1690 for Lord Grey, and a later owner – Sir Matthew Fetherstonhaugh – filled it with many rare and beautiful treasures.

In 1799 the Kennet and Avon Canal was built to link the River Avon with the River Kennet and thus make transportation between the west and east easier

Arundel, *W Sussex* TQ 0107
Arundel Castle, seat of the Duke of Norfolk, overshadows this pretty little town set on the River Arun. Many fine paintings and some rare 16th-century furniture are on display inside. Two fascinating museums are to be found in the High Street: one is a toy and military museum, and the other is the Museum of Curiosity. The latter is the work of the Victorian naturalist and taxidermist Walter Potter, who created well-known animal tableaux – such as the Death of Cock Robin – with uncanny naturalism.

Chichester, *W Sussex* SU 8605
Four streets dating from Roman times meet at the ornate octagonal Market Cross which has stood in the centre of Chichester since the 15th century. Even older is the splendid Norman cathedral notable for its detached bell-tower – the only one in England – and a fine modern tapestry by John Piper. Beautiful Georgian architecture graces nearly every street but the prettiest areas are the Pallants and Little London, where the Corn Store has been converted into the District Museum.

Guildford, *Surrey* TQ 0049
Capital of Surrey for many centuries, Guildford has a steep, attractive cobbled High Street. The 17th-century Guildhall, featuring an ornate overhanging gilded clock, stands half way up next door to Guildford House, now an art gallery. Guildford's oldest building is the three-storeyed castle keep built by Henry II during the 12th century. Castle Arch, at the entrance to the pleasant gardens around the keep, houses the town museum. Two of the town's most impressive buildings were built this century – the redbrick cathedral on Stag Hill, and the Yvonne Arnaud Theatre which overlooks the River Wey.

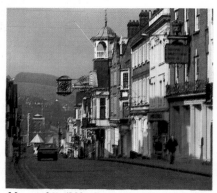

Many of Guildford's most notable buildings are to be found in the High Street

Kensington and Chelsea,
London TQ 2778
During the 18th century these were two outlying villages a day's ride away from London but now they are among the most fashionable residential and shopping areas of the capital. Kensington Palace was the birthplace of Queen Victoria and many of the apartments open to the public contain royal mementoes.

Kew, *Surrey* TQ 1877
It is the famous Royal Botanical Gardens that chiefly attract visitors to this corner of London. Great glasshouses protecting rare orchids and ferns are among the most popular features, but the beautifully maintained lawns and flowerbeds are no less delightful. Kew Palace stands in the gardens and contains many souvenirs of George III.

Littlehampton, *W Sussex* TQ 0202
Everything the holidaymaker could need seems to be available at Littlehampton. There is a splendid sandy beach with safe swimming, two sailing clubs, an 18-hole golf course, good sea and river fishing and open downland and woodland behind ideal for walking and horse-riding. A marine museum in River Road includes several paintings of local interest and old marine exhibits.

Midhurst, *W Sussex* SU 8821
Redbrick buildings dating from the 16th and 17th centuries abound in this pretty little market town and one of its many old inns, the Spread Eagle, is a particularly fine 15th-century building. The ruins of Cowdray House, built in 1530 by the Earl of Southampton and burnt down in 1793, lie on the outskirts.

Midhurst's pleasing townscape is enhanced by the church tower of St Mary and St Denys

Petworth, *W Sussex* SU 9721
Right in the centre of this charming country town is Petworth House, which was largely rebuilt during the 17th century by the Duke of Somerset. Its impressive 320ft west front overlooks the great deer park landscaped by Capability Brown. One of the finest art collections in the country is displayed in the state rooms and galleries, and the beautiful Carved Room was decorated by Grinling Gibbons in 1692.

Richmond, *Surrey* TQ 1874
Richmond has been a royal manor since Edward I built a palace here during the 13th century. The town is delightfully situated overlooking the Thames and artists such as Turner and Reynolds have been inspired to paint the fine views. 1m S of Richmond is Ham House which, together with its contents, has survived virtually unchanged since the 17th century.

Singleton, *W Sussex* SU 8713
Just outside the village of Singleton is the Weald and Downland Open Air Museum. Here all types of domestic buildings have been collected from southern England and reconstructed as faithfully to the original as possible. Traditional crafts and industries are also on display, as well as an exhibition of building techniques and materials used since medieval times.

Windsor, *Berks* SU 9676
For nearly 900 years Windsor Castle has been the home of the Royal Family and this great rambling fortress dominates the centre of the town. Various parts of the castle are open to the public, including Queen Mary's Dolls' House which was built by Sir Edwin Lutyens. One of the finest military museums in Britain is housed in the Combermere Barracks, and the Guildhall – designed by Sir Christopher Wren – houses Borough insignia and plate. Windsor Great Park includes Savill Garden and Valley Gardens, both featuring beautiful trees and flowering shrubs. The entrance to the Safari Park and Seaworld lies on the B3022 SW of the town.

Henry II built the great round tower which dominates the skyline of Windsor Castle

Worthing, *W Sussex* TQ 1402
Patronage by George III's family transformed the small 18th-century fishing hamlet of Worthing into a popular seaside resort with all the traditional entertainments. The town has suffered somewhat from over-development but there are a few corners where its dignity has survived. Worthing Museum and Art Gallery in Chapel Road includes an interesting costume collection.

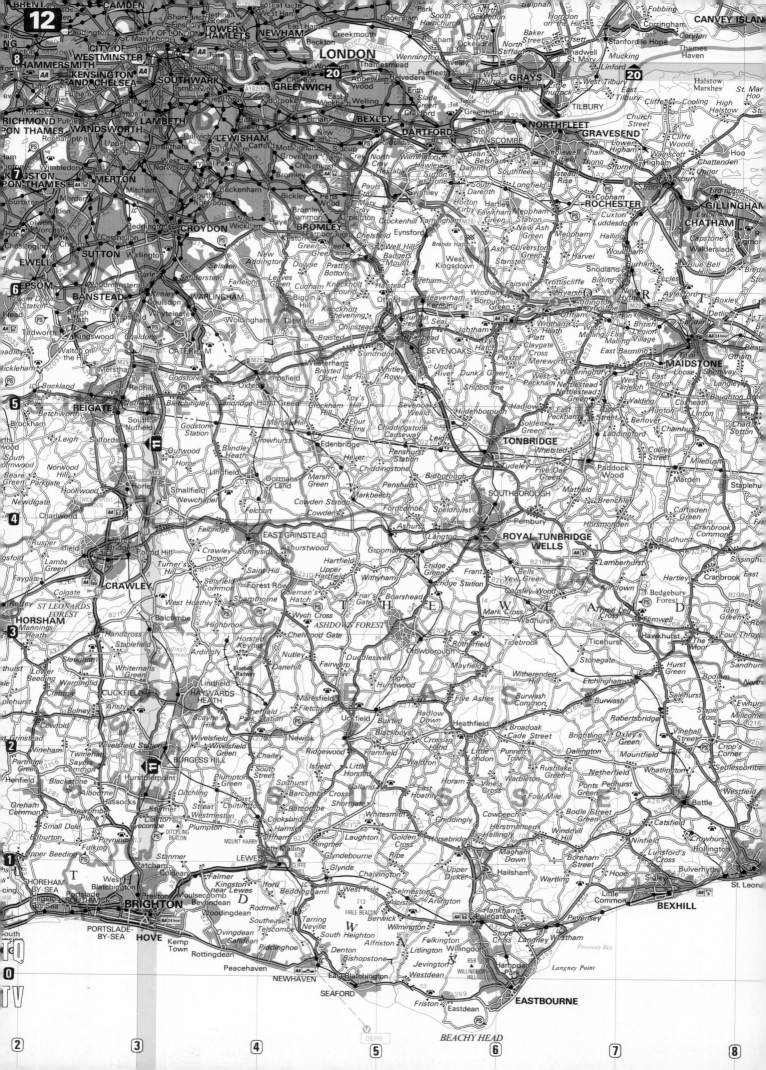

Battle, *E Sussex*   TQ 7416
Famed as the site of the Battle of Hastings which gave the town its name, Battle's past is recaptured by a diorama of the battle and a copy of the Bayeux Tapestry, both kept in Langton House. The town's chief glory is the splendid abbey gateway built in 1338.

Brighton, *W Sussex*   TQ 3105
During the 18th century the curative powers of the sea air turned the village of Brighthelmstone into a famous resort. George IV was a great patron of the town and built the fantastically exotic oriental-looking Royal Pavilion. As well as being a popular holiday town, top class night-life and huge conference facilities make it one of the most exciting towns outside London.

By adding spires, minarets and onion-shaped domes to Henry Holland's villa John Nash created the Royal Pavilion

Cranbrook, *Kent*   TQ 7735
A splendid 19th-century smock mill stands on the edge of this pretty little town built with the profits from the cloth trade. Sissinghurst Castle to the NE is famous for the series of small gardens created by Vita Sackville-West.

Eastbourne, *E Sussex*   TV 6199
Boasting more hours of sunshine than other resorts, Eastbourne has retained its popularity since the 18th century. During the Napoleonic Wars fortifications sprang up along the coast and two in the town now house military museums. The great white cliffs of Beachy Head rise 600ft to the W and provide exhilarating views of the Channel.

Goudhurst, *Kent*   TQ 7337
Attractive old houses line the hill up to the church where there are lovely views of hopfields, oasthouses and fruit orchards. Finchcocks, an early 18th-century house, lies 1½m W. Here a magnificent collection of historical keyboard instruments is of great interest.

Greenwich, *London*   TQ 4077
The most impressive of Greenwich's buildings are best appreciated from the river and one of the most striking groups is the Royal Naval College, formerly the Naval Hospital: Queen's House beyond houses the National Maritime Museum. The Royal Observatory in Greenwich Park has exhibits of astronomical, horological and navigational interest.

Hastings, *E Sussex*   TQ 8009
Ruins of the castle built by William the Conqueror overlook this ancient Cinque Port. Fishing has been the town's livelihood since medieval times and the old fishermen's quarter is a particularly attractive area where there is a fishermen's museum. Interesting local archaeological exhibits can be seen in the museums in Cambridge Road and the High Street.

Lewes, *W Sussex*   TQ 4110
Steep streets, tiny alleys known as twittens, and pretty red-roofed Georgian houses lend Lewes an unforgettable charm. Added to this are numerous features of interest, not least of which is the ruined Norman keep perched on its high, artificial mound. The 14th-century Castle Barbican houses a good museum of Sussex archaeology. Anne of Cleves House in Southover High Street, one of the most fascinating timbered houses in the country, is packed with domestic bygones of every conceivable nature.

Maidstone, *Kent*   TQ 7656
County town of Kent, Maidstone dates back to Anglo-Saxon times and has much of interest to offer. A Tudor mansion known as Chillington Manor houses a museum and art gallery, including Anglo-Saxon relics and jewellery, and the Tyrwhitt Drake Museum of Carriages in Mill Street, and Allington Castle 2m NE, are worth a visit. The castle, set on the Medway, retains its castellated curtain wall, gatehouse and great hall.

At one time Brighton had three piers but Palace Pier is the only one still in use with all the traditional amusements

Penshurst, *Kent*   TQ 5243
Wooded hills surround this distinguished village with houses up to 400 years old. Penshurst Place, screened by tall trees, has been the home of the Sidney family since the 15th century. Viscount De L'Isle, the present owner, has provided numerous attractions for the whole family in and around the house.

Rochester, *Kent*   TQ 7467
For those willing to seek it out there is much of interest in this busy Medway port and commercial centre. The city was a favourite haunt of Charles Dickens and Eastgate House has been turned into a Dickens Centre realistically displaying many characters from his novels. The remarkable castle keep is one of the delights of Rochester.

Royal Tunbridge Wells, *Kent*   TQ 5839
Tunbridge Wells grew up around the medicinal springs discovered in 1606 by Lord North. The waters can still be taken on the delightful shop-lined colonnaded walk called the Pantiles, which takes its name from the large roofing tiles laid for Queen Anne to walk on. Tunbridge Ware and Victorian toys are displayed in the museum at the Civic Centre.

Sevenoaks, *Kent*   TQ 5355
Pleasant but unexceptional in itself, Sevenoaks has one of England's largest stately homes on its doorstep. Before becoming the home of the Sackville family, Knole was an archbishop's, and later a king's, palace. Its seven courtyards, 52 staircases and 365 rooms cover some four acres.

Westerham, *Kent*   TQ 4454
Westerham claims fame as the birthplace of General James Wolfe who lived in Quebec House, now in the care of the National Trust. Another notable late 17th-century mansion is Squerryes Court, and as well as numerous art treasures there is a room of Wolfe exhibits here too. By far the most famous nearby house, however, is Chartwell — former home of Sir Winston Churchill.

Houses dating from the 15th to 17th centuries line Rye's cobbled Mermaid Street

Bell Harry Tower dominates the exterior of Canterbury Cathedral

Broadstairs, *Kent*   TR 3967
The spirit of Charles Dickens is strong in this Victorian resort. Bleak House, his home while writing *David Copperfield*, is now a Dickens museum and nearby the Dickens House Museum contains yet more Dickensia. Every June a Dickens Festival takes place and the townfolk dress up as Dickensian characters.

Canterbury, *Kent*   TR 1557
In the year 597 Canterbury became the Metropolitan See of the Church of England and the beautiful cathedral that housed Thomas à Becket's shrine drew pilgrims for centuries. There are many other religious foundations in the city, notably Greyfriars by the Stour and St Augustine's Abbey. Long stretches of the medieval city walls have survived, but only the keep of the 12th-century castle remains. The old Weavers House by the river dates from the 16th century when Flemish refugees began their industry.

Deal, *Kent*   TR 3752
The treacherous shifting Goodwin Sands offshore offered Deal considerable protection from sea invaders but nevertheless Henry VIII built a great castle here with a massive central citadel. Iron Age relics and many other intriguing exhibits can be seen in the Maritime and Local History Museum.

Dover, *Kent*   TR 3141
Dover was the chief Cinque Port and consequently has a magnificent castle guarding the harbour. Within the castle walls stands a rare example of a Roman lighthouse. Further evidence of the Roman invasion can be seen in the Roman Painted House in New Street, and another interesting museum is housed in the town hall.

Faversham, *Kent*   TR 0161
Faversham has a surprising number of historic buildings, considering it has always primarily been a port and commercial centre. One of its industries was gunpowder and a former mill has been preserved and restored. History is brought to life in the Fleur de Lis Heritage Centre occupying a 16th-century coaching inn.

Folkestone, *Kent*   TR 2336
Once a subsidiary Cinque Port, Folkestone still has a fishing fleet and fish market and has a harbour for cross-Channel steamers. The Leas – extensive lawns and gardens along the cliff top – are particularly appealing, and wooded walks lead down to the beach.

Margate, *Kent*   TR 3670
One of England's oldest and most well-known resorts, Margate rivals even Blackpool for variety and scope of entertainment. Two places of interest not concerned with the 20th century are Salmestone Grange – a restored medieval monastic grange, and Tudor House – a richly plastered and beamed 16th-century building housing a local history museum.

Ramsgate, *Kent*   TR 3865
Rather overshadowed by its more extravagant neighbour, Ramsgate is nevertheless a very busy resort. It was popular with the Victorians and the architecture from that period, together with Georgian building, predominates.

Rye, *E Sussex*   TQ 9220
Cobbled streets, Georgian and timbered houses and its lofty position above the Rother flood plain, give Rye a charm virtually unparalleled in England. One of its oldest buildings, the Ypres Tower, now contains a curious collection of bygones, many relating to the Cinque Ports of which Rye is one. Mermaid Street is probably the most picturesque of Rye's roads and is famous for the Mermaid Inn – a notorious smugglers' haunt. Lamb House was Henry James' home and now belongs to the National Trust.

Sandwich, *Kent*   TR 3358
A 2m stretch of sand-dunes now separates the town from the sea, but Sandwich is actually the oldest of the Cinque Ports. Of the wealth of attractive old buildings that grace the streets, the medieval Barbican, Fisher Gate and St Bartholomew's Hospital are particularly noteworthy.

Tenterden, *Kent*   TQ 8833
Weather-boarded houses so typical of the Kentish Weald line Tenterden's delightful main street. It has the distinction of being the principal station of Britain's first light railway in the late 1800s, and this was re-opened in 1974 with steam trains.

Whitstable, *Kent*   TR 1166
This popular seaside resort was once famous for its oyster beds. The beach is shingle, but there are plenty of amusements and facilities and it is a good centre for water-skiing and surfing. Yachtsmen flock to Whitstable as there are three top class clubs here.

Winchelsea, *E Sussex*   TQ 9017
Considerably quieter than its famous neighbour, Rye, Winchelsea has a sleepy charm that many prefer. Also a subsidiary Cinque Port, the old town was submerged by the sea and rebuilt in about 1292. One of its oldest buildings is Court Hall.

Today only the chancel and side chapels of St Thomas's in Winchelsea are still standing

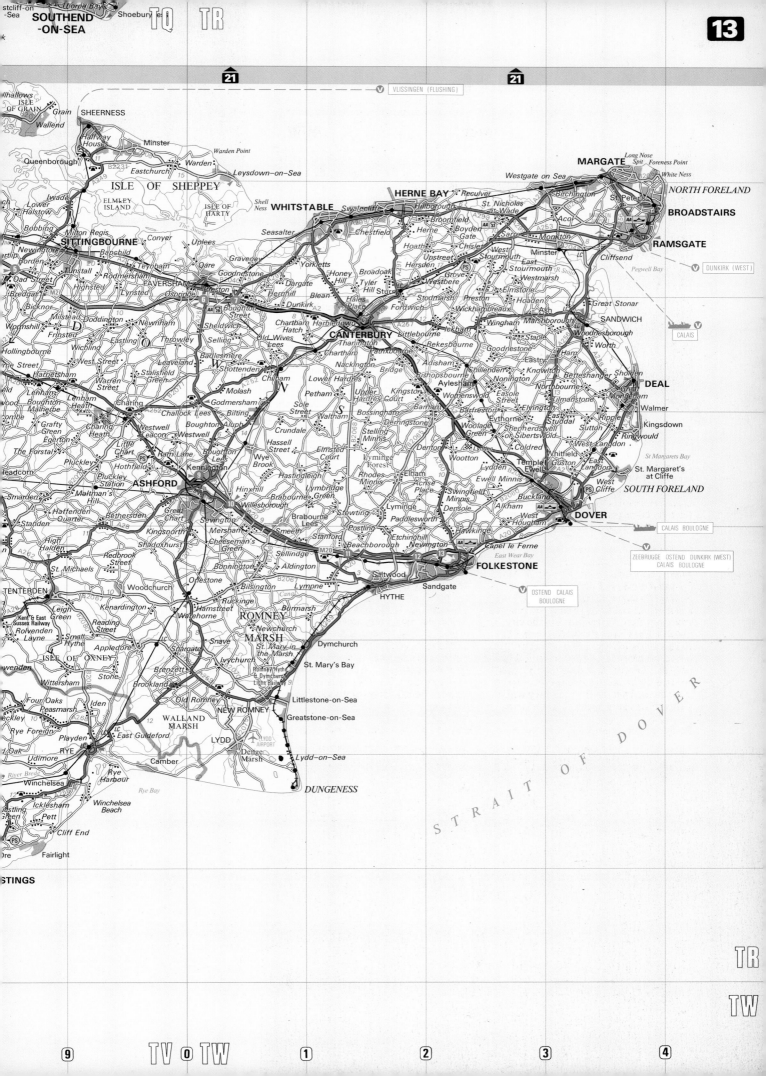

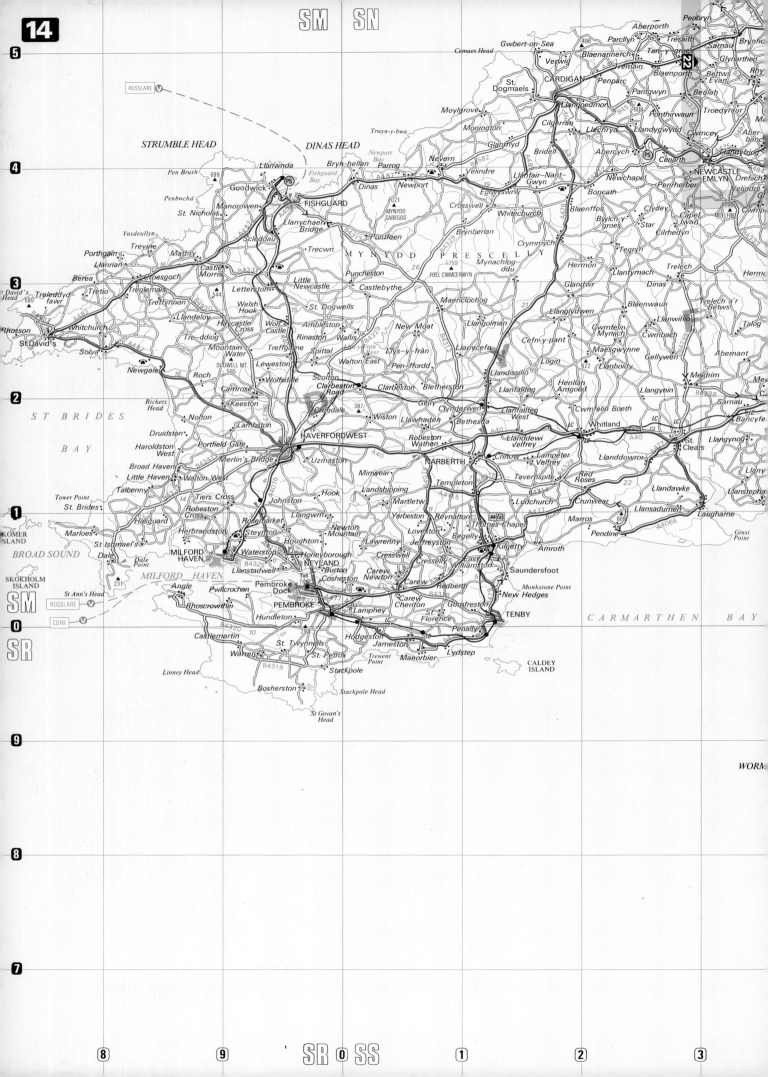

Caldey Island, *Dyfed* SR 1497
A community of Cistercian monks live on the island, and as well as farming the land they produce their own brand of perfume which is for sale. Motor boats run out to the island from Tenby 2½m away.

Cardigan, *Dyfed* SN 1846
Until the beautiful River Teifi silted up Cardigan was an important sea port exporting lead. Coracles are still able to navigate the waters and trout and salmon are caught from these time-honoured craft. A weekly market held beneath the Guildhall's arches draws visitors from far and wide.

Carew, *Dyfed* SN 0403
The overgrown ruin of Carew Castle stands on the lonely banks of the Cleddau River at the edge of the village. Nearby a tidal corn mill dating from the 18th century is open as a working museum.

Cenarth, *Dyfed* SN 2641
Cenarth Falls on the River Teifi is one of the most beautiful stretches of water in Wales. Downstream from the swirling, foaming pools, men in coracles are a familiar sight.

Fishguard, *Dyfed* SM 9637
A steep hill separates Lower Town – the oldest part of Fishguard clustering around the creek – and Upper Town. History was made here during the 18th century when a treaty was signed that ended the last invasion of British soil. The town is an ideal centre for touring the spectacular coastal scenery to either side.

Haverfordwest, *Dyfed* SM 9515
A ruined 12th-century stronghold broods over the steep slopes of this old market town that resisted Welsh rule for so long. The castle was used as a gaol until 1820 and now houses the county museum and art gallery.

Laugharne, *Dyfed* SN 3011
Dylan Thomas loved this remote village and after several visits returned in 1949 to live in The Boathouse. This romantic Georgian house, idyllically set into Cliff Walk, has been turned into a museum of his work, and the blue-painted garden shed where he worked has been kept just as he left it – cigarette ends on the floor and all!

Manorbier, *Dyfed* SS 0698
Giraldus Cambrensis – well-known 12th-century historian – was born at Manorbier's imposing stone castle in 1146. Norman barons built the castle and it resembles a baronial manor rather than a fortification. A pleasant sandy beach with inviting tidal rock pools is ideal for children.

Milford Haven, *Dyfed* SM 9006
The huge natural harbour of Milford Haven was one of Britain's great fishing ports during the 18th century and the town developed during those days. Great oil refineries have sprung up along the shoreline, but the town itself has been unspoilt and part of the Haven has been designated a nature reserve.

Pembroke, *Dyfed* SM 9901
Like so many Welsh towns, Pembroke grew up around its great castle. Impressively perched on a rocky promontory above the town, this great fortress has a huge natural cavern beneath its foundations which is reached by a twisting staircase and opens onto the sea.

Pembroke Dock, *Dyfed* SM 9603
Tidy grey buildings line the straight streets of Pembroke Dock – onetime naval dockyard but now mainly used by ship repairers and chandlers. At the Gypsy Wagon Museum in the Commons Road traditional gypsy caravans are restored on the premises and the work can be observed.

When Tenby's town walls were built in the 13th century there were probably about 20 towers like this one in South Parade

St David's, *Dyfed* SM 7525
St David, revered patron saint of Wales, was born here and his bones rest in the great cathedral begun some 500 years after his death. In about 1340 the Bishop's Palace was built to accommodate pilgrims visiting the shrine and the extensive remains show some fine architectural detail.

Tenby, *Dyfed* SN 1300
Medieval town walls, elegant Georgian houses and a busy picturesque harbour are Tenby's chief charms. The remains of the Norman castle perched on top of Castle Hill house a good museum relating to the Tenby district.

The cascading Teifi at Cenarth

Mumbles Pier, at the western end of Swansea Bay, incorporates a promenade and lifeboat station

Bridgend, *M Glam*   ss 9079

Three Norman castles lie within easy reach of this busy town at the end of the Vale of Glamorgan. The nearest is Newcastle, set up on a wooded hill near St Illtyd's Church. Its massive curtain walls enclose a polygonal courtyard and there is a richly carved Norman gateway on the south side of the rectangular tower. Coity Castle – 2m NE, Ogmore Castle – 3m SW, and the medieval manor of Candleston – 1m SW, are all of interest.

Carmarthen, *Dyfed*   SN 4120

Narrow, twisting streets weaving through tightly-packed old houses give credibility to Carmarthen's claim to be the oldest town in Wales. Its history reaches back to Celtic times and Roman relics from the area can be seen in the museum at nearby Abergwili. Coracles on the River Tywi below are a familiar sight.

Kidwelly, *Dyfed*   SN 4106

Kidwelly lies between the two Gwendraeth rivers which meander out to the sea over flat marshy land. The town's chief glory is its castle overlooking the area from higher ground. Built during Henry I's reign, it was one of a string along the coast that protected territories won by the Normans.

Llandovery, *Dyfed*   SN 7634

Three rivers meet at Llandovery which have given it its evocative name of 'church amid the waters'. A pleasing mixture of Georgian and Victorian houses and the picturesque ruin of its castle lend the town considerable appeal. In the past it was an important cattle centre and the weekly cattle market held now is a lively local event.

Llanelli, *Dyfed*   SN 5000

As far back as the 16th century Llanelli became a market town for the surrounding districts, but industrialisation took over in the early 19th century. Parc Howard is a pleasant recreational area that was presented to the town by its first mayor, Sir Stafford Howard. Here an art gallery and museum contains a permanent collection of paintings and the distinctive Llanelli pottery.

Mumbles, The *W Glam*   ss 6287

The curiously named Mumbles are actually the two tiny islands at the tip of Swansea Bay, but the whole peninsula is referred to by this name. An 800ft pier, safe bathing and a variety of amusements and entertainments all contribute to the resort's increasing popularity. Oystermouth Castle at the opposite end of the bay consists of a ruined gatehouse, chapel and great hall.

Neath, *W Glam*   ss 7597

Steel works and collieries dominate Neath and the countryside southwards, but stretching away to the NE are wooded hills and the picturesque Vale of Neath, characterised by spectacular waterfalls. Richard de Granville founded an abbey at Neath during the early 12th century but the existing ruins date from the 1300 and 1600s. Penscynor Wildlife Park 2m NW has a lovely bird garden specialising in exotic breeds which are allowed to fly free and are bred in conditions as similar to their natural habitat as possible.

Thomas Picton, British soldier, is commemorated by a monument in Carmarthen's museum.

Porthcawl, *M Glam*   ss 8176

Porthcawl enjoys the reputation of being one of the leading resorts on the south coast of Wales. The harbour forms the focal point of this attractive town and the esplanade and huge sandy beaches, plus every conceivable form of seaside entertainment, make it ideal for a lively family holiday.

Sennybridge, *Powys*   SN 9228

During the 19th century Sennybridge developed as an important sheep and cattle market centre for the surrounding area. The town lies on the northern edge of the Brecon Beacons National Park that is made up of some 500 sq m of mountains and moors. The name dates from the days when a chain of beacon hilltop fires were lit as a means of communication.

Swansea, *W Glam*   ss 6593

Bomb-damage and intensive industrialisation have left their scars on Swansea but there are three museums of interest and the Gower peninsula on its doorstep is beautiful. The thick wooded valleys, lovely beaches and rolling fields constitute some of the most beautiful and unspoilt scenery in South Wales.

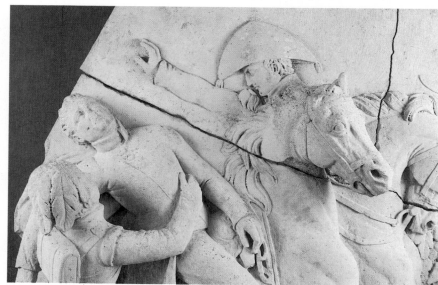

Cider-making is just one of the many traditional crafts still practised in the restored buildings at the folk museum at St Fagan's

Abergavenny, *Gwent*   SO 2914
Abergavenny, set on the banks of the River Usk, is surrounded by seven green hills and borders onto the Brecon Beacons National Park. The 12th-century castle that once guarded the valley contains a museum of rural craft tools, a Welsh kitchen, a saddler's shop, costumes and local history.

Barry, *S Glam*   ST 1168
Extensive docklands were built around Barry in the late 19th century and the population exploded from 500 to over 12,500. At the same time the Barry Island holiday resort expanded at a rapid rate and now has everything possible for the holidaymaker. A breaker's yard on the island has dozens of scrapped steam locos which are used for restoration.

Caerleon, *Gwent*   ST 3390
As the onetime base of the 2nd Augustinian Legion, Caerleon is believed to have had about 6,000 inhabitants. Excavations

have revealed various living quarters, but the most striking remain is the great oval amphitheatre. A museum on the site contains a selection of finds from the fortress.

Caerphilly, *M Glam*   ST 1587
Caerphilly is best known for its cheese and its castle. In fact the cheese-making industry has been phased out to some extent, but the castle, the second largest in Britain, continues to dominate the town and draw thousands of visitors.

Cardiff, *S Glam*   ST 1877
Cardiff, capital city and cultural centre of Wales, owes much of its development to the Bute family. It was the 3rd Marquess of Bute who restored the castle with the help of the bizarre architect, William Burges. Close to the castle, in Cathays Park, are Cardiff's principal civic buildings, one of which houses the National Museum of Wales. Now fully restored to its former splendour is the city's cathedral at Llandaff, NW of the city centre.

Chepstow, *Gwent*   ST 5393
Switchback streets and quaint old houses crowd together in the shadow of Chepstow Castle, spectacularly set above a bend of the River Wye. A Royalist stronghold during the Civil War, it was dismantled in 1690. Exhibitions of all aspects of Chepstow can be seen in the Chepstow Museum, but the wine and salmon displays are particularly good.

Clevedon, *Avon*   ST 4071
Just outside this Severn estuary resort is Clevedon Court, a superb 14th-century house typical of the period. Beautiful 18th-century terraced gardens drop away from the house and opposite, off the B3130, are 16 craft studios and a museum of countryside artefacts.

During the 19th century a romantic complex was built in the grounds of Cardiff Castle

Monmouth, *Gwent*   SO 5113
Monmouth's strategic position on the Rivers Wye and Monnow was recognised by the Normans and the fortified bridge they built in 1262 is the only one left in Britain. Their castle suffered severe damage during the Civil War, but the Duke of Beaufort built Great Castle House onto the ruins with stones from the castle. Collections of Nelson memorabilia can be seen in the town museum.

Penarth, *S Glam*   ST 1871
The Victorians adopted Penarth and transformed it into a seaside resort in the late 19th century. Pleasant gardens and lawns give the town a peaceful atmosphere, and the old harbour is now a lively water skiing and sailing centre. Turner House includes exhibits from the National Museum and has a small art gallery.

St Fagan's, *S Glam*   ST 1177
St Fagan's, an attractive village of thatched cottages beside the River Ely, is best-known for the collection of buildings rescued from all over Wales that form the National Folk Museum of Wales. Even the furnished interiors are authentic, and some still fulfil their original functions.

Usk, *Gwent*   SO 3701
Noted as an angling centre, this old market town stands on the river of the same name which means 'water'. A castle, founded by the de Clare family but eventually dismantled during the Civil War, overlooks the town.

Weston-super-Mare, *Avon*   ST 3261
Large beaches and a pier backed by seafront gardens face the Bristol Channel at Weston. As well as a boating lake and aquarium, there is an interesting museum in Burlington Street featuring displays of the typical Victorian seaside holiday.

Avebury, *Wilts*   SU 0969
The Avebury Stone Circle is one of
Europe's most famous prehistoric monuments. About 28 acres, including the
attractive village of Avebury, are enclosed within the outer standing stones.
Avebury Manor is a fine Elizabethan
mansion with grounds containing the
Alexander Keiller Museum, the Wiltshire Folk Life Society Great Barn and a
model railway.

Bath, *Avon*   ST 7464
Few cities can claim such elegance as
Bath. Some 2,000 years after the Romans
built baths around the natural hot
springs, the Georgian spa town was created which was to become the hub of
high society. The superb work of architects John Wood and son includes the
Royal Crescent – no 1 is open as a period
showpiece, the Circus, and the Assembly
Rooms – where there is a costume
museum.

Bourton-on-the-Water, *Glos*   SP 1620
This is one of the Cotswold's most
famous villages and as such caters well
for tourists. A model village in the New
Inn garden represents Bourton in miniature, and nearby is a motor museum and
the Birdland Zoo Gardens and Wildlife
Art Gallery.

Bradford-on-Avon, *Wilts*   ST 8260
Terraces of old weavers' cottages overlook this pretty town nestling by the
River Avon at the foot of a steep limestone hill. A tiny Saxon church and a
superb 14th-century tithe barn are the
main treasures of Bradford, but there are
numerous other unexpected delights.

*Three curving terraces form Bath's elegant
circle of houses known as The Circus*

Bristol, *Avon*   ST 5872
During the 16th century ships set sail
from Bristol in search of new and exotic
merchandise and international trading
flourished as never before. Brunel
launched his SS *Great Britain* here in
1843 and the ship is now back in dry
dock as a museum. Although Bristol is a
commercial 20th-century city and port,
historic buildings abound in its streets
and a wealth of interest awaits any visitor.

Cheltenham, *Glos*   SO 9422
Elegant Regency architecture arranged in
squares, avenues and crescents is Cheltenham's hallmark. The whole town was
built around the medicinal springs discovered in the 18th century, and it
became one of the most fashionable spas
in the country. Gustav Holst was born
here and his house has been turned into a
museum of his life and work, and the art
gallery and museum in Clarence Street is
excellent. The Pittville Pump Room still
dispenses the waters.

Chippenham, *Wilts*   ST 9173
Situated on the River Avon, this pleasant
town was a market centre for several
hundred years. Now industrialised, it
retains many attractive houses and
an ancient lock-up in the Yeldehall.
Nearby Sheldon Manor has a detached
15th-century chapel and beautifully
terraced gardens.

Cirencester, *Glos*   SP 0201
Cirencester was the second biggest town
in England during Roman times and the
Corinium Museum has lovely mosaics,
jewellery and domestic items which have
been excavated in the area. Its pretty old
streets and greystone cottages are dominated by the grand church built with the
profits of the wool trade.

Devizes, *Wilts*   SU 0061
Situated on the edge of Salisbury Plain,
Devizes is a good centre for exploring
Wiltshire and the town museum provides
an informative background to the area.
The Kennet and Avon Canal has a record
29 locks between Devizes and Caen Hill.

Gloucester Cathedral is one of the centres of the famous Three Choirs Festival

Gloucester, *Glos*   SO 8318
Gloucester began when the Romans built
a fort and called it *Glevum*. Later the
Saxons called it Gleawcestre and when
the Normans arrived they built the great
church which is preserved at the heart of
Gloucester's magnificent cathedral. The
city's four main streets still follow the
original Roman layout. Bishop Hooper's
Lodging in Westgate Street, traditionally
associated with the martyrdom of John
Hooper in 1555, now contains a folk
museum.

Lacock, *Wilts*   ST 9168
This beautiful village is now owned by
the National Trust and the buildings
dating from medieval times to the 18th
century are lovingly preserved. The
lovely abbey on the outskirts was built as
an Augustinian nunnery and, after the
Reformation, rebuilt as a Tudor mansion. Its tithe barn contains a museum of
Fox-Talbot's photographic work.

Painswick, *Glos*   SU 8609
Handsome greystone houses cluster
round the famous churchyard of Painswick where there are about 100 clipped
yew trees and dozens of rare tabletop
tombs. Painswick House stands ½m outside this lovely little town and Prinknash
Abbey and Bird Park towards Cheltenham are particularly attractive.

Stroud, *Glos*   SO 8504
At one time Stroud claimed to produce
the finest broadcloth in England, and one
of its chief products today is baize for
billiard tables. Some of the old mills still
stand and a few fine houses built by the
wealthier clothiers have survived. The
District Museum at Landsdown has,
among other things, a full-size model of
the dinosaur megalosaurus.

Tetbury, *Glos*   ST 8993
The most distinctive feature of this
attractive little Cotswold market town is
its 17th-century town hall raised on three
rows of pillars. Chavenage, 2m NW, is a
charming Elizabethan manor house with
some lovely 17th-century stained glass.

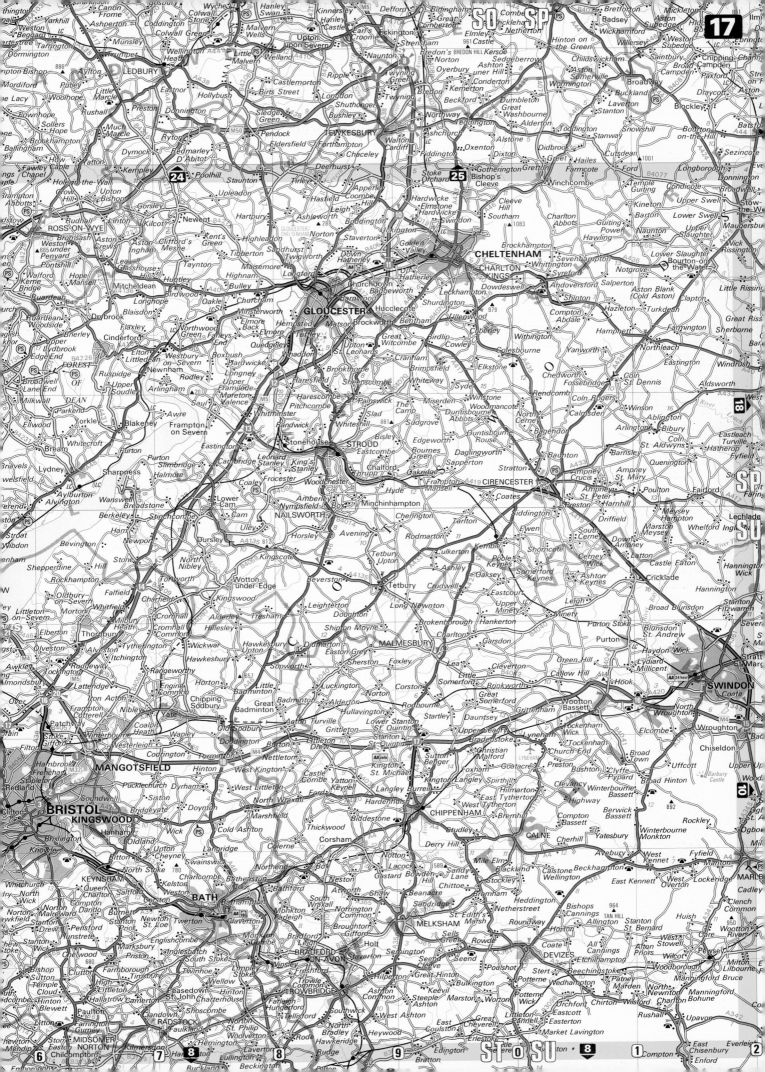

Visitors to Henley often leave the river to explore the many quaint old shops

Abingdon, *Oxon*   SU 4997
Onetime county town of Berkshire, Abingdon is a charming mixture of architectural styles dating back to the 13th century. Its Thameside position gives it a lovely peaceful atmosphere and provides pleasant towpath and water meadow walks. The elegant 17th-century County Hall houses the town museum.

Aylesbury, *Bucks*   SP 8213
This ancient market town overlooks the wide fertile vale of the same name where beef herds grow fat. The weekly cattle market, which used to be held in the town's cobbled market square, now takes place near the Victorian town hall. A charming building in Church Street – the former grammar school – houses the Bucks County Museum.

Buckingham, *Bucks*   SP 6933
King Alfred made this riverside settlement the county town of Buckinghamshire in 886 and its maze of narrow streets are packed with interest. Buildings of note include the Georgian town hall, the Manor House and the old gaol in the middle of Market Square.

Burford, *Oxon*   SP 2512
Burford's sloping main street lined with golden-coloured stone houses is the epitome of a prosperous Cotswold wool town. Local crafts, town charters, seals and ancient manuscripts in the Tolsey Museum record the history of Burford. 2m S the Cotswold Wildlife Park offers wild animals, gardens and woodlands, an adventure playground and a narrow-gauge railway.

Chipping Norton, *Oxon*   SP 3127
Chipping is a derivative of the Anglo-Saxon word for market, and for two centuries it was the commercial centre for the Evenlode valley. The town's wide market place is surrounded by handsome 16th- and 17th-century houses built by wealthy wool merchants, and there are a number of ancient inns once mainly used by cattle and sheep farmers. 3m N are the Rollright Stones – monolithic Bronze Age stone circles.

Henley-on-Thames, *Oxon*   SU 7682
The annual Henley Regatta draws more visitors than usual to this deservedly popular riverside town. Throughout the summer boats of all kinds are available for hire and there are several pleasant walks along the river. Among the picturesque inns and houses is the Kenton Theatre – the fourth oldest in England.

Moreton-in-Marsh, *Glos*   SP 2032
This pleasant little market town on the edge of the Cotswolds used to be an important coaching town and the Redesdale Arms was the chief stop. Charles I slept in another of Moreton's old inns, the White Hart.

Oxford, *Oxon*   SP 5305
Oxford has been a centre of learning since the 13th century when Edmund Hall, Merton and Balliol Colleges were founded. As well as the beautiful colleges, much of the city centre is occupied by outstanding buildings belonging to the university: the circular Sheldonian Theatre, the Radcliffe Camera and the Bodleian. Of the city's many museums its greatest is the wonderful Ashmolean, where priceless treasures from all corners of the earth are collected. Another delightful aspect of Oxford is the river where punts can be hired.

Thame, *Oxon*   SP 7006
Architecture spanning 500 years lines the streets of Thame but one of the most picturesque buildings is the 15th-century Birdcage Inn in the High Street. This exceptionally wide thoroughfare is the scene every autumn of the annual town fair. Parliamentarian John Hampton was educated at Thame Grammar School.

Waddesdon, *Bucks*   SP 7416
On the doorstep of this attractive, rambling village is a great manor house resembling a French château. Waddesdon Manor was built in the 1870s for Baron Ferdinand de Rothschild, but now in the care of the National Trust, this vast treasure-trove of priceless objects can be enjoyed by everyone.

Oxford's Radcliffe Camera is now a Bodleian Library reading room

Wallingford, *Oxon*   SU 6089
As its name suggests, the town grew up around a ford across the Thames and traces of Anglo-Saxon ramparts can still be seen. A pleasant mixture of Georgian and timber-framed buildings grace the streets, and of special interest is the 17th-century town hall which contains a portrait by Gainsborough.

Witney, *Oxon*   SP 3509
Witney blankets are a household name and the industry has flourished since the 18th century. This prosperity is reflected in the fine houses built around the green and the elaborate Butter Cross. ½m SE at Cogges an Edwardian-period farm demonstrates the agriculture of Oxfordshire.

Woodstock, *Oxon*   SP 4416
Attractive in its own right with numerous old stone houses and the famous Bear Hotel, Woodstock nevertheless tends to be eclipsed by its grand neighbour, Blenheim Palace. Sir John Vanbrugh's grandiose house occupies seven acres and the awe-inspiring grounds cover some 2,200 – including a huge lake, a Triumphal Arch and an Italian-style garden.

Long Alley Almshouses provide a pretty setting for St Helen's Church in Abingdon

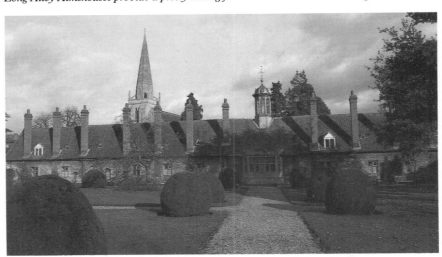

The white lion cut out of the chalky slopes of Dunstable Downs advertises Whipsnade's famous open-air zoo

Ampthill, *Beds*   TL 0337
Thatched cottages and Georgian coaching inns surround the pretty square of Ampthill. 1m N lies Houghton House – a ruined 17th-century mansion dismantled in 1794.

Ayot St Lawrence, *Herts*   TL 1916
At one end of this village is Shaw's Corner – the home of George Bernard Shaw from 1906 until his death in 1950. He donated the house to the National Trust before he died and many of the rooms have been kept as they were in the playwright's lifetime.

Cookham, *Berks*   SU 8985
River cruisers crowd the Thames at Cookham and boathouses along the banks hire out all types of craft. Stanley Spencer lived in Cookham and several of his paintings depict river scenes. A gallery in the High Street features many of Spencer's works.

Dunstable, *Beds*   TL 0221
Although Henry I established Dunstable in 1113, the present town is mostly modern with just a smattering of old buildings and a few from Victorian times. The ancient Roman roads – Watling Street and Icknield Way – meet in the town and much of the more interesting architecture is to be found around this crossroads.

Hatfield, *Herts*   TL 2309
This ancient market town is overshadowed by the splendid Jacobean home of the Marquess of Salisbury – Hatfield House. Standing within the gardens is the surviving wing of the Royal Palace in which Elizabeth I spent much of her childhood.

High Wycombe, *Bucks*   SU 8593
Lace and paper used to bring High Wycombe a respectable livelihood, but furniture-making is now its leading industry and a museum of chairmaking in Castle Hill House traces the history of this craft. Hughendon Manor, 1½m N, was the home of Disraeli and contains much of the statesman's furniture and books.

Hitchin, *Herts*   TL 1829
Hitchin became prosperous as a medieval wool town and it has preserved many of its old buildings. The museum in Paynes Park covers a variety of subjects and has monthly exhibitions.

Leighton Buzzard, *Beds*   SP 9225
Linslade and Leighton Buzzard, divided by the River Ouse, have recently been amalgamated into one town. Leighton is a pleasant place with thatched brick and timber cottages and a handsome five-sided market cross. The Light Railway (reclaimed industrial track) runs from Pages Park through nearly four miles of lovely countryside.

Luton, *Beds*   TL 0821
Luton is best known for its light industry and its airport, but something of its more interesting past can be gleaned from the museum and art gallery in Wardown Park. Just outside the town is Luton Hoo – the mansion built by Robert Adam that now houses Julius Wernher's spectacular collection of art treasures, Fabergé jewellery, and imperial robes from the Russian court.

Maidenhead, *Berks*   SU 8881
Maidenhead is a popular Thameside residential town that originally developed in the 13th century. Oldfield House, near the bridge, houses the Henry Reitlinger Bequest museum which includes ceramics, glass and paintings. 1½m W is the Courage Shire Horse Centre where about a dozen shire horses are kept and there are several other attractions including many specially for children.

Marlow, *Bucks*   SU 8587
One of the prettiest towns on the river, Marlow is a picture of unspoilt old buildings, an elegant suspension bridge and a cascading weir. The Compleat Angler Hotel by the bridge was named after Izaak Walton's famous fishing book.

St Albans, *Herts*   TL 1507
Just W of St Albans lie the remains of the Roman town of *Verulamium* and a superb museum of Roman finds. The great abbey founded in 793 sits on a hill above St Albans whose winding old streets are a delight to explore. The City Museum, St Albans Organ Museum, the Royal National Rose Society's Gardens and Kingsbury Watermill Museum each have their own fascination and are well worth a visit. Gorhambury House on the A414 was the home of Sir Francis Bacon and contains various relics relating to his life.

Whipsnade, *Beds*   TL 0117
As one of England's oldest open-air zoos, Whipsnade gained fame for providing animals with natural surroundings. The park set in the Chiltern countryside includes hundreds of animals and birds obviously enjoying their near-freedom.

Woburn, *Beds*   SP 9433
Attractive old buildings, many now occupied by antique shops, fill the village of Woburn made famous through Woburn Abbey and the Wild Animal Kingdom. Rare and exotic animals are the chief attractions of the 3,000-acre park, but numerous other family entertainments are also provided.

The abbey gatehouse at St Albans – one of many reminders of the ecclesiastical connections of this town which was named after Britain's first Christian martyr

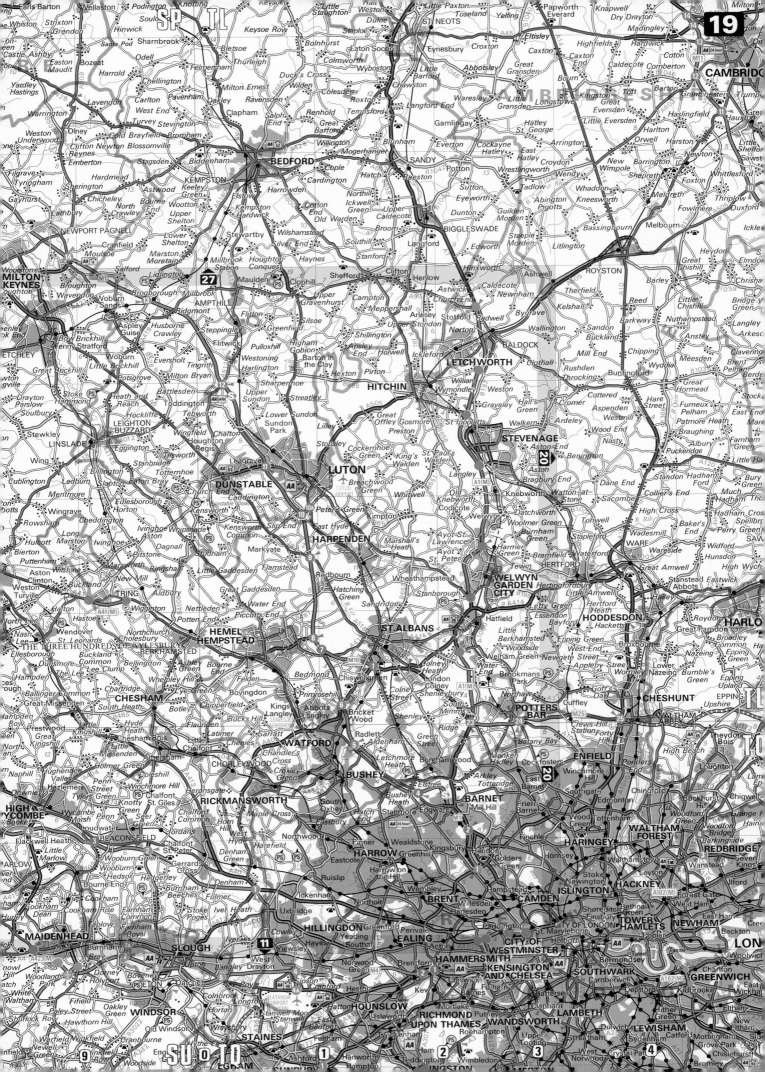

Beautiful lawns and gardens known as The Backs slope down to the River Cam behind the gracious college buildings in Cambridge

Bishop's Stortford, *Herts* TL 4821
Cecil Rhodes was born here in 1853 and the house in South Street is now a museum with exhibits relating to his life and work. Hatfield Forest 3m NE has good facilities for boating and fishing.

Cambridge, *Cambs* TL 4658
This ancient university city sits on the willow-shaded banks of the River Cam. Of the 36 colleges, King's College is perhaps the most outstanding architecturally – a medieval masterpiece with some of the finest fan-vaulting in Europe – and the lovely half-timbered Queens' College is by far the most picturesque. This city boasts many impressive museums, notably the Fitzwilliam Museum, the Museum of Archaeology and Anthropology, and the Scott Polar Research Institute which houses displays, manuscripts, photographs etc., relating to Arctic and Antarctic expeditions. The University Botanic Garden consists of 40 acres of fine botanical collections.

Chelmsford, *Essex* TL 7006
This busy county town was an important market town in earlier times and the site of the world's first radio company, set up in 1899 by the Marconi Company. Mementoes of the original company, as well as exhibits of Roman remains and local history, can be seen at the Chelmsford and Essex Museum in Oaklands Park.

Chipping Ongar, *Essex* TL 5502
Chipping Ongar grew as a market town beneath the walls of a Norman castle of which only the mound and moat remain. Missionary and explorer David Livingstone was a pupil pastor of the town's 19th-century Congregational Church.

Danbury, *Essex* TL 7805
This ancient village overlooks the Chelmer valley from a 400ft wooded hill. As the name implies, Danbury was the site of a Danish settlement after their invasion in the Dark Ages. Remains of an ancient earthwork defence can still be seen in the local churchyard, and there are unusual wooden effigies of knights inside. The National Trust land of Danbury Common lies S of the village and another beautiful stretch of countryside, Danbury Country Park, lies to the W.

Epping, *Essex* TL 4602
This small market town has managed to retain its own identity and charm despite its proximity to London. The 18th-century Winchelsea House and Epping Place, in the High Road, are of interest. Nearby Epping Forest was created by the conquering Normans who used it as a hunting ground.

Maldon, *Essex* TL 8506
The charming little town of Maldon is renowned for its natural fine quality table salt, mined from a hillside above the

Essex sailing barges and fishing smacks are moored at The Hythe in Maldon

Blackwater River. Oyster beds are another well-known feature of this picturesque port and yachting harbour, whose steep winding streets are a wonderland of fascinating shops and homely inns. A battleground to the E was the site of the Battle of Maldon in 991.

Rodings, The *Essex* TL 5913
The Rodings is the name shared by a number of attractive villages lying in the Roding valley. Leaden Roding is one, and High Roding, with its thatched and gabled cottages, is another.

Saffron Walden, *Essex* TL 5438
An autumn-flowering saffron crocus was the speciality of this delightful town at one time. There are a number of interesting timbered houses and inns in Saffron Walden, notably the Cross Keys Inn and the Rose and Crown. The magnificent 17th-century mansion, Audley End, lies 1m W of the town.

South Woodham Ferrers, *Essex* TQ 8097
An impressive new town has recently sprung up in the reclaimed marshland around the quaint market town of South Woodham Ferrers. Occupying a sheltered position overlooking the Crouch estuary, the town has been given a traditional-style market place surrounded by terraces and arcades.

Stock, *Essex* TQ 6998
The local church has a traditional wooden belfry which is said to include timbers from wrecked galleons of the Spanish Armada. Almshouses and a tower windmill are other attractions in this pleasant village.

Ware, *Herts* TL 3614
Attractive old houses and the Canon Maltings of about 1600 are features of Ware. The famous 'Great Bed of Ware' is now in the Victoria and Albert Museum, London. Ware Priory and the Regency-period town hall are two other notable buildings.

Colchester, *Essex*   TM 0025
Once a Roman capital and the oldest
recorded town in England, Colchester is
a pretty place with lots to offer the visitor.
The Emperor Claudius had a temple here
and it was on this site that the Normans
built their castle, using Roman bricks in
its construction. Today the castle houses
a museum with Roman, Iron Age and
medieval exhibits. There are five other
museums, and the art gallery is housed in
the Minories, a Georgian building of
Tudor origin. Colchester Zoo offers all
the usual attractions plus a model railway. The town's age-old traditions of
oyster cultivation and rose-growing are
celebrated each year with an oyster feast
and the Colchester Rose Show.

East Bergholt, *Suffolk*   TM 0734
The great landscape painter John Constable was born here in 1776 and it is a
fitting compliment to the area that he said
'These scenes made me a painter'.
Mellow Elizabethan cottages, set in fine
gardens, cluster around the 14th-century
church and a nearby timber-framed
belfry. Close to the village is Flatford
Mill, made famous by Constable.

Flatford Mill, near East Bergholt, is featured in several of Constable's works

Felixstowe, *Suffolk*   TM 3034
Felixstowe has been a popular seaside
resort since the late 19th century when
the German Kaiser was among the
fashionable society who were drawn
here. The 2m promenade is well laid out
with neat lawns and beautiful flowerbeds.
Felixstowe Dock is a busy car-ferry
terminus as well as a container port and
tanker terminal.

Hadleigh, *Suffolk*   TM 0242
Fine examples of pargetting adorn many
High Street buildings in this attractive
River Stour market town. The 15th-
century Guildhall is a striking combination of redbrick and timber, and the
imposing Deanery Tower is also of note.

*Gainsborough House, in Sudbury, was
given its Georgian façade in about 1727*

Harwich, *Essex*   TM 2431
A famous seaport and sailing centre,
Harwich lies at the mouths of the Stour
and Orwell. Christopher Jones, captain
of the *Mayflower*, was one of the famous
sailors born here. The Redoubt is a
circular fort, dating from 1808, which
was built to defend the port against
Napoleonic invasion. It has recently
been restored by the Harwich Society
and part of the building is used as a
museum.

Ipswich, *Suffolk*   TM 1744
Many relics of an eventful past survive in
Ipswich, a town which is not only large
and successful but which also boasts a
major port. Cardinal Wolsey was born
here and he founded the Cardinal College
of St Mary in the 16th century. The
building was never completed, but the
gateway can still be seen. One of the most
beautiful buildings is the Ancient House
which displays an outstanding example of
the East Anglian art of pargetting – an
intricate exterior decoration in plaster.
Christchurch Mansion, built by a Tudor
merchant, occupies an oasis of parkland
in the centre of town.

Needham Market, *Suffolk*   TM 0855
Set on the banks of the River Gipping,
this sleepy little town is surrounded by
lovely countryside. The local church
boasts a unique 15th-century wooden
hammerbeam nave roof.

Orford, *Suffolk*   TM 4250
Fishermen's cottages and quaint houses
huddle together beneath an imposing
castle in this picturesque village. A collection of arms can be seen in the castle
which affords excellent views of the surrounding countryside. Orford Ness, a
long shingle bank, separates the River
Ore from the sea.

Southend-on-Sea, *Essex*   TQ 8885
Southend Pier (1¼m) is the longest in
the world and the walk it provides
is a great attraction for day trippers
who flock here. Other attractions include
the quieter sandy beaches at Thorpe Bay
and the ornamental gardens and Edwardian bandstand at Westcliff. The 14th-
century Southchurch Hall – a timbered
manor house restored and furnished as
a medieval home, Prittlewell Priory –
a restored 12th-century Cluniac priory,
and the Historic Aircraft Museum ½m
away are all interesting places to
visit.

Stowmarket, *Suffolk*   TM 0458
Thomas Young, tutor to John Milton,
lived here, and the poet visited this
bustling Gipping valley market town
regularly to see him. The Museum of
East Anglian Life is an open-air museum
displaying collections of horse-drawn
vehicles and farm implements. Of special
interest are the buildings of historic and
architectural interest that have been re-
erected on this site to avoid demolition.

Sudbury, *Suffolk*   TL 8741
Birthplace of painter Thomas Gainsborough, his house at 46 Gainsborough
Street is now a local arts centre and
museum of his life and work. The town is
referred to as Eatanswill in Charles
Dickens' *Pickwick Papers*.

Woodbridge, *Suffolk*   TM 2749
The old market square at Woodbridge is
surrounded by pleasant buildings, many
of 16th-century origin and with an interesting history. The Shire Hall is a superb
example, it incorporates work from the
16th to 19th centuries and has notable
Dutch-style gables. The port was once
the scene of much ocean trade but today
it is a popular sailing centre.

Aberaeron, *Dyfed* SN 4562
The elegant and unspoilt holiday resort of Aberaeron was largely the work of 18th-century heiress Susannah Jones, who, along with her Hampshire curate husband, built the town with her inheritance. The construction of harbours, quays, stores, a town hall and streets of houses continued well into the 19th century and resulted in the charming Georgian-style town we see today.

Aberystwyth, *Dyfed* SN 5881
This popular holiday resort and university town grew up in the shadow of its Norman castle, the ruins of which stand on the headland in Cardigan Bay. Opposite the castle is a Victorian hotel that was bought in 1870 to form the nucleus of the University of Wales. University buildings east of the town on Penglais Hill include the National Library of Wales which houses the oldest Welsh manuscript in existence – the 12th-century Black Book of Carmarthen. The famous Vale of Rheidol Light Railway runs 12m through the beautiful Rheidol valley from Aberystwyth to Devil's Bridge.

Devil's Bridge, *Dyfed* SN 7477
At Devil's Bridge the Cwm Rheidol narrows to form a magnificent 500ft-deep wooded gorge through which the waters of the River Mynach tumble in spectacular cascades. The full scenic splendour of the area is best appreciated from the valley bottom reached by means of a 91-step zig-zag pathway known as Jacob's Ladder. The Devil's Bridge itself is in fact three bridges built one on top of the other – the lowest is reputed to have been erected by 12th-century monks from Strata Florida Abbey.

Machynlleth's clock-tower replaced the old market cross in 1873. It commemorates the Marquesses of Londonderry

Lampeter, *Dyfed* SN 5748
This charming little market town enjoys a pastoral setting amid a patchwork of neatly-hedged fields and gently-rolling hills. The town is best known for St David's College, founded in 1822 by the Bishop of St David's, Thomas Burgess. Burgess wanted to give Welsh scholars, prohibited by expense from attending Oxford or Cambridge, the chance of a university education.

Llanddewi Brefi, *Dyfed* SN 6655
In AD519 St David came to this beautiful Teifi valley village to refute the *Heresy of Pelagius*, which denied the biblical doctrine of the original sin. It is said that when St David rose to speak so too did the ground on which he stood, allowing his message to be heard by the large assembly. This miraculous mound is reputed to be the same one on which the 13th-century church now stands.

Llanon, *Dyfed* SN 5167
This quaint seaside village is like a setting for Dylan Thomas's famous play *Under Milk Wood*. It has the appearance of a retirement place for old sea captains with rows of shipshape little cottages named after the craft they once commanded.

Llanwrtyd Wells, *Powys* SN 8746
The Revd Theophilus Evans discovered the healing properties of Llanwrtyd's springs in 1732 after he had drunk the sulphurous waters in an effort to cure himself of chronic scurvy and soon the town was a popular spa complete with a pump room and luxury hotels. Llanwrtyd is popular today for its country holiday potential.

Machynlleth, *Powys* SH 7401
A thriving Mid Wales market town, Machynlleth is renowned for its associations with Welsh revolutionary Owain Glyndwr. The Owain Glyndwr Institute stands on the site of the building in which Glyndwr held the last Welsh parliament in 1404. Machynlleth's Centre for Alternative Technology is based in an old slate quarry overlooking Snowdonia National Park. It shows the possibilities of living with only a small share of the earth's resources and creating a minimum of pollution and waste.

Newcastle Emlyn, *Dyfed* SN 3040
Little remains of the castle that gave this attractive town its name, only a ruined gatehouse and part of the walls can still be seen. Across the River Teifi, renowned for its excellent trout and salmon fishing, is Adpar – where the first Welsh printing press was built in 1718 by Isaac Carter.

New Quay, *Dyfed* SN 3859
New Quay is a pleasant resort set on terraces cut into the wooded east-facing slopes of New Quay Head, overlooking the sands of New Quay Bay. The tiny harbour, sheltered by a stone pier, is a magnet for fishermen, yachtsmen and sightseers.

Three bridges dating from the 12th to 20th centuries have been built over the Mynach at the dramatic Devil's Bridge

Pontrhydfendigaid, *Dyfed* SN 7366
Pontrhydfendigaid is the setting for a popular annual Eisteddfod – the traditional Welsh festival of poetry and music. A quaint old bridge spans the River Teifi here.

Tregaron, *Dyfed* SN 6759
A bright green statue of Liberal MP Henry Richard dominates the square of this unspoilt Welsh market town. Born in 1812, Richard was such an outspoken supporter of disarmament that he became known as the 'Apostle of Peace'. Near the town is Tregaron Bog, a 1,898-acre National Nature Reserve and the largest peat bog in Wales.

The colourful harbour at Aberaeron is now a popular yachting centre

Bishop's Castle, *Salop* SO 3288
A hillside market town, Bishop's Castle sits on the edge of Clun Forest. Of its many interesting old buildings the most picturesque is the 16th-century House on Crutches. The 18th-century town hall stands over a medieval lock-up and the Victorian church retains a fine Norman tower.

Builth Wells, *Powys* SO 0351
Another spa town, most of Builth's architecture dates from the 18th century when the mineral springs became popular. The original town grew up around a Norman castle of which only a mound exists today. This first settlement was totally destroyed by fire in 1691 and consequently no ancient buildings can be seen.

Clun, *Salop* SO 3081
Flint implements and similar relics of early man are displayed in the museum at Clun's 18th-century town hall, indicating just how long ago this area was inhabited. A ruined Norman castle overlooks the River Clun from a small hill and a row of 17th-century almshouses add to the charm of the town.

Hay-on-Wye, *Powys* SO 2342
Described as a book-lovers' paradise, Hay has more than its fair share of bookshops, and the narrow, winding old town streets are just made for browsing. Hay was once an important centre for the flannel industry but today it is a bustling market town. A fine gateway, the keep and the walls still remain of the town's castle that was built by the Normans. The remains are attached to a 17th-century mansion.

Kington, *Herefs & Worcs* SO 2956
This small town on the River Arrow is set amid delightfully hilly scenery. The 19th-century market hall is of particular interest and Hergest Croft Gardens, off the A44, include a fine kitchen garden, trees, shrubs, herbaceous borders and a woodland valley.

Knighton, *Powys* SO 2872
Famous for its livestock sales, Knighton is an important market town. Built on a steep hillside in the Teme valley, Knighton was originally a Saxon settlement. Today it is famous as the centre of the Offa's Dyke long-distance footpath which was opened here in 1971. The Dyke itself runs through the town.

Llandrindod Wells, *Powys* SO 0561
In its heyday as a spa town at the end of the 19th century Llandrindod was accommodating some 80,000 visitors a year in plush hotels, ballrooms, dining salons and gaming places, and the spacious Edwardian streets with their elegant buildings are a reminder of that

Above: social reformer Robert Owen is commemorated in Newtown, his hometown

prosperous era. The Llandrindod Wells Museum deals with the town's Roman connections, and there is also the Paterson Doll Collection on show and a Victorian Spa gallery.

Llanfair-Caereinion, *Powys* SJ 1006
This quaint little greystone town is built on a hillside above a river with two names – Einion and Banwy. The prime attraction here is the Llanfair and Welshpool Light Railway. Run by a preservation society, the line runs 8m from Llanfair to Welshpool.

Llanidloes, *Powys* SN 9584
Standing at the confluence of the River Severn and the Afon Clywedog, Llanidloes is a pleasant combination of old and new architecture. A particularly attractive building is the 16th-century timbered Market Hall; the upper floor houses a folk museum and the arcaded lower floor is an open area that once sheltered market stalls.

Montgomery, *Powys* SO 2296
The imposing redbrick Georgian town hall dominates Montgomery's Broad Street, an aptly-named thoroughfare almost as wide as it is long. Part of Montgomery's charm lies in the diversity of its buildings; quaint corners, slopes and steps reveal masterpieces of Tudor, Jacobean and Georgian times.

Newtown, *Powys* SO 1091
Birthplace of social reformer and 'father of trade unionism' Robert Owen, a museum to his life and work is located in Broad Street. The Newtown Textile Museum gives visitors a taste of the conditions that Owen sought to change.

Rhayader, *Powys* SN 9668
There is a certain air of the 19th century in this pretty little market town, despite the fact that many of the shops and houses have been modernised. As if to redress the balance, two of Rhayader's inns. The Triangle and the Cwmdauddwr Arms, have fascinating histories that span the centuries.

Welshpool, *Powys* SJ 2207
Welshpool was built on marshy waterlogged land, hence the name Pool by which the town was originally known. The prefix Welsh was added to distinguish it from Poole in Dorset. Today the town is a commercial and industrial centre, but there is much of interest to be found, notably the Powysland Museum and a number of half-timbered buildings with Jacobean staircases. SW of Welshpool lies magnificent Powis Castle; a medieval stronghold with 16th-century plaster-work and panelling. Eighteenth-century terraced gardens and parkland that includes oak trees, probably dating back to about 1250 when the castle was founded, surround the castle.

One of the many restored locomotives of the Welshpool and Llanfair Light Railway – originally built to carry goods

Much Wenlock Priory, founded in the 7th century by St Mildburga, was later destroyed by the Danes. The present ruins date from 1080 when it was rebuilt as a Cluniac priory

Ledbury, *Herefs & Worcs*   SO 7037
Time seems to have stood still in this quaint little market town with its cobbled streets and timbered buildings. The 17th-century market house is supported on pillars of chestnut above the market place which is the setting for an annual fair of ancient origin.

Leominster, *Herefs & Worcs*   SO 4959
Black-and-white timber-framed houses abound in this attractive medieval town whose narrow streets offer interest at every turn. 4m N of the town is Berrington Hall, an 18th-century mansion set in beautiful grounds. Also nearby are Croft Castle and Eye Manor, both of which are rewarding places to visit.

Ludlow, *Salop*   SO 5175
A latterday Camelot, Ludlow and its impressive castle lie cradled in the slopes of the Shropshire hills, on the banks of the Rivers Teme and Corve. The elegant 18th-century Butter Cross in Broad Street is now a local museum.

Much Wenlock, *Salop*   SO 6199
The Guildhall is a striking example of the type of half-timbered buildings for which this region is famous; fine oak panelling and furnishings make up an equally splendid interior. Remains of Much Wenlock Priory include beautiful interlocking Norman tracery.

Shrewsbury, *Salop*   SJ 4912
Half-timbered buildings and picturesque streets are the hallmark of this beautiful, unspoilt town. An interesting 14th-century complex of cottages, shops and a meeting hall can be found in St Alkmund's Square. Fine collections of china, costume and silver are on display at the Clive House Museum.

Tenbury Wells,
Herefs & Worcs   SO 5968
Once a fashionable spa town of the 19th century, nowadays Tenbury has relaxed again into its role of quiet market centre as it was before 1839 when the mineral springs were discovered. The pump room and baths can still be seen.

Bewdley, *Herefs & Worcs*   SO 7875
A fine Telford bridge spans the Severn at Bewdley. Load Street boasts an elegant parade of handsome Georgian buildings including The Shambles, site of the Bewdley Folk Museum. The West Midland Safari and Leisure Park is situated outside the town on the Kidderminster road.

Bridgnorth, *Salop*   SO 7193
This lovely old Shropshire town is divided into two parts; Upper Town is connected by means of a funicular railways to Lower Town. Flights of steep steps also run between the two, and there is one road, Cartway, which is one of the prettiest in the town. The Severn Valley Railway runs steam locomotives from here most weekdays during summer.

Bromyard, *Herefs & Worcs*   SO 6554
2m E of the town stands Lower Brockhampton, a half-timbered 14th-century mansion with a rare 15th-century gatehouse and a medieval hall.

Church Stretton, *Salop*   SO 4593
This popular tourist watering place is situated in a designated area of outstanding natural beauty. The heatherclad mass of National Trust land, Long Mynd, provides an impressive backdrop for this attractive red-roofed town.

Coalbrookdale, *Salop*   SJ 6604
The area around Coalbrookdale is a monument to the Industrial Revolution which was born here and the world's first iron bridge can be seen at the Ironbridge Gorge Museum. Blists Hill Open Air Museum recreates the original industries of iron, coal and clay and illustrates the living conditions of the workers on a 42-acre woodland site. The famous Coalport China was made here until 1926 and the Coalport China Works Museum illustrates its history.

Eardisland, *Herefs & Worcs*   SO 4158
This picturesque village is a happy blend of quaint old brick and colour-washed cottages and the familiar black-and-white half-timbered buildings, surrounded by lush green meadows. Nearby is Burton Court, a 14th- to 18th-century mansion house which includes a fine collection of Chinese and European costumes and a model fairground exhibition.

Great Malvern,
Herefs & Worcs   SO 7845
Healing waters first brought visitors to Great Malvern in Victorian times and today visitors come to a holiday centre largely unchanged since those days. The source of the famous waters, St Anne's Well, can be reached via a steep flight of steps by the Mount Pleasant Hotel.

Hereford, *Herefs & Worcs*   SO 5040
This town, whose name is synonymous with white-faced cattle, has lots more to offer the visitor. Pink-stoned Hereford Cathedral boasts a magnificent interior with a fine collection of brasses. There are three museums in the town, and, of special interest, is the Bulmers Railway Centre located in the centre of a cider-making factory.

There are three elegant arches to Telford's bridge which was completed in 1801

Alcester, *Warwicks*   SP 0985
2m NW of this picturesque old market
town are the beautiful Pleck Gardens,
and Ragley Hall, the 17th-century home
of the Seymour family, lies 2m SW. In
the grounds of the latter are fine gardens,
an adventure wood and country trail.

Birmingham, *W Midlands*   SP 0787
Beyond the tangled motorways of 'Spa-
ghetti Junction' lies an important manufacturing city that is second only to
London in size. Places of interest include
the Birmingham Museum of Science and
Industry, the Birmingham Nature
Centre, the City Museum and Art Gallery, Aston Hall (a Jacobean mansion,
now a museum) and the 18th-century
watermill – Sarehole Mill.

Broadway, *Herefs & Worcs*   SP 0937
Fine houses and pretty cottages in Cotswold stone line Broadway's wide main
street. Broadway Tower Country Park is
the site of an 18th-century tower which
has exhibitions on three floors, an observation room, and a telescope giving magnificent views over 12 counties. The
grounds include an adventure playground, nature walks and a picnic area.

Chipping Campden, *Glos*   SP 1539
The beautifully unspoilt Cotswold town
of fine gabled stone houses is a legacy of
the 14th and 15th centuries when it was a
prosperous wool centre and the Wool-
stapler's Hall is a fine example of that
period. The Campden Car Collection
boasts 22 immaculate sports and racing
cars.

Evesham, *Herefs & Worcs*   SP 0344
Evesham is sited on the River Avon, in
the heart of the famous fruit and vege-
table growing district of the Vale of
Evesham. The Almonry in Vyne Street
houses an interesting museum of local
history.

Henly-in-Arden, *Warwicks*   SP 1465
A small town of oak-timbered buildings,
Henly-in-Arden lies in the ancient Forest
of Arden district – though little remains
of the forest today. The 15th-century
Guildhall, an attractive gabled building
with a Dutch-style garden, houses a local
history museum in the main hall.

Kidderminster, *Herefs & Worcs*   SO 8376
Carpets were the foundation of Kidderminster's prosperity, and the carpet-
weaving industry that was introduced
here in 1735 continues to be a major
concern. Sir Rowland Hill of penny-post
fame was born here in 1795.

Lichfield, *Staffs*   SK 1209
The three tall spires, known as the Ladies
of the Vale, of Lichfield Cathedral form a
notable landmark for miles around this
ancient city. The magnificent red sandstone cathedral is one of Lichfield's many
structures of architectural interest. Birthplace of Dr Johnson, a statue of the great
man stands in the market place and his
house is now a museum of his life.

Snowshill, *Glos*   SP 0933
This secluded Cotswold village is the site
of Snowshill Manor, onetime residence of
Henry VIII's wife Catherine Parr. It is
now famed for its amazing collections of
clocks, toys and musical instruments.

Tewkesbury, *Glos*   SO 8933
This picturesque town is a jumble of
traditional timber-framed buildings in a
maze of narrow winding streets. The
magnificent abbey church features one of
the finest Norman towers in England and
the interior is particularly magnificent.
Both the high altar – consecrated in 1239,
and the organ with pipework dating from
1610, are among the oldest of their type
in the country. Opposite the abbey,
down a little alleyway, is the oldest
Baptist Chapel in England. It has recently been restored and refurnished in
traditional style.

Upton-upon-Severn,
Herefs & Worcs   SO 8540
Upton is a pleasant little market town
with olde-worlde streets filled with equ-
ally old and fascinating shops and inns.
The White Lion Inn is famous for its
associations with Henry Fielding's novel
Tom Jones.

Wilmcote, *Warwicks*   SP 1658
Shakespeare's mother, Mary Arden, was
born in Wilmcote and her home, an
attractive half-timbered Tudor farmhouse, is open to the public. The barns
house an interesting farming and rural
life museum.

Worcester, *Herefs & Worcs*   SO 8555
Porcelain and a piquant sauce are Worcester's most famous exports, but there is
more to this ancient cathedral city. The
cathedral, the Tudor House, King Charles's House and the City Museum and
Art Gallery provide the visitor with a
sound historical introduction, and the
Royal Worcester Porcelain Works and
the Dyson Perrins Museum tell the story
of the porcelain industry in the city from
1751 to the present day.

*Tewkesbury's beautiful abbey was saved
from destruction in 1539 by the townsfolk*

*Above: farming implements from over two
centuries in the barns of Mary Arden's House*

The timber-roofed Market Hall in Chipping Campden's main street is medieval

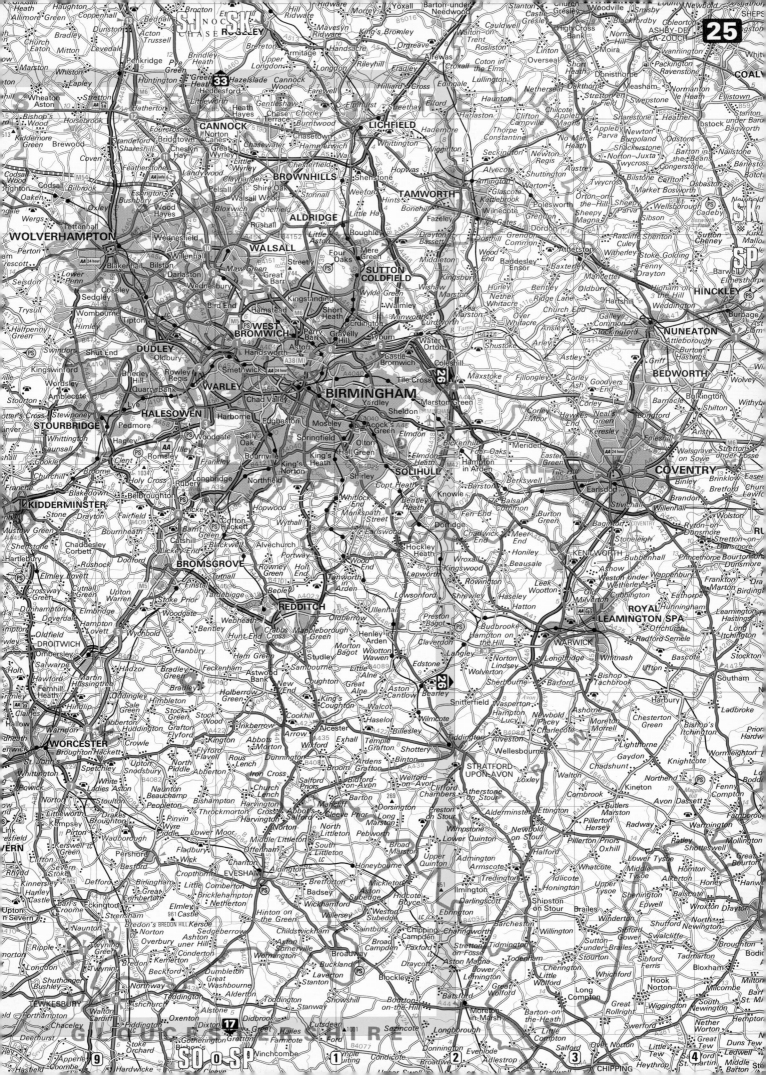

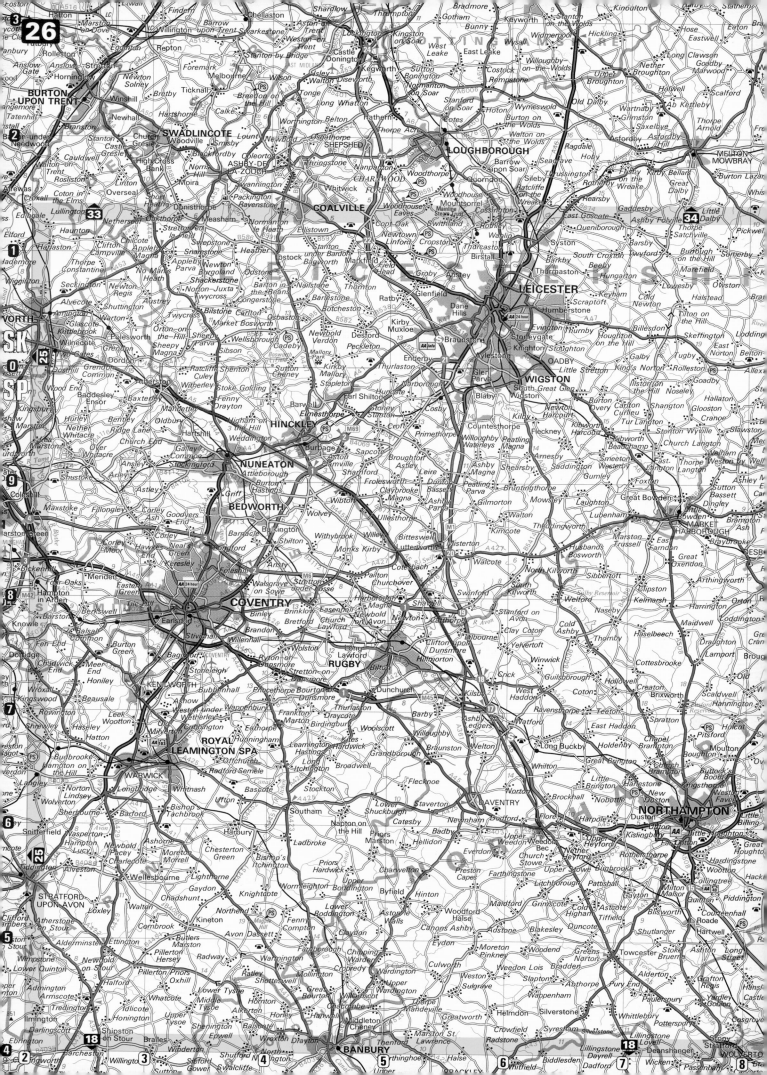

Banbury, *Oxon* SP 4520
Now a bustling industrial town and shopping centre, Banbury is of Saxon origin and it retains a charm all its own. The Banbury Cross of nursery-rhyme fame no longer exists but a replica was built in its place in 1858. A local delicacy, the Banbury Cake – a delicious concoction of puff pastry and dried, spiced fruit – can still be bought here. Banbury Museum is a small museum of local history.

Charlecote, *Warwicks* SP 2656
The highlight of this attractive old village is the elegant Elizabethan mansion of Charlecote Park which includes a museum on the first floor. The River Avon flows through the grounds where Shakespeare is said to have been caught poaching deer.

Coventry, *W Midlands* SP 3379
Badly destroyed during World War II, Coventry lost much of its history but, as if to compensate, the city is now the proud owner of a magnificent new cathedral. Among the outstanding modern works of art that adorn the interior is a vast altar tapestry by Graham Sutherland and a wall of glass (the West Screen) engraved by John Hutton.

Kenilworth, *Warwicks* SP 2872
Kenilworth, and particularly the castle, is famed for its connection with Sir Walter Scott. His historical novel, *Kenilworth*, uses the castle as the setting for many events and Scott himself may have stayed at the Kings Arms and Castle Hotel in the Square.

Leamington Spa, *Warwicks* SP 3166
As its name suggests, Leamington Spa enjoyed its heyday when the fashionable set of the 19th century discovered its healing waters. Many of the grand old buildings recall its former prosperity, notably the elegant Pump Room, rebuilt in 1925. Warwick Art Gallery specialises in British, Dutch and Flemish painters.

Leicester, *Leics* SK 5904
A county town and university city, Leicester is of Roman origin and many relics of those times are preserved in the Jewry Wall Museum. Later history, from the 16th century to Victorian times, can be traced in the Newarke Houses Museum. The University Botanic Gardens are lovely.

Market Harborough, *Leics* SP 7387
There has been a market at Market Harborough since 1204 and although today's town is mainly industrial, much remains as a reminder of earlier days. The 17th-century timbered and gabled grammar school stands high above the street on wooden pillars and the local Three Swans Inn displays one of the finest wrought-iron signs in England.

Northampton, *Northants* SP 7561
One of the largest market towns in England, Northampton is noted for its high number of fine churches. Of special note is the Holy Sepulchre, an unusual round structure founded in the early part of the 12th century. Landscaped Abington Park includes a collection of ornamental and game birds.

An elaborately decorated clock-tower of 1868 marks the centre of Leicester

Shipston-on-Stour, *Warwicks* SP 2540
Situated on the edge of the Cotswolds in the Vale of the Red Horse, this old wool town has attractive Georgian houses and inns complemented by a 19th-century church. In its heyday, Shipston-on-Stour held one of the major sheep markets in the country.

Stratford-upon-Avon,
Warwicks SP 2055
This charming old market town is a living memorial to William Shakespeare, who was born here in 1564. Celebrated actors and actresses perform his plays in the Royal Shakespeare Theatre where the Theatre Gallery contains portraits of Shakespeare and famous Shakespearian actors and actresses, as well as many theatrical relics. There is a waxwork museum in the town which specialises in scenes from the great man's plays, and his childhood home is also a museum. The idyllic thatched and timbered cottage that belonged to Shakespeare's wife, Anne Hathaway, is in nearby Shottery.

Swinford, *Leics* SP 5679
1m E of the village, on the River Avon, is Stanford Hall – a beautiful William and Mary house which was built in 1690. Attractions include a walled rose garden, a motor cycle and car museum, a crafts centre and a nature trail.

Tamworth, *Staffs* SK 2004
Elegant Tamworth Castle is of Norman origin with a fine 15th-century banqueting hall and 17th-century apartments. The latter boast fine woodwork, period furniture and a painted heraldic frieze. There is a small local history museum in the castle whose grounds contain a pleasure park and swimming pools.

Warwick, *Warwicks* SP 2865
There is much of historic interest in this fine old county town, not least the magnificent castle. This imposing medieval stronghold is one of the finest of its kind in Europe and it enjoys a picturesque position on the banks of the River Avon. Other places of interest include the lovely 15th-century timbered Lord Leycester's Hospital, the Warwick Doll Museum and the St John's House, also a museum.

The Royal Shakespeare Theatre at Stratford was the country's first National Theatre

Bedford, *Beds* TL 0449
Records of this bustling county town date back to Saxon times. A famous son of Bedford is John Bunyan, who wrote *The Pilgrim's Progress*. The Bunyan Museum includes relics of his life and work and stands on the site of the barn where he preached.

Ecton, *Northants* SP 8263
A picturesque Northamptonshire village, Ecton is the ancestral home of the Franklin family. Benjamin Franklin's father left here for New England in 1685. Features of the village include a 13th- to 14th-century church, a fine 17th-century manor house and a gothic-revival hall.

Godmanchester, *Cambs* TL 2470
Pronounced Gumchester, this ancient town stands on the site of a Roman military station. A rich variety of architectural styles stand side-by-side in the streets of Godmanchester, from the elegant lines of Georgian buildings back to the well-worn homely timber-and-plaster work of the 16th and 17th centuries.

Huntingdon, *Cambs* TL 2371
Oliver Cromwell was born here and both he and diarist Samuel Pepys attended the town's former grammar school, which is now a museum of Cromwellian relics. Hinchingbrooke House – a Tudor mansion incorporating a medieval nunnery – was the former home of the Cromwells and the Earls of Sandwich. It lies 1½m W of the town.

Oakham, *Leics* SK 8509
Renowned as a fox-hunting centre, Oakham was once the capital of the now defunct Rutland, the smallest county in England. Memories of its former status and earlier local history are preserved in the Rutland County Museum. Oakham Castle contains a splendid Norman hall where a unique collection of horseshoes can be seen. The Rutland Farm Park at Catmose Farm is a working farm with rare breeds of farm livestock and an 18-acre park alongside offers nature walks and picnic facilities.

The old country town of Oundle was established about 1,000 years ago in King Edgar's reign

Oundle, *Northants* TL 0488
A town of narrow streets and alleys, Oundle sits by the River Nene amid pleasant countryside. Its famous public school was founded by William Laxton, a onetime grocer who was born in the village and went on to become Lord Mayor of London. The Latham Almshouses of 17th-century origin are of note.

Peterborough, *Cambs* TL 1999
A town of ancient origin, Peterborough grew up on the River Nene around a magnificent cathedral whose remarkable triple-arched west front is still an attractive focal point today. Catherine of Aragon and Mary Queen of Scots were both buried here, although the remains of the latter now lie in Westminster Abbey. Local history can be studied in the City Museum and Art Gallery in Priestgate. Now a thriving New Town, Peterborough has fine leisure facilities including swimming pools, a theatre, multi-purpose leisure centres and an outdoor recreation complex.

Ramsey, *Cambs* TL 2885
All that remains of the Benedictine abbey is the 15th-century gatehouse which stands at the edge of the smooth lawns of Abbey Green. Ramsey itself is mainly 19th century, an earlier town having been devastated by a series of unhappy events such as the Civil War, the Great Plague and a number of major fires in the 17th and 18th centuries.

St Ives, *Cambs* TL 3171
St Ives was given the right to hold a fair by King Henry I in 1110 and the town grew up in the shadow of its fairground. A magnificent six-arched 15th-century bridge spans the River Ouse in the town which is a rare example of its kind. Oliver Cromwell had a farm in the surrounding countryside and his statue in the Market Place commemorates this fact.

St Neots, *Cambs* TL 1860
Beautifully compact, this ancient Ouseside market town has a wealth of attractive buildings and interesting old inns lurking discreetly in secretive back streets.

Sandy, *Beds* TL 1649
Low, wooded hills rise to the east of this large River Ivel village and provide a pleasant contrast to the flat fenland countryside. About 1m E is the Lodge Nature Reserve, an area of 100 acres which includes the headquarters of the Royal Society for the Protection of Birds. A planned nature trail provides public access.

Stamford, *Lincs* TF 0207
This ancient town, which dates back to a time when the Danes settled here, is considered to be one of the most beautiful places in England. Stamford boasts many buildings of historical and architectural interest, including Browne's Hospital, one of the finest surviving medieval almshouses in the country. More modern attractions include the Brewery Museum and Stamford Museum – a new museum of local history. Nearby Elizabethan Burghley House is open to visitors and the well-known Burghley Horse Trials are held in its grounds.

Wellingborough, *Northants* SP 8968
At the junction of the Rivers Ise and Nene, the old market centre of Wellingborough is now a rapidly expanding New Town serving numerous light industries.

St Ives' bridge chapel, dedicated to St Lawrence, was consecrated in 1426

Brancaster, *Norfolk* TF 7743
A notable golfing resort, Brancaster was once a Roman station although there are no remains now. A safe bathing beach is reached by means of a pathway from the local church or a causeway road. Scolt Head, an offshore bird sanctuary, can be reached from the village by boat.

Bury St Edmunds, *Suffolk* TL 8564
East Anglia's last king died at the hands of the Danes in AD870; his name was Edmund and he was buried here and that is how the town got its name. Bury, as it is known locally, is a pleasant little market and county town offering much to interest the visitor. The town was a fashionable spot in Regency times and Charles Dickens is known to have given readings in the 18th-century Athenaeum on Angel Hill. He also used the Angel Corner as a setting in *Pickwick Papers*. Angel House is a Queen Anne mansion which contains one of the finest collections of clocks and watches in Britain. A rare 12th-century house in Cornhill, named Moyses Hall, is now a museum of local history, archaeology and natural history. Other places of interest include the Market Cross which houses an art gallery, the remains of Bury Abbey and Gardens, and the Norton Bird Gardens where there are collections of foreign birds and waterfowl.

Ely, *Cambs* TL 5380
The splendid octagonal tower of Ely Cathedral stands out against the flat fenland landscape for miles around the town. One of the oldest religious foundations in the country, there has been a cathedral in Ely since AD600. The town was once an island and acquired its name because of the number of eels that were caught in the area; however, it became landlocked when the Fens were drained for use as agricultural land in the 18th and 19th centuries. A fascinating museum of stained glass is located in the north triforium of the cathedral.

Holkham, *Norfolk* TF 8944
By the Almshouses Gate in Holkham village is the entrance to Holkham Hall, a vast Palladian mansion which was started in 1733 by William Kent. The magnificent entrance leading to the Marble Hall is considered to be an example of Kent's genius at its peak. The whole mansion is decorated and furnished in a sumptuous style complemented by grounds laid out by Capability Brown.

Hunstanton, *Norfolk* TF 6741
Hunstanton, the only coastal town in East Anglia that faces west, is also one of the largest seaside resorts in west Norfolk. Great stretches of golden sand are backed by cliffs of mixed chalk and sand rising 60ft above the beach.

King's Lynn, *Norfolk* TF 6220
King's Lynn has been an important commercial centre since Norman times, when two markets were founded here, and 20th-century industry perpetuates the

tradition. The town's long history has left it with some of the finest medieval buildings in the country. The Hanseatic Warehouse, built in 1428, is a superb structure and the two 15th-century Guildhalls complement the two market squares. One of these is the largest medieval Guildhall extant and is now used as a theatre. Perhaps the most outstanding building in the town is the Dutch-style Custom House.

Newmarket, *Suffolk* TL 6463
Famous as a horse-racing centre, Newmarket is the headquarters of the Jockey Club and the National Stud. Riders can be seen at early morning training on the Heath. Newmarket Town Plate is one of the oldest races in existence and it attracts some women jockeys.

Sandringham, *Norfolk* TF 6928
Owned by the Royal Family, the 7,000-acre estate at Sandringham, which was bought by Queen Victoria for the Prince of Wales, includes an 18th-century house, the farms and woodlands of seven parishes and a 300-acre park. Wolferton Station, on the estate, was built specifically for, and solely used by kings and queens and their guests *en route* for Sandringham. Fine oak panelling and original fittings can be seen, as well as period railway posters and important small railway relics.

Swaffham, *Norfolk* TF 8109
The town sign depicts the 'Pedlar of Swaffham' who, legend has it, journeyed to London after having a dream urging him to seek his fortune there. A stranger told him of a dream he had had of a remote village garden in which there lay some treasure. The pedlar recognised the garden as his own and when he returned home he found two pots of gold. In the unusual triangular market place there stands a domed rotunda which was built in 1783 by the Earl of Orford as a market cross of distinction.

Thetford, *Norfolk* TL 8783
The charming town of Thetford lies on the Rivers Ouse and Thet. The mound of a motte-and-bailey castle is preserved in Castle Park and the Ancient House Museum is believed to have been a Tudor merchant's house. Thetford Heath and Thetford Chase, both national nature reserves, lie to the W.

Wells-next-the-Sea, *Norfolk* TF 9143
Charming old houses around a large green called Buttlands and a picturesque quayside form an interesting focal point in this small resort and port. Bathing may be enjoyed at Wells and about 1m away is Abraham's Bosom where there is a boating lake.

Wisbech, *Cambs* TF 4609
Fruit trees and bulbs are cultivated in the district around this River Nene town, and fruit-canning is an important local industry. The many splendid Georgian houses that line the north and south brinks form what is considered to be one of the finest riverside vistas in England. A history of life on the Fens is displayed in the Wisbech and Fenland Museum.

Brancaster's deserted beach is typical of Norfolk's almost unspoilt dune coast

The grounds of Bury's old abbey have been turned into attractive public gardens

Aylsham, *Norfolk*   TG 1926
Once a famous centre for the manufacture of worsted cloth and linen, today Aylsham is a peaceful market town on the River Bure with many charming buildings, including Dutch-gabled Georgian houses. 1½m NW of the town is 17th-century Bickling Hall which stands in a fine landscaped park.

Banham, *Norfolk*   TM 0688
This attractive village boasts an unusual zoo specialising in primates. Set in over 20 acres of grounds the Monkey Sanctuary houses such rarities as the Emperor tamarin and Goeldi's monkey. Nearby is the Banham Classic Collection displaying automobilia from motoring's past.

The 315ft spire of Norwich Cathedral is one of the city's most imposing landmarks

Cromer, *Norfolk*   TG 2142
The bustling holiday resort of Cromer boasts a fine sandy beach backed by lofty cliffs. Seafood fans will find some of the best crabs in the country, netted by the small local fishing fleet. The days when fishing was the major preoccupation in the town are relived in the museum in Tucker Street. Cromer also has a fine five-acre zoo.

Great Yarmouth, *Norfolk*   TG 5207
At the mouth of the River Yare, the popular seaside resort boasts a generous serving of holiday amenities mixed with just a dash of historic interest. Remains of the ancient town walls are still standing and close by are The Rows, a number of narrow lanes where the 300-year-old Merchant's House can be seen. Anna Sewell, the authoress of *Black Beauty*, was born here and her 17th-century house is open. The 5m of seafront are backed by colourful gardens and the quaint Merrivale Model Village stands near Wellington Pier.

Leiston, *Suffolk*   TM 4462
Leiston is distinguished as the home of Summerhill, one of the country's most

advanced schools which was set up as an experiment in self-education by educationalist A. S. Neill and is now well established and very successful. The remains of the 14th-century Leiston Abbey include the church choir and transept, and some cloisters.

Lowestoft, *Suffolk*   TM 5493
An attractive seaside resort and fishing port, Lowestoft offers the natural amenities of excellent sandy beaches and safe bathing in both sea and river. In the old town is a notable area of criss-cross alleyways known as the 'Scores'. The Maritime Museum in Sparrows Nest Park depicts the town's history as a major fishing port and the East Anglia Transport Museum is situated in nearby Carlton Colville.

North Walsham, *Norfolk*   TG 2730
The twisting lanes and charming cottages beckon you to linger a while in this pleasant little market town. Lord Nelson once attended the grammar school at Walsham, and the school's founder, Sir William Paston, is the subject of a 17th-century monument in the local church.

Norwich, *Norfolk*   TG 2308
A truly remarkable city with over 1,000 years history, Norwich is Norfolk's capital. The magnificent Norwich Castle, now an art gallery and museum, looks down from its landscaped hill in the centre of the city. It is surrounded by a maze of medieval streets, the most fascinating being Elm Hill – a charming cobbled thoroughfare famous for its craft shops. Away from the shops, amid spacious green surroundings, is the magnificent Norman cathedral whose interior is one of the finest in Britain. Norwich's past as a successful textile centre is celebrated in the many fine buildings of

that time and Stranger's Hall is an ancient merchant's house dating from the 14th century which is now a museum of English domestic life. Another merchant's house, the Brideswell Museum, covers the history of the textile industry. Places of interest are too numerous to mention, but of special note are the Colman's Mustard shop and museum and the picture-postcard house known as Pull's Ferry.

Sall, *Norfolk*   TG 1024
Pronounced 'Saul' this tiny village boasts what is thought to be one of the finest period churches in Norfolk; it is also likely to be the most under-used because of the size in relation to the parish. It was built by three wealthy local families, including the Boleyns whose daughter Anne married Henry VIII.

Sheringham, *Norfolk*   TG 1543
Like its neighbour, Cromer, Sheringham is also a popular seaside resort with an abundance of Victorian architecture. A crab-fishing industry is something else these towns have in common. The North Norfolk Railway is based here and their magnificent railway museum can be found at Sheringham Station. A 1m rhododendron drive leads to the beautiful Regency mansion of Sheringham Hall (open by appointment only).

Southwold, *Suffolk*   TM 5076
A feature of this charming resort on the River Blyth is its open green spaces. These are a result of a devastating fire during the 17th century which coincided with a drop in the town's herring industry so there was no money to rebuild. The Southwold Museum stands on Bartholomew Green and includes displays on local history and relics of the Southwold light railway.

In the 19th century Cromer developed as a resort around its splendid church

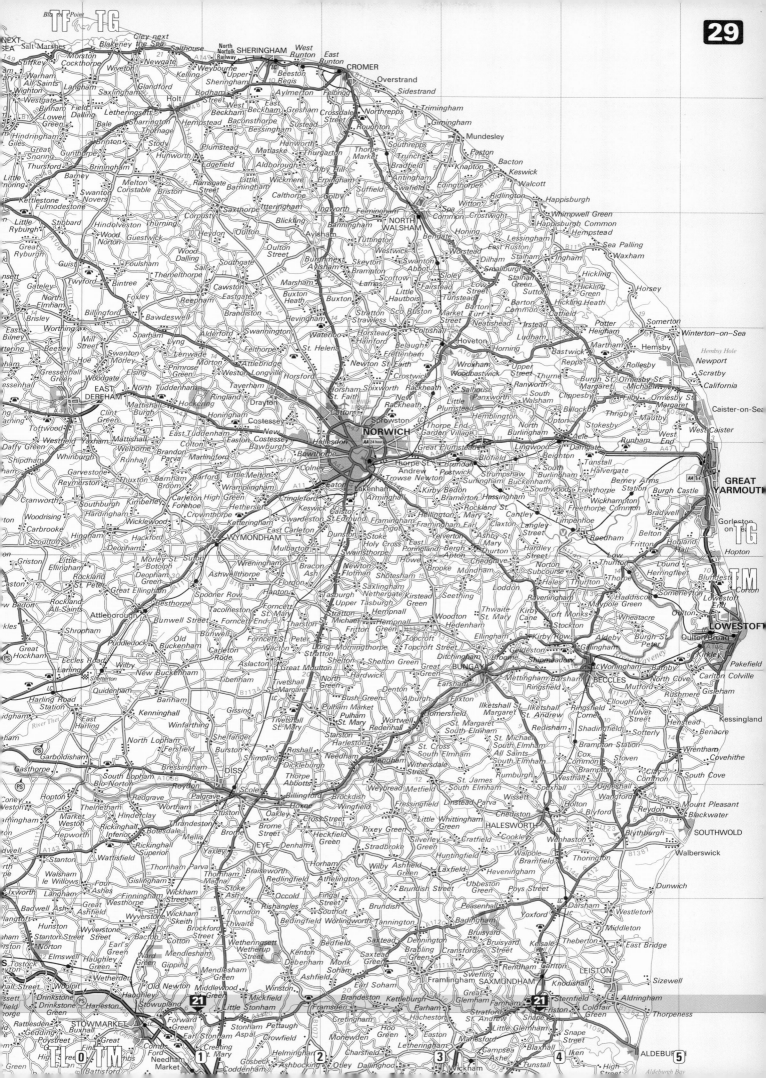

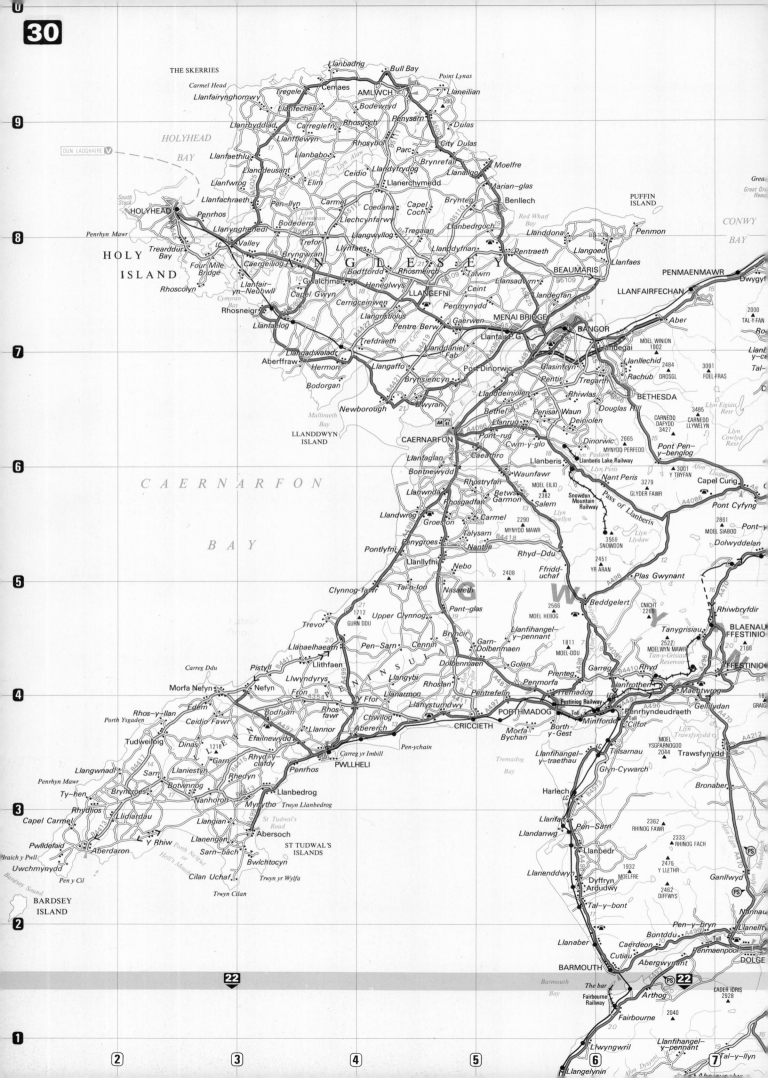

Amlwch, *Gwynedd* SH 4392
In the 18th century Amlwch was a thriving copper town and the bustling port exported the metal worldwide. The boom lasted for just over 50 years and after that Amlwch declined with its industry: the harbour, literally gouged out of the granite cliffs, is a haven for pleasure craft today. Nearby Bull Bay is an attractive little holiday resort.

Bangor, *Gwynedd* SH 5872
Rather an unassuming university city, Bangor's bustling streets drop down to the shores of the Menai Strait and a Victorian pier. Bangor Museum and Art Gallery houses collections of furniture, crafts, maps, costumes etc., pertaining to the history of North Wales. 1½m E of the city lies the neo-Norman Penrhyn Castle which stands amid beautiful open park and woodland.

Beaumaris, *Gwynedd* SH 6076
Many places of interest attract the visitor to Beaumaris, not least of which is the splendid concentric castle which is one of the finest examples of this style in Britain. The beautiful half-timbered Tudor Rose House in Castle Street is one of the few 15th-century ancient monuments in Wales. In the stark Beaumaris Gaol lie grim reminders of the harshness of justice in Victorian Britain, including prisoners' cells, a treadmill and a condemned cell.

Beddgelert, *Gwynedd* SH 5848
A local innkeeper, keen to put Beddgelert on the tourist map during the 18th century, revived a legend of the town's name. The story goes that Llewelyn the Great returned home one day to find his dog Gelert covered in blood. Assuming that the dog had attacked his baby son, Llewelyn flew into a rage and killed Gelert, only to discover that the animal had, in fact, killed a wolf that had tried to savage the boy. His son was unharmed. Today Beddgelert needs no fanciful legends to draw visitors. It stands on its own merits as probably the only genuine alpine resort in Snowdonia, completely locked in by mountains.

Blaenau Ffestiniog, *Gwynedd* SH 7045
A once thriving slate-mining industry has left its mark in the town's houses, streets, garden walls and even tombstones – all incorporate slate in their makeup. Today, visitors can enjoy a trip down a real slate mine with accompanying description of the life and times of a Victorian slate miner at the Llechwedd Slate Caverns. Also in the town is the largest slate mine in the world, Gloddfa Ganol which includes a ½m of underground workings, museum, quarryman's cottages, craft shops and a fairy grotto. There is also a narrow-gauge railway and a children's play area within this popular tourist complex.

Caernarfon, *Gwynedd* SH 4862
Possibly the finest example of medieval fortification in Britain, Caernarfon Castle is the town's most impressive attraction and one which has helped make it the most important tourist centre in Snowdonia. The castle was the birthplace of the first Prince of Wales and has seen the investiture of all successors, the latest being our own Prince of Wales in 1969. The Romans had a fort here called *Segontium* and its remains, along with a museum of excavated relics, can be visited today.

Criccieth, *Gwynedd* SH 4938
Criccieth is a pleasant seaside resort where charming Victorian buildings merge with older cottages on streets sloping steeply towards the sea. To the E and W of a headland occupied by the ruins of Criccieth Castle are sand and pebble beaches backed by short esplanades.

Harlech, *Gwynedd* SH 5831
One of Edward I's great fortresses stands at the edge of the sea at Harlech with fine views of Snowdonia and the Lleyn Peninsula. Further S along the coast of the Old Llanfair Slate Quarries – originally blasted out of the hills in the search for slate – are now open for guided tours.

Holy Island, *Gwynedd* SH 2583
Reached via the Stanley Embankment, Holy Island is the site of many prehistoric monuments. The approach is dominated by the silhouette of a giant aluminium plant but its mass is overpowered by the 720 ft height of Holyhead Mountain, the island's main natural attraction and highest point offering superb views across the island. The main town on the island, Holyhead, is also the largest in Anglesey. A major ferry terminal for Ireland, it is always filled with holidaymakers, seamen and travellers. The walls of a Roman fort surround the old parish church of St Cybi.

Llanberis, *Gwynedd* SH 5760
Typical of the slate-mining villages in North Wales, terraces of cottages huddle together against the rock faces in Llanberis. Two steam railways operate

A statue of Welshman Lloyd George, one time prime minister of England, stands opposite the castle balcony in Caernarfon

nearby: one is the narrow-gauge Lake Railway at Gilfach Ddu and the other is the Snowdon Mountain Railway which takes passengers to the summit of the famous mountain.

Menai Bridge, *Gwynedd* SH 5572
The gracious bridge which carries the London to Holyhead traffic across the Menai Strait was built by Thomas Telford and is said to be one of his finest works. It has given its name to the largely Victorian town clustered around the Anglesey end of the crossing. The town's Tegfryn Art Gallery in Cadnant Road stands in pleasant grounds near the shores of the Menai Straits and includes the work of many local artists. Historical exhibits in the Museum of Childhood in Water Street span 150 years.

Pwllheli, *Gwynedd* SH 3735
The unofficial capital of the Lleyn Peninsula, Pwllheli is a market town and seaside resort with an old harbour. Activity in the harbour reached its peak in the days of the sailing ships when Pwllheli was an important port building fine ships and producing excellent seamen. Today pleasure-craft find a haven here.

Beddgelert seen nestling at the foothills of Snowdon from Moel Hebog

Punch and Judy shows have a lasting appeal that Llandudno fully exploits

Bala, *Gwynedd*   SH 9236
In the 18th century Bala became famous for the quality of its hand-knitted stockings, a reputation enhanced by the fact that George III would wear no others. Behind the quaint tree-lined High Street stands the mound of Tomen-y-bala, a Norman castle. A local farmer's son, Tom Ellis, became Liberal Chief Whip, and was a tireless campaigner for Welsh home-rule, but he died at the age of 44 and now a dramatic statue of him stands in the High Street.

Betws-y-coed, *Gwynedd*   SH 7956
Popularised by Victorian artists, Betws-y-coed is a charming little town on the River Conwy much loved by today's tourists. Standing amid wooded slopes and tumbling white waters, the area is renowned for its waterfalls – notably the fairy-tale cascades of the Swallow Falls.

Colwyn Bay, *Clwyd*   SH 8478
Colwyn Bay is a refined Victorian resort with many fine parks and attractive shopping arcades. Its promenade stretches for 3 m around the bay to Rhos-on-Sea. The town rises gradually to wooded heights where the Welsh Mountain Zoo is located, and other attractions include the 50-acre Eirias Park, and, at Rhos-on-Sea, an open-air swimming pool and the Harlequin Puppet Theatre.

Conwy, *Gwynedd*   SH 7777
Conwy the river, Conwy the castle and Conwy the vale are thought by many to be the three most memorable sights in Wales. The majestic Afon Conwy is spanned here by three bridges, the oldest of which was built in 1826 by Thomas Telford. The magnificent 13th-century Conwy Castle is arguably one of the greatest works of Edward I's military architect, Master James of St George. Among the medieval buildings of interest in the town is the Tudor House of Plas Mawr which houses the Royal Cambrian Academy of Art.

Denbigh, *Clwyd*   SJ 0566
The 13th-century Denbigh Castle towers above the town's charming streets and the original town walls remain largely intact to this day. The magnificent tri-partite gatehouse is perhaps the most impressive feature of this fortress. Henry Morton Stanley, best remembered as the speaker of 'Dr Livingstone, I presume', was born in this small market town and a model of his demolished birthplace is on show in the castle. Nearby Denbigh Moors have undergone a dramatic change in recent years with the construction of huge reservoirs and the planting of forests.

Llandegla, *Clwyd*   SJ 1952
A peaceful moorland town, Llandegla was once an important place for cattle drivers who herded Welsh cattle through here *en route* to English markets. An elaborate ritual associated with the cure of epilepsy was carried out here at St Tecla's Well.

Llandudno, *Gwynedd*   SH 7782
During the 1850s Llandudno grew from a tiny cluster of fishermen's cottages into a classic Victorian seaside resort, justifiably described as the 'Queen of Welsh Resorts'. Great Orme's Head, with its gardens, an ancient church, cable railway and windswept grassy slopes, separates the resort's two superb beaches.

Llangollen, *Clwyd*   SJ 2141
Since 1947 this picturesque town has played host to the world at the International Eisteddfod, a festival of music and culture that takes place annually in July, when the sound of the world's best choirs echo through surrounding hillsides. On the edge of the town is Plas Newydd, a handsome black-and-white house with an interesting history.

Llanrwst, *Gwynedd*   SH 7961
This pleasant market town is noted for the fine triple-arched bridge which spans the River Conwy here. It was built in 1636 and is said to be the work of Inigo Jones, although the claim is in dispute. The beautiful Gwydir chapel is also attri-buted to Inigo Jones. Attached to the parish church, it houses memorials of the Wynnes – one of the foremost land-owning families in Wales.

Oswestry, *Salop*   SJ 2829
The English and Welsh fought over Oswestry for centuries but in 1535 it was officially made part of England. Offa's Dyke, built in the 8th century by the Anglo-Saxons to keep out the Welsh, can be seen to either side of the town and at Old Oswestry to the N are remains of an Iron Age hill-fort. The Civil War and three bad fires between the 13th and 18th centuries destroyed much of Oswestry but there are still some survivors from its past, including Oswestry School in Upper Brook Street which is thought to be the oldest secular school in England.

Pentrefoelas, *Clwyd*   SH 8751
Moorland and mountain surround this sleepy 19th-century hamlet. Points of interest include an old watermill and the site of the Levelinus Stone. This 8ft-high pillar marked the spot where a Welsh prince fell in battle in 1023 but the stone itself has now been removed to the National Museum of Wales, Cardiff.

Prestatyn, *Clwyd*   SJ 0682
Although a most important seaside resort in its own right, Prestatyn is on the doorstep of many interesting places: Dyserth Falls, the remains of Basingwerk Abbey, the ancient Maen Achwyfan – a carved standing stone – and Ewloe Castle are but a few. There are nature trails in the nearby foothills of the Clwydian Range.

Rhyl, *Clwyd*   SJ 0181
Definitely a holiday fun centre, 'Sunny Rhyl' offers the seaside tourist all possible amenities, plus 3m of sandy beach. Since the town's development from a pair of fishermen's cottages in 1833, Rhyl has come a long way and now caters better for the family holiday than almost any of its rivals in Britain. Among its entertainment facilities are a large fairground, theatres, the Royal Floral Hall and the newly-opened Sun Centre.

Strategically placed Conwy Castle is one of Britain's best-preserved strongholds

Bangor-is-y-coed, *Clwyd* SJ 3945
This picturesque village was the site of a monastery but in AD651 King Aethelfrith of Northumbria ordered that the monastery be razed to the ground and all the monks killed. Little of the monastery can be seen today, but an ancient stone bridge is a notable attraction.

Chester, *Cheshire* SJ 4066
Chester was a principal military station and trading town in Roman times, when it was called *Deva*. One of the finest collections of Roman remains in Britain is to be found in the Grosvenor Museum in Grosvenor Street. The town today is a pleasing mix of medieval and Victorian architecture but the source of its distinctive character is undoubtedly The Rows – galleried tiers of shops in black and white located in Bridge Street, Watergate Street and Eastgate Street. Part of the Rows comprises Chester Heritage Centre which includes displays relating to Chester's 2,000-year-old history. Chester Zoo, one of the finest in Europe, has over 100 acres of natural enclosures.

Holt, *Clwyd* SJ 4053
An eight-arched 15th-century bridge spans the River Dee at Holt and alongside the bridge remains of a Norman castle can be seen. An elaborate font is one of the interesting items in the local 13th-century church.

Knutsford, *Cheshire* SJ 7578
The charming old-world town of Knutsford, with its excellent hotels and guesthouses, offers an ideal base from which to explore the delights of the Cheshire countryside. May Day celebrations are a special event here and have had royal patronage on two occasions. The town has many associations with the famous; Knutsford was the birthplace of Edward Penny R.A., a founder member of the Royal Academy, and author Mrs Gaskell lived there. It was while Sir Henry Royce was living here in 1904 that he met Charles Stewart Rolls – and so the famous partnership was born. One of the National Trust's most visited stately homes, Tatton Hall, is nearby.

A tower of coloured glass crowns the conical roof of Liverpool's RC Cathedral

Liverpool, *Merseyside* SJ 3591
Situated on the Mersey estuary, Liverpool is an important shipping, university and cathedral city. Although not immediately recognisable as a tourist city, Liverpool has much to offer the visitor. The famous dockyard is the setting for some impressive architecture, the centrepoint being the 17-storey Royal Liver Building which displays two towers surmounted by the legendary Liver Birds. Also in the dockyard is the Mersey Maritime Museum, standing on restored 19th-century quays by the waterfront. The magnificent red sandstone Anglican Cathedral stands in lofty elegance, a tribute to the architect Sir Giles Gilbert Scott who died in his 80th year, in 1960, still supervising it. The city has many fine museums and art galleries and the Liverpool University Botanic Garden includes a scented garden for the blind.

Market Drayton, *Salop* SJ 6734
The ancient town of Market Drayton is famous as the birthplace of Robert Clive – Clive of India. He attended the local grammar school and a desk on which his initials are carved is still preserved. The town itself stands on the River Tern and the Shropshire Union Canal and has many notable houses.

Nantwich, *Cheshire* SJ 6552
A onetime salt-mining town, Nantwich is in the heart of an area renowned for its production of Cheshire cheese. Many of the black-and-white buildings common to this region can be seen in Nantwich and a particularly fine example is the Welsh Row. The Bridgemere Wildlife Park has many exotic birds and animals in its 35 acres.

Northwich, *Cheshire* SJ 6573
Northwich is an important salt-producing town beneath which dissolving rock salt has created underground caverns. A Salt Museum in London Road traces the industry's history from Roman times. Vale Royal Abbey which was constructed around a 13th-century monastery is reached via a beautiful beech-lined drive and lies a few miles SW of Northwich.

Sandbach's two Anglo-Saxon crosses are thought to mark Paeda's – son of the king of Mercia – conversion to Christianity

Overton, *Clwyd* SJ 3741
One of the seven great wonders of Wales can be found in this pleasant small town in the shape of some stately old yew trees in the grounds of the local church.

Sandbach, *Cheshire* SJ 7560
Two magnificent carved crosses which are believed to date from the 9th century stand side by side in the market place and are the main attraction in Sandbach. An old salt-mining town, its industries now include lorry production and fabric manufacture.

Warrington, *Cheshire* SJ 6088
Known as the Gateway to Cheshire, Warrington is an industrial town of some importance with factories producing soap to ironworks. Several old timber houses can still be seen and the Barley Mow is a fine example of a half-timbered inn. The town hall, once the 18th-century Bank Hall, was designed by James Gibbs.

Wrexham, *Clwyd* SJ 3349
Wrexham has seen many changes over the years as it has outgrown the role of border market town to become a major administrative commercial and shopping centre for a concentrated industrial area. One of the fastest growing towns in North Wales, with much new development, Wrexham has few buildings of historic note. The parish church of St Giles is one exception, it includes an altar piece given by Elihu Yale – of Yale University fame, whose family came from nearby Ial.

33

Derbyshire well-dressing was originally a pagan ceremony of thanksgiving

Astbury, *Cheshire*   SJ 8461
Astbury's 14th- and 15th-century church displays some fine Jacobean woodwork and the 18th-century village rectory is of note. The main attraction – Little Moreton Hall – lies 2m or so S of the village. Its famous exterior of beautifully-carved gables and distinctive black-and-white Elizabethan wood and plasterwork have made Little Moreton Hall perhaps the most photographed building of its kind in Britain. The beauty of this splendid manor house is enhanced by the striking reflection in its own moat.

Bakewell, *Derbys*   SK 2168
The only town in the Peak District National Park, Bakewell sits sheltered on three sides by wooded hills on the banks of the River Wye. The five-arched medieval bridge that spans the Wye is reputedly one of the oldest structures of its kind in Britain. An unusual sponge and jam tart took its name from this town after a harassed cook at the Rutland Arms mistakenly added an egg to the jam. The resultant concoction was thoroughly enjoyed by guests and Bakewell tarts are with us to this day.

Beeley, *Derbys*   SK 2667
Just beyond this ancient village lie the grounds of Chatsworth House, home of the Duke and Duchess of Devonshire. This 17th- and 18th-century mansion stands in a magnificent park complete with mature chestnut avenues and water gardens, and inside is a superb collection of antiques and works of art.

Buxton, *Derbys*   SK 0673
Sitting on the edge of the Peak District National Park, Buxton is the highest village in England, and one of the most elegant. The Romans were first to discover the medicinal qualities of the spas in these parts and the town itself grew with the popularity of the mineral springs. The beautiful Crescent and the Pump Room were built by the 5th Duke of Devonshire who was largely responsible for the town's development. The waters can still be sampled today at a public well in the Crescent or it can be bought bottled at the Tourist Information Centre. The Pavilion is a superb ameni-

ties complex standing in 23 acres of enchanting gardens.

Macclesfield, *Cheshire*   SJ 9173
The town centre of this silk manufacturing town is criss-crossed with steep streets and includes many 18th- and 19th-century mills. West Park Museum contains a small exhibition of the town's associations with the silk industry, as well as a collection of intriguing Egyptian antiquities.

Matlock, *Derbys*   SK 3060
Another spa town, Matlock stands on the River Derwent to the east of the national park amidst gritstone moors and high ridges. Derbyshire County Council now occupies an impressive building which originally functioned as a hydrotherapy centre for the fashionable 19th-century set who came to take the waters.

Peak Forest, *Derbys*   SK 1179
This charming little village bears the name that once applied to a medieval hunting ground that encompassed most of northern Derbyshire. The original church had the power to grant marriage licences and at one time the village was known as the 'Gretna Green' of the Peak District. To the N of the village on the southern slope of Eldon Hill lies a sheer-sided pothole named Eldon Hole.

Rugeley, *Staffs*   SK 0418
Dr William Palmer was the infamous resident of Rugeley during the 19th century. Known as the 'Prince of Poisoners', his case made national news when he was found guilty of poisoning a bookmaker to whom he owed money. What made this case special was the fact that Dr Palmer was discovered to have murdered many others previously. Today Rugeley is a bustling town, worlds removed from these sinister goings-on.

Sheffield, *S Yorks*   SK 3587
Sheffield is world famous for its cutlery, in particular stainless-steel and silver-plated cutlery which was originated here

Buxton's grand Edwardian Opera House – recently restored to its former glory – reflects the town's cultural heritage

in about the 18th century. The city was badly damaged during World War II and consequently few buildings of historic interest remain. The world's largest collection of Sheffield Plate is housed in the City Museum at Weston Park and Cutler's Hall, built in 1832, boasts a fine display of silver from 1773 to the present day. Nearby is the magnificent Peak District.

Tissington, *Derbys*   SK 1752
This lovely village features a triangular green around which greystone houses cluster. Beside the houses a fine church of Norman origin has an unusual two-tier pulpit dating from the 18th century. Five different wells in the area are the scenes of the traditional Derbyshire well-dressing ceremonies that take place on Ascension Day.

Wormhill, *Derbys*   SK 1274
Wormhill enjoys panoramic views across the River Wye from its prominent position. The narrow Chee Dale lies in a curve of the river beneath the village and is popular with walkers. One of the village's most notable buildings is a 17th-century hall with mullioned windows.

Views of the Peak District from Bakewell's hillside churchyard

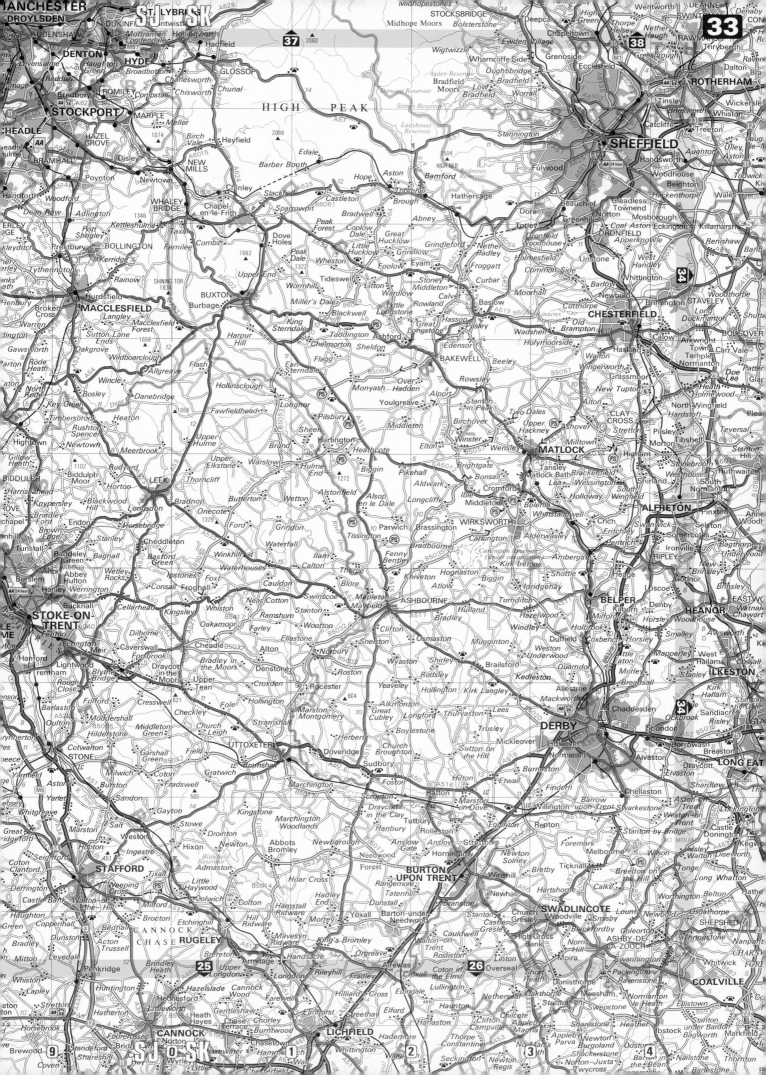

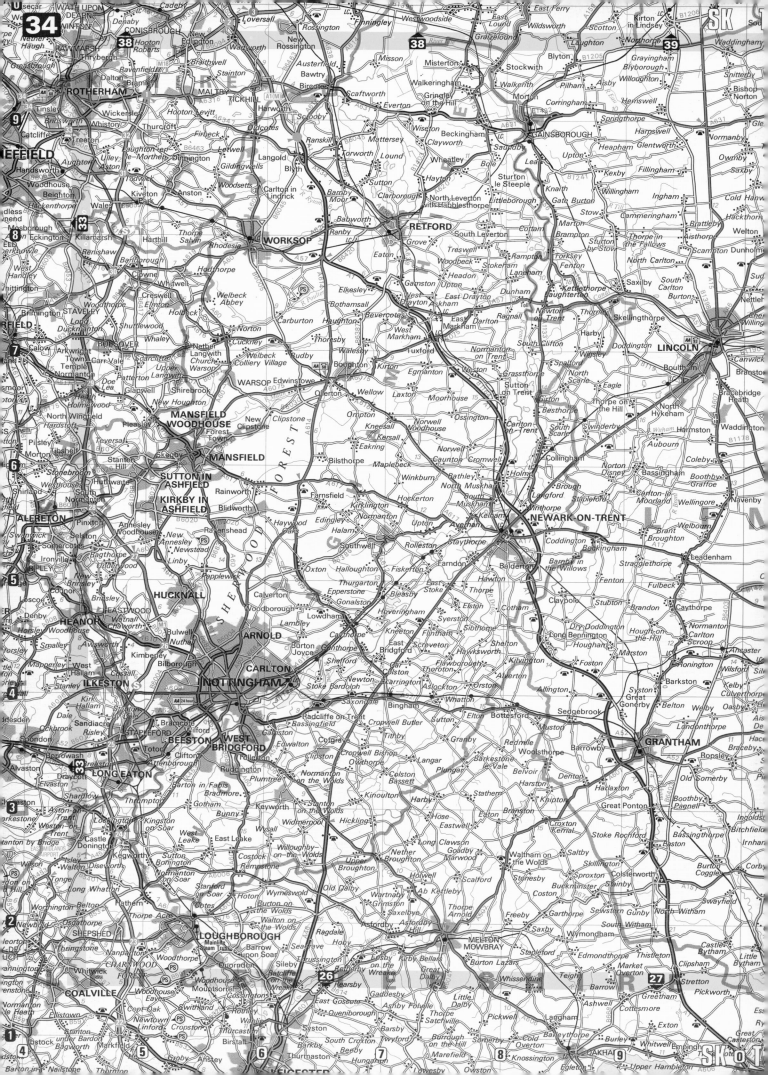

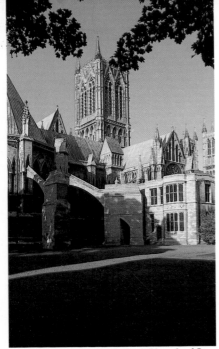

Lincoln's majestic Cathedral Church of St Mary is the third largest in England

Ancaster, *Lincs* SK 9843
The village of Ancaster sits on the old Roman road of Ermine Street which was built to allow ease of access from London to the east of England: the name was derived from that of a local Saxon tribe. In the surrounding wooded countryside are the remains of a Roman camp called *Causennae*. The famous Ancaster stone that was used to build many of Lincolnshire's beautiful churches was taken from quarries some 2m S of the village.

Barrow upon Soar, *Leics* SK 5717
As its name suggests, this attractive village is situated on the east bank of the River Soar. The unusual village sign depicts an aquatic prehistoric reptile. Historic architecture includes a 17th-century hospital, and almshouses dating from 1825.

Blidworth, *Notts* SK 5855
Blidworth is a mining village that has been linked with some of Robin Hood's associates. It is supposed to be the home of Friar Tuck and Maid Marian, characters that add the essential touch of humour and romance to the legend. Will Scarlet, fellow outlaw and friend of Robin, is said to be buried in the local churchyard.

Bottesford, *Leics* SK 8035
Bottesford boasts one of the finest village churches in the country and one that contains an outstanding collection of monuments. A whipping post and some old stocks are preserved here and the attractive Fleming's Bridge dates from the 17th century. A few miles S of Bottesford, overlooking the Vale of Belvoir, is the elegant 19th-century Belvoir Castle.

Honington, *Lincs* SK 9443
The Norman church in Honington is of note and about ¾m SE of this village is an Iron Age hillfort called Honington Camp. A find of Roman coins in the 17th century suggests that the Romans, based

at Ancaster, must have used this camp.

Kinoulton, *Notts* SK 6730
One of the best cricket greens in the county – that is the claim made by the villagers of Kinoulton. They can also claim to have one of the best viewpoints across the rich Vale of Belvoir and the dense woodlands known as the Borders. The Earl of Gainsborough built the local church, which stands opposite a forge, in about 1793.

Leadenham, *Lincs* SK 9452
An interesting feature of this delightful Lincolnshire village is Leadenham Old Hall – an unusual 18th-century structure built entirely of golden ironstone. The village also boasts a 19th-century drinking fountain beneath a hexagonal canopy.

Lincoln, *Lincs* SK 9771
The striking landmark of Lincoln Cathedral with its three towers and impressive west front dominates this ancient city. It holds one of the four original copies of the *Magna Carta* among its many treasures. Around the cathedral cobbled streets wind their way past fascinating antique shops and many quaint old buildings, including the oldest inhabited house in England – Aaron's House, to the banks of the River Witham. Lincoln was an important Roman station and Newport Arch, the only surviving Roman gateway to span an English street, remains as a relic of that ancient walled city. Founded in 1068 by William the Conqueror, Lincoln Castle is a majestic structure surrounded by six acres of grounds.

Melton Mowbray, *Leics* SK 7518
Famous for a special type of pork pie and its fine Stilton cheese, Melton Mowbray is never short of tourists. Anne of Cleve's House is of ancient origin and a local history museum can be found at Thorpe End. Foxhunting thrives in the area and the local villages are often alive with the sound of horns, hounds and horses.

Navenby, *Lincs* SK 9857
Navenby is a charming little village of stone and pantiled houses clustered around a restored church. Of particular note inside the church is the finely-carved Easter Sepulchre which includes the figures of three Roman soldiers in its decoration.

Nottingham, *Notts* SK 5741
A county, university and manufacturing town on the River Trent, Nottingham is renowned for its hosiery, lace, bicycle and tobacco industries. The mainly 17th-century castle is now a museum and art gallery. There are many museums dealing with the city's industrial history, notably the museum of Costume and Textiles in Castlegate and the Industrial Museum in Wollaton Hall. Magnificent oak trees still survive in Sherwood Forest, famous for its associations with the legendary Robin Hood and his band of charitable robbers.

Robin Hood commemorated in Nottingham

Quorndon, *Leics* SK 5616
The most famous hunt in England, the Quorn, is named after this pretty village where there is a station for the Main Line Steam Railway which runs for 5m between Loughborough Central and Rothley. Valuable Tudor relics can be seen in the Farnham Chapel of Quorndon's fine granite church. The rocky Charnwood Forest, once an important hunting ground, lies to the W of the village.

Widmerpool, *Notts* SK 6327
This charming little village is set in some of the finest woodland scenery in the county. The picturesque restored church has a 14th-century tower and contains an exquisite marble sculpture.

An inn built into the cliffside below Nottingham Castle recalls the city's links with King Richard's crusades

Alford, *Lincs* TF 4575
This town includes many fine Georgian and later houses, and Merton Lodge is a fine example. Alford boasts one of Lincolnshire's most notable windmills. The brick tower is six storeys tall and has five sails and an ogee cap on top. Still in working order although no longer in use, it dates from 1837.

Bourne, *Lincs* TF 0920
This ancient market town is reputed to be the birthplace of Hereward the Wake. Today Bourne's fame lies in its racing car industry at BRM and its pure water which produces excellent watercress. Fine domestic architecture is everywhere in Bourne and the Tudor cottages in South Street are of particular note. A Roman canal known as the Car Dyke runs close to the town.

Burgh-le-Marsh, *Lincs* TF 5056
A majestic five-sailed tower windmill is a well-known landmark hereabouts. Another prominent building is the local church which carries an impressive tower decorated with 16 iron crosses. Some 2½m NW of the village is the 18th-century redbrick mansion of Gunby Hall. Behind an austere façade lies a treasure-trove of fine interior decorating, antique furniture and paintings by Reynolds.

Donington, *Lincs* TF 2135
A popular touring base, Donington grew up on a part of Lincolnshire reclaimed from the fens in Roman times. The town was an important centre for the flax and hemp industry and it boasts a charming cobbled market square surrounded by Georgian houses. Inside the local church is a commemorative plaque to Captain Matthew Flinders, a son of the town and a great sailor who travelled with Captain Bligh after the *Bounty* mutiny.

Horbling, *Lincs* TF 1135
An outstanding collection of Georgian houses constitutes the bulk of this charming fenland village. Just N of Horbling's Norman and later church lies Spring Well which used to be a communal washing trough in days gone by.

Horncastle, *Lincs* TF 2669
This village is the scene of a ten-day horse fair held annually in August and featured in George Burrows' *Romany Rye*. In earlier days a Roman settlement called *Banovallum* stood where Horncastle now stands and the modern library incorporates the fort that once guarded that settlement.

Huttoft, *Lincs* TF 5176
Yet another of the tall tower windmills stands out against the skyline of this pleasant village. An early Victorian grain store is also of interest.

Mablethorpe, *Lincs* TF 5085
This popular seaside resort used to have a woodland village for a neighbour, until it was swamped by the sea in 1287. Old tree stumps can still be seen at low tide, and the only surviving building is the old Church of St Mary. The church which contains notable medieval relics is now protected from the sea by a concrete promenade.

Skegness, *Lincs* TF 5663
A onetime peaceful fishing village, Skegness found itself in the centre of a seaside holiday boom with the advent of the railway in 1863. Crowds from the industrial Midlands flocked to enjoy the excellent sands and bathing facilities; and, indeed, they still do today. Beautiful seafront gardens border the long promenade, and fairgrounds, swimming pools and various other seaside attractions vie for attention

Sleaford's malthouses are an impressive example of industrial architecture

with 3½m of golden beach, although the pier was destroyed in storms during 1979. Nearby Gibraltar Point is a dune nature reserve and bird observatory. Church Farm Museum, by way of complete contrast to the town, depicts the life and work of a Lincolnshire farmer in the 19th century.

Sleaford, *Lincs* TF 0645
Sleaford is a charming little market town which enjoys a peaceful situation on the banks of the River Slea. The 12th- to 15th-century church possesses one of the earliest stone spires in England, and other notable buildings in the town include a 15th-century timber-framed vicarage, the 19th-century Corn Exchange and the elegant Carre's Hospital.

Somersby, *Lincs* TF 3472
This tiny Wolds village is famous as the birthplace of poet Alfred Lord Tennyson. Memorials to the Tennyson family can be seen in the local church and their house still stands, but it is not open to the public.

Spalding, *Lincs* TF 2422
Famous for its bulb growing, the springtime array of lovely tulips and daffodils in Spalding are rivalled only by the bulbfields of Holland. Every May this historic fenland town holds a spectacular Flower Parade that attracts visitors from all over the world. Springfields Gardens is a unique 25-acre flower spectacle on the eastern outskirts of the town including a great variety of roses in the magnificent Rose Garden. The town itself is historically interesting with many fine old buildings, including the 15th-century Ayscoughfee Hall, now a museum of British birds.

Woodhall Spa, *Lincs* TF 1963
The only championship standard golf course in the county brings fame to Woodhall Spa today. In Victorian times however it was the mineral springs and fine pump room and bathing facilities that drew visitors to the town.

Ayscoughfee Hall – a philanthropist's former home, now a bird museum

Blackburn, *Lancs* SD 6827
Blackburn has always been an industrial town and one aspect of its past is illustrated in the Lewis Museum of Textile Machinery where period rooms portray the development of the textile industry. The six parks scattered throughout the town relieve its rather sombre atmosphere, and the museum and art gallery in Library Street which features manuscripts, watercolours and Japanese prints is interesting.

Blackpool, *Lancs* SD 3035
Blackpool has gained the reputation of being the biggest, most extravagant and busiest resort in Britain. The famous tower, miles of sandy beaches and spectacular illuminations merely represent the tip of the entertainment iceberg that caters for thousands of visitors each year. Grundy Art Gallery in Queen Street provides a respite from the noisy seaside activities.

Bolton, *Gt Manchester* SD 7108
Prosperity came to Bolton when the cotton industry boomed during the era of the spinning mule, invented by Bolton native Samuel Crompton. His original model, together with an Arkwright's water frame and Hargreave's Spinning Jenny, are kept in the Tonge Moor Textile Museum in Tonge Moor Road.

Carnforth, *Lancs* SD 4970
The former British Rail depot at Carnforth has been turned into the Steamtown Railway Museum where the famous *Flying Scotsman* is kept. About 30 other locos from Britain, Germany and France can also be seen. Leighton Hall, 3m N, belonged to the Gillow family for many generations and much of the work of furniture-maker Richard Gillow is on display in the house. A collection of birds of prey are kept in the extensive grounds and, weather permitting, eagles are flown each afternoon.

Heysham, *Lancs* SD 4161
The village of Heysham dates back hundreds of years and it is thought that the church was built during the 7th century. Heysham Head, however, is the site of a gigantic new entertainments centre that caters for families on a vast scale.

Lancaster, *Lancs* SD 4761
During the 18th century Lancaster was England's chief trading port with America and the prosperity of this era is reflected in the town's elegant Georgian architecture. The attractive streets are overshadowed by the great, square Norman keep of the castle which has been used as a gaol for centuries. Housed in the 17th-century Judges' Lodgings is the fascinating Museum of Childhood and Gillow Museum. The Barry Elder doll collection is also kept here. Hornsea Pottery Co Ltd, set in some 42 acres of landscaped parkland off Wyresdale Road, includes a children's playground, farmyard and picnic area.

Lytham St Anne's, *Lancs* SD 3427
Four championship golf-courses and six miles of sandy beaches draw holiday-makers to this pleasant resort. Of the many parks and gardens laid out in the town, the Alpine Gardens offer particularly enjoyable walks. Situated on Lytham Creek, overlooking the Ribble estuary, is the Motive Power Museum and Lytham Creek Railway where industrial steam locos and a variety of internal combustion engines are displayed.

Morecambe, *Lancs* SD 4364
Morecambe, facing the great sweep of Morecambe Bay, is one of the major holiday resorts in the north. The scale of seaside entertainments comes second only to Blackpool, and here too lavish illuminations draw the holiday season to a spectacular close. At the vast Marineland Oceanarium and Aquarium dolphin shows are a summer attraction.

Seven miles of promenade stretch out beneath 518ft-high Blackpool Tower

Preston, *Lancs* SD 5329
John Horrocks began Preston's cotton industry in 1786 when he established the town's first cotton mill. Later another Preston man, Sir Richard Arkwright, revolutionised the industry when he invented the spinning frame. Housed in an impressive neo-Classical building is the Harris Museum and Art Gallery specialising in Fine and Decorative Arts.

Ribchester, *Lancs* SD 6435
The Roman fort of *Bremetennacum* used to occupy the site of the village of Ribchester and its ruins have been extensively excavated. Pottery, coins and jewellery are displayed in the local museum, together with a replica of a rare parade helmet now housed in the British Museum. Exposed remains of a Roman granary are also open to view.

Southport, *Merseyside* SD 3316
Beautiful gardens complement this elegant resort noted for the many sporting events which take place. Amenities for holidaymakers include a huge pier, a model village and railway, the Steamport Transport Museum, a zoo and the Botanic Gardens Museum. The latter, set in a public park, has a rare example of an early dug-out canoe from nearby Martin Mere.

Wigan, *Gt Manchester* SD 5805
Despite its industrial image, Wigan is a historic town dating back to Roman times when coal was being mined in the area. The town also developed as a weaving and later a clock-making centre. When the Leeds and Liverpool Canal was built in 1774 linking Wigan to Liverpool, its future was sealed. The well-known Wigan Pier is a loading point on the canal. Haigh Country Park 1½m NE has a conference centre, an information centre and a zoo.

Foundations of the Roman fort at Ribchester which guarded the area for 300 years

A memorial to William Gladstone in Manchester's Albert Square

Skipton Castle gateway is all that remains of the original Norman fortress

Bradford, *W Yorks*   SE 1633
Noted as one of Yorkshire's great wool towns, Bradford is predominately Victorian although new development is rapidly altering its atmosphere. The industrial museum at Eccleshill illustrates the growth of the worsted industry in the area. Modern artist David Hockney was born in Bradford and many of his paintings can be seen in the City Art Gallery and Museum in Cartwright Memorial Hall. Two parks in the city are of special interest – Lister and Bowling park. Bolling Hall, opposite the latter, is a period 15th-century house.

Burnley, *Lancs*   SD 8332
Burnley's roots stretch back to the 8th century and in the 13th century it prospered as a wool market. The Industrial Revolution, however, transformed the town and it expanded to its present size. Townley Hall (14th century), is a memorial to the Townley family who figured in the town for centuries. Adjacent is a museum of local crafts and industries.

Grassington, *N Yorks*   SE 0064
A cobbled market place and intriguing alleyways make this Wharfedale village one of the most attractive in the Dales. Displays of conservation and estate management can be seen at the National Park Centre in Hebden Road.

Halifax, *W Yorks*   SE 0825
Halifax is the proud possessor of the only surviving cloth hall in Yorkshire. Now restored and converted into a tourist complex and museum, Piece Hall, dating from the 18th century, has 315 rooms built round a quadrangle and forms an exciting focal point to the town. Another fascinating building in the town is Shibden Hall, a 15th century half-timbered house with period rooms.

Haworth, *W Yorks*   SE 0337
The parsonage home of the three Brontë sisters has become a literary shrine and brought fame to this grim little town on the moors. At the top of the steep main street stands the Black Bull Hotel where their dissolute brother, Branwell, spent most of his time.

Hebden Bridge, *W Yorks*   SD 9927
Deep in the Pennines' heart Hebden Bridge is a dour mill town now reborn as the tourist centre of the Calder Valley. No corduroy making remains but visitors can see clogs being made. The town is the unlikely venue of an annual Anglo-Swiss rally, and a way-marked nature trail skirts the nearby, imposing Hardcastle Crags.

Huddersfield, *W Yorks*   SE 1416
Built on the slopes of the Colne valley, Huddersfield's streets are among the steepest in England. Its reputation was built on worsted which began as a cottage industry in the nearby villages. The first cloth market was held in Almondbury one of the prettiest of these communities. There are two museums and an art gallery in the town, but the Museum of Hand Tools in Halifax Road is particularly interesting.

Ilkley, *W Yorks*   SE 1147
During the 1840s the spring water here was found to have medicinal properties and Ilkley became a popular spa town. Most of its buildings date from the 19th and 20th centuries, but there is a nucleus of older houses around the church. One of these, Manor House, is an Elizabethan house built on the site of a Roman fort and has of Roman material on display.

Keighley, *W Yorks*   SE 0641
The Brontë girls used to walk to this pleasant 19th-century town from Haworth to do their shopping. A great attraction nowadays is the Keighley and Worth Valley Light Railway which has been restored and provides trips to Oxenhope and back. Just NW of the town on the A629, Cliffe Castle, a late 19th-century mansion, contains numerous interesting bygones and there are craft workshops in the grounds. East Riddlesden Hall 1m NE is a lovely stone manor which has a fine tithe barn.

Manchester, *Gt Manchester*   SJ 8397
Manchester developed during the Industrial Revolution as Britain's leading cotton centre and, despite extensive redevelopment, its character is essentially Victorian. Fascinating and diverse museums can be found throughout this city, and the John Rylands University Library is a paradise for lovers of antiquarian books and manuscripts.

Settle, *N Yorks*   SD 8263
Georgian houses, tiny courtyards and narrow streets characterise this delightful Ribblesdale town which is an ideal centre for touring the hills and crags of the area. Nearby Giggleswick Scar is particularly impressive, and 300 ft-high Castleberg Crag dominates the town itself.

Skipton *N Yorks*   SD 9851
An imposing medieval castle overshadows this interesting town on the edge of the Wharfedale Moors. Opposite the huge castle gateway is the Craven Museum which specialises in the geology and folk life of the district. Milling has been carried out in Skipton since the 12th century and the George Leatt Industrial and Folk Museum occupies an old four-storey mill in Chapel Hill.

Terraces of stone cottages – often several storeys high – were built into the hillside at Hebden Bridge to house mill workers

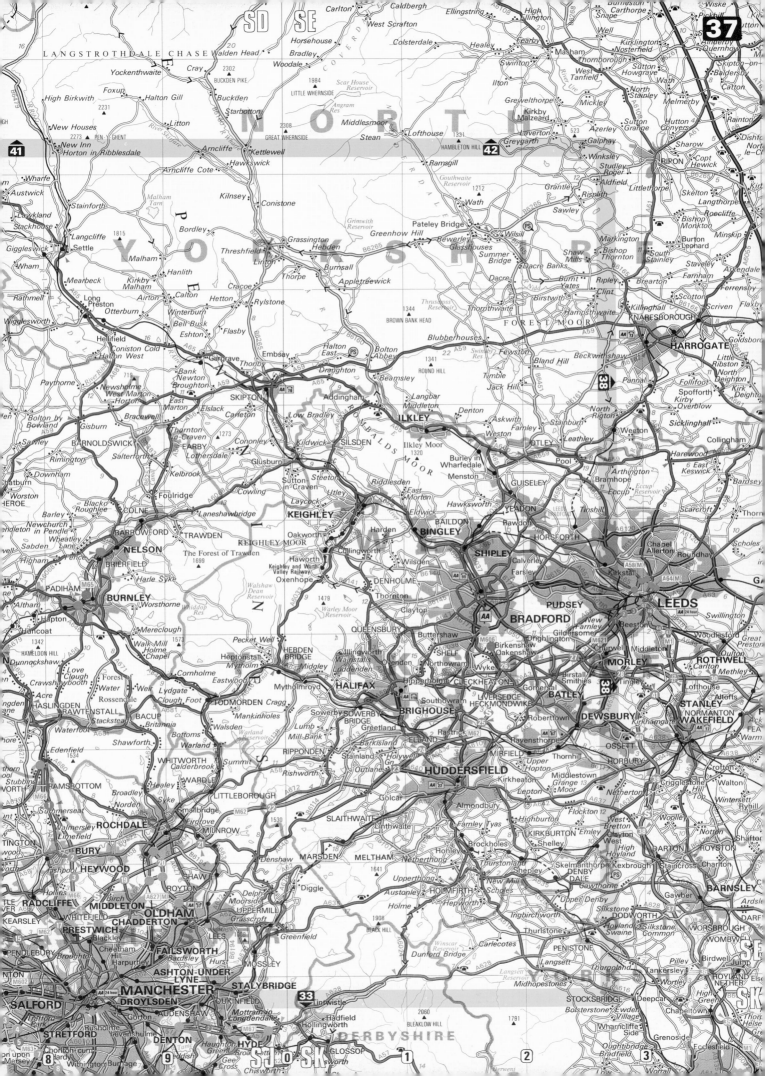

St John's Church tower and the railway viaduct are distinctive landmarks in Knaresborough

Barnsley, *S Yorks* SE 3406
Situated in the middle of the South Yorkshire coalfield, Barnsley has suffered the consequences. There are few buildings over 100 years old and re-development is replacing many of those. Worsbrough Mill Museum 2½ m S has been turned into a working industrial site museum and is set in a country park. To the E, the ruins of Monk Bretton Priory give a good picture of how a Cluniac house with its associated buildings must have looked.

Doncaster, *S Yorks* SE 5803
Doncaster is well known for its race-course and the St Leger race has been run since 1778. A Roman station – *Danum* – stood on the site of the town and several relics from this can be seen in the Museum and Art Gallery in Chequer Road. Coal mining supports Doncaster today, and exhibits in Cusworth Hall on the outskirts trace its history in the area.

Harewood, *W Yorks* SE 3245
Harewood House, home of the Earl and Countess of Harewood, was originally designed by John Carr of York and Robert Adam in 1759. Capability Brown landscaped the grounds which offer lakeside and woodland walks and there is a separate Bird Garden. Here tropical birds, amphibians and small mammals are housed under cover, and there is also an adventure playground and picnic area.

Harrogate, *N Yorks* SE 3055
Dignified Victorian stone buildings and lovely gardens reflect Harrogate's 19th-century popularity as a spa town. Its most famous spa – originally known as The Stinking Spaw – lies beneath the Royal Pump Room which was built in 1804: the water can still be tasted here. The Royal Baths were opened nearby in 1897 and became one of the largest hydrotherapy complexes in the world. Although the baths were closed down in 1969, the elegant Assembly Rooms are still used for conferences. Harrogate's main entertainment and conference centre, however, is the Royal Hall, which seats 1,350. A glass-covered 600 ft-long walkway in Valley Gardens leads to the Sun Pavilion and the lovely Harlow Car Gardens are used for experimental horticulture.

Knaresborough, *N Yorks* SE 3557
Buildings climb higgledy-piggledy up a rocky outcrop above the River Nidd at Knaresborough and set right at the top are the castle ruins from which the views are spectacular. Part of the keep is used as a museum. The town claims two records: it has the oldest linen-mill and the oldest chemist's shop in England. Other places of interest include the grounds of Conyngham Hall where there is a zoo.

Leeds, *W Yorks* SE 3034
Leeds, at one time acknowledged capital of the wholesale clothing trade, is a big, busy, modern city. A scattering of substantial Victorian buildings give Leeds a certain identity, but modern office blocks and housing are rapidly submerging this. Railway enthusiasts will enjoy the Middleton Colliery Railway at Garnet Road, and Temple Newsam House and Park on the SE outskirts is rewarding.

Malton, *N Yorks* SE 7871
Old Malton and New Malton are separated by the site of a Roman station, finds from which are kept in the museum in the old town hall. New Malton was built in 1138 when the old village was largely burnt down and its large market square is the centre of activity for the surrounding farming district.

Pontefract, *W Yorks* SE 4522
Liquorice-flavoured Pontefract cakes became famous at the turn of the century and although the liquorice is no longer grown here, two local firms still produce them. There are several attractive 18th- and 19th-century buildings in the town and the local history museum in Salter Row provides a good background to Pontefract and its historically important castle – now in ruins in a public park.

Ripon, *N Yorks* SE 3171
Known as the Gateway to the Dales, this attractive city stands at the junction of the Rivers Ure, Skell and Laver. The small cathedral is a lovely 12th-century building with a Saxon crypt and fine local woodcarving. 3m SW the ruins of Fountains Abbey, among the finest in England, stand in the grounds of Studley Royal. Landscaped in the 18th century, the park features statues, a temple folly and grazing herds of deer and livestock.

Selby, *N Yorks* SE 6132
Selby's pride and joy is its 900-year-old abbey, founded by Benedict of Auxerre after he had been sent in a vision to the spot where it stands. Begun in about 1100, the nave of the present abbey took 100 years to complete and consequently represents Norman to early English styles of architecture.

York, *W Yorks* SE 6052
Two thousand years of history can be traced in this beautiful city dominated by the largest Gothic church in England – York Minster. Among its treasures are over 100 stained-glass windows spanning 800 years. The medieval streets – epitomized by the famous Shambles – enclosed within the great city walls hold a wealth of interest backed up in the city's numerous museums and public buildings that cover every aspect of a rich past. Britain's finest Heritage Centre, in Castlegate, interprets the social and architectural history of the city of York and the 'Walk Around York' guides visitors to the major buildings in the city.

York Minster – seen from the medieval walls which provide a 2½m walk around the city

Beverley, *Humberside*   TA 0339
Two exceptionally beautiful churches
soar up above this lovely old East Riding
town. One is the twin-towered minster,
and the other is St Mary's – begun as a
chapel to the minster in the 12th century.
At one time a ditch and five gates protected the town, of which only one, the
North Bar, survives. Lairgate Hall, built
in 1700, has lovely hand-painted Chinese
wallpaper adorning the drawing-room.

Bridlington, *Humberside*   TA 1766
The busy working harbour of Bridlington provides a colourful focal point to this
popular resort which has long stretches of
sand to either side. A mile inland the
church of St Mary is of great interest and
includes the nave of an Augustinian
priory. Bayle Gate, originally a priory
building, has had many uses over the
years but is now occupied by a museum.
Sewerby Hall set on the cliffs to the NE is
surrounded by grounds which include a
zoo and a cliff-top railway.

Burton Agnes, *Humberside*   TA 1063
The great Elizabethan mansion, Burton
Agnes Hall, outshines the rest of this
quiet village. Built in 1598, its contents
have been collected over five centuries
and there are fine examples of many
periods; not least of these are the 20th-
century paintings which have been
collected by the present owner. Simple
gardens and herbaceous borders provide
a pleasing setting for this lovely redbrick
house. Next door is a much smaller
building that is often overlooked – this is
Burton Agnes Old Hall which was built
in about 1170. A stone-vaulted store-
room occupies the ground floor which is

*Spurn Head lightship coming into dock at
Hull for an overhaul*

linked by a spiral staircase to the hall
above.

Cleethorpes, *Humberside*   TA 3008
In just over a hundred years Cleethorpes
has been transformed from a small
fishing village into a large resort able to
cater for a million visitors each season. A
huge open-air swimming pool, a zoo with
a Marineland featuring performing dol-
phins, a boating lake and the popular
Lincolnshire Coast Light Railway are just
a few of the attractions here.

Great Driffield, *Humberside*   TA 0257
Driffield, situated on the edge of the
Yorkshire Wolds, has always been a busy
agricultural town and its two weekly
markets still attract buyers from the area.
A small private museum provides a good
background to local history. Anglers
come to Driffield to fish for trout in the
numerous streams which flow down from
the Wolds into the River Hull.

Hornsea, *Humberside*   TA 2047
Hornsea Pottery has become known
nationwide and tours of the factory in
Rolston Road are available. Landscaped
gardens here include a model village and
lake. The town itself is a popular family
holiday centre with a fine promenade and
a fascinating museum in the main street.
This, housed in Burn's Farm, is the
North Holderness Museum of Village
Life. It consists of a kitchen, a parlour
and bedroom furnished in the 1880s
style, and sometimes old skills such as
lace-making are demonstrated.

Kingston upon Hull, *Humberside*   TA 0929
More commonly known just as Hull, this
important industrial and commercial
centre is one of England's biggest deep-
sea fishing ports. War damage resulted in
extensive new development, but one of
the older buildings that survived is Mal-
ster House, which now belongs to the
National Trust. Hull's fishing and whaling industry can be traced in the Town
Docks Museum, and archaeology and
transport are well covered at the museum
in the High Street.

Pocklington, *Humberside*   SE 8048
The Yorkshire Wolds rise up behind the
friendly little town of Pocklington whose
most attractive feature is the garden of
Burnby Hall on the edge of the town.
The Hall is used as local council offices
but the gardens were given to Pocklington by the late Major P. M. Stewart. He
first laid out the lovely water gardens as
trout ponds and they were turned into
lily ponds in 1935. The Major also spon-
sored the building of an exhibition hall to
house his collection of sporting trophies
and treasures acquired from trips around
the world.

Scunthorpe, *Humberside*   SE 8910
In about 1864 extensive ironstone beds
were discovered in the area and as a
result Scunthorpe developed from a few
villages into a vast industrial town. The
Borough Museum and Art Gallery covers

local history from Stone Age to recent
times, but there is little else for the visitor
in Scunthorpe. Normanby Hall 5m N,
however, is an interesting early 19th-
century house. The architect, Sir Robert
Smirke, designed it as a group of inter-
secting cubes which gives it a rather
ungainly appearance. Scunthorpe
Corporation acquired the house, empty,
in 1963 and furnished the rooms in
the style of the 1820s.

Sledmere, *Humberside*   SE 9364
The village of Sledmere belongs to the
estate attached to Sledmere House. This
Georgian mansion filled with elegant furniture is surrounded by a lovely park
designed by Capability Brown. Sir
Tatton Sykes, a well-known member of
the family who have owned the house for
many years, is commemorated by a spire
on Garton Hill.

Sproatley, *Humberside*   TA 1934
1½m N of this little village is an Elizabethan house called Burton Constable
Hall. Several architects worked on the
house during the 18th century and the
diversity of styles is one of its charms.
The splendid Chinese room and the long
gallery are especially striking.

Withernsea, *Humberside*   TA 3328
A 127ft-tall lighthouse – no longer in use
– stands in the middle of this quiet family
resort. Typical seaside entertainments
are provided here, including the ever-
popular donkey rides along the beach,
and there are good sports facilities.
During Victorian times the town had a
pier but all that remains is a castellated
gateway.

*Beverley Minster's beautiful vaulted nave is
carved from magnesium limestone*

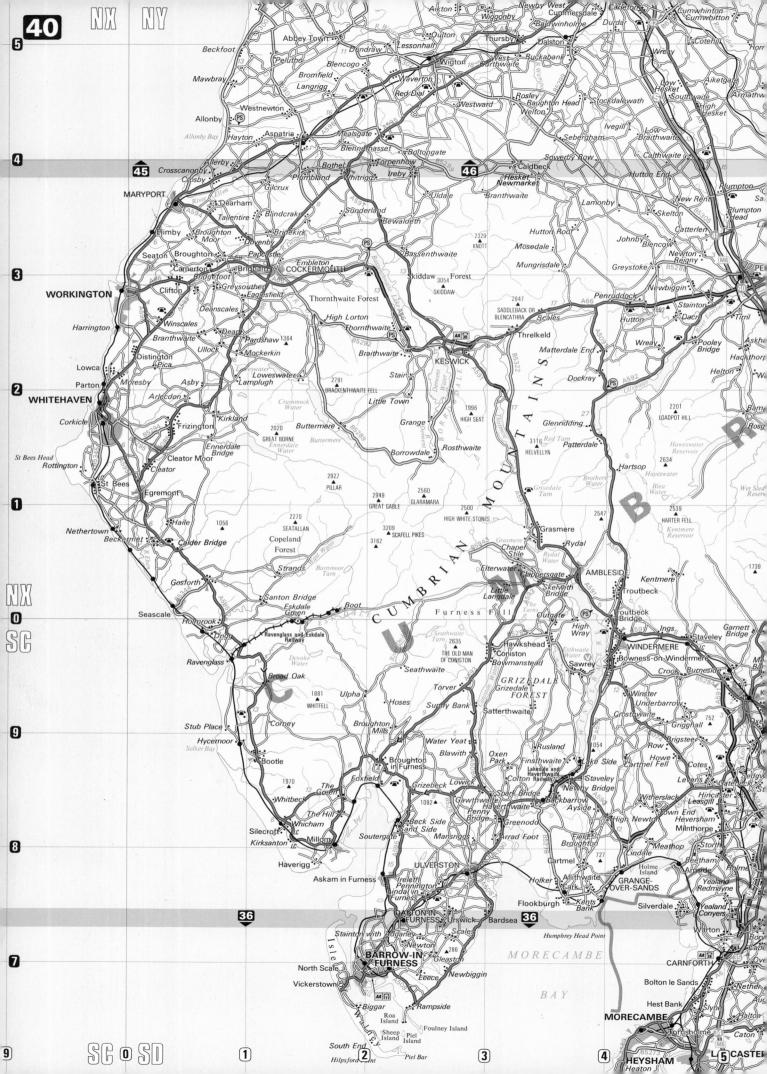

Ambleside, *Cumbria*   NY 3704
Anglers, walkers and climbers flock to Ambleside to enjoy their various pursuits for which the town is well placed. Stagshaw Gardens 1m S overlook Lake Windermere and the beauty of one complements the other splendidly.

Buttermere, *Cumbria*   NY 1717
Buttermere Lake, which gave the village its name, is one of the loveliest in the Lake District, and together with Crummock Water on the other side sandwiches the pretty village. Scale Force, the highest waterfall in Lakeland, can be reached by a footpath from Buttermere.

Cartmel, *Cumbria*   SD 3778
At one time this attractive old village was one of the most important religious centres in the area, but there is little left of the great priory now apart from the gatehouse and the church. The former, facing the market cross, was used as a grammar school from 1624 to 1790.

Cockermouth, *Cumbria*   NY 1230
Cockermouth, an attractive market town standing at the junction of the Rivers Cocker and Derwent, is famous as the birthplace of William Wordsworth. His old home on Main Street, Wordsworth House, now belongs to the National Trust which has kept it much as it was in the poet's day.

Grange-over-Sands, *Cumbria*   SD 4077
Lovely wooded hills rise up behind this pleasant seaside resort which overlooks Morecambe Bay, and the mild local climate allows ornamental gardens to flourish throughout the town. At nearby Holker Hall there is a motor museum, a baby animal farm, and a countryside museum and aquarium, as well as several other attractions.

Grasmere, *Cumbria*   NY 3307
Every August traditional lakeland events take place at the Grasmere Sports held in a nearby natural arena. The village's most popular building is 17th-century Dove Cottage in which Wordsworth lived from 1799 to 1808, when it became the home of writer Thomas de Quincey. A Wordsworth Museum is attached to the house.

Kendal, *Cumbria*   SD 5192
Greystone buildings have given Kendal its nickname of the Auld Grey Town, although it is in fact a combination of both old and modern architecture. The ruins of Kendal Castle, birthplace of Catherine Parr, overlook the narrow old streets and the River Kent, lined by neat gardens, meanders through the town. Housed in a stable block designed by Carr of York are displays of Lakeland life, trade, social and economic history, and the Kendal Museum specialises in natural history and archaelogy. Another house designed by Carr is occupied by the Abbot Hall Art Gallery.

Keswick, *Cumbria*   NY 2723
With some of Lakeland's most beautiful scenery on its doorstep, Keswick is a favourite touring centre. During Victorian times it was popular with poets and artists, including Wordsworth and Coleridge whose works and possessions can be seen in the Fitz Park Museum. Lingholm Gardens about 2m away are laid out on the shores of Derwent Water and in spring are ablaze with daffodils.

Maryport, *Cumbria*   NY 0336
Lord of the Manor Colonel H. Senhouse developed the town during the Industrial Revolution and named it after his wife, Mary. There are miles of sandy beaches to either side of the town and a Maritime

Museum in Shipping Brow includes a photographic display illustrating Maryport's history.

Bridge House in Ambleside, built in the 18th century as a summerhouse, is now a National Trust information centre

Penrith, *Cumbria*   NY 5130
It is thought that Penrith was occupied by the Celts in about 500BC, and in the 9th century it was capital of the independent state of Cumbria. During the 14th century the castle was built to defend the town from the Scots but only ruins are left. Among several interesting old buildings is the Gloucester Arms which claims to be one of the oldest inns in England.

Ravenglass, *Cumbria*   SD 0896
Lying at the head of an estuary formed by three rivers is the small village of Ravenglass. Just to the S are the ruined walls of a Roman fort, known as Walls Castle, measuring 12½ft high in places. These are some of the best preserved remains in northern England. The Ravenglass and Eskdale Railway established in 1875 to carry iron ore is now a passenger line covering some 7m. Nearby Muncaster Castle and Bird Garden are delightful.

Whitehaven, *Cumbria*   NX 9718
In 1690 Sir John Lowther industrialised the sleepy village of Whitehaven and it developed into the busy seaport that exists today. A museum and art gallery in Market Place has changing exhibitions as well as permanent collections.

Windermere, *Cumbria*   SD 4198
Beautiful Lake Windermere, studded with tiny islands and fringed by well-wooded slopes, has drawn tourists since the 19th century. Belle Isle, in the middle of the lake, has the first completely round house built in England and it can be reached by motor launch from Bowness-on-Windermere. Recalling the days when steamboats plied up and down the 10m lake is the Steamboat Museum.

The harbour at Whitehaven dates from the town's days as an important port

Appleby, *Cumbria*   NY 6820
Until 1092 Appleby belonged to Scotland but under severe subsequent Scottish attacks was virtually destroyed by about 1388. The castle survived from the 12th century and later it was restored by Lady Anne Clifford who was a notable figure in Westmorland during the 17th century – her tomb is in St Lawrence's church. Several old buildings line Boroughgate – the main thoroughfare – including the Moot Hall dated 1596.

Barnard Castle, *Co Durham*   NZ 0516
Set up on a rocky bluff with lovely views of Teesdale, the attractive old town of Barnard Castle grew up around its medieval castle. This, built by Guy de Balliol then rebuilt by his nephew Bernard – hence the town's name – was destroyed during the Civil War but there are extensive remains covering 6½ acres. The town is well known for the huge Bowes Museum which resembles a French château and houses one of the finest art collections in Britain. John Bowes, son of the Earl of Strathmore, and his wife spent a lifetime acquiring the treasures, but sadly they both died before the building was finished and their dream of their own museum realised.

Brough, *Cumbria*   NY 7914
Brough's history reaches back about 2,000 years but the oldest building is the castle which is thought to date from the early 12th century – the keep was added between 1175 and 1200. This was another of the strongholds restored by Lady Anne Clifford. Every September a horse fair takes place which was first held in the 19th century when Brough was a busy coaching town.

Castle Bolton, *N Yorks*   SE 0391
The village and much of the surrounding area is, rather confusingly, dominated by Bolton Castle. Built in the 14th century to guard the approach to Wensleydale, it is set on the side of the valley and has far-reaching views. Although now partly in ruins and overgrown, there is still enough of the castle to gain a vivid impression of the living conditions it provided.

Kirkby Lonsdale, *Cumbria*   SD 6178
This lovely little market town is a centre for touring the Lune valley which 19th-century writer and painter John Ruskin loved so much. Some of his favourite walks are signposted to the north of the churchyard and nearby is the view which he described as 'one of the loveliest in England and therefore in the world'.

Leyburn, *N Yorks*   SE 1190
A short walk from the town centre of Leyburn takes you to the Shawl – a wooded mile-long limestone terrace that provides beautiful views over Wensleydale. The town makes an ideal base for touring the surrounding switchback countryside.

Middleton-in-Teesdale,
Co Durham   NY 9425
The London Lead Company which first developed Teesdale's lead mines in the mid 18th century was run by Quakers and they had a strong influence on the running of the town which is still in evidence in the stern architecture.

Sedbergh, *Cumbria*   SD 6592
Sedbergh, lying in the shadow of the Howgill Fells, is largely Victorian in character. At the National Park Centre in Main Street permanent displays cover the topography of the area which are particularly interesting to walkers.

Shap, *Cumbria*   NY 5615
To the west of the village of Shap, which lies nearly 1,000 ft above sea level, are the ruins of Shap Abbey. It was founded by Premonstratensian canons in about 1191 but the remains date from the early 13th century to 1540 when the abbey was dissolved. 1m SW off the A6 is a small pre-Reformation chapel belonging to the National Trust.

Bolton Castle, a fine castellated manor house, was dismantled after the Civil War

Staindrop, *Co Durham*   NZ 1220
The village which grew up beside nearby Raby Castle, seat of the Neville family, consists of a single street and an unusually long village green. There are many monuments to the Nevilles in the village church which is proud to possess the only pre-Reformation screen in England. Raby Castle, with its nine towers, battlements and moat, is all a castle should be. Parts of it may date back to the 12th century, but its overall appearance was established in the 14th and subsequent alterations have created the atmosphere of a rambling mansion.

Stanhope, *Co Durham*   NY 9939
High moorland surrounds the quiet town of Stanhope which is known as the 'capital' of Weardale. It dates back to about 1200 when the church was built, but predating this by millions of years is the huge fossilized tree stump standing in the churchyard. Nearby Heathery Burn Cave is famous for the various Bronze Age weapons and artefacts discovered in 1843 by workmen which are kept in the British Museum.

Bowes Museum in Barnard Castle stands in a 21-acre park and has 22 exhibition rooms displaying thousands of beautiful treasures

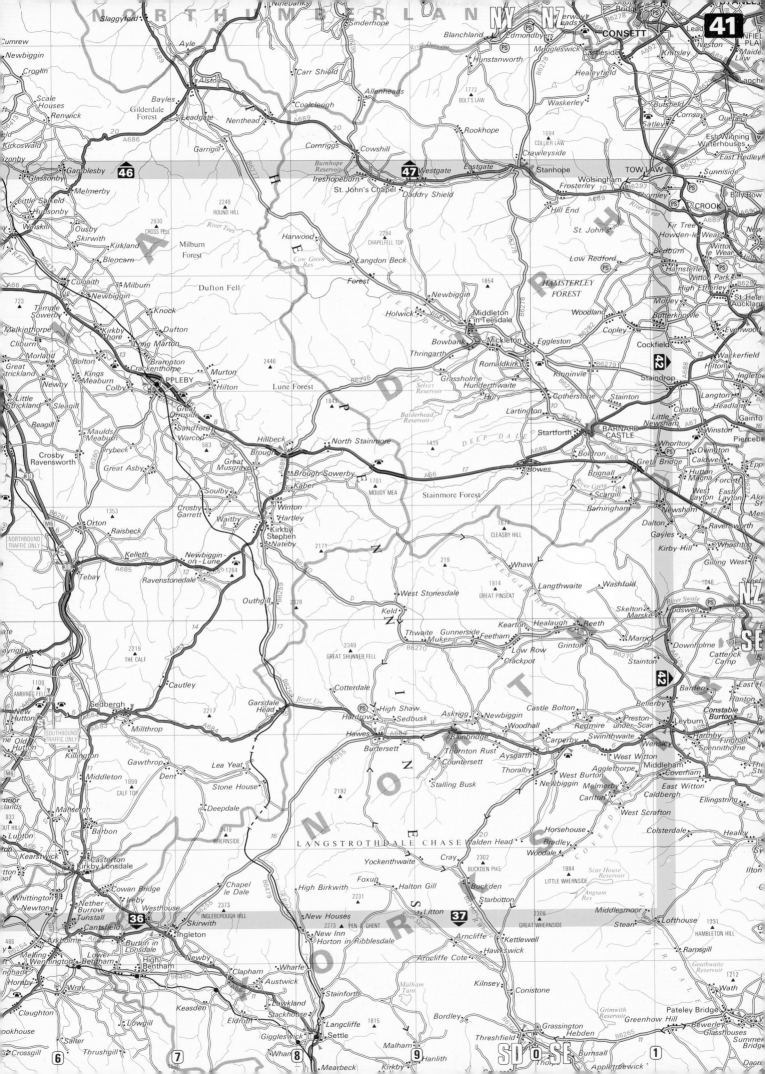

Steam locos from the golden age of steam are preserved at Darlington's museum

Ampleforth, *N Yorks*   SE 5878
Set into the Hambleton Hills, Ampleforth is well known for its Roman Catholic public school founded in 1802 by Benedictine monks. Both the college and the Abbey of St Lawrence stand at one end of the main street of this pleasant stone-built village. Gilling Castle, which can just be seen across the valley at Gilling East, is now a preparatory school for Ampleforth College. Some of Robert Thompson's work can be seen in the library here: his signature was a tiny carved mouse hidden on each piece of work. Lovely gardens surround the house and the great hall and chamber are noted for their panelling and painted glass.

Castleton, *Derbys*   SK 1582
A group of limestone caverns round about Castleton draws visitors in their hundreds to this little village. Speedwell Cavern is floodlit and has a bottomless pit and the Blue John Cavern has veins of the bright blue semi-precious Blue John stone. A ruined keep built by Henry II is an impressive medieval landmark in the village.

Coxwold, *N Yorks*   SK 5377
Golden stone cottages set behind broad grass verges and a lovely octagonal church tower have gained Coxwold just fame as a beauty spot. Another attraction is Shandy Hall, the former home of Laurence Stern – author of *The Life and Opinions of Tristram Shandy* – who was a rector in the village for seven years. Nearby Newburgh Priory is an 18th-century hall standing on the site of an Augustinian foundation. To the NE of

Coxwold are the striking ruins of Byland Abbey. At one time it was the largest Cistercian church in the county but was sacked by the Scots in the aftermath of the Dissolution.

Darlington, *Co Durham*   NZ 2914
When the Darlington to Stockton line was opened as Britain's first public railway in 1825, Darlington's modern history began. The Railway Museum at North Road Station has many early models and exhibits connected with the line, including Stephenson's famous *Locomotion 1* which opened it. For non-railway enthusiasts there is a museum in Tubwell Row and an art gallery in Crown Street.

Guisborough, *Cleveland*   NZ 6115
Rising up above the trees in the grounds of Guisborough Hall are the fine ruins of the east end of Gisborough Priory. Robert the Bruce founded it in about 1120 and it grew very prosperous before the Dissolution of the monasteries by Henry VIII. Chapel Beck Gallery in Fountain Street has changing exhibitions on the local history of Cleveland and the work of local craftsmen.

Helmsley, *N Yorks*   SE 6183
Gracious stone houses surround the spacious market square at Helmsley. In 1689 Charles Duncombe, a wealthy banker, bought the town and built Duncombe Park. Standing in the grounds are the ruins of Helmsley Castle which dates from the 12th century. It was built by Walter d'Espec and its strength is still evident in the great keep, tower and curtain walls that remain.

Northallerton, *N Yorks*   SE 3793
This was an important posting town and it still has many of the big old inns that once sheltered stagecoach travellers. The curving main street widens out in the middle to form a market square where a market is held twice a week.

Richmond, *N Yorks*   NZ 1701
Dramatically situated above the River Swale, this historic town is a maze of little alleys, known as Wynds, distinguished by much Georgian architecture. A massive Norman castle dominates the picturesque streets and the large cobbled market place which is one of the largest in the country. The most outstanding Georgian building is the Little Theatre which, beautifully restored, is the oldest theatre in the country to have survived in its original condition. Green Howard's Museum by the market place illustrates the colourful history of the regiment. One of the best of many lovely walks around Richmond is along the Swale to the parklands at Lowenthwaite Bridge.

Rievaulx, *N Yorks*   SE 5785
Set in the thickly wooded valley of the River Rye are the magnificent ruins of Rievaulx Abbey. It was the first church the Cistercians built in the north of England and the remains of the chapels,

chapter house, choir and transepts indicate the scale and richness of their work. To the south, from Rievaulx Terrace, there are beautiful views of the abbey. Garden temples were built here in the 18th century so the gentry could rest during their promenade along the ½m terrace.

Stockton-on-Tees, *Cleveland*   NZ 4419
Twice a week (Wednesdays and Saturdays) Stockton High Street – the broadest in England – is the scene of an open-air market that has been held since the 14th century. Stockton developed as a shipbuilding and engineering centre in the 19th century but something of the charm of the old town can still be seen at its centre. Preston Hall Museum on the Farm Road at Eaglescliff illustrates Victorian social history and has a reconstructed 19th-century street.

Stokesley, *N Yorks*   NZ 5208
Two greens mark each end of the long market place in Stokesley which lies at the foot of the Cleveland Hills. Narrow cobbled lanes weave between its redbrick houses and the River Leven, spanned by several footbridges, flows along one side of the town and provides a lovely tree-shaded walk.

Thirsk, *N Yorks*   SE 4282
Thirsk took its name from an old local family who lived in the area for centuries and it was Robert Thirsk who founded the chantry of the parish church in the 15th century. Old inns surrounding the cobbled market square recall the heyday of the coaching era when Thirsk was an important staging post.

At its most prosperous Rievaulx Abbey housed about 140 monks and 50 lay brothers

Weathered red tiles contrast effectively with the stone cottages in Hutton-le-Hole

Danby, *N Yorks*   NZ 7009
Lying deep in Eskdale, the wide, beautiful valley of the River Esk, Danby is surrounded by moorland. 1m SE is the ruin of 14th-century Danby Castle, now part of a farmhouse but formerly owned by Catherine Parr's second husband, Lord Latimer. Duck Bridge, a medieval clapper bridge of the same era, crosses the Esk nearby, and nearly 1,000 prehistoric cairns litter the moorland round the village. Danby Lodge, once a shooting lodge, is set in 13 acres of woodland and riverside meadow close by, and serves as a visitor centre for the North Yorks Moor National Park.

Filey, *E Yorks*   TA 1180
The old village of narrow streets and charming houses is now largely eclipsed by the modern but pleasant seaside resort which has grown up around it – and added a promenade and neat gardens to the natural attractions of the coast. Old St Oswald's church with a 'weatherfish' on top of its stolid tower has a circular window commemorating all Filey men lost at sea. From the headland stretches a natural pier of weathered rock which provides a wonderful assortment of caves bays and pools inviting exploration.

Goathland, *N Yorks*   NZ 8301
Goathland is very much a typical moorland village, the old and new houses scattered haphazardly around a green of rough pasture. A custom here calls for the men and boys of the village to perform longsword and plough stort dances to celebrate special events. Men pulling a plough, normally pulled by a bullock or stort, tour the village collecting contributions for the great celebrations which occur here on Plough Monday. From the green a path leads to the 70ft-high waterfall, Mallyn Spout.

Hutton-le-Hole, *N Yorks*   SE 7090
The Ryedale Folk Museum relates in great detail the history of this village and the surrounding area through a fine display of finds from prehistoric times to the end of the 19th century. Housed in farm buildings, once the home of prosperous 17th-century Quakers, the largest exhibits are concerned with agricultural and domestic history, and include reconstructed cruck-framed houses. The

village is a popular beauty spot, with old houses scattered around a large green and the course of the beck which flows through it is marked by a series of small white bridges.

Kirby Misperton, *N Yorks*   NE 7779
The 18th-century Kirby Misperton Hall and its 350-acre park, situated at the heart of the Vale of Pickering, has been turned into Flamingoland – a zoo and flamingo park. There are over 1,000 animals, birds and reptiles, and attractions include a jungle cruise, a children's farm, Gnomeland and a fairground. There is also a model railway and holiday village.

Pickering, *N Yorks*   SE 7983
This greystone Yorkshire market town is now a tourist and trade centre for the Vale of Pickering and the North York Moors. Set in beautiful countryside, the town does boast its own attractions – a restored medieval church with remarkable wall paintings, and the ruins of Pickering Castle, founded by William the Conqueror. A pleasant Georgian House, Beck Isle, houses a museum of folk exhibits of the area. The North Yorks Moors Railway which travels 18m to Grosmont across glorious moorland scenery has its terminus at Pickering, where there is an information centre.

Scarborough, *N Yorks*   TA 0388
Although best-known as a popular holiday town, Scarborough is a fine old town in its own right. It is centred around two fine sandy bays, separated by a 300 ft-high headland upon which are perched the remains of a 12th-century castle. From this vantage point the roofs of the medieval town can be seen clustered below, stretching down to the jolly harbour. Splendid Victorian buildings house the natural history museum, art gallery and baths. On the seafront promenades, gardens and a zoo and dolphinarium complement the traditional seaside entertainments. Woodend, once the holiday home of the Sitwell family, houses a general museum.

Whitby, *N Yorks*   NZ 8911
The great 18th-century navigator, Captain James Cook, kept his home in Grape Lane, and learnt his seamanship on the

The medieval heart of Scarborough clusters around the old fishing harbour

local colliers here when the town was a foremost whaling port. These maritime industries have long disappeared, but the seagoing atmosphere Cook knew then is still strong, and Whitby remains a busy fishing town. Red-roofed houses upon the steep banks of the River Esk echo to the cries of seagulls, both on the East Cliff, the older part of the town above the harbour, and on the West Cliff on the opposite bank, developed by the Victorians along a wide, sandy beach. The gaunt ruins of Whitby Abbey stand on the cliff above the old town – a centre of learning in Saxon times. In Pannet Park the town's museum and gallery record the local history and display examples of carved jet, a local craft.

Isle of Man

Castletown, *Isle of Man*   SC 2667
True to its name, the former capital of the island is built around Castle Rushen, a medieval fortress. The narrow streets separate quaint old houses squashed together in a medley of stone and tile, spilling down to the spacious beach of Castletown Bay. The National Museum's pride and joy is the *Peggy*, a splendid schooner-rig yacht, probably the oldest in the British Isles. The museum is housed in an 18th-century boathouse by the harbour.

Douglas, *Isle of Man*   SC 3876
On a clear day England, Scotland, Ireland and Wales are visible from the Isle of Man; but Douglas, the capital and chief resort, has a Continental air. Horse-drawn trams sedately meander along streets between ranks of old houses beneath the watchful eyes of policemen in white helmets. The Tynwald, the island's ancient parliament, meets in the House of Keys on Prospect Hill. On a bluff above St Thomas' Church is Manx Museum, 'a national museum of the Island', as much an institution as the tailless Manx cat, specially bred in Noble's Park to preserve the strain.

Peel, *Isle of Man*   SC 2484
A fishing port from another age, and seemingly untouched by time, Peel is especially famous for its Manx Kipper, smoked over oak woodchips. Tynwald Hill nearby is a small hill from which all new island laws must be proclaimed in English and the Manx tongue.

Ramsey, *Isle of Man*   SC 4594
The Isle of Man belonged briefly to Scotland, for Robert the Bruce landed here in 1313 to claim it for himself. Ramsey is now the second largest town on the island, sheltered from the northerly winds by tall hills. The port boasts a magnificent public park, 400 acres in extent, with a large marine lake and a palm-tree lined drive. 'The Grove' Rural Life Museum in Andreas Road is a Victorian house with early agricultural equipment displayed in the outbuildings. At Laxey, between Ramsey and Douglas, is the world's largest waterwheel.

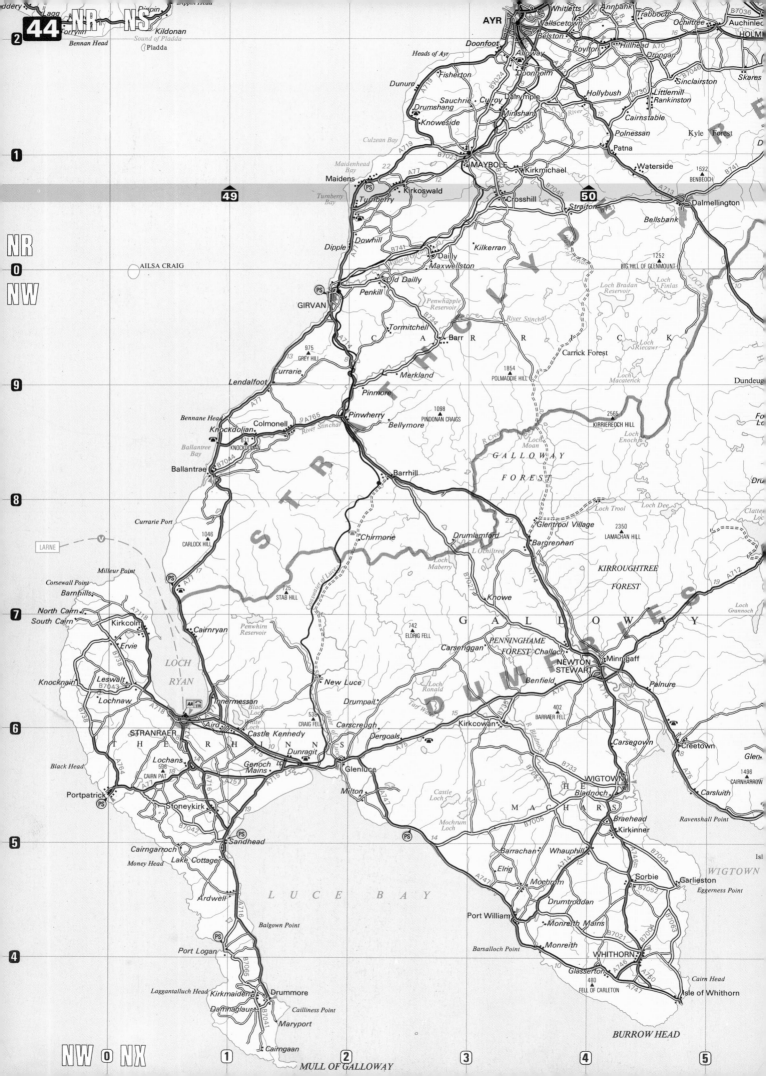

Ballantrae, *Strath*   NX 0882
Due to its position at the mouth of the River Stinchar, Ballantrae was well placed for smuggling and prospered well from this notorious practice in the 18th century. Near the river bridge stands ruined Ardstinchar Castle which used to belong to the influential Kennedy family. Robert Louis Stevenson visited the castle and subsequently took the village name for his novel *The Master of Ballantrae.*

Carsluith, *Dumf & Gall*   NX 4854
Apart from a few farm buildings there is little at Carsluith except for the ruins known as Carsluith Castle. This roofless, 16th-century tower house belonged to the Brouns of Carsluith, whose most famous member was Abbot Gilbert Broun of Sweetheart Abbey.

Castle Kennedy, *Dumf & Gall*   NX 1059
Standing to the N of the village between Black Loch and White Loch is Lochinch Castle, seat of the Earl of Stair. It is surrounded by some 70 acres of beautiful gardens which the 2nd Earl of Stair created in the 18th century. After his death in 1747 the gardens were neglected for some years but restoration was begun in 1840 by the 8th Earl. A pinetum and an avenue of 79ft-high monkey-puzzle trees are among the numerous splendid features of the gardens.

Creetown, *Dumf & Gall*   NX 4758
Overlooking the Cree estuary and the wide expanse of Wigtown Sands, Creetown shelters beneath the cliff and hills behind. It was originally called Ferrytown of Cree but a local laird, McCulloch of Barholm, decided to change it. The village boasts the largest private collection of gem rocks in Britain and this can be seen at the Museum and Art Gallery. Lapidary workshops are also open to view here.

Drummore, *Dumf & Gall*   NX 1336
Situated in Kirkmaiden, the southern-most parish in Scotland, Drummore is a small fishing port facing Luce Bay. An unusual gravestone in the churchyard of the 17th-century church is shaped in the form of a lighthouse. Fragments of St

Whithorn Priory stands on the site of Scotland's earliest Christian church

Medan's Chapel, the oldest in Galloway, lie at the foot of cliffs 4m S of Drummore.

Girvan, *Strath*   NX 1897
The town of Girvan developed from a small fishing port at the mouth of the River Girvan into a flourishing holiday resort. Sea-trout fishing in the Girvan is virtually unsurpassed in the west of Scotland and other sports are well catered for too.

Glenluce, *Dumf & Gall*   NX 1957
Lovely wooded countryside surrounds the pretty little village of Glenluce set on the banks of the Water of Luce. 2m NW the ruins of Glenluce Abbey, a Cistercian house founded in 1192, occupy a particularly beautiful spot. The vaulted chapter house has survived virtually intact and a medieval drainage system has been excavated which could function today.

Newton Stewart, *Dumf & Gall*   NX 4165
William Stewart, son of the Earl of Galloway, founded the town on the River Cree in 1677 and obtained a charter from Charles II giving it the status of burgh of barony. Later Sir William Douglas bought the town and tried, without

success, to change the name to Newton Douglas. The main street runs so close to the Cree that many of the attractive old houses seem to rise out of the water. A five-arched bridge crossing over the river to Minnigaff was built by engineer John Rennie in 1813.

Stranraer, *Dumf & Gall*   NX 0660
Situated at the head of the huge natural harbour provided by Loch Ryan, Stranraer is a royal and municipal burgh as well as a seaport. As the nearest Scottish port, the town does a lot of trade with, and is a busy ferry port for, Northern Ireland. At the centre of the attractive old town stands the mid 16th-century castle which served as the town gaol during the 18th and 19th centuries. A house near the pier known as the North-West Castle was built by Sir John Ross, the Arctic explorer. At low tide the town's two sandy bathing beaches are revealed.

Whithorn, *Dumf & Gall*   NX 4440
This remote town at the tip of The Machars peninsula is distinguished as one of the earliest centres of Christianity in Britain. St Ninian landed here in about AD 397 and built an oratory. In the 12th century Fergus, Lord of Galloway, built the priory whose ruins can be viewed. The nearby Priory Museum has a small collection of early Christian relics including carved stone crosses.

Wigtown, *Dumf & Gall*   NX 4355
Before 1914 when the harbour silted up, Wigtown flourished as a seaport but has since mainly catered for tourists of The Machars peninsula. A cross dating from 1816 stands in the town's central square commemorating the Iron Duke's victory at Waterloo. Windy Hill, a viewpoint in the town, bears a memorial to five Covenant martyrs – two of which were drowned by the tide while they were tied to the stake. The saltings, marshes and sands around Wigtown are rich in birdlife and attract many ornithologists from all over Britain.

Fire-gutted old Castle Kennedy, near Stranraer, is a backdrop to rich formal gardens

Castle Douglas, *Dumf & Gall*   NX 7662
This onetime commercial capital of the county was founded in the 18th century on the shores of Loch Carlingwark. In 1765 traces of prehistoric crannogs – lake dwellings – and several Bronze Age relics were found around the loch. To the W of Castle Douglas stand the ruins of Threave Castle, built in about 1360 by Archibald the Grim, 3rd Earl of Douglas. Threave Estate, to the SE of this, includes a baronial mansion now used by the National Trust for Scotland as their School of Practical Gardening, and there are beautiful gardens as well.

Dalbeattie, *Dumf & Gall*   NX 8361
Local granite quarries brought considerable prosperity to Dalbeattie in the 19th century when it was shipped down the Urr Water to all parts of the world. The town itself is mostly built of this shiny-grey stone and is very attractive. 2½m N is the 80ft-high Mote of Urr – a well-preserved Norman fortification.

Dumfries, *Dumf & Gall*   NX 9775
Known by the Scots as 'Queen of the South,' Dumfries is a town of old red sandstone buildings and spacious parks set in a loop of the River Nith. The centre is marked by the Midsteeple which was built in 1707 as a courthouse and prison. Robert Burns lived in the town from 1759 until his death in 1796 and his house, Burns House, contains many of the poet's personal possessions. There is also a mausoleum to Burns and his family in St Michael's churchyard. Dumfries Museum includes a camera obscura which brings the town to life and The Old Bridge House, also part of the museum, has been furnished to portray local life in different periods. One of the town's oldest buildings is Lincluden College which stands on the site of a Benedictine nunnery founded in 1164.

Gatehouse of Fleet,
Dumf & Gall   NX 5956
Walter Scott used Gatehouse of Fleet in his novel *Guy Mannering* and Robert Burns wrote some of his poetry while walking on the surrounding moors. Cardoness Castle stands on the road to Creetown overlooking Fleet Bay, Murray's Isles and the Islands of Fleet. The picturesque ruins consist of a 15th-century tower house.

Kirkbean, *Dumf & Gall*   NX 9859
The 1,868ft-high mass of Criffel overshadows this little village. Paul Jones, the colourful United States naval officer, was born 1m SE at Arbigland and next door to his cottage is Arbigland Garden where he worked as a boy under his father, who was gardener here during the 1740s. Woodland, water and formal gardens are arranged around a sandy bay.

Kirkcudbright, *Dumf & Gall*   NX 6851
This used to be one of Scotland's major ports but is now little more than a small harbour at the mouth of the Dee. Much of Kirkcudbright's local history can be

traced in the Stewartry Museum. Dominating the town are the impressive ruins of 16th-century MacLellan's Castle, and 18th-century Broughton House contains a fine collection of paintings by E.A. Hornel.

Lochmaben, *Dumf & Gall*   NY 0882
Three large lochs and two smaller ones surround this ancient royal burgh. Rammerscales House, 3m S off the B7020, is one of the great mansions in the area that were built with wealth acquired through the China tea trade. The house has links with Flora Macdonald and contains several Jacobite relics and, in contrast, there is a small collection of works by modern artists.

Lockerbie, *Dumf & Gall*   NY 1381
It is an annual sheep fair held since 1680 until recently, from which Lockerbie's main landmark, Lamb Hill, takes its name. A great battle was fought in Lockerbie in 1593 which marked the end of one of the last Border family feuds: the Johnstones killed Lord Maxwell and some 700 of his clan followers.

Moffat, *Dumf & Gall*   NT 0805
During the 18th and 19th centuries Moffat was a popular spa town due to the sulphur springs nearby. Today visitors come to explore the lovely Annandale countryside and Lowther Hills. Ladyknowe Mill, a small modern weaving unit, continues making traditional Scottish cloth and the workshops are open to view.

Moniaive, *Dumf & Gall*   NX 7791
The market cross in the centre of this village is all that remains to indicate Moniaive was a chartered burgh in 1636. To the E lies Maxwellton House – former stronghold of the Earls of Glencairn. Recently restored, the house has its own chapel and contains a museum of ancient domestic utensils.

New Abbey, *Dumf & Gall*   NX 9665
Whitewashed cottages and an 18th-century water-mill form a picturesque group in the village of New Abbey, but by far its greatest treasure is the beautiful

MacLellan's Castle is a gaunt memorial to a military Kirkcudbright family

ruined Sweetheart Abbey. Lady Devorguilla of Galloway founded it in honour of her husband, John Balliol, in 1273 and she was buried there with the embalmed heart of her husband.

Thornhill, *Dumf & Gall*   NX 8795
Long associations with the Dukes of Queensberry and Buccleuch have earned Thornhill the nickname of 'the ducal village'. Tangible evidence of this is a column crowned by a statue of the Queensberry emblem – a winged horse – in North Drumlanrig Street. Drumlanrig Castle 4m NW was built by William Douglas, 1st Earl of Queensberry, in the 17th century. It is filled with valuable art treasures, including furniture given to the house by Charles II.

Tongland, *Dumf & Gall*   NX 6953
Famous engineer Thomas Telford designed the bridge which spans the Dee here. The river plays a vital part in the life of Tongland as a generating station and dam have been built across the water, part of the Galloway hydro-electricity scheme. Tours include a visit to the dam – where there is a fish ladder – and the power station.

Only six arches remain of 15th-century Dumfries Old Bridge, a footway over the Nith

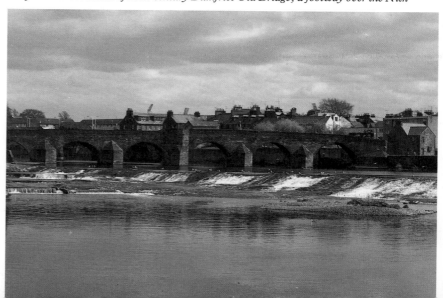

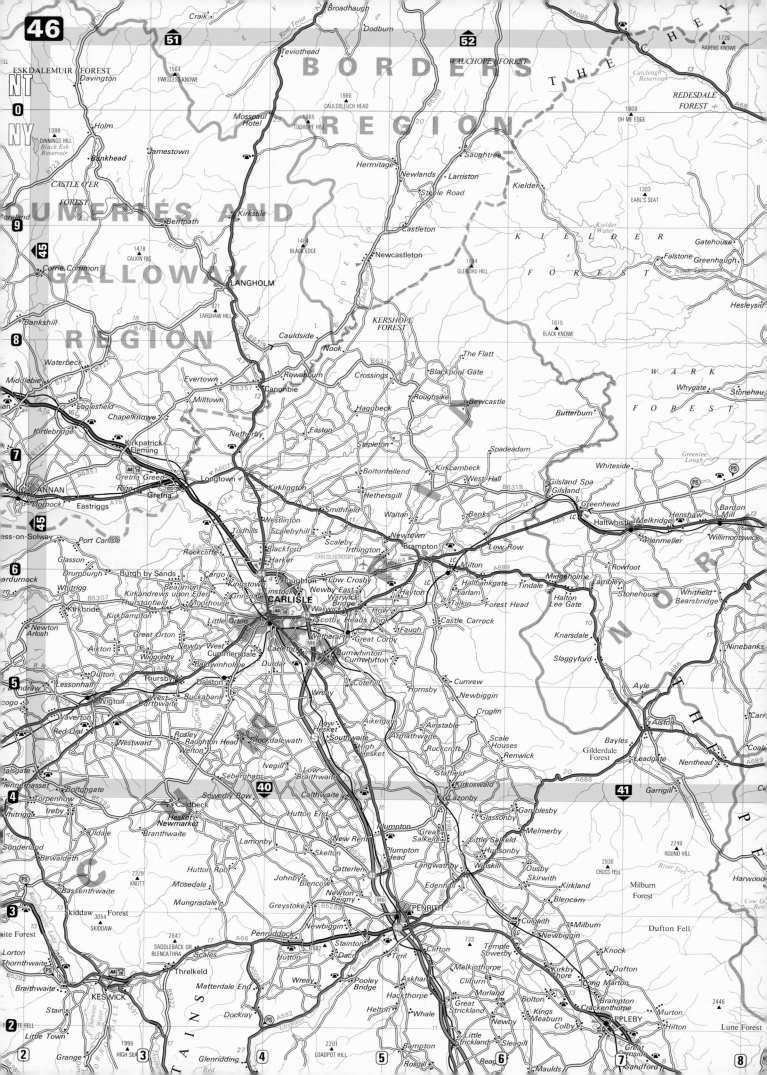

The smithy at Gretna Green where for 100 years Scottish law allowed English couples to be married without their parents' consent

Annan, *Dumf & Gall*   NY 1966
Beautiful countryside surrounds the town of Annan which overlooks the Solway Firth and has become a popular touring centre. Among its own attractions are the Kinmount Gardens where there are signposted woodland walks taking up to two hours. Two people associated with the town are lighthouse engineer Robert Stevenson who built the river bridge, and historian and essayist Thomas Carlyle who attended the old grammar school.

Brampton, *Cumbria*   NY 5361
One outstanding building in Brampton's attractive cobbled-edged main street is the picturesque octagonal Moot Hall which is crowned by a clock and bell-tower. Another noteworthy feature in the town is the stained glass designed by the Victorian artist – Sir Edward Burne-Jones – in the local church. Extensive remains of Lanercost Priory lie 2½m NE of Brampton. Founded in about 1166 by William de Vaux, the priory was partly built with stones taken from nearby Hadrian's Wall.

Carlisle, *Cumbria*   NY 3955
Due to its position just below the Scottish border, Carlisle has been strategically important for centuries. The Romans built Hadrian's Wall between Bowness and Wallsend-on-Tyne to defend themselves from attacks by the Picts and great stretches of it can still be seen E of Carlisle. Later the Normans built Carlisle Castle as added defence and its well-restored remains include St Mary's Tower where the Border regiments' museum is housed. Carlisle has one of the smallest cathedrals in England and its treasures include a fine east window, a painted barrel-vault ceiling and superbly carved choir stalls. Prior's Tower which stands in the cathedral grounds houses a museum covering 850 years of the cathedral's history. The city's museum

and art gallery occupies Tullie House – a handsome Jacobean building – and the 15th-century Guildhall, renovated in 1978, is also open as a museum.

Gilsland, *Northumb*   NY 6366
Sulphur springs brought popularity to this little town during the heyday of spa towns, but it never achieved fashionable status. More people visit the town now to visit one of the several milecastles built along Hadrian's Wall – Poltross Burn Milecastle – which is incorporated into a nearby railway embankment.

Great Corby, *Cumbria*   NY 4754
A pele tower had guarded Great Corby for 300 years and in 1611 the Howards – a local family – transformed it into a large L-shaped house. Further work took place in the 19th century. Its setting by the River Eden is particularly lovely and the grounds are open.

Gretna Green, *Dumf & Gall*   NY 3268
The forge at Gretna Green is famous as the place where runaway couples could be legally married without parental consent. For over a century these marriages took place over the smithy's anvil, but in 1856 a law was passed dictating that one party had to live in Scotland for at least three weeks, and in 1940 the ceremony was finally declared invalid.

Haltwhistle, *Northumb*   NY 7064
Hadrian's Wall lies to the N of Haltwhistle and the town is a good place from which to explore it. A milecastle has been excavated here. Light industry has taken over from the area's former coal-mining industry.

Langholm, *Dumf & Gall*   NY 3684
In the late 18th century Langholm's first cotton-mill was founded and within a few years the town was an important clothmaking centre—there are now several tweed mills. Every year a

Common Riding ceremony takes place in the town which began in 1759 as an inspection of the boundaries by foot.

Port Carlisle, *Cumbria*   NY 2461
In about 1820 the Carlisle Canal Navigation Company built a canal from Carlisle to a tiny hamlet called Fisher's Cross – later Port Carlisle – but the plan was not successful and only a few cottages remain. Nearby the Glasson Moss Nature Reserve occupies over 140 acres of the marshlands overlooking the Solway Firth.

Wigton, *Cumbria*   NY 2548
King Henry III granted Walter de Wigton permission to hold a market here in 1262 and markets have taken place regularly ever since: an annual horse fair is also held every autumn. Charles Dickens visited Wigton with his companion Wilkie Collins and he included the ancient parish pump and lofty gas lamp in his novel entitled *The Lazy Tour of Two Idle Apprentices*.

A Norman battle catapult replica, called a 'wild ass', at Carlisle's Tullie House

Bellingham, *Northumb*   NY 8383
Border raids were frequent in Bellingham (pronounced Bellinjam) when Scotland and England were forever falling
out, but there is no sign of trouble now in
this quiet little town. St Cuthbert's
Church has a unique stone roof of such
weight that the building had to be but-
tressed during the 18th century to with-
stand its pressure. St Cuthbert's Well,
reached by a path from the churchyard,
is locally supposed to still have healing
powers.

Blanchland, *Northumb*   NY 9650
Greystone cottages surround the L-
shaped square of this little village set
deep in wild moorland which is one of
the most enchanting in England. A
monastery was built on the site in the
12th century and the square was probably the abbey courtyard and the Lord
Crewe Arms includes parts of the abbey
guesthouse. Blanchland was named after
the Premonstratensian White Canons
who founded the abbey.

Chester-le-Street, *Co Durham*   NZ 2751
An important Roman station originally
occupied the site of Chester-le-Street and
the monks of Lindisfarne brought the
remains of St Cuthbert to the wooden
Anglo-Saxon church here before finally
removing them to Durham. Other than
these historic points of interest there is
surprisingly little to show for the town's
great age. 1½m to the NE the Lambton
Pleasure Park was created in the grounds
of Lambton Castle – a romantic 19th-
century replica of a medieval castle.

Corbridge, *Northumb*   NY 9964
The town has had good and bad periods
throughout its history but it has survived
as a charming place with stone houses
and shady trees beside the River Tyne.
Several old buildings are scattered
throughout the town and these include St
Andrew's Church, parts of which date
from Anglo-Saxon times. *Corstopitum,*
½m W, was built by the Romans and
excavations of the site have revealed that
the fort was probably a legion headquarters. Finds are on display in a museum
on the site. At the Hunday National

*Originally, Black Gate guarded the only
level approach to Newcastle's castle*

*A Roman arch leading into the nave has been
preserved in Corbridge's old church*

Tractor and Farm Museum at Stocksfield
over 250 tractors and engines show the
development of agriculture from 1900 to
the post-war period. There are also
collections of hand tools, harness and
farm equipment.

Durham, *Co Durham*   NZ 2742
Two great legacies from the Normans
dominate this lovely city – the castle and
the cathedral. They stand side by side
high on a sandstone bluff which is practi-
cally encircled by a loop of the River
Wear. The site of the cathedral was
determined when the body of St Cuthbert was brought here from Lindisfarne
in 875 to escape Viking raids, and a
shrine was built. No trace of the monks'
church has survived, but the magnificent
cathedral founded by William de St
Carileth is one of the finest Norman
buildings in Europe. Sharing the promontory with these giants are the buildings
of the university that was established in
1832. In 1836 the castle was given to the
university and since then 14 colleges have
been built to integrate with their historic
neighbours. A modern pedestrian-only
shopping centre has transformed the old
city centre but there are several handsome 18th-century houses around the
market place. The Gulbenkian Museum
of Oriental Art in Elvet Hill Road is one
of the most spectacular in England.

Hexham, *Northumb*   NY 9364
St Wilfred founded an abbey here in 674
and the town grew up around its gates.
The crypt of this first church is retained
in the present abbey church which was
begun by Augustinian canons in the 12th
century. Its treasures include an Anglo-
Saxon stone chair known as the Frith
Stool, and a dramatic Roman monument
to Flavinus. Other interesting buildings
near the abbey are the Moot Hall –
reputedly the gatehouse of a 12th-century
castle – and the medieval Manor Office
which was a prison until 1824. Hexham
is a great shopping and social centre for
the area and its agricultural traditions are
reflected in the annual shows, steeple-
chase meetings, sheepdog trials and
other farming festivals.

Houghton-le-Spring,
Tyne & Wear   NZ 3450
A busy mining town, Houghton was
where Bernard Gilpin, the evangelist
known as the Apostle of the North,
practised. He was rector at St Michael
and All Angels Church from 1556 until
his death in 1583. At the time this had the
richest living in England and he used it
unstintingly to help his parishioners.
Every October the Houghton Feast
remembers his hospitable traditions.

Newcastle upon Tyne,
Tyne & Wear   NZ 2464
Newcastle, which began as a fort on
Hadrian's Wall, is now a great university
and engineering city with shipbuilding as
its key industry. The 19th century saw
the real growth of the city and two of the
six great bridges which span the Tyne
date from that time. Robert Stephenson
built his High Level Bridge in 1849 and
Lord Armstrong built his Swing Bridge
in 1876. Much of the city centre too is
19th century and Richard Grainger, John
Dobson and John Clayton were largely
responsible for the elegance of the commercial centre. Grey Street curving
round to the Theatre Royal is particularly
fine. Among the rambling university
buildings is the Hancock Museum
famous for its natural history collection,
and the Museum of Antiquities with a
valuable collection of Roman finds.

Peterlee, *Co Durham*   NZ 4440
One of Durham's most successful New
Towns, Peterlee was built for about
30,000 inhabitants and to attract industry. Its most distinctive feature is its own
nature reserve – Castle Eden Dene. In
the 3m it stretches towards the coast,
unspoilt woodlands harbour wild
flowers, trees, grasses and animal life that
is badly threatened elsewhere in eastern
Durham. The town's name commemorates Peter Lee – President of the Miners'
Federation.

Stanley, *Co Durham*   NZ 1953
Near Stanley, 200 acres of the old Beam-
ish Hall estate have been opened as the
North of England Open Air Museum.
Four county councils administer the
museum which opened in 1971 and is
still expanding. Buildings of all kinds
have been rebuilt and furnished.
There is a traditional north-eastern
railway network and a mining village
and colliery complete with working
steam locos. Home Farm has animals,
tools and machinery and skills such
as bread-making on a range and hand
printing are demonstrated.

Whitley Bay, *Northumb*   NZ 3572
Unlike most of Northumberland's lovely
coast, Whitley Bay, within a day's reach
of Tyneside, has been subjected to considerable commercialism. Entertainments include one of the biggest amusement parks in the NE, golf courses,
bowling clubs and, of course, the
long sandy beach is a lasting attraction
for the whole family.

The Mull of Kintyre lighthouse at the southern tip of the Kintyre peninsula

Ardminish, *Isle of Gigha,*
Strath   NR 6448
Gigha is only 6m by 1½m but it offers
quite of lot of interest. One of its few
towns is Ardminish and Achamore
House Gardens here defy the Atlantic
conditions. Sir James Horlick designed
them and high belts of trees protect the
azaleas, rhododendrons and camellias
that provide the chief beauty of the
gardens.

Bowmore, *Isle of Islay,*
Strath   NR 3159
The largest village on the Isle of Islay,
and its unofficial capital, Bowmore was
built in 1768 along spacious, open
streets. One of these leads up to the
round parish church at Killarrow –
allegedly built so the devil had no

corners to hide in. Whether this is true or
not this unusual church was built in 1769
by Daniel Campbell of Islay, one of very
few examples in Scotland.

Campbeltown, *Strath*   NR 7120
Situated at the southern end of the long,
narrow Kintyre peninsula, Campbeltown
stands at the head of a deep sheltered bay
known as Campbeltown Loch. Towards
the end of the 19th century the town was
a busy centre of commerce and industry
with a 500-strong herring fleet. There
were also about 30 distilleries in the area
but only two of these remain. Now
Campbeltown is a quiet resort popular
with golfers and anglers. St Kieran's
Cave, about 3½m SE, may be the earliest
Christian chapel in Scotland as St Kieran
is thought to have arrived in Scotland

before St Columba. Relics from these
and prehistoric times can be seen in
Campbeltown's museum. Offshore
Davaar Island can be reached by boats
hired from the harbour. Its great attraction is the painting inside a cave of the
Crucifixion scene by the 19th-century
artist Archibald MacKinnon.

Kilmory, *Strath*   NR 7075
This tiny, remote little village overlooks
the Sound of Jura towards the conical
outlines of the Paps of Jura. Castle
Sween, 2½m N, is possibly the earliest
stone castle in Scotland. Built in the 12th
century, it was devastated by Sir Alexander Macdonald. Launches can be hired
from Kilmory to Eilean Mor, an islet W
of the village where there is a tiny
medieval chapel with an upper chamber
only accessible by ladder, and a fine
sculpture of a priest.

Machrihanish, *Strath*   NR 6220
A salt-producing village in the past,
Machrihanish is now mainly a holiday
resort. One of its great assets is the fine
golf course which was laid out in 1876.
The beach, offering 5m of sand between
long stretches of rocky coast, is another
great attraction.

Port Askaig, *Isle of Islay,*
Strath   NR 4369
Port Askaig is important as one of the
gateways to the island: a passenger ferry
operates to Feolin Ferry on the Isle of
Jura and there are steamers to the mainland. All that lies N of this little township
is the Bunnahabhainn where there is a
small distillery. The coastline southwards
of Port Askaig is almost completely deserted for over 12m and no roads serve
this part of the island.

Saddell, *Strath*   NR 7832
Interesting remains of an abbey and a
castle can be seen in this pleasant village
on the rocky east Kintyre coast. The
abbey was said to be founded by Somer-
led, Lord of the Isles, for Cistercian
monks in about 1160. Celtic tombstones
and the boundary walls are included
among the ruins. Privately-owned Saddell Castle, a large, square battlemented
tower, dates from the 16th century when
it was used as the residence of the
Bishops of Argyll. Saddell Glen forms
part of the lovely South Kintyre Forest
that merges with Carradale Forest.

Southend, *Strath*   NR 6908
Right at the southern tip of the long
Kintyre peninsula, Southend has
sandy beaches and a golf course which
make it a popular holiday resort. Traditionally, this was where St Columba
arrived when he came from Ireland on
his first mission to Scotland. Near the
ruined chapel of Keil is a flat stone
bearing the imprint of a pair of footsteps
– supposedly belonging to the saint.
Scant ruins of Dunaverty Castle remain
perched on top of a precipitous cliff. It
was an early stronghold of the Lords of
the Isles, the Macdonald clan.

Fish boxes litter Tayinloan's quay where boats depart for tiny Gigha on the horizon

Hill House in Helensburgh was designed by the innovative Scottish architect Charles Rennie Mackintosh who lived from 1868 to 1928

Ayr, *Strath*   NS 3321

Scotland's most famous poet, Robert Burns, was born at Alloway on the outskirts of Ayr in 1759 and the town has many associations with him. One is the Tam O'Shanter Museum where relics of his life and work can be seen and there is a statue of him near the station. Ayr has a lot to offer the visitor as it is an ancient royal burgh and long-time fishing port with a number of interesting buildings. One of these is 16th-century London Hall which was saved from demolition in 1938. The town's fine parks and gardens are a particularly attractive feature and the race-course is considered one of the best in Britain.

Brodick, *Isle of Arran, Strath*   NS 0136

Officially named Invercloy, Brodick takes its name from Brodick Bay on which it is situated. Steamers from Ardrossan call at the pier here and, as it is Arran's chief town, it has become popular with holidaymakers from Glasgow and southern Scotland. Housed in a former croft at Rosaburn is the Isle of Arran Heritage Museum illustrating the island's way of life – past and present. Brodick Castle was the ancestral home of the Duke of Hamilton and contains an impressive art collection. The 600-acre grounds are magnificent and include a formal 18th-century walled garden.

Dunoon, *Strath*   NS 1777

Up until the 19th century Dunoon was little more than a village that had grown up around the castle and the harbour. Now it is a popular holiday resort and the present castle – traces of the old 13th-century building can still be seen on Castle Hill – was built in 1822 as a villa for James Ewing, Provost of Glasgow, and is now used as municipal offices. Robert Burns' sweetheart, 'Highland Mary', is commemorated by a statue at the foot of Castle Hill. Every August the holiday season reaches a spectacular peak when the Cowal Highland Gathering is held in the town's sports stadium and the March of a Thousand Pipers takes place.

Helensburgh, *Strath*   NS 2982

Sir James Colquhoun of Luss first established the town of Helensburgh in about 1776 on the shores of the Lower Clyde. Not until the 19th century did it become a holiday centre as well as a suburb of Glasgow, and Victorian architecture is therefore much in evidence. Several steamer tours operate from Helensburgh and Henry Bell, designer of Europe's first steamship – the *Comet* – lived in the town for a while. He is commemorated by an obelisk on the quayside and the *Comet's* flywheel stands in Hermitage Park.

Irvine, *Strath*   NS 3239

Port, manufacturing town and former royal burgh, Irvine's origins are in the 13th century. Robert Burns lived in the town for a while and his house bears a plaque recording his subsequent venture into the trade of flax-dressing. Eglinton Castle and Gardens at nearby Kilwinning were built in the late 18th century but the castle is now in ruins.

Largs, *Strath*   NS 2058

Largs is ideal as a cruising and yachting centre and steamers travel from here to all the piers on the Clyde, and even to Loch Fyne and the Kilbrennan Sound. Skelmorlie Aisle, a splendid example of a Renaissance monument, is one of Largs' treasures. It is the only surviving part of the old Church of Columba and was built by Sir Robert Montgomery of Skelmorlie in 1636. The monument, built of stone, consists of a gallery raised above a partially sunk burial chamber.

Maybole, *Strath*   NS 3009

At one time there were as many as 28 baronial mansions in the parish of Maybole as it was the stronghold of the Earls of Cassillis. They lived in the old town house known as the 'castle' in the High Street and it is still used as offices. Crossraguel Abbey 2m SW was founded by Duncan, Earl of Carrick, in 1244 and the extensive ruins include the church, cloisters, abbot's house and gatehouse.

Millport, *Great Cumbrae Island, Strath*   NS 1655

This tiny island is linked by car ferry to Largs. Its only town is Millport which became something of a resort in the 18th century when the harbour was built and the ferry provided. Occupying Garrison House is the Museum of the Cumbraes which tells the story of life on and around the Cumbraes and features many old photographs and objects of particular local interest.

Port Glasgow, *Strath*   NS 3274

In 1668 a harbour was founded here to serve Glasgow and in 1710 the chief Customs House for the Clyde was built. However, when the Clyde was deepened at the end of the 18th century trade declined, but with the advent of the Industrial Revolution it regained importance as a ship-building centre. The village was originally called Newark after Newark Castle – a large, turreted mansion overlooking the Clyde which was the former home of the Maxwells.

Rothesay, *Isle of Bute, Strath*   NS 0864

Historic town and Clyde holiday resort, Rothesay is also the county town of Bute. The town's castle was built in about 1098 and it is an outstanding example of a medieval Scottish castle with a unique circular plan. Seaside entertainment and leisure facilities abound in the resort and for a comprehensive history of the island the Bute Museum in Rothesay is first-class. As well as a natural history room, there are models of Clyde steamers, an assortment of early bygones, and a collection of early Christian crosses.

Tarbert, *Strath*   NR 8668

Tarbert stands on the tiny neck of land that separates West Loch Tarbert from Loch Fyne and just saves Kintyre from being an island. Although a popular resort, Tarbert is also the centre of the Loch Fyne herring industry. Remains of a 14th-century castle that served as a stronghold of Robert Bruce and James II overlook the harbour it once guarded.

Balloch, *Strath*   NS 3981
Situated on the River Leven at the S end
of lovely 23m-long Loch Lomond,
'Queen of the Scottish Lakes', this little
village is a popular place for holidaymakers and yachtsmen. Boat trips on the loch
can be made from here. Of the 30
wooded islands to be seen, five form part
of a nature reserve. Balloch Castle Park
on the shore of the loch has nature trails
through extensive woodland, and bears
and bison are among animals to be seen
in Cameron Loch Lomond Wildlife Park.
Cameron House contains much to
interest visitors.

Clydebank, *Strath*   NS 5069
Almost destroyed by bombing in 1941,
the town has also suffered unemployment
problems in recent years but her ship-
yards will always be famous for building
Lusitania, Queen Mary, Queen Elizabeth
and *QE2.*

Dumbarton, *Strath*   NS 4075
The 240ft basalt volcanic plug, Dumbarton Rock, dominates this town at the
confluence of the Rivers Leven and
Clyde. The medieval castle which once
stood on the Crag has gone, but 17th- and
18th-century fortifications are still visible. Whisky rather than shipbuilding is
now the town's main industry, but the
famous clipper *Cutty Sark* was built in
the shipyard here.

Falkirk, *Central*   NS 8880
To the W of this busy industrial centre is
Rough Castle, best-preserved of the 19
forts that once stood on the Antonine
Wall built by the Romans across Scotland in the 2nd century to keep out the
northern tribes. The remarkable site
covers one acre and is enclosed by double
ditches and defensive pits.

Glasgow, *Strath*   NS 5865
Scotland's largest city, seaport and administrative centre, Glasgow's prosperity
was based on shipbuilding and heavy
engineering but more recently there has
been a switch to lighter engineering. The
city is fortunate in having more than 70
parks and other open spaces. Among
those of special interest are: Rouken Glen
with waterfall and lake; Victoria Park
with fossilised tree stumps; Linn Park
with a children's zoo and a ruined castle,
and the Botanic Garden where there is an
outstanding collection of plants. The
Hunterian Art Gallery, belonging to the
university which was founded in 1451,
has paintings by Whistler as well as many
17th- and 18th-century paintings by
European artists. One of the finest civic
art collections in Britain is housed in
the Glasgow Art Gallery and Museum.
Haggs Castle contains a special museum
for children, there is a fascinating visual
record of Glasgow's history in the People's Palace, and the Transport Museum
is well worth visiting. Glasgow Cathedral
is the only complete medieval cathedral
on the Scottish mainland. Well-restored
15th-century Provand's Lordship may be
the city's oldest house, the city centre

being dominated by handsome Victorian
buildings including the palatial City
Chambers.

Kilmarnock, *Strath*   NS 4237
Kilmarnock is an industrial centre whose
wide range of industries includes whisky
distilling. There is a Burns Museum in
the town with an outstanding Burns
Memorial, and Dean Castle in Dean
Road is an interesting fortified tower. It
was built in the 14th century – the keep,
great hall and upper hall are in perfect
condition. There are a variety of exhibitions here and extensive gardens.

Mauchline, *Strath*   NS 4927
Poet Robert Burns lived in and near the
town for several years and was married at
the parish church. A memorial tower
stands 1m N on the Kilmarnock road and
houses a Burns museum containing many
of his personal possessions.

Paisley, *Strath*   NS 4864
One of Scotland's major towns, and the
world's largest thread-manufacturing
centre, Paisley was famous for its unique
shawl-weaving industry. The distinctive
designs were inspired in the 18th century
by Indian and Turkish shawls and the
pattern is now widely copied. Early examples of the shawls can be seen in the
museum and art gallery. The abbey
church, mainly dating from the mid 15th
century, is well worth a visit.

Stirling, *Central*   NS 7993
Now the regional headquarters, and with a
university founded in 1967, Stirling has
for centuries been an important market
town for the fertile Forth valley. In the
late Victorian period it grew affluent as a
commercial centre. Steep streets of 16th-
to 18th-century buildings in the Old
Town lead up to the 250ft fortified crag

*Templeton Carpet Factory in Glasgow is a
stunning example of Victorian architecture*

which dominates the town. Parts of the
present castle date back to the 13th
century and from the 15th century the
castle became a regular residence of
Stuart kings. Today it houses the regimental museum of the Argyll and Sutherland Highlanders, whose headquarters it
now is, and there are fine views from the
ramparts. Places of interest in the town
include the Landmark Centre, with a
multi-screen presentation of the history
of Stirling, and Mar's Wark, a partly
ruined Renaissance mansion. 1m NE are
the beautiful ruins of 12th-century Cam-
buskenneth Abbey, burial place of James
III. Bannockburn, 2m S, is the site of
Robert the Bruce's victory over Edward
II in 1314.

Stirling's Old Bridge, built across the Forth in 1415, is for use by pedestrians only now

Aberdour, *Fife*   NT 1885
2m of fine sandy beaches have made the
town a popular holiday resort. Aberdour
Castle, still partly roofed, dates from the
14th to 17th century and on Inchcolm
Island, 1½m S, are the remains of the
Augustinian abbey of St Columba
founded in about 1123.

Culross, *Fife*   NS 9885
The well-preserved 16th- and 17th-cen-
tury houses in this attractive small town
in Torry Bay have crow-stepped gables
and red pantiled roofs. Little Culross
Palace was built between 1597 and 1611
and is noted for its painted rooms and
terraced gardens. The Cistercian abbey
was founded in 1215 but only the choir
and parts of the nave remain.

Dunfermline, *Fife*   NT 0987
Now a linen-manufacturing town, Dunfermline was Scotland's capital for two
centuries and has many royal associations. Benedictine Dunfermline Abbey
was founded by Queen Margaret in the
11th century. Robert the Bruce is buried
at the site of an old abbey now occupied
by a modern church. The monastic
guesthouse was reconstructed as a palace
and here Charles I was born, but only
ruins now remain. The cottage where
millionaire and philanthropist Andrew
Carnegie was born in 1835 is preserved as
a museum and Dunfermline and
Pittencrieff House museums are also of
interest.

Edinburgh, *Lothian*   NT 2674
Superbly situated near the Firth of
Forth, with steep streets on seven hills
dominated by the castle, Edinburgh has
been Scotland's capital for over 500 years
but has only expanded outside the picturesque Old Town in the last two centuries.
The Old Town huddles against Castle
Rock, crowned by its centuries-old fortress. From here the sea and distant
Highlands can be seen. Leading down
from the castle to the Palace of Holyrood
is the historic cobbled Royal Mile. Begun
by James IV in the mid 16th century,
much of the Palace was built for Charles
II. Mary Queen of Scots lived here in
1561–7 when she witnessed the death of
her secretary Rizzio and married
Bothwell. In contrast, the spacious
New Town, built around 1800, is a fine
example of neo-Georgian town
planning, begun after the Nor' Loch
was drained. The city has two
universities and is a cultural centre,
especially during the world-renowned
Edinburgh Festival at the end of each
summer, when theatres and concert
halls are packed, and the castle is
floodlit for the Military Tattoo each
night. The city contains a wealth of
excellent museums, art galleries,
houses and other places of interest for
the tourist: the National Gallery of
Scotland; the Scottish National Gallery
of Modern Art; the Royal Scottish
Museum; the Scottish National Portrait
Gallery; the Royal Botanic Garden and
Edinburgh Zoo are just a few of these.

The National Trust for Scotland owns Culross Palace and most of the ancient town

Innerleithen, *Borders*   NT 3336
This pleasant woollen manufacturing
town sits on the Leithen Water near its
confluence with the Tweed. 1m S is
Traquair House, dating from the 10th
century. Scotland's oldest inhabited
house it has many royal associations
particularly concerning Mary Queen of
Scots: 27 Scottish and English monarchs
have stayed here in all. Fine collections of
historical treasures adorn the house and
there is a unique 18th-century brew-
house licensed to sell its own beer.

Kirkaldy, *Fife*   NT 2791
A busy industrial and coal-mining town
and seaport, Kirkaldy became a boom
town in the last century with the invention of linoleum. The town's 4m-long
main street has given it the name 'the
Lang Toun' and provides excellent shopping facilities. Parallel to it is the mile-
long esplanade and pebble beach. The
town has three museums and impressive
ruined 15th-century Ravenscraig Castle
lies to the N.

Linlithgow, *Lothian*   NS 9977
Beautifully-situated on a promontory jutting into Linlithgow Loch, the ruined

15th- to 17th-century palace, birthplace
of Mary Queen of Scots, is the main
attraction in this ancient royal burgh. 4m
E is the magnificent 17th-century House
of The Binns. It used to be the home of the
Dalyell family and in 1681 General Tam
Dalyell raised the Royal Scots Greys here.
Views from the grounds are spectacular.

Musselburgh, *Lothian*   NT 3472
Mussels were once gathered at this
fishing and manufacturing town situated
on the banks of the River Esk amid
wooded scenery. The shingle beach has
outcrops of rock and some sand and there
is a good golf course. Horse-racing and
archery take place on the nearby links.
Pinkie House is a fine Jacobean building
and the Tolbooth dates from about 1590.

Peebles, *Borders*   NT 2540
Pleasantly situated on a lovely stretch of
the River Tweed and surrounded by
green hills, this quiet former county town
has become popular with anglers. It is
also well-known for tweeds and knitwear. Above the river is 13th-century
Neidpath Castle. To the E lies 2,000-acre
Glentress Forest and to the S the unspoilt
valley of Glensax.

Edinburgh Castle esplanade is where the famous Military Tattoo takes place every year

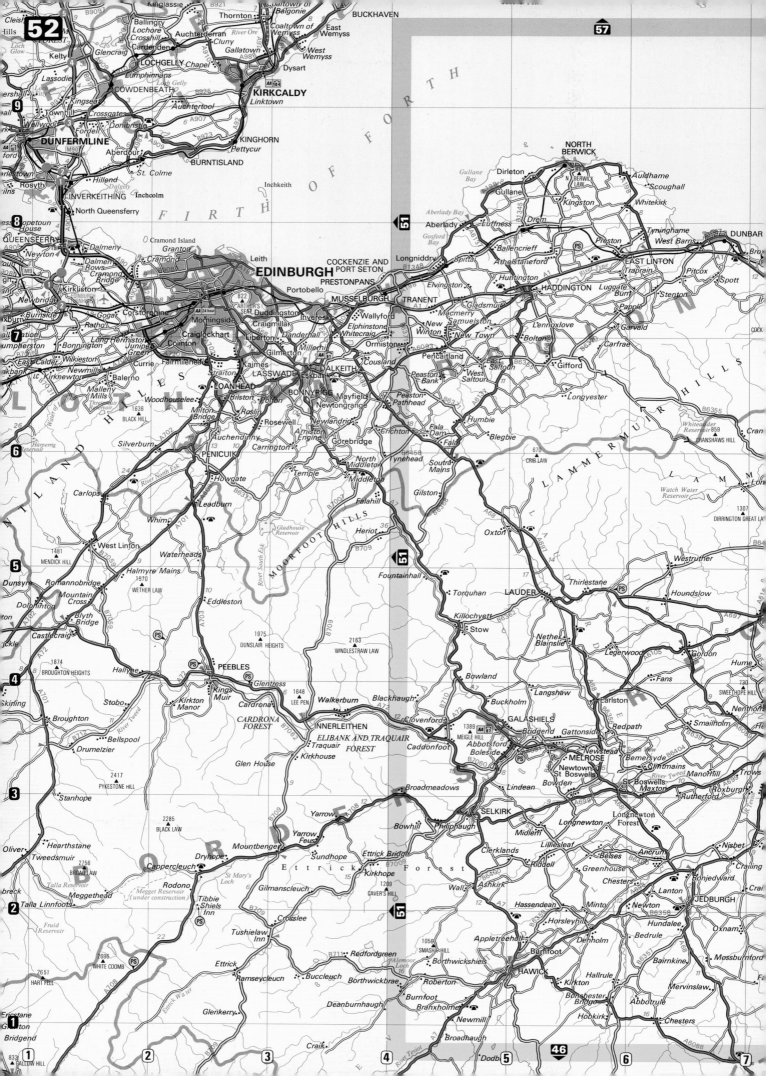

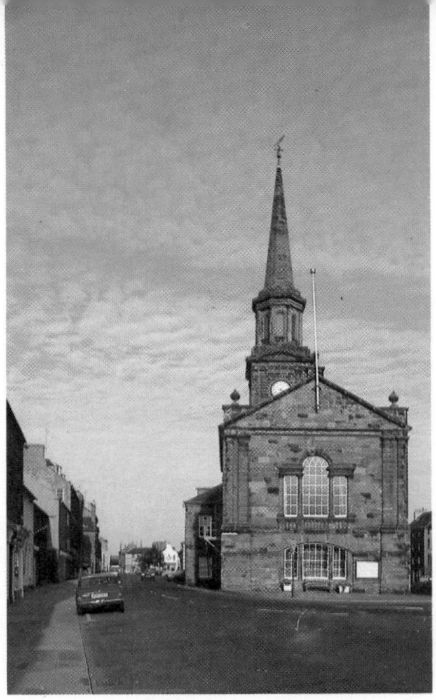

The Town House, with its graceful spire, in Court Street, Haddington

Aberlady, *Lothian* NT 4679
This seaside village has a sandy beach and a nature reserve where more than 200 species of bird have been recorded. Myreton Motor Museum is a large collection of cars, motorcycles, commercial and military vehicles—another part of the collection can be seen at Dunbar.

Dunbar, *Lothian* NT 6878
Now a holiday resort with good facilities for golfing, this ancient fishing port was created a royal burgh in 1370. The town's ruined castle, perched high above the harbour, has associations with Mary Queen of Scots. She stayed here in 1566 with Darnley, and in 1567 with Bothwell before surrendering to the nobles. The castle was destroyed the following year. The Town House, the oldest public building in continuous use in Scotland, was built in 1620 and has a six-sided tower.

East Linton, *Lothian* NT 5977
Near this unspoilt village on the River Tyne is attractive 17th-century Preston Mill – the oldest working water-driven meal mill in Scotland. Hailes Castle, an old fortified manor house 1½m SW, was dismantled by Cromwell in 1650 but a fine 16th-century chapel has survived.

Galashiels, *Borders* NT 4936
Pleasantly situated on both sides of the Gala Water, Galashiels is a busy manufacturing town noted for its tweeds and woollens. The centre for wool studies in Scotland, the Scottish Woollen Technical College, was founded here in 1883. The town's charter was granted in 1599 and its history since then is re-enacted in a pageant, the Braw Lad's Gathering, every June or July.

Haddington, *Lothian* NT 5174
A well-preserved former county town on the River Tyne, Haddington is rich in architectural interest. William Adams, father of the famous Robert, designed the splendidly-proportioned 18th-century Town House and also several other houses. The red sandstone 14th-century Parish Church of St Mary's is known as the 'Lamp of the Lothians'.

Hawick, *Borders* NT 5014
Set in the heart of Teviotdale, Hawick is the market town for an extensive farming area and is also well-known for its knitwear. The Museum and Art Gallery in Wilton Lodge contains many items of local interest.

Jedburgh, *Borders* NT 6520
An attractive town, rich in historical associations and a centre for exploring the surrounding hills and moorland, Jedburgh is best known for the magnificent ruins of its red sandstone abbey. Built in the 16th century, picturesque Mary Queen of Scots House, home to the queen during a month-long illness, now contains a museum. Monteviot House, 3¼m N, is set in beautiful grounds by the River Teviot.

Lauder, *Borders* NT 5347
A good touring centre on the Leader Water in Lauderdale, Lauder has been a royal burgh since 1502. One of the oldest horse-riding festivals in the country, the Lauder Common Riding, is held here in late summer. NE, in a parkland and riverside setting, is imposing Thirlestane Castle, once the seat of the Earls of Lauderdale. The castle has a splendidly decorated interior and houses a fine collection of furniture, china and paintings, while outside the Border Country Life Museum has both static and working displays of rural activities.

Melrose, *Borders* NT 5433
Melrose's outstanding attraction is the Cistercian abbey. Built in 1136, the vulnerable Border abbey was wrecked during the 14th-century wars of independence and finally destroyed in raids during the 16th century. The beautiful ruins, mostly belonging to the 15th-century reconstruction, were described and made famous by Sir Walter Scott in the *Lay of the Last Minstrel*. The heart of Robert the Bruce is said to be buried within the church. In the abbey grounds is the Abbey Museum and nearby Priorwood Garden is a special garden featuring flowers for drying and a picnic area. Abbotsford House, 2m W on the B6360, was owned by Sir Walter Scott in the 19th century and was the place of his death. It contains his library and a collection of historical relics.

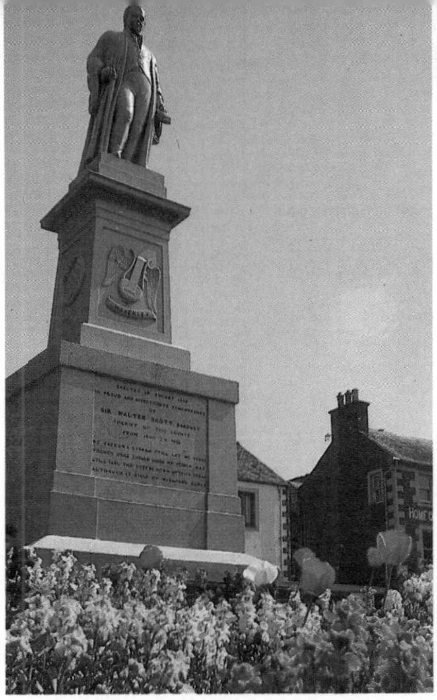

Sir Walter Scott, Selkirk's sheriff for 33 years, still stands before his old court house

North Berwick, *Lothian* NT 5485
This ancient royal burgh and fishing village has become a popular resort. Two good sandy bays flank the harbour and there are facilities for golf and sailing. The ruin of a Napoleonic watch tower tops grassy 613ft North Berwick Law, 1m S, while 2m E on the A198 is 14th-century Tantallon Castle, a dramatically-situated clifftop stronghold of the Douglas clan. 3m out to sea is the lonely 350ft Bass Rock.

Selkirk, *Borders* NT 4728
Noted for the manufacture of tweeds and woollens, Selkirk lies on Ettrick Water at the edge of the old Ettrick Forest—a good centre for exploring the lovely Yarrow and Ettrick valleys. Items of local interest can be found in the Selkirk Museum and 2½m W off the A708 is Bowhill, splendid home of the Scotts of Buccleuch, which has an outstanding collection of pictures, porcelain and period furniture.

David I founded Jedburgh Abbey, one of his four important Border monasteries

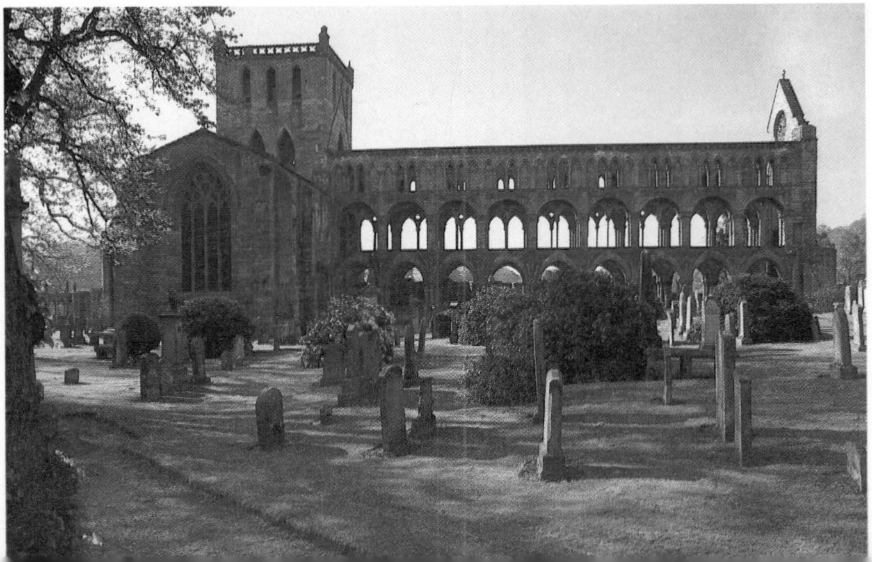

16th-century Lindisfarne Castle was restored by Sir Edwin Lutyens in 1903

Chillingham, *Northumb* NU 0625
In the grounds of the castle (not open to the public) can be seen a unique herd of some 50 truly wild, white cattle, believed to be the descendants of wild oxen trapped here when the park was originally enclosed in 1220.

Coldstream, *Borders* NT 8439
James IV of Scotland died when the Scots were defeated in 1513 at the bloody Battle of Flodden Field, 3m SE of the town on the English side of the border. 2m NW is the Hirsel, home of Sir Alec Douglas Home. Dundock wood, 1½m W on the A697, has a magnificent display of rhododendrons and azaleas in season and there is also a large bird sanctuary.

Craster, *Northumb* NU 2519
Well-known for the quality of its oak-smoked kippers, this small fishing village is the starting point for an interesting 1¼m cliff-top walk to the 14th-century Dunstanburgh Castle, splendidly isolated on a rocky promontory.

Duns, *Borders* NT 7853
In 1545 English invaders destroyed the old town of Duns set on Duns Law, and the present market town has developed at the foot of the hill. The Jim Clark Room, Newtown Street, houses motor racing trophies won by the famous driver. Manderston, 1¼m E, is a fine Edwardian house with magnificent state rooms, stables, a marble dairy, gardens and lovely lakeside walks.

Eyemouth, *Borders* NT 9464
Two hundred years ago the narrow passageways and small courtyards of this busy fishing port and holiday resort were used by smugglers evading customs men as they brought their goods from hiding places in the caves of the neighbouring picturesque cliffs. The resort has sand and shingle beaches dotted with teeming rock pools.

Holy Island (Lindisfarne),
Northumb NU 1342
Access to the island is via a causeway impassable at high tide: tide times should be noted before crossing from the main-

Bamburgh Castle facing the North Sea over Budle Bay at low tide

land. Known as the Cradle of Christianity, the island provided a refuge for monks from Iona, led by St Aidan in the 7th century, and ruins of an 11th-century Benedictine priory can be seen today. Lindisfarne Castle sits on a rock outcrop overlooking the harbour. It is National Trust owned and has displays of 17th-century furniture. A variety of wildfowl and wading birds can be seen on the island's nature reserve.

Kelso, *Borders* NT 7333
An excellent touring centre for the Cheviot Hills, this town on the Tweed has a wide cobbled square and was described by Scott (who lived here in 1783) as 'the most beautiful if not the most romantic, village in Scotland'. Imposing fragments are all that remain of the church of Kelso Abbey, destroyed in 1545 when garrisoned as a fortress. Floors Castle on the B6089 was originally designed by William Adam in 1721 and contains superb French and English furniture, tapestries and paintings. There is also a particularly fine walled garden and a garden centre.

Alnwick, *Northumb* NU 1912
The town is an excellent touring centre for the Cheviot and Simonside Hills, the Northumberland National Park and the magnificent coastline to the N, designated an Area of Outstanding Natural Beauty. The impressive Norman castle with its massive keep, walls and towers dominates the town. For centuries it was the powerful Percy family's border stronghold, and is still home of the Duke of Northumberland. It contains much of interest ranging from state rooms with an outstanding picture collection, to an armoury and Roman antiquities.

Bamburgh, *Northumb* NU 1834
Superbly situated on a rocky outcrop above the shore, Bamburgh's restored Norman castle dominates this unspoilt fishing village. The castle's collections of armour are especially worth seeing. In 1838 a local heroine, Grace Darling, helped her father, keeper of the Longstone lighthouse, rescue survivors of a ship wrecked in a gale: a museum in the village was founded by the RNLI in her memory.

Berwick-upon-Tweed,
Northumb NT 9953
Now England's northernmost town, this busy seaport and holiday resort at the mouth of the Tweed was the object of bitter fighting between Scots and English for many centuries, being captured or sacked on at least 14 occasions. The defensive medieval town walls, rebuilt in the 16th century, remain intact as a 2m circuit round the old town which contains many well-preserved houses. From the ramparts there are fine views of the Northumberland moors and Cheviot Hills. Three attractive bridges, the earliest being 17th century, span the Tweed, and there are fine, sandy beaches. Much of the nearby coastline is designated an Area of Outstanding Natural Beauty.

Robert Stephenson built the Royal Border Bridge at Berwick in 1850

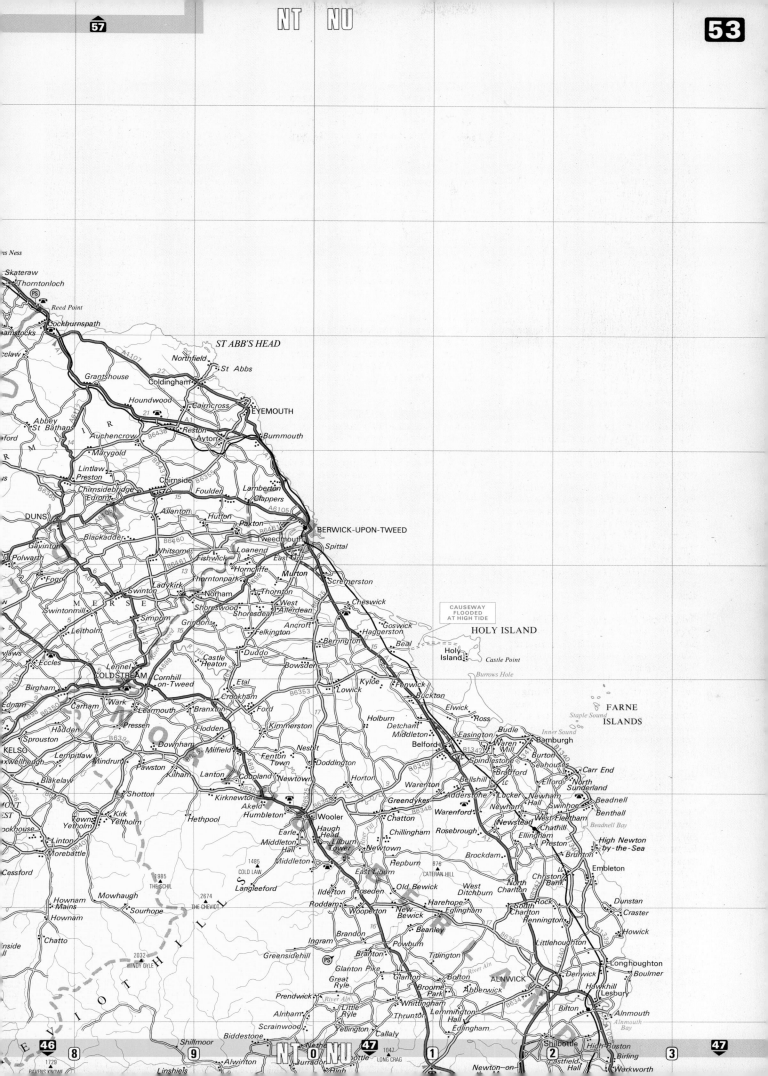

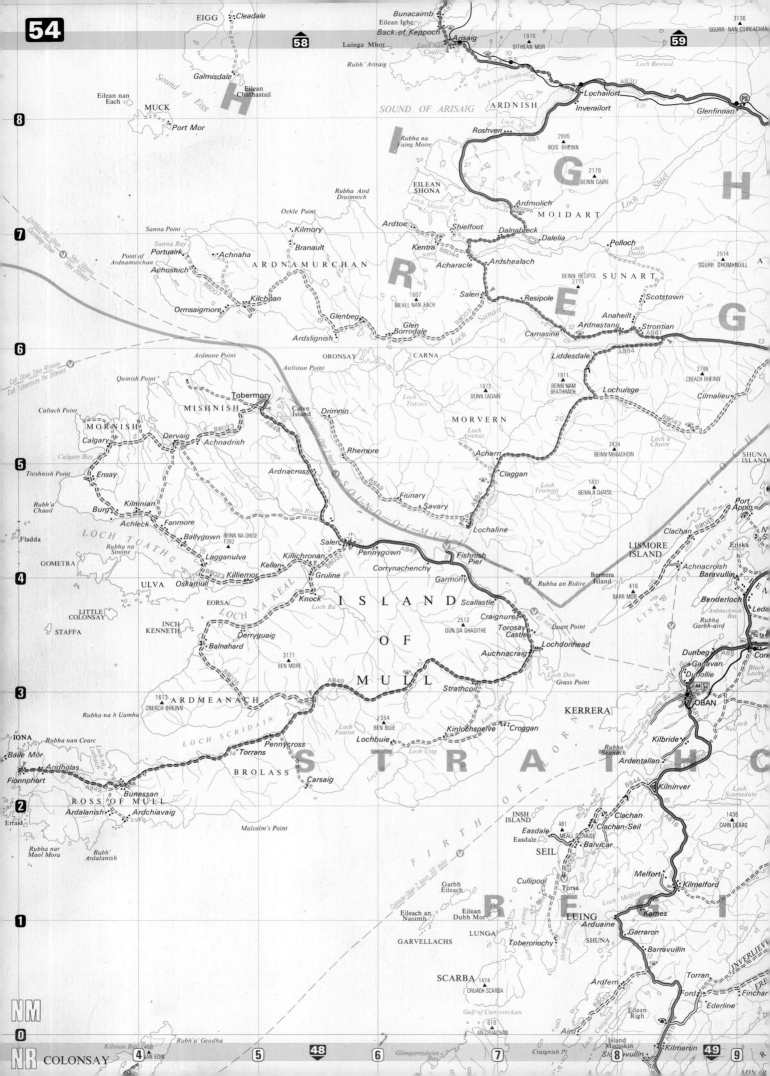

A craft shop in Strontian – a village at the eastern end of Loch Sunart

Balvicar, *Strath*   NM 7616
Seil Island hugs the coast S of Oban as close as any offshore land can – only the narrow Clachan Bridge carrying the B844 from Kilniver over the Clachan Sound to Balvicar attaches Seil to the mainland. Tiny Balvicar is the island's main settlement but it hosts tourists passing through to Seil's own satellite islet – Easdale, where there are the beautiful water and rock gardens of An Cala – and Luing, the island which provided the slate to roof Iona Cathedral. Breathtaking views of this island trio can be seen from the viewpoint 1m W of the village.

Bunessan, *Isle of Mull, Strath*   NM 3821
A village with a small harbour, nearby Ardtun has famous fossil beds. 5m W is Fionnphort from where passenger ferries cross the narrow Sound of Iona to the little Inner Hebridean island. In the Sound is mile-square Erraid Island, accessible by foot at low tide, which was the inspiration for Stevenson's famous novel *Kidnapped*.

Craignure, *Isle of Mull, Strath*   NM 7236
The car-ferry from Oban calls at the village pier, and from here there are views of the distant mountains of Appin on the mainland and the peak of Ben Nevis. 3½m SE Duart Point is the splendid setting for restored Duart Castle, ancestral home of the Macleans, dating from 1250. Torosay Castle, 2m S of Craignure, is a 19th-century house containing, among other items of interest, a superb collection of stags' 'heads' (antlers). The 11 acres of Italian gardens and grounds include a plantation of Australian gum trees.

Glenfinnan, *Highland*   NM 9080
Here the 'Road to the Isles' passes the head of beautiful Loch Shiel, framed by spectacular mountain scenery. There is a fine view down the 18m length of the loch from the parapet of a statue-topped monument erected in 1815 to commemorate the Highlanders who followed Prince Charles Edward Stuart in 1745. Glenfinnan was the rallying point for loyal clans after the Prince landed from France. The National Trust Visitor Centre traces the Prince's campaign from Glenfinnan to Derby and back to Culloden.

Kilninian, *Isle of Mull, Strath*   NM 3945
In the churchyard of this quiet village can be found stones with carved Celtic inscriptions. To the NW the B8073 climbs through hairpin bends and over moorland to reach Calgary, where there is a fine sandy beach. 3½m SE Eas Fors waterfalls face Loch Tuath and the island of Ulva.

Oban, *Strath*   NM 8630
Well-situated on a sheltered bay fronted by the island of Kerrera, Oban has grown over the last two centuries from a small fishing village to a major tourist centre for the west Highlands and islands. But while visitors come in their thousands to depart by ferry for Mull, Tiree, Coll, Barra and South Uist, or explore the surrounding hills and mountains, the fishing fleet is still busy and Oban is the market town for the surrounding area. Demonstrations of one local industry can be seen at McDonald's Mill, ½m S, which contains an exhibition of spinning and weaving. 3m N is Dunstaffnage Castle. Originally a 13th-century stronghold of the Campbells, parts of the ruin date from a later period but the two round towers, a curtain wall and gate-

Oban Harbour glimpsed through an arch of McCaig's Folly on Battery Hill

This viaduct near Glenfinnan matches the scale of the superb mountain scenery

house remain. Flora Macdonald was held prisoner here in 1746. A chapel nearby is the burial place of the Campbells. On a hill behind the town, overlooking the harbour, McCaig's Folly contrasts strangely with the solid Scottish buildings below, especially at night when floodlit. Intended to be a replica of Rome's Colosseum, the building was started in 1897 to relieve local unemployment, but was never finished.

Salen, *Highland*   NM 6864
On the shores of Loch Sunart, this small fishing and boating centre has a beautiful setting of moorland and pine plantations. To the S are several sandy bays.

Strontian, *Highland*   NM 8161
The rare Scottish wildcat survives in the Ariundle Forest Nature Reserve close to the village, and a nature trail leads through the Ariundle oak wood in Strontian Glen to old lead mines. A rare mineral found here was called strontian after the village. There are superb views of Loch Shiel to the N and Morven to the S from 2,774ft Ben Resipol which can be climbed from the glen.

Tobermory, *Isle of Mull, Strath*   NM 5055
The main tourist centre of Mull, Tobermory's early 19th-century houses curve colourfully round the harbour, backed by sycamore-wooded hills. The town's importance as a fishing port has declined, but the bay provides a safe anchorage for yachts. A Spanish galleon containing 30 million ducats, a survivor of the Armada, sank in the bay in 1588 after being blown up. Repeated attempts to salvage the ship have not yet been successful.

Inveraray, often described as one of Scotland's most attractive towns

Ardanaiseig, *Strath*   NN 0824
Here 3m NE of Kilchrenan, at the end of
an unclassified road, there are gardens
with magnificent views across Loch Awe
which include a garden centre.

Balquhidder, *Central*   NN 5320
Rebel and Highland hero Rob Roy,
whose exploits were romanticised by Sir
Walter Scott in his book of the same
name, lies buried in the graveyard of
Balquhidder's old roofless church at the
eastern end of Loch Voil. Rob Roy
became chief of the MacGregor clan but
as a staunch Jacobite he was outlawed
and his exploits became legend in the
district. To the N of Loch Voil are
beautiful steep-sided valleys known as
the Braes of Balquhidder (pronounced
Balwhidder). A single track road leads
through the braes to Loch Doine.

Bridge of Gaur, *Tayside*   NN 5056
To the SW lies Rannoch Moor. This
desolate area of bog, moor, lochans and
mountains covers 56sq m and was described by Robert Louis Stevenson as
being 'as waste as the sea'. The largest

moor in Scotland, 3,500 acres in the NE
corner form a nature reserve, where red
deer or even a golden eagle may be seen.

Cairndow, *Strath*   NN 1810
Strone Gardens here feature rhododendrons, azaleas, conifers and daffodils in
season. A 190ft-high tree is claimed to be
the tallest in Britain.

Dalmally, *Strath*   NN 1527
Situated on the River Orchy, in its
beautiful wooded valley near Loch Awe,
the village has become a holiday centre
for anglers. 2m SW is a monument to the
18th-century Gaelic poet Duncan Ban
MacIntyre.

Fort William, *Highland*   NN 1074
Now a major resort and touring centre
for the west Highlands, the town takes
its name from a stone stronghold built on
the order of William III in 1690. The fort
was garrisoned until the mid 19th century, then demolished. The town mainly
dates from the arrival of the railway in the
Victorian period. Superbly situated near
the west end of Great Glen and the head

of Loch Linnhe, the town lies at the foot
of 4,406ft Ben Nevis, Britain's highest
mountain. It may be climbed by the
sensibly-equipped tourist in good
summer weather, but allow six to eight
hours if attempting the whole route.
Cross the River Nevis NE of Fort William and keeping to the E bank reach a
rough but well-defined path which starts
from Achintee Farm in Glen Nevis. The
West Highland Museum contains much
of local interest and in particular an
exhibition of the 1745 rising. A famous
'secret' portrait of Prince Charles Edward
Stuart can only be seen if reflected onto
the polished surface of a cylinder. Inver-
lochy Castle, dating from the 13th century and later, has been converted into a
luxury hotel.

Glencoe, *Highland*   NN 1058
Glencoe village is situated at the Loch
Leven end of one of Scotland's most
famous glens. Protected by the National
Trust for Scotland, Glen Coe is a starkly
beautiful mountain wilderness ascending
1,100ft in 10 miles to the vast expanse of
Rannoch Moor. The brooding atmosphere of the often mist-shrouded glen is a
reminder of the notorious massacre of 38
Macdonalds in the lower part of the
valley in 1692. After being entertained
for 12 days by the Macdonalds, Campbell
soldiers turned on their hosts, who had
failed to sign an oath of allegiance to
William III. Close to the site of the
massacre is the Glen Coe Visitor Centre,
and the Glencoe and North Lorn Folk
Museum in the village contains Macdonald and Jacobite relics.

Inveraray, *Strath*   NN 0908
Created a royal burgh in 1648, Inveraray
is one of the most attractive small towns
in western Scotland. White-walled buildings cluster together on the banks of
Loch Fyne and it is surrounded by lovely
woodland. The original fishing village
was destroyed by fire and the town
largely dates from the mid 18th century,
including some finely restored tall buildings known as 'lands'. At the junction of
Front and Main streets there is a tall
Celtic cross from Iona. Impressive 18th-
century Inveraray Castle stands in well-
wooded parkland and is the ancestral
home of the Dukes of Argyll. Damaged
by fire in 1975, it is now restored and its
many treasures are on show again to the
public. There is an excellent view of the
surrounding countryside from the roof of
the parish church bell-tower.

Lochawe, *Strath*   NN 1227
Kilchurn Castle, 1½m E, can be viewed
from the outside. Built in the 15th century with later additions, the castle was at
one time on an island before the level of
Loch Awe dropped 10ft. Water is
pumped from Loch Awe up to the spectacularly high Corrie Reservoir on Ben
Cruachan. Water from the reservoir
drives the turbines of Cruachan Power
Station, set in a huge man-made cave in
the mountain, which may be visited by
the public.

The wilds of famous Glen Coe, with the crags of Stob Coire nan Lochan towering above

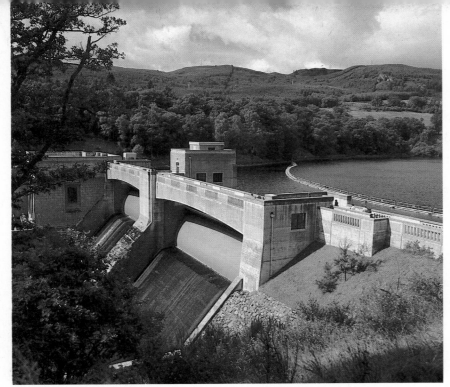

Pitlochry's power station and dam overlooking Loch Faskally in the Tummel valley

Aberfeldy, *Tayside*   NN 8549
Ramblers will find this little market town
on the River Tay a good centre for
exploration. There is a nature trail
through the Birks of Aberfeldy, forest
walks, and archaeological and historical
walks. 1½m W is the line of General
Wade's 18th-century military road. His
five-arched bridge, built in 1733, still
spans the River Tay.

Blair Drummond, *Central*   NS 7398
In the grounds of a turreted Victorian
castle (not open to the public) is Scotland's only safari park, where wild
animals can be seen in 100 acres of
woodland. As well as lions, camels,
elephants and zebras, there is a pets'
corner, a boat safari and picnic areas.

Bridge of Allan, *Central*   NS 7897
Now a touring centre for the Trossachs,
and site of Stirling University, the town
was a popular spa for 150 years after
mineral springs were found to have
medicinal properties in 1820. The baths
and pump room still stand.

Callander, *Central*   NN 6208
A busy little town on the edge of the
Highlands, Callander is ideally situated
for touring the Trossachs and Loch Kat-
rine. Kilmahog Woollen Mill was once
famous for hand-woven blankets and
tweed and its old water-wheel is still in
working order.

Comrie, *Tayside*   NN 7722
The comprehensive Museum of Scottish
Tartans in the centre of town is well
worth visiting. Exhibits trace the history
of tartans and there are spinning, weaving and dyeing demonstrations.

Crieff, *Tayside*   NN 8621
A town of steep streets and parks, beautifully situated on a hillside overlooking
the River Earn, Crieff was almost completely burnt down in the 1700s. There is

an extensive view of surrounding
countryside from the 911ft Knock of
Crieff N of the town. 2m S are the
beautiful formal gardens of 15th-century
Drummond Castle.

Doune, *Central*   NN 7201
A town once famous for the manufacture
of pistols, Doune's main attraction for
the tourist is its well-preserved medieval
castle, whose two fine towers overlook
the River Teith. Once a royal palace, the
castle belongs to the Earls of Moray. At
Doune Motor Museum there is a display
of approximately 40 vintage and veteran
cars – most are in running order.

Dunblane, *Central*   NN 7801
Worth visiting in this attractive old residential town of narrow streets is the
mainly 13th-century cathedral. John
Ruskin considered the west front to be a
masterpiece of Scottish church architecture. A single-arch 16th-century bridge
spans the Allan Water.

Dunkeld, *Tayside*   NO 0242
The restored 14th-century choir of Dunkeld's beautiful ruined cathedral now
serves as the parish church. The town
was rebuilt after the battle of Dunkeld in
1689, and its restored 'Little Houses'
date from this time. A variety of wild
birds can be viewed from special hides at
the Loch of Lowes Wildlife Reserve.

Kinross, *Tayside*   NO 1102
Situated near Loch Leven, world-
famous for its trout, the town is popular
with anglers. Mary Queen of Scots was
imprisoned for a year in the island
stronghold of 16th-century Loch Leven
Castle before escaping. The castle was
dismantled in 1640.

Perth, *Tayside*   NO 1123
The 'Fair City' of Perth stands at the
head of the River Tay estuary, the oldest
part, including 15th-century St John's

Kirk, lying between two open spaces
known as the North Inch and South
Inch. Centre for a wide area, this ancient
city is rich in historical associations and
was frequently a royal residence. Places
of interest include the Black Watch Regimental Museum; 16th-century Elcho
Castle; 15th- and 16th-century Huntingtower Castle; the Perth Musuem and Art
Gallery; Branklyn Garden and Fair Maid's
House – now a centre for Scottish crafts.

Pitlochry, *Tayside*   NN 9458
Situated in the beautiful wooded
Tummel valley, this attractive little town
has become a well-known tourist centre,
with a festival theatre giving plays in the
summer. A modern attraction for visitors
has proved to be the huge hydro-electric
power station. There is a permanent
exhibition about hydro-electricity, a
viewing gallery, and an observation
chamber from which salmon can be seen
making their way up-river to their
spawning beds. 1½m SE is a fine Pictish
slab thought to be 8th century.

Scone (New and Old), *Tayside*   NO 1226
Scone Palace, dating from the 1800s,
stands on the site of the famous 12th-
century abbey. Destroyed about 400
years ago, this was the coronation place
of all Scottish kings up to James I. They
were crowned on the famous Stone of
Scone, which had probably been brought
to Scone from Iona in the 9th century.
Edward I moved it to Westminster
Abbey in 1297, where it became part of
the coronation chair. The old village
which had grown up round the abbey
was moved to a new site 1½m away in
1805 by the then Earl of Mansfield, to
make room for a park.

*During 1746 Bonnie Prince Charlie kept
prisoners inside grim Doune Castle*

A glimpse of Sir James Barrie's childhood recreated at his birthplace in Kirriemuir

Arbroath, *Tayside*   NO 6340
As a fishing port Arbroath is well-known for its delicious 'smokies', oak-smoked haddock. The town, a busy industrial and commercial centre, is also a holiday resort with sandy beaches on one side, and on the other spectacular cave-riddled, red sandstone cliffs. The 13th-century abbey is now in ruins, but it was here that Scotland's Declaration of Independence was signed by Robert the Bruce in 1320.

Brechin, *Tayside*   NO 5960
Brechin's red sandstone houses rise steeply up the hillside from the South Esk River. Particularly worth visiting is the well-preserved 87ft-high round tower attached to a mainly 13th-century church. Dating from the 10th or 11th century it served as a watchtower and place of refuge. It is one of only two on the Scottish mainland, but similar structures are found in Ireland.

Carnoustie, *Tayside*   NO 5634
This popular holiday resort with 5m of sandy beaches is perhaps best known for its three fine golf courses, the championship course being of international standard.

Cupar, *Fife*   NO 3714
The Hill of Tarvit Mansion House lies 2m S of this market centre for the fertile Howe of Fife. Remodelled in 1906, the house contains notable collections of furniture, tapestries and paintings.

Dundee, *Tayside*   NO 4030
A bustling industrial and university city, Scotland's fourth largest, Dundee also had an extensive dockland area on the Firth of Tay. The Barrack Street Museum contains shipping and industrial exhibits of local interest. Dundee marmalade has been famous since it was first made here by Mrs Keiller in the early 18th century – the city's jam industry uses fruit from the fertile Carse of Gowrie to the NE. For centuries the town was subjected to repeated sackings by the English and most of the city dates from the mid 18th century onwards, when it began to flourish with linen and jute industries. A focal point of the city is the 15th-century church steeple, St Mary's Tower. The city has four golf courses and Spalding Golf Museum traces the history of golf. The residential suburb of Broughty Ferry, 4m E, is also a popular holiday resort. Claypotts is an unusual 16th-century castle here, and exhibits in Broughty Castle and Museum include those relating to whaling.

Fettercairn, *Grampian*   NO 6573
A surprising royal arch in this village on the edge of the Howe of Mearns was built in 1861 to commemorate the visit of Queen Victoria and Prince Albert. Nearby Fasque was the home of four-times Prime Minister William Gladstone from 1829 to 1851.

Glamis, *Tayside*   NO 3846
This attractive village is famous as the site of splendid Glamis Castle. Ancestral seat of the Earl of Strathmore and Kinghorne, it was the childhood home of HM Queen Elizabeth, The Queen Mother, and birthplace of HRH Princess Margaret. Its history may have inspired Shakespeare's *Macbeth*, 'Thane of Glamis', for Malcolm II was murdered here. The Angus Folk Museum in the village houses a collection of agricultural and domestic equipment in a row of restored 17th-century cottages.

Kirriemuir, *Tayside*   NO 3854
Writer Sir James Barrie, best-known as creator of *Peter Pan*, was born in this small town of picturesque narrow streets. His birthplace in 1860 is preserved as a personal museum.

Montrose, *Tayside*   NO 7157
This pleasant town is bordered by water on three sides. The South Esk River forms the Montrose Basin, a 5sq m tidal lagoon, with a 5m-long sandy margin. Sandy beaches backed by sand-dunes extend N from the river mouth for several miles, making the whole area a popular one for holiday-makers, sailors, anglers, and ornithologists. The particularly spacious High Street is paralleled by a grassy belt, the Links, and narrow, twisting closes lined with charming 18th-century houses lead from the High Street.

St Andrew's, *Fife*   NO 5016
Once the ecclesiastical centre of Scotland, this beautiful old university town has a fascinating history, but it is also a seaside resort with 2m of sandy beaches. The world's ruling authority on golf is the Royal and Ancient Golf Club, founded here in 1754, and the town's five golf courses include the Old Course, where the game has been played for 500 years. Only ruins remain of the 12th-century cathedral, Scotland's largest church by the time it was completed in 1318. The university, with several interesting buildings, is Scotland's oldest, founded in 1412, and students still wear traditional red gowns. Behind the harbour, on a craggy promontory, are the remains of the 13th-century castle that was once the archbishop's palace.

Stonehaven, *Grampian*   NO 8685
Houses of the old town curving round the yacht-filled harbour make an attractive sight in this popular small holiday resort. The beach is mainly shingle and there is lovely cliff scenery to the N and S. The new town has grown up on the other side of the Carron Water. Stonehaven Tolbooth is now a fishing and local museum, while 1½m S is 14th- to 16th-century Dunnottar Castle.

Command of St Andrew's Bay did not prevent the castle's fall to French sailors in 1547

Ardvassar, *Isle of Skye*
Highland   NG 6303
A short distance from this hamlet on the
fertile Sleat peninsula is Armadale Pier
from which there are frequent ferry services to Mallaig. Armadale Castle, once
seat of the Macdonalds, Lords of the
Isles, dates from the early 18th-century.
Now reconstructed, it houses the Clan
Donald Centre with a Museum of the
Isles and there are marked woodland
walks. The region to the S of Ardvassar is
wild, bare and barren, but has wonderful
panoramic views.

*View of Dunvegan Loch from the
battlements of the 13th-century castle*

Colbost, *Isle of Skye,*
Highland   NG 2148
Here the Skye Black House is an example
of a typical island dwelling. It gets its
name from the lack of a chimney – having
only a hole in the roof above the peat fire.
The house was divided into two rooms –
one for people, the other for animals.

Dunvegan, *Isle of Skye,*
Highland   NG 2548
On a rock overlooking island-studded
Dunvegan Loch is the castle, ancestral
home of the Clan Macleod for 700 years.
The mainly 19th-century exterior hides
much older sections dating from the 15th
century including a dreadful pit dun-
geon. Well-known treasures include the
Fairy Flag. This fragment of silk is
thought to have been woven on the Island
of Rhodes in the 7th century, but tradition has it that a fairy gave it, endowed
with magical properties, to the 4th Chief
in the 14th century. Boat trips can be
taken from Dunvegan Pier to see colonies
of seals on the islands.

Elgol, *Isle of Skye,*
Highland   NG 5214
Magnificent views from this hamlet
include the Cuillins to the N, and the
mountains of Rhum, Canna and Eigg to

the S. From here a short powerboat trip
will take you to within ½m of famous
Loch Coruisk. This isolated stretch of
water lies in a 2m-long glacial basin,
completely encircled by the Cuillins.

Kilvaxter, *Isle of Skye,*
Highland   NG 3869
To the N, at Kilmuir, four thatched
cottages comprise the Kilmuir Croft
Museum, portraying the croft house of
100 years ago. An improvement on the
'black' house, these had a chimney and
the second room was used as a bedroom.
The graveyard at Kilmuir, superbly
situated overlooking the sea, contains a
Celtic cross, the Flora Macdonald
Monument, marking the site where the
heroine was buried in 1790.

Kyleakin, *Isle of Skye,*
Highland   NG 7526
This is the main arrival point for visitors
to Skye. Sixty miles long, with a coastline
intricately indented by sea lochs forming
rocky peninsulas, this lovely island is the
largest of the Inner Hebrides group, but
no part of it is more than 5m from the
sea. The grandly austere, often mist-
enshrouded Cuillin Mountains are
famous for climbing, but the centre of the
island has miles of rolling moorland. In
the north grazing land supports crofting
communities.

Kyle of Lochalsh, *Highland*   NG 7627
Only a few hundred yards lie between
this busy fishing and shipping village and
the Isle of Skye. Consequently it is the
main ferry-stage for Skye, and the rail-
head of the line from Inverness.

Mallaig, *Highland*   NM 6796
A busy herring and lobster port on the
rocky shores of north Morar, Mallaig is

the western end of one 'Road to the
Isles'. Car ferries carry visitors to Armadale on Skye and also other islands of
the Inner and Outer Hebrides. Tourists
can also be taken by motor launch to
remote Inverie on Loch Nevis.

Portree, *Isle of Skye,*
Highland   NG 4843
Well situated around a bay sheltered by
high cliffs, this fishing village is the
island's capital, and a busy touring centre
in summer. There are views from here of
the wooded, hilly Island of Raasay. To
the N is the Old Man of Storr, a 160ft-
high pillar of rock, backed by a 2,000ft
cliff-face.

Sligachan, *Isle of Skye,*
Highland   NG 4829
Near the head of Loch Sligachan, this
hamlet provides access to the ebony
granite Black Cuillins, and is popular
with mountaineers and geologists. The
area is also a good one for anglers, the
River Sligachan, well-known for salmon
and sea-trout, flowing into the sea near
here. Nearer its source it forms a
boundary between the Black Cuillins and
the pink granite Red Cuillins. Glen
Sligachan, an excellent example of a U-
shaped glacial valley, extends S into the
Black Cuillins, and a long-distance path
eventually reaches the spectacular Loch
Coruisk.

Staffin, *Isle of Skye,*
Highland   NG 4967
The village lies in the sandy curve of
Staffin Bay. Nearby is a cliff known as
the Kilt Rock because the vertical forma-
tion of the strata resemble the pleats of a
kilt. To the NW is the strange group of
stone stacks and pinnacles known as the
Quiraing.

Scratching a living on Skye – the Kilmuir Croft Museum shows just how hard it was

Achnasheen, *Highland* NH 1658
The hotel in this little hamlet between Strath Bran and Glen Carron is part of the old railway station. To the N is the 3,060ft granite peak of Fionn Bheinn, behind which is lonely Loch Fannich. Water from the surrounding area is used to generate hydro-electricity.

Balmacara, *Highland* NG 8028
Two-thirds of the 8,000-acre Balmacara estate are now owned by the National Trust for Scotland. There is a woodland garden open all year, and guided and self-guided walks to Plockton peninsula. In the coach house there is also a natural history display.

Dornie, *Highland* NG 8826
Some of the most beautiful scenery in the West Highlands is to be found here, where Loch Duich meets Loch Long. This is the idyllic setting for the well-restored Eilean Donan Castle. Linked to the mainland by a causeway, this island castle remained intact until reduced to ruins by the English navy in 1719 when garrisoned by Spanish Jacobite troops.

Fort Augustus, *Highland* NH 3709
Situated at the SW end of Loch Ness, near where it is entered by the Caledonian Canal, this village on the Great Glen is popular with anglers. It gets its name from a fort built here by General Wade in 1730, who named it after William Augustus, Duke of Cumberland. Only a small part of the fort remains in a corner of a 19th-century Benedictine abbey. 2m S the Great Glen Exhibition traces the history and traditions of the people of the the Great Glen, with current information on the search for the Loch Ness Monster.

Glenelg, *Highland* NG 8119
This hamlet on Glenelg Bay, facing the Isle of Skye, can be reached by only one road which climbs over a high ridge via the steep and winding Mam Ratagan Pass. From here there are fine views of the Five Sisters of Kintail. 1m S on Glen Beg are the remains of two 30ft-high Iron Age brochs, Dun Telve and Dun Troddan. Among the best preserved in Scotland, they contain entrance passages, stairs and galleries. The rough coast road to Arnisdale has fine views of Skye over the Sound of Sleat.

Invergarry, *Highland* NO 3101
Some of the most spectacular scenery in Scotland surrounds this hamlet on the W side of Loch Oich. One of the Roads to the Isles runs W from here through Cluanie and Glen Shiel to the Kyle of Lochalsh, first passing through the richly wooded valley of the River Garry. Ruined Invergarry Castle, to the S on the shores of Loch Oich, was once the seat of the MacDonells of Glengarry. Badly damaged in 1654 and 1716, the ill-fated castle was finally destroyed by the Duke of Cumberland in 1745. This was an act of revenge because Prince Charles Edward had stayed here before and after the Battle of Culloden.

The Caledonian Canal near Fort Augustus, where it enters Loch Ness

Lochcarron, *Highland* NG 9039
Scarves and ties are woven in this small, attractive village on the north shore of the sea loch of Loch Carron. To the NW is the thickly-wooded Alt-nen-Carnan National Nature Reserve. 3m SE are the fragmentary ruins of Strome Castle, blown up in 1602.

Achnasheen is built around its railway station – lifeline to the outside world

Shiel Bridge, *Highland* NG 9318
At the head of the lovely sea loch of Duich, the village is situated at the W edge of the beautiful 15,000-acre Kintail estate, protected by the National Trust for Scotland. From road level in Glen Shiel the mountain range known as the Five Sisters of Kintail rises abruptly, four of the peaks exceeding 3,000ft. At the estate's northern limit are the Glomach Falls where a burn tumbles 370ft over two rock lips. They are a vigorous 3½m walk from the end of the Strath Coe forest track.

Shieldaig, *Highland* NG 8154
Once prosperous because of special privileges, this bright little fishing and crofting village facing W over the bay of Loch Shieldaig became poverty-stricken when deprived of its privileges in the mid-19th century. Isolated from the outside world for centuries, the village now has good road links, the most recent being W to Applecross. The hamlet faces tree-covered Shieldaig Island, protected by the National Trust for Scotland.

Torridon, *Highland* NG 9055
The hamlet of Torridon is situated at the W end of Glen Torridon, one of the finest and wildest of the Wester Ross glens. The Corrie of a Hundred Hills in the glen is a curious glacial moraine, and some of the red sandstone mountains which rise from the glen are capped by white quartzite. The National Trust for Scotland owns 14,000 acres of this beautiful district, and there is a visitor centre.

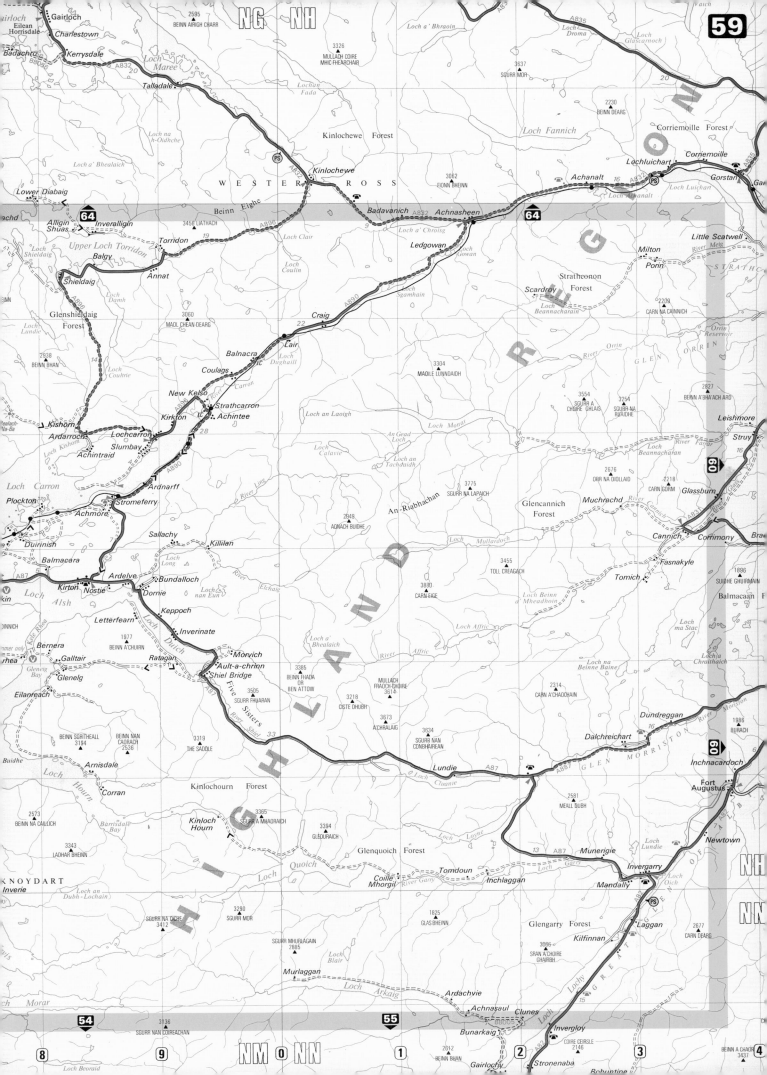

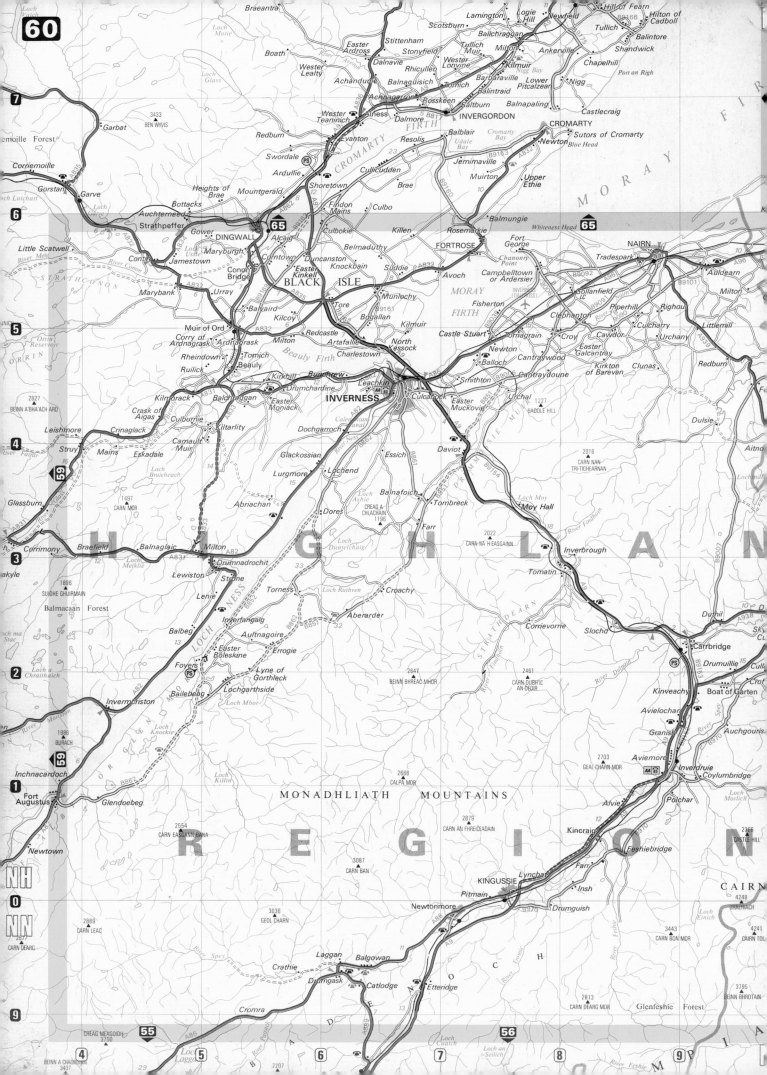

The altar of St Andrew's Cathedral, Inverness, which was built in 1866-9

Aviemore, *Highland*   NH 8912
Well-known as the heart of Britain's main winter-sports area, this Speyside village is the site of a multi-million pound, all-year-round holiday complex developed in the 1960s. There is a wide range of accommodation and leisure facilities, as well as provision for many indoor and outdoor sports. A 100 sq m national nature reserve is situated nearby, and to the E is the 12,500-acre Glenmore Forest Park. Steam trains of the Strathspey Railway run to Boat of Garten 5m away.

Beauly, *Highland*   NH 5426
Traditionally both the town and the salmon river on which it is so well situated obtained their shared name from the French *beau lieu* – beautiful place. The remains of a priory built in 1230 can be seen. It was adopted as the burial place of the Mackenzies of Kintail.

Carrbridge, *Highland*   NH 9022
Summer touring centre and winter ski-resort, the village is well-known for its award-winning Landmark, Europe's first Visitor Centre. An audio-visual display tells the story of the Highlands from the last Ice Age to the present day, and other attractions include treetop and nature trails and a woodland adventure playground.

Cawdor, *Highland*   NH 8450
The village stands at the foot of the castle, one of Scotland's finest medieval buildings and home of the Thanes of Cawdor since the early 14th century.

Dingwall, *Highland*   NH 5458
Formerly county town of Ross and Cromarty, Dingwall was created a royal burgh in 1226. A good touring centre for the N and W, it mainly consists of one long street and a harbour. In front of the Tolbooth, built in 1730, is the shaft of the old mercat cross and an iron yett (gate) taken from the old town gaol.

Drumnadrochit, *Highland*   NH 5029
A fine tourist centre, the village lies on the River Enrick, 2m W of Loch Ness. The dark waters of the loch are 700ft deep in places, and stories of a monster

date back to the 7th century. The A82 was opened in 1933 and there have been many reported sightings since then — the Official Loch Ness Monster Exhibition even includes photographs. The impressive ruins of mainly 14th-century Urquhart Castle, destroyed before the 1715 rising, overlooks the loch at the entrance to lovely Glen Urquhart.

Fort George, *Highland*   NH 7656
Covering 12 acres, the present fort was built in 1748-63. Considered one of Europe's finest examples of late artillery fortification, it is still garrisoned by the Queen's Own Highlanders and a regimental museum is open to the public.

Inverness, *Highland*   NH 6645
A large and busy city on the tree-lined banks of the River Ness, Inverness is the administrative headquarters of the Highland Region, and has a harbour. A stone keep was first built on Castle Hill in the 12th century but the present imposing castle dates from 1834 and is now used as a courthouse and administrative centre. A 19th-century monument to Flora Macdonald stands on the terrace, and from here there are lovely views of the surrounding hills. Abertarff House (16th-century) is the headquarters of An Comunn Gaidhealach, an association concerned with preserving Gaelic language and culture. It has an exhibition of the origins and history of the Gaels. In 1746 the great Battle of Culloden was fought on Culloden Moor (Drumossie Muir), 5m SE off the B9006. During a 40-minute battle 1,200 Scotsmen and 310 Englishmen died. With over a quarter of his Highland army slaughtered by the Duke of Cumberland's men, Prince Charles Edward's hopes of restoring the Stuart monarchy were finally dashed. Old Leanach Farmhouse, round which the fierce battle raged, is now a museum, and there is also a Trust Visitor Centre. A huge 19th-century cairn marks the site of the battle and simple head-stones distinguish the graves of the clans. 1m SE of the

The original 18th-century bridge over the River Dulnain at Carrbridge

battlefield are the Stones of Clava, a group of neolithic or Bronze Age burial cairns and markers.

Kincraig, *Highland*   NH 8305
An interesting attraction in this holiday centre at the NW end of Loch Insh is the Highland Wildlife Park. Native animals of Scotland past and present can be seen here, including wolves, bears, reindeer, European bison and wildcat.

Kingussie, *Highland*   NH 7500
Beautifully situated in wooded Strath Spey to the W of the Cairngorm Mountains, the town is a good centre for pony-trekking, walking, touring and fishing, as well as water-sports. The Highland Folk Museum has an interesting display of Highland crafts and furnishings; a farming museum; and a reconstructed Hebridean mill and 'black' house. ½m S across the Spey are the ruins of Wade's 18th-century Ruthven Barracks.

Nairn, *Highland*   NH 8756
Sheltered by mountains to the N and W and with good sandy beaches and a dry, sunny climate, Nairn has become a popular holiday resort. Lovely wooded countryside is within easy reach.

Beauly's salmon attract wealthy anglers but, near the village, permits are cheaper

Glenlivet, produced at this Dufftown distillery, is one of several local malt whiskies

Ballater, *Grampian*   NO 3695
This pleasant little town was not established until 1770 when mineral wells with
supposedly health-giving properties were
found 2m SE. It is now a popular
Deeside summer resort where Highland
Games are held each year. In August and
September, when the Royal Family is in
residence at Balmoral, the Victoria Barracks house the royal guard of honour.
Glen Muick, to the SW, is a particularly
attractive glen. Situated here is Birkhall,
a royal home used by The Queen Mother.

Braemar, *Grampian*   NO 1491
Standing among heather-covered hills at
1,100ft Braemar has a bracing climate. It
is best known for its Royal Highland
Gathering held every September.
Initiated in 1832, the Gathering was
popularised by Queen Victoria's attend-
ance and the present Queen often attends
this display of piping and athletic events.
Built in 1628, picturesque Braemar
Castle overlooking the River Dee was
burned down in 1689 and largely rebuilt
in 1748.

Crathie, *Grampian*   NO 2695
½m W of Crathie Church, lying on a
curve of the River Dee in a large wooded
estate, is Balmoral Castle, the Royal
Family's Highland home. The original
house bought by Queen Victoria was
pulled down in 1853 and rebuilt in
Scottish baronial style.

Dufftown, *Grampian*   NJ 3240
Famous now for its whisky distilleries,
including Glenfiddich, the town was laid
out by James Duff, 4th Earl of Fife, in
1817. 1m N are the picturesque 15th- and
16th-century ruins of moated Balvenie
Castle.

Duffus, *Grampian*   NJ 1668
On a great mound 1½m SE of the village
are the ruins of Duffus Castle, its eight-
acre bailey surrounding the rebuilt 15th-
century hall and 14th-century tower, now
split in two. To the NE is Gordonstoun
School where the Duke of Edinburgh
and his three sons were educated.

Elgin, *Grampian*   NJ 2162
This ancient city is the market town for
the fertile Laich of Moray and a popular
touring centre, but is perhaps best
known for its fine ruined cathedral.
Dating from the 13th century, the cathedral was burnt in 1390 by the notorious
outlawed son of Robert II, the 'Wolf of
Badenoch', and later suffered further
damage, even becoming a quarry for
building stone. Despite this, much of
early interest remains. The Elgin
Museum contains a world-famous
collection of fossils.

Forres, *Grampian*   NJ 0358
In a sheltered situation near where the
scenic River Findhorn enters Findhorn
Bay, Forres is mentioned in Shakespeare's play *Macbeth* as the site of King
Duncan's court. The Falconer Museum
has displays of local history, wildlife,

geology, ethnography and archaeological
finds from Culbin, near Findhorn. From
19th-century Nelson Tower on the den-
sely-wooded Cluny Hill there are magnificent views of the Moray Firth, Black
Isle and inland mountains. The sculpted
20ft-high Sueno's Stone, 1m NE, may
commemorate the victory won by Sueno,
son of the King of Denmark, over
Malcolm II in 1008.

Grantown-on-Spey, *Highland*   NJ 0327
Situated on the beautiful salmon-filled
River Spey, this elegant granite Georgian
town has long been popular with anglers.
Now it is also a year-round resort, with
skiers finding it convenient for the Cairngorm snow-slopes.

Huntly, *Grampian*   NJ 5339
An attractive little market town surrounded by hills, Huntly lies in the angle
between the River Deveron and its
tributary, the Bogie, and so is popular
with anglers. In a beautiful wooded park,
on a green mound overlooking a gorge of
the Deveron, stands roofless Huntly
Castle. The castle dates largely from 1602
but the Norman motte and medieval keep
are evidence of its earlier history. The
Agricultural Museum, 3½m SE, contains a large, varied collection including
farm implements and dairy utensils.

Keith, *Grampian*   NJ 4350
Keith consists of the Old Town, whose
oldest building is the Milton Tower, built
in 1480, and the New Town built in the
mid 18th century and full of character.
The town is an agricultural centre, with
woollen mills and distilleries, including
the oldest working distillery in Scotland,
dating from 1786. The picturesque Auld
Brig O'Keith dates from 1609 and joins
the town with Fife Keith on the opposite
bank of the River Isla.

Lossiemouth, *Grampian*   NJ 2370
A resort and fishing port with sandy
beaches to the W, sand-dune-backed
beaches to the E, and a rocky harbour
area, Lossiemouth was the birthplace in
1866 of Ramsay MacDonald, first
Labour Prime Minister. 2m W there are
caves displaying remarkable rock
formations.

Rothes, *Grampian*   NJ 2749
Pleasantly situated on the River Spey
between Ben Aigan (1,544ft) and the
wooded viewpoint of Conerock Hill,
Rothes is the home of the well-known
Glen Grant Distillery, established in
1840. Regarded as one of the best malt
whiskies in the world, Glen Grant is still
distilled in the traditional way although
the most modern equipment is used.

Traditional Scottish souvenirs on display in a village shop in Braemar

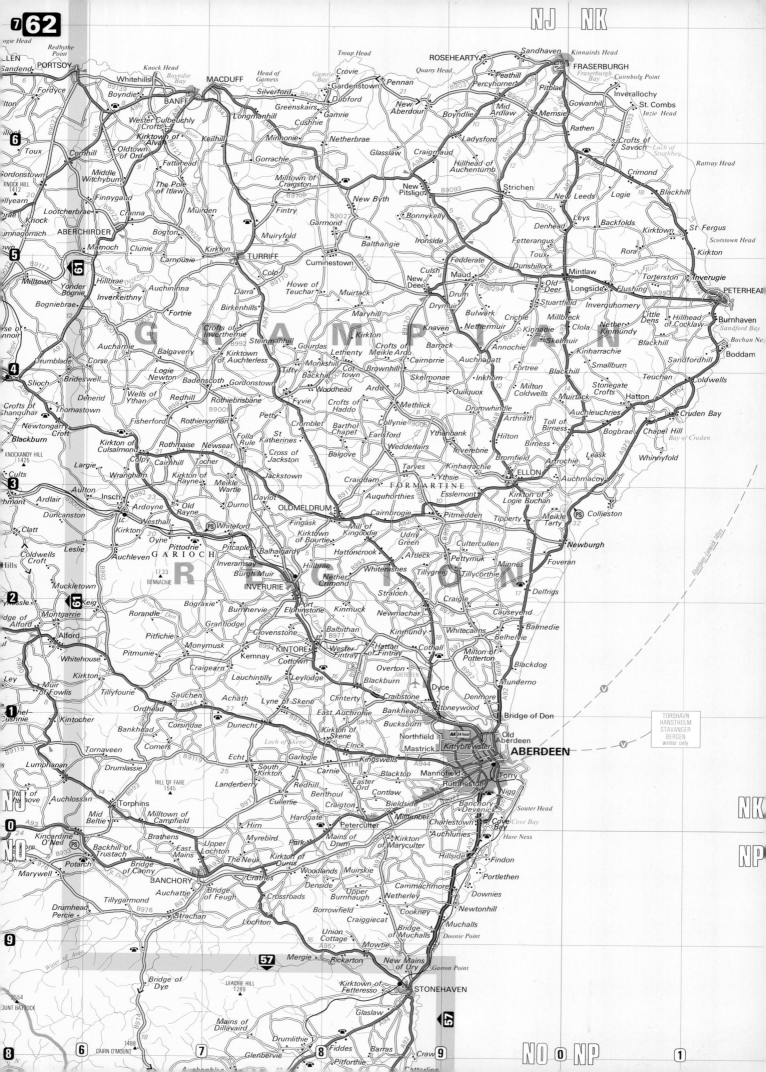

Aberdeen, *Grampian* NJ 9305
Scotland's third largest city, the 'granite city' of Aberdeen has a very varied character. Administrative, commercial and educational centre for the north of Scotland, the city's industries include engineering and paper-making, but in addition it has a splendid harbour and the largest fishing port in Scotland. Since the mid 1970s it has become Europe's North Sea oil capital, necessitating extensive new provision of housing and other facilities, yet it still remains one of Scotland's most popular seaside holiday resorts, with 2m of sandy beaches backed by a wide expanse of grassland. The attractive parks in the city have won several 'Britain in Bloom' trophies and there are many facilities for amusement and sport. The Old Town is dominated by the ancient university colleges, Marischal (founded in 1593) and King's (1494) with many interesting buildings added through the centuries. Little remains of the Norman origins of St Machar's Cathedral. The nave dates from the 15th century and the twin spires and heraldic ceiling from about 1520. Places to visit include the art gallery and museum; Cruickshank Botanic Gardens; James Dun's House – a museum with changing exhibitions; 16th-century Provost Ross's House which contains a maritime museum; and Provost Skene's House, a museum of local history and social life.

Banff, *Grampian* NJ 6863
Steep terraced streets rise from the pleasure-craft-filled harbour in this ancient seaport and resort. The 18th-century castle which overlooks the sea stands on the site of a 12th-century royal residence. Duff House was never completed but ranks among the finest works of Georgian Baroque architecture in Britain. Banff Museum has an exhibition of British birds and exhibits of local interest. To the N the coast is rocky, but Boyndie Bay to the W is a mixture of sand and rocks.

Crathes, *Grampian* NO 7596
Set in a magnificent early 18th-century

A distinctive lantern tower crowns King's College Chapel in Old Aberdeen

Ruins of 13th-century Deer Abbey stand in the lovely grounds of Pitfour House

formal garden with ancient yew hedges, picturesque Crathes Castle is an L-plan tower house. Completed in 1596 and undamaged, it is noted for its painted ceilings. Nature trails through the wooded grounds are especially attractive.

Fraserburgh, *Grampian* NJ 9966
Although situated in an exposed position on a rocky headland, the town is a popular holiday resort with an extensive stretch of sand. Since the decline of the herring industry the fishing port now deals mainly with white fish. A lighthouse was built on the lower floors of a 15th-century castle on Kinnairds Head and another guards the harbour entrance.

Kemnay, *Grampian* NJ 7315
Now a dormitory town for Aberdeen, the village developed after 1830 when its first granite quarry was opened. The granite was of such a quality that it found its way all over the world. 3m S is Castle Fraser. Completed in 1636, it is considered by many to be the most spectacular of the Castles of Mar.

Macduff, *Grampian* NJ 7064
A picturesque fishing port and holiday resort, Macduff's steep streets lead to a large and busy harbour. There is a fine outdoor sea-water swimming pool, with remarkable rocky outcrops nearby.

Old Deer, *Grampian* NJ 9747
An attractive village in the wooded valley of the South Water of Ugie, Old Deer was once the site of a monastery founded in AD520 by the Celts. Nearby is the Cistercian Deer Abbey founded in 1219.

Peterhead, *Grampian* NK 1346
With its splendid harbour, Peterhead's major importance was, until recently, as a fishing port for herring and white fish. At one time it was also the whaling capital of Scotland, and the Arbuthnot Museum and Art Gallery has exhibits illustrating in particular the fishing and whaling industries. Since the mid 1970s however North Sea oil exploration has

made Peterhead a boom town as a supply base for oil rigs, extensive developments taking place at Buchan Ness, 3m S.

Pitmedden, *Grampian* NJ 8927
The 100-acre Pitmedden estate contains a fine recreated 17th-century garden with elaborate floral designs, sundials, pavilions and fountains. There is also a museum of farming life. 2m NE, off the B999, is Tolquhon Castle, a roofless late 16th-century quadrangular mansion enclosing a tower built 100 years earlier. Haddo House, 2m further N, was designed by William Adam in 1731 for the 2nd Earl of Aberdeen.

Turriff, *Grampian* NJ 7249
Overlooking the confluence of the River Deveron and the Water of Idoch, this small red sandstone town is the centre of an area rich in castles and tower-houses. Delgatie Castle, 2m E, has a 97-step turnpike stair and two interesting 16th-century painted ceilings. Craigston Castle, 4m NE, has altered little since its construction in the early 17th century.

Old Aberdeen's Marischal College, rebuilt in 1844, is considered to be one of the finest granite buildings in the world

Balivanich, *Benbecula,*
Western Isles   NF 7755
Once the site of a monastery, the village
is now used by the army as a headquarters and near here there is an airport. The
island, fairly flat and dotted with lochs, is
joined to South Uist by a bridge and to
North Uist by a causeway. Prince
Charles Edward Stuart escaped from
here to Skye in a rowing boat in 1746,
dressed as Flora Madonald's maid, Betty
Burke.

Carloway, *Isle of Lewis,*
Western Isles   NB 2042
The well-preserved Dun Carloway Broch
(Pictish tower) stands 30ft high and was
built as a defensive structure between
100BC and 300AD.

Castlebay, *Barra,*
Western Isles   NL 6698
The island's village 'capital' of substantial stone houses, reached by ferry from
Oban, Castlebay takes its name from
early 12th-century Kisimul Castle set on
a small islet in the harbour. This restored
stronghold can be visited by rowing boat.
The village has a large harbour and
herring station. Another part of the island's economy is its succulent cockles,
whose shells are crushed for grit and
poultry-feed. Twelve miles of road encir-
cle the island, and the varied landscape
includes barren mountains and cattle
pasture. At Great Cockle Strand, a 2m
stretch of sand, there is an airstrip, and
there are fine views from 1,260ft Heaval
in the S. The Gaelic spoken on the island
is considered to be particularly pure.

Garynahine, *Isle of Lewis,*
Western Isles   NB 2331
On bleak moorland stand the remarkable
Standing Stones of Callanish. Second
only to Stonehenge in importance, the
arrangement includes a circle of 13 large
stones, a chambered cairn, and a double
row of 19 stones forming an avenue.
Their function is not known.

Kirkwall, *Orkney Islands*   HY 4410
On the largest of the 67 islands that make
up Orkney, Kirkwall has been capital for
centuries. This attractive old town of
narrow twisting streets clustering round
the cathedral (dating from the 12th century) is a busy port that was made a royal
burgh by James III in about 1486.
Although at their nearest point the islands

are about 6½m from the Scottish mainland, until 1468 they were ruled by
Norway and Denmark. The land is green,
treeless and fertile, and the islanders
are cattle farmers rather than fishermen.
With an ancient history, the island
contains much of archaeological interest,
including Skara Brae, a neolithic village
settlement. Tankerness House is now
occupied by a museum of Orkney history
with archaeological collections.

Lerwick, *Shetland*   HU 4741
110m from the Scottish mainland, the
100 islands that make up the Shetlands
are nearer the Arctic circle than London.
Seventeen islands are inhabited and
Lerwick, on the largest island, is the administrative and commercial capital, its
sheltered harbour busy with fishing boats
from several countries. The summer days
are long, with only two hours of twilight
in mid June.

Lochboisdale, *S Uist,*
Western Isles   NF 7820
Chief village and port for the island,
Lochboisdale is also becoming a sea-
angling centre. Angling is available on 18
lochs as well, but on the whole the
islanders (who are mainly Roman
Catholic and stongly Celtic) rely on farming and crofting for their livelihoods. The
22m-long island is only 8m wide and
bisected by the A865. To the W is flat
'machair' (sand and marram grass) and to

the E virtually inaccessible hills where
Prince Charles Edward hid for three
weeks in 1746.

Lochmaddy, *N Uist*
Western Isles   NF 9268
With a pier on the trout and salmon-rich
Loch Maddy, this is the island's main
village and there are several surprisingly
large residential buildings. The island,
predominantly Protestant, has over 150
lochs and the barren hills of the south are
riddled with prehistoric remains.
Balranald Nature Reserve has a wide
variety of bird life.

Stornoway, *Isle of Lewis,*
Western Isles   NB 4333
'Capital' of the Western Isles and largest
town and seaport in the Hebrides, Stornoway has good shopping and leisure
facilities. There are good ferry services to
the mainland and a large airport. Oil
explorations are in progress near the
Isles, but the traditional production of
Harris Tweed and knitted garments
continues.

Stromness, *Orkney Islands*   HY 2509
In its sheltered harbour backed by steep
hills, the town became a trading port in
the 17th century and grew in importance
in the 18th century. The museum deals
mainly with Orkney maritime and
natural history.

Sullom, *Shetland*   HU 3573
The exploration of vast oil reserves and
the siting of one of the world's great oil
terminals at Sullom Voe (loch) have
made profound changes in the Shetlands.

Tarbert, *Isle of Harris,*
Western Isles   NB 1500
A single terraced street on an isthmus
between East and West Loch Tarbert,
with a steamer pier on the former, makes
up the isle's only proper village. Sheds
here sell the famous Harris Tweed.
Harris and Lewis are not separated by
water but by the rugged mountains of
Harris.

Overlooking Stornoway Harbour is the clock-tower of the splendid town hall

Sunset over the Western Isles from Lochboisdale, South Uist's main village

SHETLAND ISLANDS

ORKNEY ISLANDS

SCALE
0 5 10 mls
0 5 10 15 kms

Outer Hebrides (Isle of Lewis)

Butt of Lewis
Foropie
Lionel Port of Ness
Dell Skigersta
Ness
Cellar Head
Shader Borve
Brue Borve
Bragar Barvas
Arnol MUIRNEAG 813
Shawbost A858 Tolsta Head
North Tolsta
Garenin Tolsta
Carloway BEINN MHOLACH 955
Gt Bernera Chaolais Back
Gallan Head W Loch Roag Aird Tong
Valtos Newmarket B895
Timsgarry Breasclete STORNOWAY
Ardroil Miavaig Achmore Eye Peninsula
Cruhlivig Garnahine Garrabost
Islivig Garynahine Knock Bayble
Aird Brenish Balallan Chicken Head
Brenish Loch Suainaval Laxay
Loch Grunavat Kershader Crossbost
Mealasta I Anivuaich Cromore
Scarp Gravir
Hushinish TIRGA MOR 2227 Kebock Hd
Hushinish Pt Forest of Harris PARK Loch Odhairn
Amhuinnsuidhe Ardvourlie Lemreway
Taransay Seaforth
Glorigs CLISHAM 2622 BEINN MHOR 1874
Taransay West Loch Tarbert Loch Seaforth
HARRIS Tarbert
Toe Head Carnach
Shilay Scalpay
Pabbay Northton Grosebay
Ensay Finsbay Shiant Islands
Berneray Rodel
Sound of Pabbay Killegray
Renish Point

THE MINCH
THE LITTLE MINCH
SEA OF THE HEBRIDES

Stornoway-Ullapool 3hrs 15mins
Lochmaddy-Uig 2hrs
Lochmaddy-Tarbert 2hrs
Tarbert-Uig 2hrs

North Uist / Benbecula / South Uist / Barra

Griminish Pt Vallay
Tigharry Sollas
Bayhead NORTH UIST
Lochmaddy
SOUTH LEE 920
Locheport
Baleshare EAVAL 1139
Carinish Ronay
Balivanich BENBECULA
B892
BENBECULA
Creagorry
Ardivachar Pt Wiay
Stilligarry
Verran I HOWMORE
HECLA 1988 Usinish
SOUTH UIST
Daliburgh BEINN MHOR 2033
Lochboisdale Loch Eynort
Kilbride Stuley
A888
Fiaray Eriskay
Scurrival Pt Fuday
Barra Stack Islands Gighay
Eirean Head Hellisay
Borve HEAVAL 1260 Bruernish Pt
Castlebay Muldoanich
Sandray Vatersay
Rosinish

Haskeir
Gasker
Monach Islands
Sound of Monach
Sound of Harris
Sound of Barra

Castlebay-Lochboisdale-Oban
Castlebay-Oban 5hrs 20mins

Shetland Islands

Muckle Flugga The Noup
Herma Ness Lamba Ness
Burrafirth Norwick
Baltasound The Nev
Westing BALTASOUND
Gloup Holm Uyea
North Neaps Huney
Ramna Stacks Gloup Hascosay
Point of Fethaland Cullivoe Belmont
Uyea Gutcher Linga FETLAR
North Roe YELL Funzie
South-haa Herra Tresta The Snap
The Faither Mid Yell Rams Ness
Muckle Ossa West Sandwick Otterswick
Collafirth Ulsta Burravoe
Heylor Brae Muckle Skerry
Esha Ness Sullom Housay
Stenness Oil Terminal Out Skerries
Hillswick Mossbank The Guens
Skaw Taing
ST MAGNUS BAY
Ve Skerries Laxo Whalsay
Muckle Roe Voe The Haa
Fogla Skerry Vementry Neap
Papa Stour Papa Little South Nesting Bay
Sandness Clousta Moul of Eswick
Dale Aith Gletness
ZETLAND Tresta
Wats Ness Walls Gruting
Vaila Sand Gunnista
Culswick Score Head
The Deeps LERWICK
Skelda Ness Scalloway Isle of Noss
Foula Oxna Kirkabister
Ham Hamnavoe BRESSAY
West Burra Quarff Bard Ness
Fladdabister
South Havra Helli Ness
St Ninians Isle Mousa
B9122
Scousburgh Sandwick
Fora Ness Boddam
Quendale SUMBURGH
Fitful Head Toab
Ladys Holm Pool of Virkie
Horse Island Sumburgh Head
Sumburgh Roost

SCALE
0 5 10 mls
0 5 10 15 kms

Lerwick-Aberdeen 14hrs

Orkney Islands

Mull Head Dennis Hd
Bow Head Papa Westray North Ronaldsay
Noup Head Hollandstoun
Pierowall Strom Ness
THE NORTH SOUND
Westray Stanger Hd Sanday
Midbea Rapness Broughtown
Berst Ness Calf Overbister
Sacquoy Hd Faray Braeswick Start Pt
Rousay Eday Spur Ness Northwall
Warbister Backaland SANDAY SOUND
Brough Head Egilsay Holm of Huip
The Barony Brinyan Linga Holm Papa Stronsay
Twatt Wyre Aith Whitehall Mill Bay
Redland Gairsay Rothiesholm STRONSAY
B9056 Sound Lamb Head
Downby Gorseness Bay of Holland
Bay of Skaill Balfour SHAPINSAY
Yesnaby Sandgarth
Finstown Wide Firth
STROMNESS Rerwick Head
Graemsay KIRKWALL Mull Head
St Johns Head Skaill Point of Ayre
Old Man of Hoy Orphir St Marys Copinsay
WARD Whaness Glims Holm
Rackwick Cava Hunda
HOY Fara Burray
Lyness Flotta St Margarets Hope
Little Ayre Swithia
Hurliness Waterinhouse South Walls
South Ronaldsay
Swona Burwick
Brough Ness
Stroma Pentland Skerries

SCAPA FLOW
PENTLAND FIRTH

Stromness-Scrabster 2hrs

SCALE
0 5 10 mls
0 5 10 15 kms

Ardmair, *Highland*   NH 1198
The village of Ardmair lies above Loch
Kanaird – a bay of outer Loch Broom. St
Martin built his chapel on the 397ft-high
round hill of Isle Martin which fills the
bay's mouth. The island once had a small
population, but like the Summer Isles to
the N, it was deserted by the end of
the last war when the herring shoals
diminished.

Aultbea, *Highland*   NG 8789
The pier of this neat little crofting village
on Loch Ewe is sheltered by the Isle of
Ewe. Formerly a war-time base, the sea-
loch is being further developed by
NATO.

Braemore Junction, *Highland*   NH 2278
Near here well-grown woods hide the
200ft-deep gorge of Corrieshalloch,
carved from solid rock by the River
Droma which plunges 150ft as the Falls
of Measach towards Loch Broom. A
19th-century suspension bridge a little
way downstream from the falls provides a
safe vantage point. To the NE the vertical
cliffs of 3,041ft Seana Bhraigh rise between the Inverlael and Freevater forests.

Gairloch, *Highland*   NG 8076
Now developed as a tourist centre, this
small village on Loch Gairloch still has a
busy harbour; salmon are landed in the
morning; whitefish, prawns, lobsters and
crabs in the evening. Safe sandy beaches
stretch away to the W and there are
distant views of the Outer Hebrides. The
Gairloch Heritage Museum traces the
way of life in the village from earliest
times to the present day.

Kinlochewe, *Highland*   NH 0261
At the foot of 3,309ft Beinn Eighe and at
the head of beautiful 12m-long Loch
Maree, this scattered village lies amidst
magnificent scenery. Thousands of acres,
including Beinn Eighe, have been protected as a nature reserve since 1951. On
the west bank of the loch, the 700-acre
woodlands of Coille na Gas-Leitre are a
remnant of the ancient Caledonian Forest
which once spread right across the Highlands. Pine marten, wildcat, otter, fox,
deer, golden eagle, buzzard and pere-
grine falcon are all established here. Beinn
Eighe is composed of 750-million-year-
old red sandstone, topped by quartzite.
The slopes of Letterewe Forest and
3,217ft Slioch (the Spear) rise from the
eastern shore of the loch. To the N and E
is one of the most spectacular and remote
mountain districts in Scotland. Plentiful
sea- and loch-trout and salmon also
attract many anglers to the area.

Little Gruinard, *Highland*   NG 9489
The road round scenically beautiful
Gruinard Bay closely follows the beach.
The bay has a dozen mainly rocky coves,
but several have sweeps of unusual pink
sand. Gruinard Island, a grim place in so
lovely an area, is still infected by anthrax
deposited during germ warfare testing in
World War II and access is therefore
strictly prohibited.

In the 19th century many Highlanders sailed from Lochinver to Australia

Lochinver, *Highland*   NC 0922
This busy little fishing village lies on
Loch Inver on the rocky Assynt coast.
The beach is pebble but there are sandy
coves at Achmelvich, Clachtoll and
Clashnessie on the Rhu Stoer peninsula.
The village is a good angling centre with
300 small lochs within easy reach, as well
as the salmon-filled Rivers Inver and
Kirkaig. For walkers there is the wild
hinterland of Glencanisp Forest, and for
climbers 2,399ft Suilven, known as the
Matterhorn of Scotland because of its
dangerous cliff faces.

Poolewe, *Highland*   NG 8580
Situated at the head of Loch Ewe,
Poolewe also has excellent views down
the entire length of Loch Maree, the
largest entirely natural loch in Scotland.
With both lochs so near, the village is a
good centre for anglers. Remarkable 64-
acre Inverewe Gardens, on a headland
jutting into Loch Ewe, were created just
over a century ago from barren ground.
Planned as a wild garden it is now one of
the best sub-tropical gardens in North
West Europe – extraordinary as the

garden lies near the 58th parallel, shared
by Hudson Bay and Siberia.

Red Point, *Highland*   NG 7368
The outermost point on Loch Torridon,
this croft, and those at Opinan and Port
Henderson, have sandy beaches safe for
bathing. In clear weather there are views
down the Inner Sound to the Cuillins of
Skye and SE across Loch Torridon to the
Kintail Mountains.

Ullapool, *Highland*   NH 1294
This neatly laid-out village on Loch
Broom was founded by the British
Fishery Society in 1788 to expand the
herring industry. A large fleet still uses
the long pier, also used by a daily car-
ferry to Stornoway in Lewis and motor-
boats operate regular cruises to the
Summer Isles. The village is unrivalled
on the west coast for sea-angling and
shark-fishing, and although the beach is
shingle, superb scenery makes Ullapool a
popular touring centre. Several ruined
brochs can be seen in the vicinity of the
village, particularly Dun Canna 4m N on
the Kanaird estuary.

Trips to the Summer Isles are among the many cruises available from Ullapool

Ardgay, *Highland*   NH 5990
The White Stone of Kincardine in the
market square of this small village has a
strange history. The stone once marked
the site of a winter market whose location
varied from year to year. The inhabitants
of Ardgay decided to keep the market in
their own village and the stone is now
sited on the village green.

Bonar Bridge, *Highland*   NH 6191
Travellers once crossed the firth by ferry
but after 99 people died in the 1809
Meikle Ferry disaster, Thomas Telford
built a bridge here. Touring areas near
the village include picturesque Strath
Carron to the W and Strath Oykell to the
NW. Loch Migdale lies in a wooded
setting to the E and there are several hut
circles and Stone Age burial cairns in the
neighbourhood.

Cromarty, *Highland*   NH 7766
A small attractive seaport at the mouth of
Cromarty Firth, for seven centuries the
town was a royal burgh. At one time a
busy fishing port, much of the area has
now been developed in connection with
North Sea oil. The sandy beaches are
scattered with shingle and bathing is safe
except after heavy rain when there are
strong currents in the Cromarty Firth.
Many of the old buildings in the town
have been restored. Of particular interest
is a low white-harled thatched cottage
dating from 1711, birthplace in 1802 of
Hugh Miller who became a well-known
geologist. The cottage is open as a
personal museum and belongs to the
National Trust for Scotland.

Dornoch, *Highland*   NH 7989
Formerly county town of Sutherland,
this ancient royal burgh is popular with
holiday-makers and golfers. To the N
and S there are extensive sandy beaches
and the world-renowned golf course
dates from 1616 – one of the first courses
established. The much-renovated and rebuilt cathedral was founded in 1224 for
the Bishop of Caithness and, now a
parish church, is a landmark for miles
around. A stone marks the site where a
woman was burnt to death for witchcraft
in 1722, the last such execution to take
place in Scotland.

Edderton, *Highland*   NH 7184
On the NW edge of the village is a 10ft-
high red sandstone Pictish symbol stone
and there are the remains of a large cairn
traditionally supposed to commemorate a
battle against Norse invaders 2m NW.

Golspie, *Highland*   NH 8399
A busy centre for the farms and crofts of
the hinterland, and one of the Highland
Region's administrative centres, Golspie
is also a tourist resort with a sandy beach
dotted with outcrops of rock. Trout and
salmon-fishing are available, with nearby
walks on wooded 1,293ft Ben Bhraggie.
Further off lofty moorland rises to
1,464ft Ben Lundie. Dunrobin Castle,
1m NE along the coast, is the ancient seat
of the Earls and Dukes of Sutherland and

The fishing village of Portmahomack lies at the mouth of Dornock Firth

contains a wide variety of furniture,
paintings and exhibits. An inscribed
Gaelic stone on the old bridge in the town
marks the rallying point of the Clan
Sutherland.

Invergordon, *Highland*   NH 7168
A castle stood here in the 13th century
and the area was known as Inverbreakie.
The present town only grew up after the
castle and estate were bought by Sir
William Gordon in the early 18th century, who gave the town his name.
Cromarty Firth is one of the deepest and
safest anchorages in the British Isles and
so the seaport became a vital dockyard
and fuelling station for the Royal Navy's
biggest ships during both world wars.
The town is now also a busy industrial
centre.

Nigg, *Highland*   NH 8071
Due to deep channels the extensive
sands here are hazardous to swimmers
and walkers. In 1972 the world's largest
dock was built here on reclaimed land for
the construction of North Sea oil-
production platforms.

Portmahomack, *Highland*   NH 9184
This small fishing village is now a resort
with a sheltered sandy bay. 4m NE at the
tip of the peninsula there is a lighthouse
and there are wide views from here. The
area has the distinction of having the
lowest rainfall in Scotland.

Tain, *Highland*   NH 7782
On the shores of Dornoch Firth, Tain is
an ancient royal burgh and agricultural
centre. For centuries it was a place of
pilgrimage. St Duthus, born here in
about AD1000, died in Ireland but
his remains were later returned to a
chapel here, destroyed by fire in 1427.

King James IV regularly visited the
shrine and the road leading S is still
called King's Causeway. Tain's sandy
beach, dotted with shingle and rock, is
reached via a footbridge over the river.

*Oil platforms at Nigg seen across
Nigg Bay from the churchyard at Kilmuir
where the grave and monument of
Flora Macdonald can be seen*

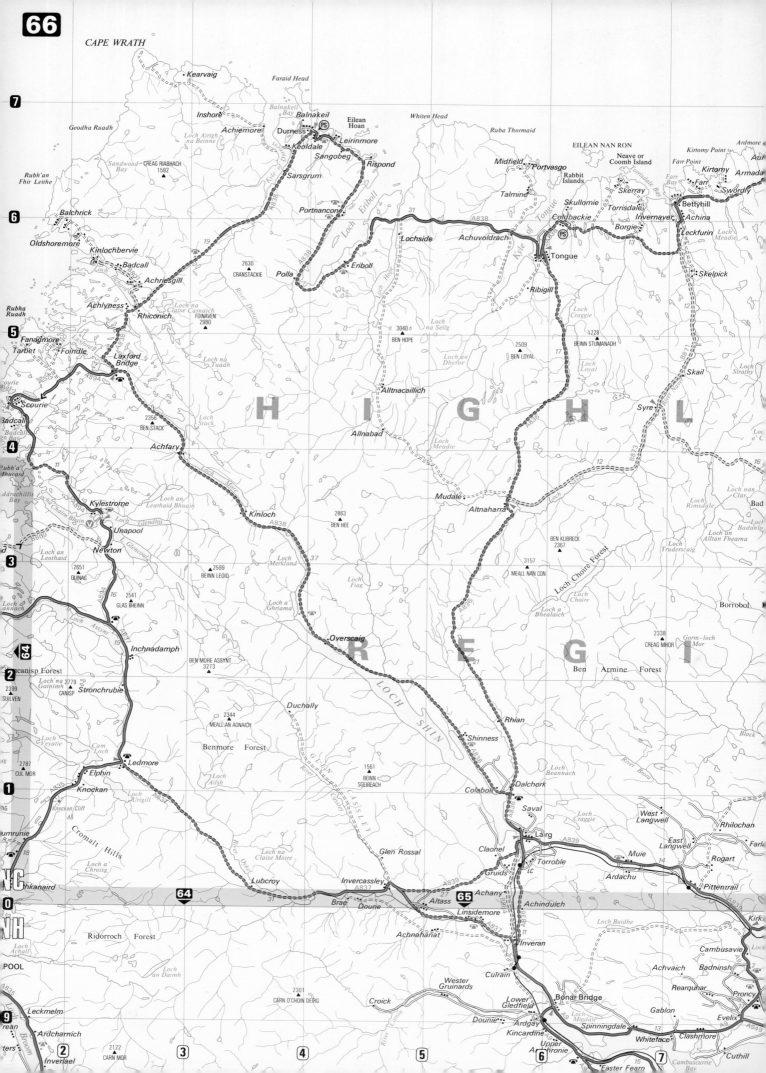

The wild, unspoilt shoreline of Scotland's northernmost coast provides numerous deserted beaches such as these at Bettyhill

Balnakeil, *Highland*   NC 3968
The 12th-century ruins of Durness Old
Church overlook the fine sandy shores of
the bay. Puffins can be seen on the
spectacular cliffs of the headland. Bal-
nakiel Craft Village is a community of
artist and craftsmen, established during
1964 in an old radar station.

Bettyhill, *Highland*   NC 7061
Named after Elizabeth, Countess of
Sutherland, who founded it for crofters
evicted by the clearances, this small village at the mouth of the River Naver is
now an angling centre. Strathnaver
Museum contains a collection of of home-
made furnishings, domestic and farm
implements and Gaelic books. The Invernaver Nature Reserve to the W has a
wide range of wildlife and plants within a
small area, and there is a bird sanctuary
at Torrisdale Bay.

Durness, *Highland*   NC 4067
A scattered crofting community set on
top of limestone bluffs above Sango Bay,
Durness is the nearest village to lonely
Cape Wrath and its lighthouse. The Cape
lies 11m away over bleak uninhabited
moorland known as The Parph. A small
boat crosses the narrow kyle and in
the summer months the Cape can be
reached by mini-bus. There is no land
between the Cape and, due N, the North
Pole. The 900ft-high cliffs of Clo Mor
near Durness are the highest in Britain.

Eriboll, *Highland*   NC 4356
On the E side of the wildly beautiful
10m-long Loch Eriboll, the tiny village
has a magnificent setting. The loch is
deep and well-sheltered by the surrounding mountains. In the war it provided a
safe naval anchorage and Nazi U-boats
eventually surrendered here. S of Whiten
Head, on the E side of the loch, there are
very fine cliffs and caves, the latter being
the only breeding ground on the mainland of the rare Atlantic grey seal.

Inchnadamph, *Highland*   NC 2522
This crofting community lies in an area
of interest to both geologists and anglers.
The land to the NW is formed by Arch-
ean gneiss, the oldest type of rock in the
world and 3,200 acres of limestone are

preserved as a nature reserve. Here, on
the lower slopes of 3,273ft Ben More
Assynt, 4m SE of the village, are the Allt
nan Uamh caves where two 8,000-
year-old human skeletons have been
found. 1m W on the shores of Loch
Assynt are the ruined towers of Ardvreck
Castle where the famous Marquis of
Montrose was imprisoned in 1649.
Further W the loch, with wooded bays
and tiny islands, becomes more
interesting.

Kinlochbervie, *Highland*   NC 2158
Beautifully situated on a hill above Loch
Inchard, this tiny village is the most
important fishing port of the North West
Highlands. It has two bays with harbours
and piers. To the N the narrow road
continues to the fishing village of Sheigra,
beyond which a track leads to the
beautiful, and deserted, 2m-wide
Sandwood Bay.

Lairg, *Highland*   NC 5806
A thriving little market village, Lairg
stands at the junction of roads leading W
and N into some of the wildest, most
dramatic scenery in the Highlands. To
the NW is 17m-long Loch Shin, used to
produce hydro-electricity but nevertheless popular with anglers.

Laxford Bridge, *Highland*   NC 2347
Not really a village but a scattering of
cottages at the head of Loch Laxford, the
area is at the heart of superb angling

country – *lax* is in fact the Norse word for
salmon. Nearby Loch Stack, lying beneath 2,346ft Ben Stack, is certainly one
of Scotland's finest fishing lochs, while
the surrounding country contains a variety of wildlife including black-throated
divers, otters, pine martens and deer.

Leirinmore, *Highland*   NC 4267
A cliff-top path near this little settlement
leads to 203ft-long Smoo Cave, one of the
most dramatic natural features in northern Scotland. The cave, in limestone
cliffs, is 130ft wide and 30ft high. Two
further chambers can only be reached by
expert potholers. The cave probably gets
its name from the old Norse word,
smuga, meaning cleft.

Rhiconich, *Highland*   NC 2552
The strange landscape round this tiny
hamlet is almost lunar in character:
moorland littered with ancient rocks and
pock-marked by countless lochs and
lochans. To the SE stretches the largely
uninhabited expanse of the Forest of
Reay. Dominated by 2,980ft Foinaven,
this is a land of bogs and craggy hills.

Tongue, *Highland*   NC 5957
A little angling resort on the sandy shores
of the Kyle of Tongue. Ruined Castle
Varrich may have been the fortress of an
11th-century Norse king and later
became a Mackay stronghold. It stands
on a headland where the little stream of
Allt and Rhian enters the Kyle.

Durness – a remote sheep-farming community in the lonely Highlands

The River Helmsdale provides some of the Highland's best trout and salmon fishing

Altnaharra, *Highland*   NC 5635
Spectacular mountain scenery surrounds this tiny angling resort at the extreme western tip of Loch Naver. The ruins of cottages forcibly abandoned during the infamous 19th-century clearances can be seen on the fertile land beside the loch. There are also several prehistoric remains near the loch, including a Celtic cross and Pictish brochs.

Brora, *Highland*   NC 9003
With an extensive sandy beach surrounded by magnificent mountain and moorland scenery, and with many more attractive bays along the nearby indented rocky coastline, Brora has become a holiday centre. Situated at the mouth of the salmon- and trout-filled River Brora, the town is popular with anglers and there is also a golf course. The coal mine, now closed, was the earliest in Scotland, being worked from 1529. Other small industries include a whisky distillery and woollen mills. The small fishing harbour is now little used.

Dunbeath, *Highland*   ND 1629
This scattered little fishing village takes its name from the nearby ancient broch known as Dun Beath. 1m S lies the imposing cliff-top Dunbeath Castle. Thatched Laidhay Croft Museum in Dunbeath is a typical Caithness-type longhouse furnished in traditional style.

Helmsdale, *Highland*   ND 0215
Lying between high moorland ridges, this little fishing village has a natural harbour and employed many crofters during the 19th century. The A9 reaches 700ft above sea level near the rocky Ord of Caithness, with splendid views of cliffs and ravines, and desolate moorland stretching away to the NW.

John O'Groats, *Highland*   ND 3874
Near the NE tip of the Scottish mainland, this spot, named after a Dutchman Jan de Groot who settled here in about 1500, is 864m from Land's End by road. The most northerly point is in fact Dunnet Head with its lighthouse. To the S are spectacular 200ft-high sandstone cliffs and on the beach pretty cowrie shells known as Groatie Buckies may be found.

Lybster, *Highland*   ND 2435
One of the largest fishing villages on this wild, rocky coast of steep grey cliffs, Lybster's spacious well-planned streets of dignified houses stand above a busy little harbour. To the NE of the harbour is a Celtic cross set in a block of sandstone, and the area is rich in other antiquities. 5m N are two megolithic chambered cairns of about 3,000-2,000BC, known as the Grey Cairns of Camster.

Mey, *Highland*   ND 2872
Dating from 1568, the Castle of Mey is a holiday home of Queen Elizabeth the Queen Mother. From the gardens, which are open to the public, there are fine views across the Pentland Firth to the Orkneys.

Reay, *Highland*   NC 9664
In 1955 an area 2m E of the village became the coastal site of the first British experimental atomic fast reactor, the Dounreay Fast Reactor. The spectacular steel sphere in which it is housed is 135ft in diameter and the United Kingdom Energy Authority has a summer exhibition. An earlier settlement by Sandside Bay was engulfed by sand-dunes in the early 18th century but the present dune-backed sandy beach with rock pools makes the area a very popular one with tourists.

Scrabster, *Highland*   ND 0970
Steamers leave the pier at Scrabster for Stromness in the Orkneys. The harbour in wide sandy Thurso Bay is sheltered from the turbulent Pentland Firth by the jagged cliffs of Holburn Head, spectacularly split from top to bottom in many places by steep chasms. A Pictish broch known as 'Things Va' lies at the foot of Scrabster Hill.

Thurso, *Highland*   ND 1168
Mainland Britain's most northerly town, Thurso is well situated. It lies on the salmon-rich River Thurso which flows into Thurso Bay with its good sandy beach between the towering cliffs of Holburn Head and Clairdon Head. Once

Holburn Head and lighthouse sheltering the harbour and pier at Scrabster

an important port, the small town is now an expanding residential area for employees of Dounreay Fast Reactor, and a resort popular with anglers. Old fishermen's houses near the harbour have been well-restored and to the NE is roofless Thurso Castle.

Wick, *Highland*   ND 3650
Wick's two harbours, situated where the Wick Water enters Wick Bay, were built to cater for the once-prosperous herring industry, and are still busy. The previous county town of Caithness and market town for the fertile hinterland, Wick has much of interest for the tourist and is well-served by air and rail links: the airport 2m NE has flights to the Orkneys and Shetland. A modern factory produces beautiful Caithness glass and all aspects of glass-blowing can be seen on the guided tours. The history of the town, and especially of the fishing industry, is illustrated at the Wick Heritage Centre. 1½m SE, on a headland overlooking the sea, is the ruined 14th-century square tower of Castle of Wick, once known as Castle Oliphant. 3m N, in a striking cliff-top setting at Noss Head, are two adjacent ruined castles; Girnigoe dating from the 15th century and Sinclair from the early 16th century. Both were abandoned during the 1600s.

A former fisherman's cottage at John O'Groats is famous as Scotland's last house

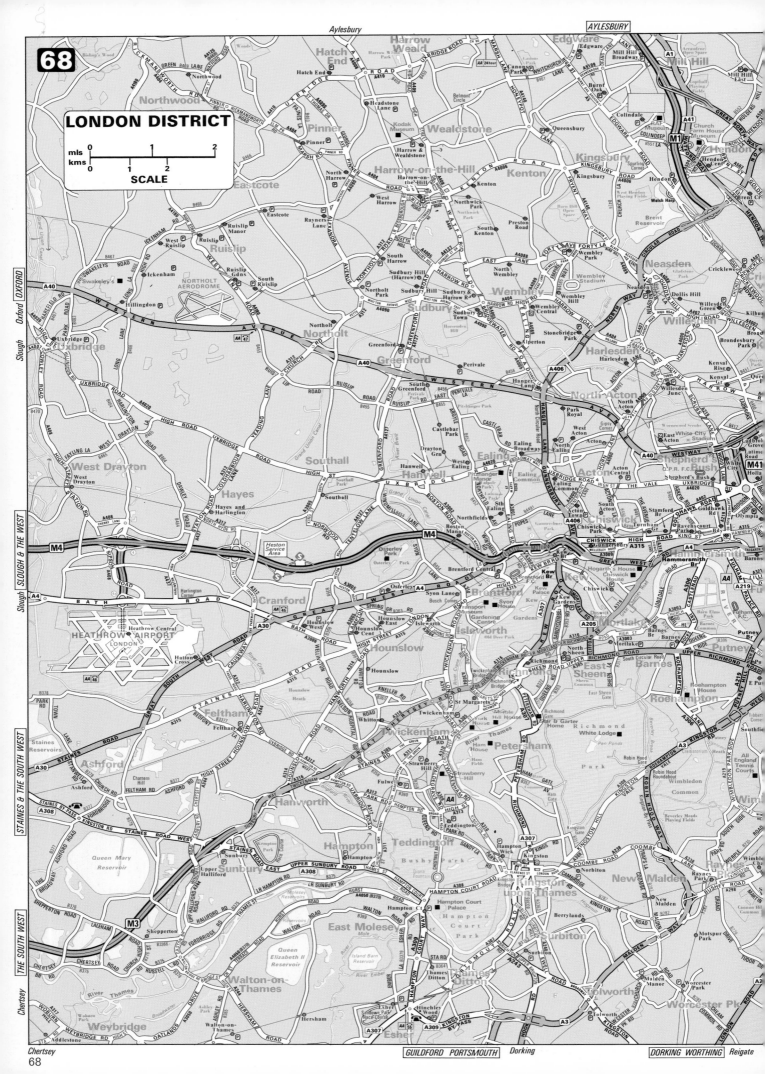

INNER LONDON

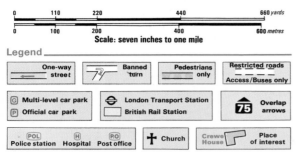

0 110 220 440 660 yards
0 100 200 400 600 metres

Scale: seven inches to one mile

Legend

One-way street	Banned turn	Pedestrians only
		Restricted roads Access/Buses only
G Multi-level car park	**↔** London Transport Station	**75** Overlap arrows
P Official car park	British Rail Station	
POL Police station	**H** Hospital	**P.O** Post office
✝ Church	Crewe House	Place of interest

The one—way streets and banned turns shown on this map are in operation at time of going to press. Some of these are experimental and liable to change. Only the more important banned turns are shown, some of which operate between 7am and 7pm only, and these are sign—posted accordingly. No waiting or unilateral waiting restrictions apply to many streets. All such restrictions are indicated by official signs.

Key to Pages

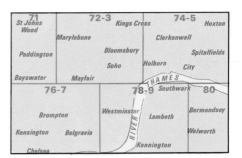

71 St Johns Wood	72-3 Kings Cross	74-5 Hoxton
Marylebone	Clerkenwell	
Paddington	Bloomsbury	Spitalfields
	Soho Holborn	City
Bayswater Mayfair		
76-7	Westminster 78-9	80
Brompton	Lambeth	Bermondsey
Kensington Belgravia		Walworth
Chelsea	Kennington	

THEATRELAND

0 110 220 yards
Scale
0 100 200 metres

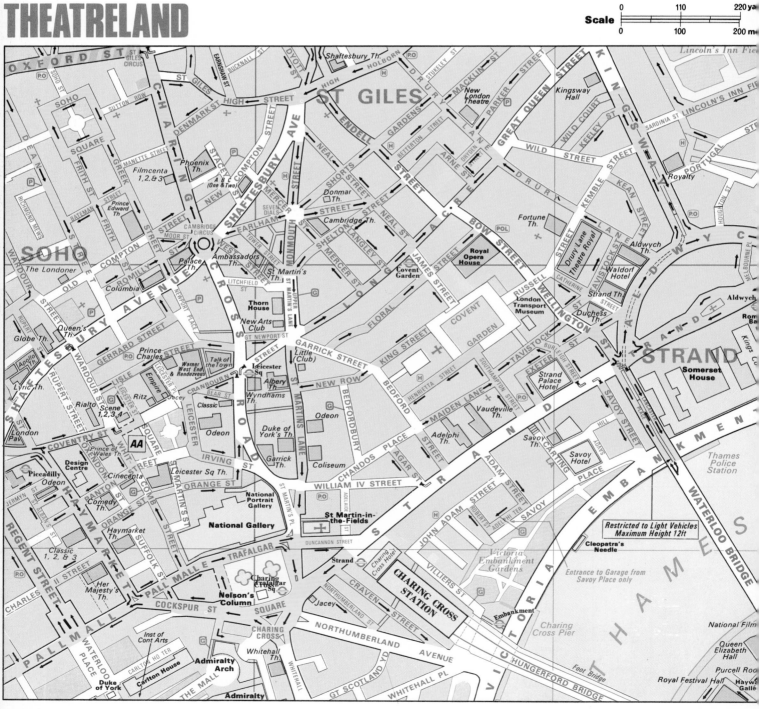

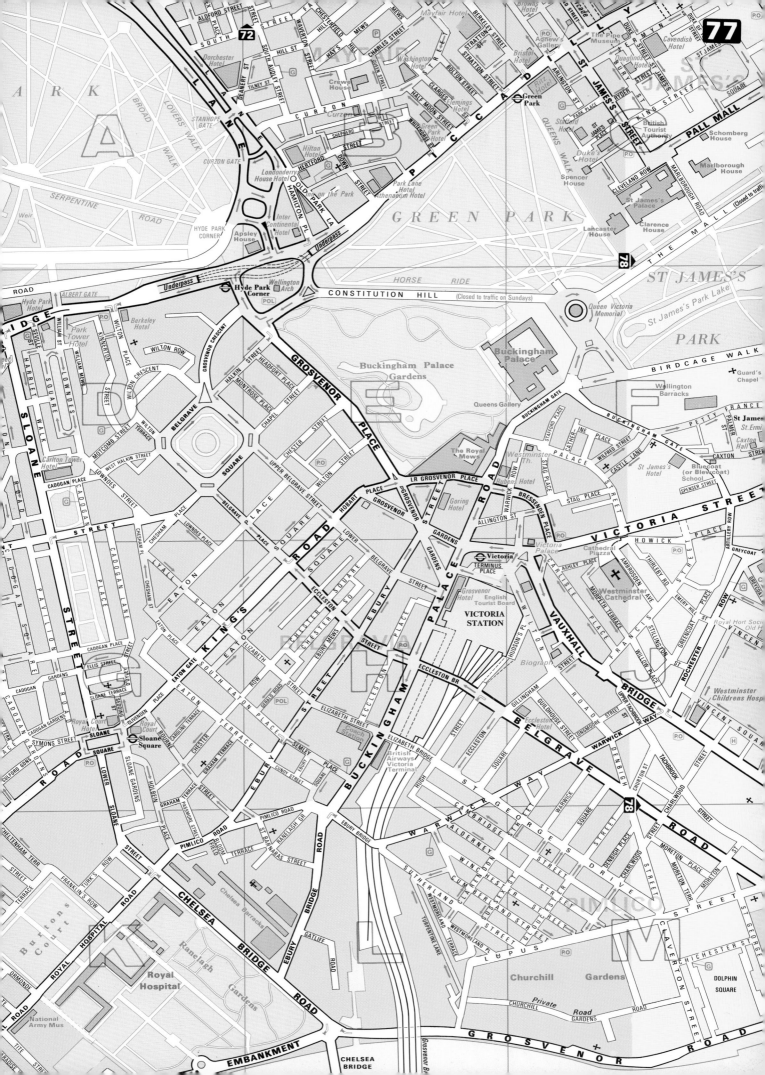

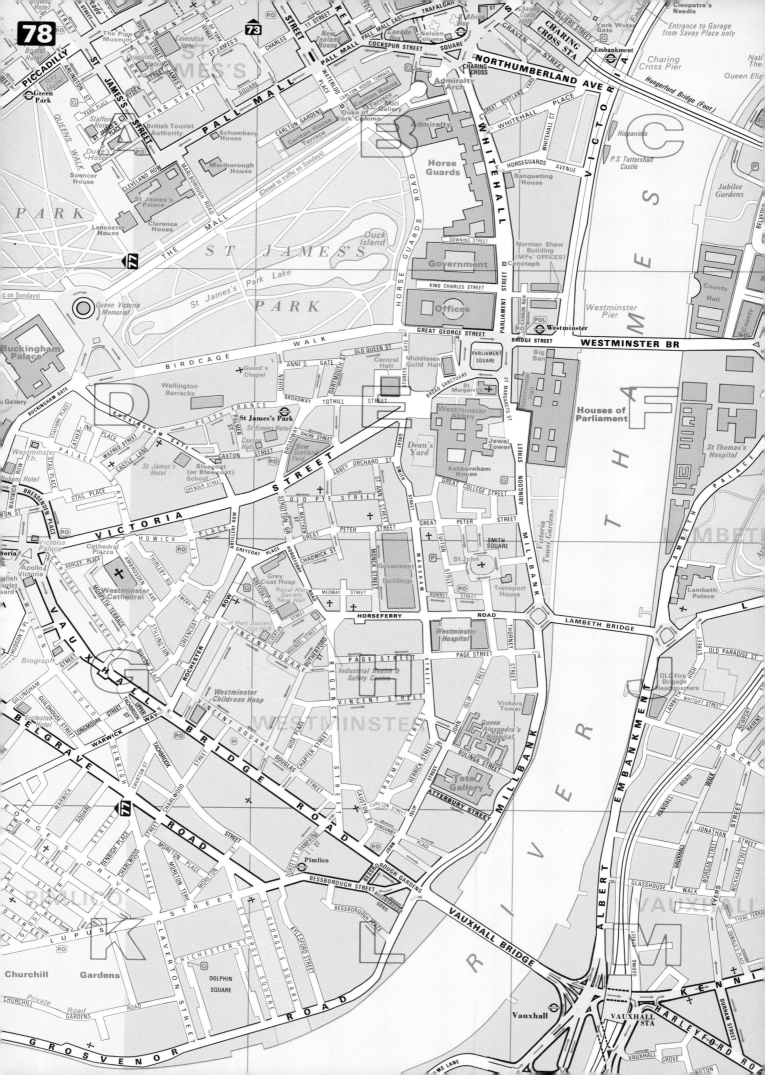

INDEX To Inner London Maps

This map employs an arbitrary system of grid reference. Pages are identified by numbers and divided into twelve squares. Each square contains a blue letter; all references give the page number first, followed by the letter of the square in which a particular street can be found. Reference for Exhibition Road is *76* E, meaning that the relevant map is on page *76* and that the street appears in the square designated E.

Ashbury

Barton-on-the-Heath

Ashbury (Oxon.)	18	SU 2685
Ashby	39	SE 9008
Ashby by Partney	35	TF 4266
Ashby cum Fenby	39	TA 2500
Ashby de la Launde	35	TF 0455
Ashby-de-la-Zouch	33	SK 3516
Ashby Foville	26	SK 7012
Ashby Magna	26	SP 5690
Ashby Parva	26	SP 5288
Ashby St. Ledgers	26	SP 5768
Ashby St. Mary	29	TG 3202
Ashchurch	25	SO 9233
Ashcombe	5	SX 9179
Ashcott	7	ST 4336
Ashdon	20	TL 5842
Asheldham	21	TL 9701
Ashen	20	TL 7442
Ashendon	18	SP 7014
Ashfield (Central)	56	NN 7803
Ashfield (Suff.)	29	TM 2062
Ashfield Green	29	TM 2673
Ashford (Derby.)	33	SK 1969
Ashford (Devon.)	6	SS 5335
Ashford (Kent)	13	TR 0142
Ashford (Surrey)	11	TQ 0671
Ashford Bowdler	24	SO 5170
Ashford Carbonel	24	SO 5270
Ashford Hill	10	SU 5562
Ashgill	50	NS 7849
Ashiesteel Hill	52	NT 4134
Ashill (Devon.)	7	ST 0811
Ashill (Norf.)	28	TF 8804
Ashill (Somer.)	7	ST 3217
Ashingdon	21	TQ 8693
Ashington (Northum.)	47	NZ 2687
Ashington (W Susx)	11	TQ 1315
Ashkirk	52	NT 4722
Ashleworth	17	SO 8125
Ashley (Cambs.)	28	TL 6961
Ashley (Devon.)	5	SS 6411
Ashley (Glos.)	17	ST 9394
Ashley (Hants.)	9	SU 3831
Ashley (Northants.)	26	SP 7991
Ashley (Staffs.)	32	SJ 7536
Ashley Green	19	SP 9705
Ashley Heath	8	SU 1105
Ash Magna	32	SJ 5739
Ashmansworth	10	SU 4156
Ashmansworthy	4	SS 3317
Ash Mill	6	SS 7823
Ashmore	8	ST 9117
Ashorne	26	SP 3057
Ashover	33	SK 3463
Ashow	26	SP 3170
Ashperton	24	SO 6441
Ashprington	5	SX 8157
Ash Priors	7	ST 1429
Ashreigney	5	SS 6213
Ashtead	11	TQ 1858
Ash Thomas	5	ST 0010
Ashton (Ches.)	32	SJ 5069
Ashton (Corn.)	2	SW 6028
Ashton (Devon.)	5	SX 8584
Ashton (Here. and Worc.)	24	SO 5164
Ashton (Northants.)	26	SP 7649
Ashton (Northants.)	27	TL 0588
Ashton Common	17	ST 8958
Ashton-in-Makerfield	36	SJ 5799
Ashton Keynes	17	SU 0494
Ashton under Hill	25	SO 9938
Ashton-under-Lyne	37	SJ 9399
Ashton upon Mersey	32	SJ 7792
Ashurst (Hants.)	9	SU 3310
Ashurst (Kent)	12	TQ 5038
Ashurst (W Susx)	11	TQ 1716
Ashurstwood	12	TQ 4236
Ashwater	4	SX 3895
Ashwell (Herts.)	19	TL 2639
Ashwell (Leic.)	27	SK 8613
Ashwellthorpe	29	TM 1397
Ashwick	8	ST 6447
Ashwicken	28	TF 7018
Askam in Furness	40	SD 2177
Askern	38	SE 5613
Askerswell	7	SY 5292
Askett	18	SP 8105
Askham (Cumbr.)	40	NY 5123
Askham (Notts.)	34	SK 7374
Askham Bryan	38	SE 5548
Askham Richard	38	SE 5347
Askrigg	41	SD 9491
Askwith	37	SE 1648
Aslackby	35	TF 0830
Aslacton	29	TM 1591
Aslockton	34	SK 7440
Asloun	62	NJ 5414
Aspatria	45	NY 1442
Aspenden	20	TL 3528
Aspley Guise	19	SP 9436
Aspley Heath	19	SP 9334
Aspull	36	SD 6108
Asselby	38	SE 7127
Assington	21	TL 9338
Astbury	33	SJ 8461
Astcote	26	SP 6753
Asterley	24	SJ 3707
Asterton	24	SO 3991
Asthall	18	SP 2811
Asthall Leigh	18	SP 3012
Astley (Here. and Worc.)	24	SO 7867
Astley (Salop)	32	SJ 5218
Astley (Warw.)	26	SP 3189
Astley Abbots	24	SO 7096
Astley Cross	24	SO 8069
Astley Green	36	SJ 7099
Aston (Berks.)	18	SU 7884
Aston (Ches.)	32	SJ 5578
Aston (Ches.)	32	SJ 6046
Aston (Derby.)	33	SK 1883
Aston (Here. and Worc.)	24	SO 4571
Aston (Herts.)	19	TL 2722
Aston (Oxon.)	18	SP 3302
Aston (Salop)	32	SJ 5228
Astom(Salop)	24	SJ 6109
Aston (Staffs.)	32	SJ 7540
Aston (Staffs.)	33	SJ 9131
Aston (S Yorks.)	34	SK 4685
Aston (W Mids)	25	SP 0789
Aston Abbotts	19	SP 8420
Aston Blank (Cold Aston)	17	SP 1219
Aston Botterell	24	SO 6284
Aston Cantlow	25	SP 1359
Aston Clinton	19	SP 8812
Aston Crews	17	SO 6723
Aston End	19	TL 2724
Aston Eyre	24	SO 6594
Aston Fields	25	SO 9669
Aston Flamville	26	SP 4692
Aston Ingham	17	SO 6823
Aston juxta Mondrum	32	SJ 6556
Aston le Walls	26	SP 4950
Aston Magna	25	SP 1935
Aston on Clun	24	SO 3981
Aston-on-Trent	33	SK 4129
Aston Rogers	23	SJ 3406
Aston Rowant	18	SU 7299
Aston Sandford	18	SP 7507
Aston Somerville	25	SP 0438
Aston Subedge	25	SP 1341
Aston Tirrold	18	SU 5586
Aston Upthorpe	18	SU 5586
Astwick	19	TL 2138
Astwood	27	SP 9547
Astwood Bank	25	SP 0362
Aswarby (Lincs.)	35	TF 0639
Aswardby (Lincs.)	35	TF 3770
Atcham	24	SJ 5408
Athelington	29	TM 2170
Athelney	7	ST 3428
Athelstaneford	52	NT 5377
Atherington	6	SS 5923
Atherstone	26	SP 3097
Atherstone on Stour	26	SP 2050
Atherton	36	SD 6703
Atlow	33	SK 2248
Attenborough	34	SK 5134
Attleborough (Norf.)	29	TM 0495
Attleborough (Warw.)	26	SP 3790
Attlebridge	29	TG 1216
Atwick	39	TA 1850
Atworth	17	ST 8565
Aubourn	34	SK 9262
Auchagallon	49	NR 8934
Auchallater	61	NO 1588
Aucharnie	62	NJ 6341
Auchattie	62	NO 6994
Auchenblae	57	NO 7278
Auchenbowie	50	NS 7988
Auchenbreck	49	NS 0281
Auchencairn	45	NX 7951
Auchencarroch	50	NS 4182
Auchencrow	53	NT 8560
Auchendinny	51	NT 2561
Auchengray	51	NS 9953
Auchengruith	45	NS 8209
Auchenhalrig	61	NJ 3661
Auchenheath	50	NS 8043
Auchentiber	50	NS 3647
Auchgourish	60	NH 9315
Auchindrain	55	NN 0303
Auchindrean	64	NH 1980
Auchininna	62	NJ 6446
Auchinleck (Dumf. and Galwy.)	44	NX 4570
Auchinleck (Strath.)	50	NS 5422
Auchinloch	50	NS 6670
Auchintore	55	NN 0972
Auchintool	61	NJ 5316
Auchleuchries	62	NK 0136
Auchleven	62	NJ 6224
Auchlochan	50	NS 8037
Auchlossan	61	NJ 5702
Auchlyne	55	NN 5129
Auchmillan	50	NS 5129
Auchmithie	57	NO 6744
Auchmuirbridge	56	NO 2101
Auchnacree	57	NO 4663
Auchnagatt	62	NJ 9341
Auchronie	57	NO 4480
Auchterarder	56	NN 9312
Auchterderran	51	NT 2195
Auchterhouse	57	NO 3337
Auchtermuchty	56	NO 2311
Auchterneed	60	NH 4959
Auchtertool	51	NT 2190
Auchtoo	55	NN 5620
Auckingill	67	ND 3764
Auckley	38	SE 6501
Audenshaw	33	SJ 9196
Audlem	32	SJ 6543
Audley	32	SJ 7950
Auds	62	NJ 6564
Aughton (Humbs.)	38	SE 7038
Aughton (Lancs.)	36	SD 3804
Aughton (Lancs.)	36	SD 5467
Aughton (S Yorks.)	34	SK 4586
Aughton Park	36	SD 4106
Auldearn	60	NH 9155
Aulden	24	SO 4654
Auldhame	52	NT 5984
Auldhouse	50	NS 6250
Ault-a-chrinn	59	NG 9420
Aultbea	64	NG 8789
Aultgrishan	64	NG 7485
Aultiphurst	67	NC 8065
Aultmore (Grampn.)	61	NJ 4053
Aultnagoire	60	NH 5423
Aulton	62	NJ 6028
Aundorach	60	NH 9716
Aunsby	35	TF 0438
Auquhorthies	62	NJ 8329
Aust	17	ST 5789
Austerfield	34	SK 6594
Austonley	37	SE 1207
Austrey	26	SK 2906
Austwick	37	SD 7668
Authorpe	35	TF 3980
Authorpe Row	35	TF 5373
Avebury	17	SU 0969
Aveley	20	TQ 5680
Avening	17	ST 8797
Averham	34	SK 7654
Aveton Gifford	5	SX 6947
Avielochan	60	NH 9016
Aviemore	60	NH 8912
Avington	10	SU 3767
Avoch	60	NH 6955
Avon	8	SZ 1498
Avonbridge	50	NS 9072
Avon Castle	8	SU 1303
Avon Dassett	26	SP 4150
Avonmouth	16	ST 5177
Avonwick	5	SX 7158
Awbridge	9	SU 3323
Awkley	17	ST 5885
Awliscombe	7	ST 1301
Awre	17	SO 7008
Awsworth	34	SK 4843
Axbridge	16	ST 4254
Axford (Hants.)	10	SU 6043
Axford (Wilts.)	10	SU 2369
Axminster	7	SY 2998
Axmouth	7	SY 2591
Aylburton	17	SO 6101
Ayle	46	NY 7149
Aylesbeare	7	SY 0391
Aylesbury	18	SP 8213
Aylesby	39	TA 2007
Aylesford	12	TQ 7359
Aylesham	13	TR 2352
Aylestone	26	SK 5701
Aylmerton	29	TG 1839
Aylsham	29	TG 1926
Aylton	24	SO 6537
Aymestrey	24	SO 4265
Aynho	18	SP 5133
Ayot St. Lawrence	19	TL 1916
Ayot St Peter	19	TL 2115
Ayr	49	NS 3321
Aysgarth	41	SE 0088
Ayside	40	SD 3983
Ayston	27	SK 8601
Aythorpe Roding	20	TL 5815
Ayton (Berwick.)	53	NT 9260
Ayton (N Yorks.)	43	SE 9884
Aywick (Yell)	63	HU 5386
Azerley	42	SE 2574
Babbinswood	32	SJ 3329
Babcary	7	ST 5628
Babel	15	SN 8235
Bebell	31	SJ 1574
Babraham	20	TL 5150
Babworth	34	SK 6880
Back	63	NB 4840
Backaland	63	HY 5630
Backbarrow	40	SD 3584
Backford	32	SJ 3971
Backhill of Clackriach	62	NJ 9246
Backies	67	NC 8302
Backmuir of New Gilston	57	NO 4308
Back of Keppoch	58	NM 6587
Backwell	16	ST 4868
Backworth	47	NZ 2972
Bacon End	20	TL 6018
Baconsthorpe	29	TG 1237
Bacton (Here. and Worc.)	24	SO 3732
Bacton (Norf.)	29	TG 3434
Bacton (Suff.)	29	TM 0466
Bacup	37	SD 8622
Badachro	64	NG 7873
Badbury	17	SU 1980
Badby	26	SP 5559
Badcall (Highld.)	66	NC 1541
Badcall (Highld.)	66	NC 2355
Badcaul	64	NH 0191
Baddeley Green	33	SJ 9250
Baddesley Ensor	26	SP 2798
Baddidarach	64	NC 0923
Badenscoth	62	NJ 7038
Badenyon	61	NJ 3419
Badger	24	SO 7699
Badgers Mount	12	TQ 5061
Badgeworth (Glos.)	17	SO 9019
Badgworth (Somer.)	16	ST 3952
Badingham	29	TM 3067
Bedlesmere	13	TR 0154
Badluarach	64	NG 9994
Badminton	17	ST 8082
Badrallach	64	NH 0691
Badsey	25	SP 0743
Badsworth	38	SE 4614
Badwell Ash	29	TL 9969
Bagby	42	SE 4680
Bagendon	17	SP 0006
Bagillt	31	SJ 2175
Baginton	26	SP 3474
Baglan	15	SS 7493
Bagley	32	SJ 4027
Bagnall	33	SJ 9250
Bagshot (Surrey)	11	SU 9163
Bagshot (Wilts.)	10	SU 3165
Bagthorpe (Norf.)	28	TF 7932
Bagthorpe (Notts.)	34	SK 4751
Bagworth	26	SK 4408
Bagwy Llydiart	16	SO 4427
Baildon	37	SE 1539
Bailebeag	60	NH 5018
Baile Boidheach	48	NR 7473
Baile Mor	54	NM 2824
Baillieston	50	NS 6764
Bail Uachdraich	63	NF 8160
Bainbridge	41	SD 9390
Bainton (Cambs.)	27	TF 0906
Bainton (Humbs.)	39	SE 9652
Bairnkine	52	NT 6515
Baker's End	20	TL 3917
Baker Street	20	TQ 6381
Bakewell	33	SK 2168
Bala	31	SH 9236
Balallan	63	NB 2720
Balbeg	60	NH 4924
Balbeggie	56	NO 1629
Balbithan	62	NJ 7917
Balblair	65	NH 7066
Balchladich	64	NC 0330
Balchraggan	60	NH 5343
Balchrick	66	NC 1960
Balcombe	12	TQ 3130
Balcurvie	57	NO 3400
Baldersby	42	SE 3578
Balderstone	36	SD 6332
Balderton	34	SK 8151
Baldhu	2	SW 7743
Baldinnie	57	NO 4311
Baldock	19	TL 2434
Baldrine	43	SC 4281
Baldwin	43	SC 3581
Baldwinholme	46	NY 3351
Baldwin's Gate	32	SJ 7939
Bale	29	TG 0136
Balemartine	48	NL 9841
Balephuil	48	NL 9640
Balerno	51	NT 1666
Balfield	57	NO 5468
Balfour	63	HY 4716
Balfron	50	NS 5488
Balgaveny	62	NJ 6640
Balgavies	57	NO 5351
Balgedie	56	NO 1603
Balgonar	51	NT 0293
Balgove	62	NJ 8133
Balgowan	60	NN 6394
Balgown	58	NG 3868
Balgray	57	NO 4138
Balgrochan	50	NS 6278
Balhalgardy	62	NJ 7623
Balhary	57	NO 2646
Baliasta	63	HP 6009
Baligill	67	NC 8566
Balintore (Highld.)	65	NH 8675
Balintore (Tays.)	57	NO 2859
Balintraid	65	NH 7370
Balivanich	63	NF 7755
Balkeerie	57	NO 3244
Balkholme	38	SE 7828
Balkissock	44	NX 1381
Ball	31	SJ 3026
Ballabeg	43	SC 2470
Ballacannell	43	SC 4382
Ballacarnane Beg	43	SC 3088
Ballajora	43	SC 4790
Ballamodha	43	SC 2773
Ballantrae	44	NX 0882
Ballantrushal	63	NB 3853
Ballasalla (I. of M.)	43	SC 2870
Ballasalla (I. of M.)	43	SC 3497
Ballater	61	NO 3695
Ballaugh	43	SC 3493
Ballchraggan	65	NH 7775
Ballechin	56	NN 9353
Ballencrieff	52	NT 4878
Ballevullin	48	NL 9546
Ball Hill	10	SU 4263
Balliekine	49	NR 8739
Balliemore (Strath.)	54	NM 8228
Ballig	43	SC 2882
Ballinaby	48	NR 2267
Ballindean	57	NO 2529
Ballinger Common	19	SP 9103
Ballingham	24	SO 5731
Ballingry	51	NT 1797
Ballinluig	56	NN 9852
Ballintuim	56	NO 1054
Balloch (Highld.)	60	NH 7346
Balloch (Strath.)	50	NS 3981
Balloch (Tays.)	56	NN 8419
Balloch (Tays.)	57	NO 3557
Ballochan	61	NO 5290
Ballochroy	48	NR 7252
Balls Cross	11	SU 9826
Ballygown	54	NM 4343
Ballygrant	48	NR 3966
Ballymichael	49	NR 9231
Balmacara	59	NG 8028
Balmaclellan	45	NX 6578
Balmacneil	56	NN 9850
Balmae	45	NX 6845
Balmaha	50	NS 4290
Balmalcolm	57	NO 3108
Belmartin	63	NF 7273
Balmedie	62	NJ 9617
Balmerino	57	NO 3524
Balmerlawn	9	SU 3003
Balmore	50	NS 6073
Balmullo	57	NO 4220
Balmungie	60	NH 7359
Balnabodach	63	NF 7101
Balnacra	59	NG 9746
Balnafoich	60	NH 6835
Balnaguard	56	NN 9451
Balnaguisich	65	NH 6771
Balnahard	54	NM 4534
Balnahard	54	NR 4199
Balnakeil	66	NC 3968
Balnaknock	58	NG 4162
Balnamoon	57	NO 5463
Balnapaling	65	NH 7969
Balquhidder	55	NN 5320
Balranald	63	NF 7169
Balsall Common	26	SP 2377
Balscote	26	SP 3841
Balsham	20	TL 5850
Baltasound (Unst)	63	HP 6208
Balterley	32	SJ 7550
Balthangie	62	NJ 8351
Baltonsborough	7	ST 5434
Balvaird	60	NH 5452
Balvarran	56	NO 0762
Balvicar	54	NM 7616
Balvraid	60	NH 8231
Bamburgh	53	NU 1834
Bamford	33	SK 2083
Bampton (Cumbr.)	40	NY 5118
Bampton (Devon.)	7	SS 9522
Bampton (Oxon.)	18	SP 3103
Banavie	55	NN 1177
Banbury	18	SP 4540
Banc Cwmhelen	15	SN 6811
Banchory	62	NO 6995
Banchory-Devenick	62	NJ 9101
Bancyfelin	14	SN 3218
Banc-y-ffordd	22	SN 4037
Banff	62	NJ 6863
Bangor	30	SH 5872
Bangor-is-y-coed	32	SJ 3945
Banham	29	TM 0688
Bank	9	SU 2807
Bankend (Dumf. and Galwy.)	45	NY 0268
Bankend (Strath.)	50	NS 8033
Bankfoot	56	NO 0635
Bankglen	50	NS 5912
Bankhead (Grampn.)	62	NJ 6608
Bankhead (Grampn.)	62	NJ 8910
Band Newton	37	SD 9152
Banknock	50	NS 7779
Banks (Cumbr.)	46	NY 5664
Banks (Lancs.)	36	SD 3820
Bankshill	45	NY 1981
Bank Street	24	SO 6362
Banningham	29	TG 2129
Bannister Green	20	TL 6920
Bannockburn	50	NS 8190
Banstead	11	TQ 2559
Bantham	5	SX 6643
Banton	50	NS 7479
Banwell	16	ST 3959
Bapchild	13	TQ 9363
Baramore	54	NM 6474
Barassie	49	NS 3232
Barbaraville	65	NH 7471
Barber Booth	33	SK 1184
Barbon	41	SD 6282
Barbrook	6	SS 7147
Barby	26	SP 5470
Barcheston	18	SP 2639
Barcombe	12	TQ 4214
Barcombe Cross	12	TQ 4216
Barden	42	SE 1493
Bardfield Saling	20	TL 6826
Bardister	63	HU 3577
Bardney	35	TF 1169
Bardon Mill	46	NY 7764
Bardowie	50	NS 5873
Bardrainney	49	NS 3372
Bardsea	40	SD 3074
Bardsey	38	SE 3643
Bardsley	37	SD 9201
Bardwell	29	TL 9473
Barewood	24	SO 3856
Barford (Norf.)	29	TG 1007
Barford (Warw.)	26	SP 2660
Barford St. Martin	8	SU 0531
Barford St. Michael	26	SP 4332
Barfreston	13	TR 2650
Bargoed	16	SO 1500
Bargrennan	44	NX 3476
Barham (Cambs.)	27	TL 1375
Barham (Kent)	13	TR 2050
Barham (Suff.)	21	TM 1451
Barholm	27	TF 0811
Barkby	26	SK 6309
Barkestone-le-Vale	34	SK 7734
Barkham	10	SU 7866
Barking (Gtr London)	20	TQ 4785
Barking (Suff.)	21	TM 0653
Barkingside	20	TQ 4489
Barkisland	37	SE 0419
Barkston (Lincs.)	34	SK 9241
Barkston (N Yorks.)	38	SE 4936
Barkway	20	TL 3835
Barkwith	35	TF 1681
Barlaston	33	SJ 8938
Barlavington	11	SU 9716
Barlborough	34	SK 4777
Barlby	38	SE 6334
Barlestone	26	SK 4205
Barley (Herts.)	20	TL 4038
Barley (Lancs.)	37	SD 8240
Barleythorpe	27	SK 8409
Barling	21	TQ 9289
Barlow (Derby.)	33	SK 3474
Barlow (N Yorks.)	38	SE 6428
Barlow (Tyne and Wear)	47	NZ 1560
Barmby Moor	38	SE 7748
Barmby on the Marsh	38	SE 6828
Barmer	28	TF 8133
Barmouth	30	SH 6115
Barmpton	42	NZ 3118
Barmston	39	TA 1659
Barnack	27	TF 0705
Barnacle	26	SP 3884
Barnard Castle	41	NZ 0516
Barnard Gate	18	SP 4010
Barnardiston	20	TL 7148
Barnburgh	38	SE 4803
Barnby	29	TM 4789
Barnby Dun	38	SE 6109
Barnby in the Willows	34	SK 8552
Barnby Moor	34	SK 6684
Barnes	11	TQ 2276
Barnet	19	TQ 2494
Barnetby le Wold	39	TA 0509
Barney	29	TF 9932
Barnham (Suff.)	28	TL 8779
Barnham (W Susx)	11	SU 9604
Barnham Broom	29	TG 0807
Barnhead	57	NO 6657
Barnhill	61	NJ 1457
Barnhills	44	NW 9871
Barningham (Durham)	41	NZ 0810
Barningham (Suff.)	29	TL 9676
Barnoldby le Beck	39	TA 2303
Barnoldswick	37	SD 8746
Barns Green	11	TQ 1227
Barnsley (Glos.)	17	SP 0705
Barnsley (S Yorks.)	38	SE 3406
Barnstaple	6	SS 5533
Barnston (Essex)	20	TL 6519
Barnston (Mers.)	31	SJ 2783
Barnt Green	25	SP 0073
Barnton	32	SJ 6374
Barnwell	27	TL 0485
Barnwood	17	SO 8518
Barr	44	NX 2794
Barrachan	44	NX 3649
Barrack	62	NJ 8942
Barraglom	63	NB 1634
Barrapoll	48	NL 9542
Barras	57	NO 8580
Barrasford	47	NY 9273
Barregarrow	43	SC 3288
Barrhead	50	NS 5058
Barrhill (Strath.)	44	NX 2382
Barrington (Cambs.)	20	TL 3949
Barrington (Somer.)	7	ST 3918
Barripper	2	SW 6338
Barrmill	50	NS 3651
Barrock	67	ND 2571
Barrow (Lancs.)	36	SD 7338
Barrow (Leic.)	34	SK 8815
Barrow (Salop)	24	SJ 6500
Barrow (Somer.)	8	ST 7231
Barrow (Suff.)	28	TL 7663
Barroway Drove	28	TF 5703
Barrowby	34	SK 8736
Barrowden	27	SK 9400
Barrowford	37	SD 8538
Barrow Gurney	16	ST 5267
Barrow-in-Furness	36	SD 1969
Barrow Street	8	ST 8330
Barrow upon Humber	39	TA 0721
Barrow upon Soar	34	SK 5717
Barrow upon Trent	33	SK 3528
Barry (Tays)	57	NO 5334
Barry (S Glam.)	16	ST 1168
Barry Island	16	ST 1166
Barsby	26	SK 6911
Barsham	29	TM 3989
Barston	26	SP 2078
Bartestree	24	SO 5641
Barthol Chapel	62	NJ 8134
Barthomley	32	SJ 7652
Bartley	9	SU 3012
Bartlow	20	TL 5845
Barton (Cambs.)	20	TL 4055
Barton (Ches.)	32	SJ 4454
Barton (Devon.)	5	SX 9067
Barton (Glos.)	17	SP 0925
Barton (Lancs.)	36	SD 5136
Barton (N Yorks.)	42	NZ 2208
Barton (Warw.)	25	SP 1051
Barton Bendish	28	TF 7105
Barton Common	29	TG 3522
Barton Hartshorn	18	SP 6431
Barton in Fabis	34	SK 5232
Barton in the Beans	26	SK 3906
Barton in the Clay	19	TL 0831
Barton-le-Street	43	SE 7274
Barton-le-Willows	38	SE 7163
Barton Mills	28	TL 7273
Barton Moss	32	SJ 7397
Barton on Sea	9	SZ 2493
Barton-on-the-Heath	18	SP 2532

Brill Callaly

Brill 18 SP 6513
Brilley 23 SO 2549
Brimfield 24 SO 5267
Brimington 33 SK 4073
Brimpsfield 17 SO 9312
Brimpton 10 SU 5564
Brims 63 ND 2888
Brind 38 SE 7430
Brindister (Shetld.) 63 HU 2757
Brindister (Shetld.) 63 HU 4337
Brindle 36 SD 5924
Brindley Ford 33 SJ 8754
Brindley Heath 25 SJ 9914
Brineton 24 SJ 8013
Bringewood Chase 24 SO 4573
Bringhurst 27 SP 8492
Brington 27 TL 0875
Briningham 29 TG 0334
Brinkhill 35 TF 3773
Brinkley 20 TL 6254
Brinklow 26 SP 4379
Brinkworth 17 SU 0184
Brinscall 36 SD 6321
Brinsley 34 SK 4548
Brinsop 24 SO 4344
Brinsworth 33 SK 190
Brinton 29 TG 0335
Brinyan 63 HY 4327
Brisley 29 TF 9421
Brislington 17 ST 6170
Bristol 17 ST 5872
Briston 29 TG 0632
Britannia 37 SD 8821
Britford 8 SU 1528
British Legion Village 12 TQ 7257
Briton Ferry 15 SS 7394
Britwell Salome 18 SU 6792
Brixham 5 SX 9255
Brixton 4 SX 5452
Brixton Deverill 8 ST 8638
Brixworth 26 SP 7470
Brize Norton 18 SP 2907
Broad Blunsdon 17 SU 1490
Broadbottom 33 SJ 9993
Broadbridge 10 SU 8105
Broadbridge Heath 11 TQ 1431
Broad Campden 25 SP 1537
Broad Chalke 8 SU 0325
Broadclyst 5 SX 9897
Broadford 58 NG 6423
Broad Green 24 SO 7656
Broadhaugh 52 NT 4509
Broad Haven 14 SM 8613
Broadheath (Gtr Mches.) 32 SJ 7689
Broadheath (Here. and Worc.) 24 SO 6665
Broadheath (Here. and Worc.) 25 SO 8156
Broadhembury 7 ST 1004
Broadhempston 5 SX 8066
Broad Hill (Cambs.) 28 TL 5976
Broad Hinton 17 SU 1076
Broad Laying 10 SU 4362
Broadley (Grampn.) 61 NJ 4161
Broadley (Gtr Mches.) 37 SD 8716
Broadley Common 20 TL 4207
Broad Marston 25 SP 1346
Broadmayne 8 SY 7286
Broadmeadows 52 NT 4130
Broadmere 10 SU 6247
Broad Oak (Cumbr.) 40 SD 1194
Broadoak (Dorset) 7 SY 496
Broadoak (E Susx) 12 TQ 6022
Broad Oak (E Susx) 12 TQ 8320
Broad Oak (Here. and Worc.) 16 SO 4721
Broadoak (Kent) 13 TR 1661
Broadrashes 61 NJ 4354
Broadstairs 13 TR 3967
Broadstone (Dorset) 8 SZ 0095
Broadstone (Salop) 24 SO 5389
Broad Street 12 TQ 8356
Broad Town 17 SU 0977
Broadwas 24 SO 7555
Broadwater 11 TQ 1504
Broadway (Here. and Worc.) 25 SP 0937
Broadway (Somer.) 7 ST 3215
Broadway Hill 25 SP 1136
Broadwell (Glos.) 18 SP 2027
Broadwell (Oxon.) 18 SP 2503
Broadwell (Warw.) 26 SP 4565
Broadwell Lane End 17 SO 5811
Broadwey 8 SY 6683
Broadwindsor 7 ST 4302
Broadwood-Kelly 5 SS 6105
Broadwoodwidger 4 SX 4089
Brobury 23 SO 3444
Brockbridge 9 SU 6018
Brockdam 53 NU 1624
Brockdish 29 TM 2179
Brockenhurst 9 SU 2902
Brocketsbrae 50 NS 8239
Brockford Street 29 TM 1166
Brockhall 26 SP 6362
Brockham 11 TQ 2049
Brockhampton 24 SO 5932
Brockholes 37 SE 1411
Brocklesby 39 TA 1311
Brockley 16 ST 4666
Brockley Green 20 TL 8254
Brockton (Salop) 23 SJ 3104
Brockton (Salop) 24 SJ 7103
Brockton (Salop) 23 SO 3285
Brockton (Salop) 24 SO 5793
Brockweir 16 SO 5301
Brockwood Park 9 SU 6226
Brockworth 17 SO 8916
Brocton 33 SJ 9619
Brodick 49 NS 0136
Brodsworth 38 SE 5007
Brogborough 19 SP 9638
Brokenborough 17 ST 9189
Broken Cross (Ches.) 32 SJ 6872
Broken Cross (Ches.) 33 SJ 8973
Bromborough 32 SJ 3582
Brome 29 TM 1376
Brome Street 29 TM 1576
Bromeswell 21 TM 3050
Bromfield (Cumbr.) 45 NY 1746
Bromfield (Salop) 24 SO 4876
Bromham (Beds.) 27 TL 0051
Bromham (Wilts.) 17 ST 9665
Bromley (Gtr London) 12 TQ 4069
Bromley (Gtr London) 12 TQ 4365
Bromley Common 12 TQ 4266
Brompton (Kent) 12 TQ 7668
Brompton (N Yorks.) 42 SE 3796
Brompton (N Yorks.) 43 SE 9482
Brompton-on-Swale 42 SE 2199
Brompton Ralph 7 ST 0832
Brompton Regis 6 SS 9531
Bromsash 17 SO 6424
Bromsgrove 25 SO 9570
Bromstead Heath 32 SJ 7917
Bromyard 24 SO 6554
Bromyard Downs 24 SO 6655
Bronaber 30 SH 7131
Bronant 22 SN 6467
Bronington 32 SJ 4839
Bronllys 23 SO 1435
Bronygarth 31 SJ 2636
Brook (Hants.) 9 SU 2713
Brook (Hants.) 9 SU 3428
Brook (I. of W.) 9 SZ 3983
Brook (Kent) 13 TR 0644
Brook (Surrey) 11 SU 9338
Brooke (Leic.) 27 SK 8405
Brooke (Norf.) 29 TM 2999
Brookfield 50 NS 4164
Brookhouse 36 SD 5464
Brookhouse Green 32 SJ 8061
Brookland 13 TQ 9825
Brookmans Park 19 TL 2404
Brooks 23 SO 1499
Brook Street 20 TQ 5792
Brookthorpe 17 SO 8312
Brookwood 11 SU 9557
Broom (Beds.) 27 TL 1743
Broom (Warw.) 25 SP 0953
Broome (Here. and Worc.) 25 SO 9078
Broome (Norf.) 29 TM 3591
Broome (Salop) 24 SO 3981
Broomer's Corners 11 TQ 1221
Broomfield (Essex) 20 TL 7009
Broomfield (Grampn.) 62 NJ 9532
Broomfield (Kent) 13 TQ 8452
Broomfield (Kent) 13 TR 2066
Broomfield (Somer.) 7 ST 2231
Broomfleet 39 SE 8727
Broom Hill (Dorset) 8 SU 0302
Broomhill (Northum.) 47 NU 2400
Brora 67 NC 9003
Broseley 24 SJ 6701
Brothertoft 35 TF 2746
Brotherton 38 SE 4825
Brotton 42 NZ 6819
Broubster 67 ND 0360
Brough (Cumbr.) 41 NY 7914
Brough (Derby.) 33 SK 1882
Brough (Highld.) 67 ND 2273
Brough (Humbs.) 39 SE 9326
Brough (Notts.) 34 SK 8358
Brough (Shetld.) 63 HU 4377
Brough (Shetld.) 63 HU 5141
Brough (Whalsay) 63 HU 5564
Brough (Yell) 63 HU 5179
Broughalt 32 SJ 5641
Brough Sowerby 41 NY 7912
Broughton (Borders) 51 NT 1136
Broughton (Bucks.) 27 SP 8940
Broughton (Cambs.) 27 TL 2878
Broughton (Clwyd) 32 SJ 3363
Broughton (Cumbr.) 40 NY 0731
Broughton (Gtr Mches.) 37 SD 8201
Broughton (Hants.) 9 SU 3132
Broughton (Humbs.) 39 SE 9508
Broughton (Lancs.) 36 SD 5234
Broughton (Mid Glam.) 15 SS 9271
Broughton (Northants.) 27 SP 8375
Broughton (N. Yorks.) 37 SD 9451
Broughton (N Yorks.) 43 SE 7673
Broughton (Oxon.) 26 SP 4238
Broughton (Westray) 63 HY 4448
Broughton Astley 26 SP 5292
Broughton Gifford 17 ST 8763
Broughton Hackett 25 SO 9254
Broughton in Furness 40 SD 2087
Broughton Mills 40 SD 2290
Broughton Moor 40 NY 0533
Broughton Poggs 18 SP 2303
Broughtown 63 HY 6540
Broughty Ferry 57 NO 4630
Browland 63 HU 2650
Brown Candover 10 SU 5839
Brown Edge 33 SJ 9053
Brownhill (Grampn.) 62 NJ 8640
Brownhills (W Mids) 25 SK 0405
Brownlow Heath 32 SJ 8360
Brownmuir 57 NO 7477
Brownston 5 SX 6952
Broxbourne 20 TL 3707
Broxburn (Lothian) 51 NT 0872
Broxburn (Lothian) 52 NT 6977
Broxted 20 TL 5727
Broxwood 24 SO 3654
Bruan 67 ND 3039
Brue 63 NB 3349
Bruera 32 SJ 4360
Bruernish 64 NF 7102
Bruichladdich 48 NR 2661
Bruist 63 NF 9282
Bruisyard 29 TM 3266
Bruisyard Street 29 TM 3365
Brund 33 SK 1061
Brundall 29 TG 3208
Brundish 29 TM 2669
Brundish Street 29 TM 2671
Bruntingthorpe 26 SP 6090
Brunton (Fife.) 57 NO 3220
Brunton (Northum.) 53 NU 2024
Brushford 6 SS 9225
Brushford Barton 5 SS 6707
Bruton 8 ST 6834
Bryanston 8 ST 8706
Brydekirk 45 NY 1870
Brymbo 31 SJ 2953
Bryn (Gtr Mches.) 36 SD 5600
Bryn (Powys) 22 SN 9055
Bryn (Salop) 23 SO 2985
Bryn (W Glam.) 15 SS 8192
Brynamman 15 SN 7114
Brynberian 14 SN 1035
Bryncae 16 SS 9983
Bryncethin 15 SS 9184
Bryncir 30 SH 4641
Bryn-coch 15 SS 7499
Bryncroes 30 SH 2231
Bryncrug 22 SH 6003
Bryneglwys 31 SJ 1447
Brynford 31 SJ 1774
Bryn Gates 36 SD 5901
Bryngwran 30 SH 3477
Bryngwyn (Gwent) 16 SO 3909
Bryngwyn (Powys) 23 SO 1849
Bryn-henllan 14 SN 0139
Brynhoffnant 22 SN 3351
Brynmawr 16 SO 1911
Brynmenyn 15 SS 9084
Brynna 16 SS 9883
Brynrefail 30 SH 4786
Brynsadler 16 ST 0380
Brynsiencyn 30 SH 4867
Brynteg 30 SH 4982
Bryn-y-maen 31 SH 8376
Bualintur 58 NG 4020
Bubbenhall 26 SP 3672
Bubwith 38 SE 7136
Buccleuch 51 NT 3214
Buchanty 56 NN 9328
Buchlyvie 50 NS 5793
Buckabank 46 NY 3749
Buckden (Cambs.) 27 TL 1967
Buckden (N Yorks.) 41 SD 9477
Buckenham 29 TG 3505
Buckerell 7 ST 1200
Buckfast 5 SX 7367
Buckfastleigh 5 SX 7466
Buckhaven 57 NT 3598
Buckholm 52 NT 4838
Buckhorn Weston 8 ST 7524
Buckhurst Hill 20 TQ 4193
Buckie 61 NJ 4265
Buckies 67 ND 1063
Buckingham 18 SP 6933
Buckland (Bucks.) 19 SP 8812
Buckland (Devon.) 5 SX 6743
Buckland (Glos.) 25 SP 0836
Buckland (Herts.) 20 TL 3533
Buckland (Kent) 13 TR 2942
Buckland (Oxon.) 18 SU 3497
Buckland (Surrey) 11 TQ 2250
Buckland Brewer 6 SS 4120
Buckland Common 19 SP 9306
Buckland Dinham 8 ST 7550
Buckland Filleigh 4 SS 4609
Buckland in the Moor 5 SX 7273
Buckland Monachorum 4 SX 4868
Buckland Newton 8 ST 6905
Buckland St. Mary 7 ST 2713
Buckland-Tout-Saints 5 SX 7546
Bucklebury 10 SU 5570
Bucklerheads 57 NO 4636
Bucklers Hard 9 SZ 4099
Bucklesham 21 TM 2442
Buckley 31 SJ 2764
Buckminster 34 SK 8722
Bucknall (Lincs.) 35 TF 1668
Bucknall (Staffs.) 33 SJ 9147
Bucknell (Oxon.) 18 SP 5525
Bucknell (Salop) 23 SO 3574
Bucksburn 62 NJ 8909
Buck's Cross 6 SS 3422
Bucks Green 11 TQ 0732
Bucks Hill 19 TL 0500
Bucks Horn Oak 10 SU 8142
Buck's Mills 6 SS 3523
Buckton (Here. and Worc.) 24 SO 3873
Buckton (Northum.) 53 NU 0838
Buckworth 27 TL 1476
Budbrooke 26 SP 2565
Budby 34 SK 6169
Bude 4 SS 2006
Budlake 5 SS 9700
Budle 53 NU 1534
Budleigh Salterton 7 SY 0682
Budock Water 2 SW 7832
Buerton 32 SJ 6843
Bugbrooke 26 SP 6757
Bugle 3 SX 0158
Bugthorpe 38 SE 7757
Builth Road 15 SO 0253
Builth Wells 23 SO 0351
Bulby 35 TF 0526
Buldoo 67 NC 9967
Bulford 8 SU 1643
Bulkeley 32 SJ 5254
Bulkington (Warw.) 26 SP 3986
Bulkington (Wilts.) 17 ST 9458
Bulkworthy 4 SS 3914
Bulley 17 SO 7519
Bullwood 49 NS 1674
Bulmer (Essex) 20 TL 8440
Bulmer (N Yorks.) 38 SE 6967
Bulmer Tye 20 TL 8438
Bulphan 20 TQ 6385
Bulverhythe 12 TQ 7809
Bulwell 34 SK 5345
Bulwick 27 SP 9694
Bumble's Green 20 TL 4005
Bunacaimb 58 NM 6588
Bunarkaig 59 NN 1887
Bunaveneadar 63 NB 1304
Bunbury 32 SJ 5658
Bunchrew 60 NH 6145
Buncton 11 TQ 1413
Bundalloch 59 NG 8927
Buness (Unst) 63 HP 6309
Bunessan 54 NM 3821
Bungay 29 TM 3389
Bunnahabhainn 48 NR 4173
Bunny 34 SK 5829
Buntingford 20 TL 3629
Bunwell 29 TM 1293
Bunwell Street 29 TM 1194
Burbage (Derby.) 33 SK 0472
Burbage (Leic.) 26 SP 4492
Burbage (Wilts.) 10 SU 2261
Burcombe (Wilts.) 8 SU 0630
Burcot 18 SU 5595
Burdale 39 SE 8762
Bures 21 TL 9034
Burford 18 SP 2512
Burgar 63 HY 3427
Burgess Hill 12 TQ 3118
Burgh 21 TM 2251
Burgh by Sands 46 NY 3259
Burghclere 10 SU 4660
Burghead 61 NJ 1168
Burghfield 10 SU 6668
Burghfield Common 10 SU 6466
Burghfield Hill 10 SU 6567
Burgh Heath 11 TQ 2458
Burghill 24 SO 4744
Burgh Le Marsh 35 TF 5065
Burgh Muir 62 NJ 7622
Burgh next Aylsham 29 TG 2125
Burgh on Bain 35 TF 2186
Burgh St. Margaret 29 TG 4413
Burgh St. Peter 29 TM 4693
Burghwallis 38 SE 5312
Burham 12 TQ 7262
Buriton 10 SU 7319
Burland 32 SJ 6153
Burlawn 3 SW 9970
Burleigh 11 SU 9069
Burlescombe 7 ST 0716
Burleston 8 SY 7794
Burley (Hants.) 8 SU 2103
Burley (Leic.) 27 SK 8810
Burleydam 32 SJ 6042
Burley Gate 24 SO 5947
Burley in Wharfedale 37 SE 1646
Burley Street 8 SU 2004
Burlingjobb 23 SO 2558
Burlton 32 SJ 4526
Burmarsh 13 TR 1032
Burmington 18 SP 2637
Burn 38 SE 5928
Burnage 33 SJ 8692
Burnaston 33 SK 2832
Burnby 39 SE 8346
Burneside 40 SD 5095
Burneston 42 SE 3084
Burnett 17 ST 6665
Burnfoot (Borders) 52 NT 4113
Burnfoot (Borders) 52 NT 5116
Burnfoot (Tays.) 56 NN 9804
Burnham (Berks.-Bucks.) 19 SU 9382
Burnham (Humbs.) 39 TA 0517
Burnham Beeches 19 SU 9585
Burnham Deepdale 28 TF 8044
Burnham Green 19 TL 2616
Burnham Market 28 TF 8342
Burnham Norton 28 TF 8243
Burnham-on-Crouch 21 TQ 9496
Burnham-on-Sea 7 ST 3049
Burnham Overy 28 TF 8442
Burnham Thorpe 28 TF 8541
Burnhaven 62 NK 1244
Burnhead 45 NX 8595
Burnhervie 62 NJ 7319
Burnhill Green 24 SJ 7800
Burnhope 47 NZ 1948
Burnhouse 50 NS 3850
Burniston 43 TA 0193
Burnley 37 SD 8332
Burnmouth 53 NT 9560
Burnopfield 47 NZ 1756
Burnsall 37 SE 0361
Burnside (Fife.) 56 NO 1607
Burnside (Lothian) 51 NT 0971
Burnside (Shetld.) 63 HU 2778
Burnside (Strath.) 50 NS 5811
Burnside (Tays.) 57 NO 4259
Burnside (Tays.) 57 NO 5050
Burnside of Duntrune 57 NO 4434
Burnt Fen 28 TL 6085
Burntisland 51 NT 2385
Burntwood 25 SK 0609
Burnt Yates 37 SE 2461
Burpham (Surrey) 11 TQ 0151
Burpham (W Susx) 11 TQ 0408
Burradon (Northum.) 47 NT 9806
Burradon (Tyne and Wear) 47 NZ 2772
Burra Firth 63 HP 6113
Burravoe (Shetld.) 63 HU 3666
Burravoe (Yell) 63 HU 5280
Burrelton 56 NO 1936
Burridge 9 SU 5110
Burrill 42 SE 2387
Burringham 39 SE 8309
Burrington (Avon) 16 ST 4759
Burrington (Devon.) 5 SS 6316
Burrington (Here. and Worc.) 24 SO 4472
Burrough Green 20 TL 6355
Burrough on the Hill 26 SK 7510
Burrow Bridge 7 ST 3530
Burrowhill 11 SU 9763
Burry Port 15 SN 4400
Burscough 36 SD 4310
Burscough Bridge 36 SD 4411
Bursea 39 SE 8033
Burshill 39 TA 0948
Bursledon 9 SU 4809
Burslem 33 SJ 8749
Burstall 21 TM 0944
Burstock 7 ST 4202
Burston (Norf.) 29 TM 1383
Burston (Staffs.) 33 SJ 9330
Burstow 12 TQ 3141
Burstwick 39 TA 2228
Burtersett 41 SD 8989
Burton (Ches.) 32 SJ 3174
Burton (Ches.) 32 SJ 5063
Burton (Cumbr.) 40 SD 5276
Burton (Dorset) 8 SZ 1794
Burton (Dyfed) 14 SM 9805
Burton (Lincs.) 34 SK 9574
Burton (Northum.) 53 NU 1732
Burton (Somer.) 7 ST 1944
Burton (Wilts.) 17 ST 8179
Burton Agnes 39 TA 1063
Burton Bradstock 7 SY 4889
Burton Coggles 34 SK 9725
Burton Constable 39 TA 1836
Burton Fleming 39 TA 0872
Burton Green (Clwyd) 32 SJ 3458
Burton Green (Warw.) 26 SP 2675
Burton Hastings 26 SP 4189
Burton in Lonsdale 36 SD 6572
Burton Joyce 34 SK 6443
Burton Latimer 27 SP 9074
Burton Lazars 34 SK 7716
Burton Leonard 38 SE 3263
Burton on the Wolds 34 SK 5821
Burton Overy 26 SP 6798
Burton Pedwardine 35 TF 1142
Burton Pidsea 39 TA 2431
Burton Salmon 38 SE 4827
Burton upon Stather 39 SE 8617
Burton upon Trent 33 SK 2423
Burtonwood 32 SJ 5692
Burwardsley 32 SJ 5156
Burwarton 24 SO 6185
Burwash 12 TQ 6724
Burwash Common 12 TQ 6423
Burwell (Cambs.) 28 TL 5866
Burwell (Lincs.) 35 TF 3579
Burwick (Shetld.) 63 HU 3940
Burwick (South Ronaldsay) 63 ND 4384
Bury (Cambs.) 27 TL 2883
Bury (Gtr Mches.) 37 SD 8010
Bury (Somer.) 6 SS 9427
Bury (W Susx) 11 TQ 0113
Bury Green 20 TL 4521
Bury St. Edmunds 28 TL 8564
Burythorpe 38 SE 7964
Busbridge 11 SU 9842
Busby (Strath.) 50 NS 5856
Busby (Tays.) 56 NO 0327
Buscot 18 SU 2297
Bushbury 25 SJ 9202
Bushey 19 TQ 1395
Bushey Heath 19 TQ 1594
Bush Green 29 TM 2187
Bushley 25 SO 8734
Bushton 17 SU 0677
Busta 63 HU 3466
Butcher's Pasture 20 TL 6024
Butcombe 16 ST 5161
Butleigh 7 ST 5233
Butleigh Wootton 7 ST 5034
Butlers Marston 26 SP 3150
Butley 21 TM 3651
Butsfield 47 NZ 1044
Buttercrambe 38 SE 7358
Butterknowle 41 NZ 1025
Butterleigh 5 SS 9708
Buttermere (Cumbr.) 40 NY 1717
Buttermere (Wilts.) 10 SU 3361
Buttershaw 37 SE 1329
Butterstone 56 NO 0646
Butterton 33 SK 0756
Butterwick (Humbs.) 39 SE 8305
Butterwick (Lincs.) 35 TF 3845
Butterwick (N Yorks.) 43 SE 7377
Butterwick (N Yorks.) 39 SE 9971
Butt Green 32 SJ 6651
Buttington 23 SJ 2408
Buttock's Booth 26 SP 7864
Buttonoak 24 SO 7578
Buxhall 21 TM 0057
Buxted 12 TQ 4923
Buxton (Derby.) 33 SK 0673
Buxton (Norf.) 29 TG 2222
Buxton Heath 29 TG 1821
Bwlch 16 SO 1422
Bwlchgwyn 31 SJ 2653
Bwlchllan 22 SN 5758
Bwlchtocyn 30 SH 3126
Bwlch-y-cibau 31 SJ 1717
Bwlch-y-ffridd 23 SO 0695
Bwlch-y-groes (Dyfed) 14 SN 2436
Bwlch-y-sarnau 23 SO 0274
Byers Green 42 NZ 2234
Byfield 26 SP 5153
Byfleet 11 TQ 0461
Byford 24 SO 3943
Bygrave 19 TL 2636
Byker 47 NZ 2763
Bylchau 31 SH 9762
Byley 32 SJ 7269
Bythorn 27 TL 0575
Byton 24 SO 3664
Byworth 11 SU 9921
Cabourne 39 TA 1301
Cabrach (Grampn.) 61 NJ 3826
Cadbury 5 SS 9105
Cadbury Barton 5 SS 6918
Cadder 50 NS 6172
Caddington 19 TL 0619
Caddonfoot 52 NT 4534
Cadeby (Leic.) 26 SK 4202
Cadeby (S Yorks.) 38 SE 5100
Cadeleigh 5 SS 9107
Cade Street 12 TQ 6021
Cadgwith 2 SW 7214
Cadham 57 NO 2701
Cadishead 32 SJ 7091
Cadle 15 SS 6297
Cadley 10 SU 2066
Cadmore End 18 SU 7892
Cadnam 9 SU 2913
Cadney 39 TA 0103
Cadole 31 SJ 2062
Caeathro 30 SH 5061
Caehopkin 15 SN 8212
Caeo 22 SN 6739
Caerau (Mid Glam.) 15 SS 8594
Caerau (S Glam.) 16 ST 1375
Caerdeon 30 SH 6418
Caergeiliog 30 SH 3178
Caergwrle 31 SJ 3057
Caerleon 16 ST 3390
Caernarfon 30 SH 4862
Caerphilly 16 ST 1587
Caersws 23 SO 0392
Caerwent 16 ST 4790
Caerwys 31 SJ 1272
Caethle 22 SN 6099
Cairnbaan 49 NR 8390
Cairnbrogie 62 NJ 8527
Cairncross 53 NT 8963
Cairndow 55 NN 1810
Cairness 62 NK 0360
Cairneyhill 51 NT 0486
Cairngaan 44 NX 1232
Cairngarroch 44 NX 0649
Cairnhill 62 NJ 6732
Cairnie 61 NJ 4945
Cairnorrie 62 NJ 8640
Cairnryan 44 NX 0668
Caister-on-Sea 29 TG 5212
Caistor 39 TA 1101
Caistor St. Edmund 29 TG 2303
Caistron 47 NT 9901
Caitha 52 NT 4540
Calbost 63 NB 4117
Calbourne 9 SZ 4286
Calcot 10 SU 6672
Caldbeck 40 NY 3239
Caldbergh 41 SE 0984
Caldecote (Cambs.) 27 TL 1488
Caldecote (Cambs.) 20 TL 3456
Caldecote (Herts.) 19 TL 2338
Caldecott (Leic.) 27 SP 8693
Caldecott (Northants.) 27 SP 9968
Calderbank 50 NS 7662
Calder Bridge 40 NY 0405
Calderbrook 37 SD 9418
Caldercruix 50 NS 8167
Calder Mains 67 ND 0959
Caldermill 50 NS 6641
Calder Vale 36 SD 5345
Caldhame 57 NO 4748
Caldicot 16 ST 4888
Caldwell 42 NZ 1613
Caldy 31 SJ 2285
Caledrhydiau 22 SN 4753
Calgary 54 NM 3751
Califer 61 NJ 0857
California (Central) 50 NS 9076
California (Norf.) 29 TG 5114
Calke 33 SK 3722
Callaly 53 NU 0509

Chilson Coppathorne

Chilson	18	SP 3119
Chilsworthy (Corn.)	4	SX 4172
Chilsworthy (Devon.)	4	SS 3206
Chilthorne Domer	7	ST 5219
Chilton (Bucks.)	18	SP 6811
Chilton (Durham)	42	NZ 3031
Chilton (Oxon.)	18	SU 4885
Chilton Buildings	42	NZ 2929
Chilton Cantelo	7	ST 5621
Chilton Foliat	10	SU 3170
Chilton Polden	7	ST 3739
Chilton Street	20	TL 7547
Chilton Trinity	7	ST 2939
Chilworth	9	SU 4018
Chimney	18	SP 3500
Chineham	10	SU 6554
Chingford	20	TQ 3893
Chinley	33	SK 0382
Chinnor	18	SP 7500
Chipnall	32	SJ 7231
Chippenham (Cambs.)	28	TL 6669
Chippenham (Wilts.)	17	ST 9173
Chipperfield	19	TL 0401
Chipping (Herts.)	20	TL 3532
Chipping (Lancs.)	36	SD 6243
Chipping Campden	25	SP 1539
Chipping Hill	20	TL 8215
Chipping Norton	18	SP 3127
Chipping Ongar	20	TL 5502
Chipping Sodbury	17	ST 7282
Chipping Warden	26	SP 4948
Chipstable	7	ST 0427
Chipstead (Kent)	12	TQ 5056
Chipstead (Surrey)	11	TQ 2756
Chirbury	23	SO 2598
Chirk	31	SJ 2937
Chirmorie	44	NX 2076
Chirnside	53	NT 8756
Chirnsidebridge	53	NT 8556
Chirton	17	SU 0757
Chisbury	10	SU 2766
Chiselborough	7	ST 4614
Chisledon	17	SU 1879
Chislehampton	18	SU 5999
Chislehurst	12	TQ 4470
Chislet	13	TR 2264
Chiswellgreen	19	TL 1303
Chiswick	11	TQ 2077
Chisworth	33	SJ 9991
Chithurst	10	SU 8423
Chittering	28	TL 4970
Chitterne	8	ST 9843
Chittlehamholt	6	SS 6420
Chittlehampton	6	SS 6325
Chittoe	17	ST 9666
Chivelstone	5	SX 7838
Chobham	11	SU 9761
Cholderton	10	SU 2242
Cholesbury	19	SP 9307
Chollerton	47	NY 9372
Cholsey	18	SU 5886
Cholstrey	24	SO 4659
Choppington	47	NZ 2583
Chopwell	47	NZ 1158
Chorley (Ches.)	32	SJ 5650
Chorley (Lancs.)	36	SD 5817
Chorley (Salop)	24	SO 6983
Chorley (Staffs.)	25	SK 0711
Chorleywood	19	TQ 0396
Chorlton	32	SJ 7250
Chorlton-cum-Hardy	37	SJ 8093
Chorlton Lane	32	SJ 4547
Chowley	32	SJ 4756
Chrishall	20	TL 4439
Christchurch (Cambs.)	28	TL 4996
Christchurch (Dorset)	8	SZ 1593
Christchurch (Glos.)	17	SO 5713
Christian Malford	17	ST 9678
Christleton	32	SJ 4365
Christmas Common	18	SU 7193
Christon	16	ST 3956
Christon Bank	53	NU 2122
Christow	5	SX 8385
Chudleigh	5	SX 8679
Chudleigh Knighton	5	SX 8477
Chulmleigh	5	SS 6814
Chunal	33	SK 0391
Church	36	SD 7428
Churcham	17	SO 7618
Church Aston	24	SJ 7317
Church Brampton	26	SP 7165
Church Broughton	33	SK 2033
Church Crookham	10	SU 8152
Churchdown	17	SO 8819
Church Eaton	33	SJ 8417
Church End (Beds.)	19	SP 9921
Church End (Beds.)	19	TL 1937
Church End (Cambs.)	27	TF 3909
Church End (Cambs.)	20	TL 4857
Church End (Essex)	20	TL 5841
Churchend (Essex)	20	TL 6323
Churchend (Essex)	21	TR 0092
Church End (Hants.)	10	SU 6756
Church End (Warw.)	26	SP 2892
Church End (Wilts.)	17	SU 0278
Church Fenton	38	SE 5136
Church Gresley	33	SK 2918
Church Handborough	18	SP 4212
Churchill (Avon)	16	ST 4359
Churchill (Here. and Worc.)	25	SO 8779
Churchill (Oxon.)	18	SP 2824
Churchingford	7	ST 2112
Church Knowle	8	SY 9481
Church Langton	26	SP 7293
Church Lawford	26	SP 4476
Church Lawton	32	SJ 8255
Church Leigh	33	SK 0235
Church Lench	25	SP 0251
Church Minshull	32	SJ 6660
Church Norton	11	SZ 8695
Churchover	26	SP 5080
Church Preen	24	SO 5398
Church Pulverbatch	24	SJ 4303
Churchstanton	7	ST 1914
Church Stoke	23	SO 2694
Churchstow (Devon.)	5	SX 7145
Church Stowe (Northants.)	26	SP 6357
Church Street	12	TQ 7174
Church Stretton	24	SO 4593
Churchtown (I. of M.)	43	SC 4294
Churchtown (Lancs.)	36	SD 4842
Churchtown (Mers.)	36	SD 3618
Church Warsop	34	SK 5668
Churt	10	SU 8538
Churton	32	SJ 4156
Churwell	37	SE 2729
Chwilog	30	SH 4338
Chyandour	2	SW 4731
Cilcain	31	SJ 1765
Cilcennin	22	SN 5160
Cilfor	30	SH 6237
Cilfrew	15	SN 7600
Cilfynydd	16	ST 0892
Cilgerran	14	SN 1943
Cilgwyn	15	SN 7430
Ciliau-Aeron	22	SN 5058
Cilmalieu	54	NM 8955
Cilmery	23	SO 0051
Cilrhedyn	14	SN 2734
Ciltalgarth	31	SH 8840
Cilwendeg	14	SN 2238
Cilybebyll	15	SN 7404
Cilycwm	22	SN 7540
Cinderford	17	SO 6513
Cioch Mhor	65	NH 5063
Cirean Geardail	64	NC 0034
Cirencester	17	SP 0201
City Dulas	30	SH 4687
Clachaig	49	NS 1181
Clachan (Benbecula)	63	NF 7746
Clachan (Lismore Island)	54	NM 8543
Clachan (North Uist)	63	NF 8163
Clachan (Raasay)	58	NG 5436
Clachan (Strath.)	54	NM 7819
Clachan (Strath.)	48	NR 7656
Clachan Mor	48	NL 9847
Clachan of Campsie	50	NS 6179
Clachan of Glendaruel	49	NR 9984
Clachan-Seil	54	NM 7718
Clachbreck	48	NR 7675
Clachtoll	64	NC 0427
Clackavoid	56	NO 1463
Clackmannan	50	NS 9191
Clacton-on-Sea	21	TM 1715
Claddach Kirkibost	63	NF 7865
Cladich	55	NN 0921
Claggan	54	NM 7049
Claigan	58	NG 2354
Claines	25	SO 8559
Clandown	17	ST 6955
Clanfield (Hants.)	9	SU 6916
Clanfield (Oxon.)	18	SP 2801
Clannaborough Barton	5	SS 7402
Clanville	10	SU 3148
Clanyard	44	NX 1037
Claonaig	49	NR 8656
Claonel	66	NC 5604
Clapgate	8	SU 0102
Clapham (Beds.)	27	TL 0252
Clapham (Gtr London)	11	TQ 2875
Clapham (N Yorks.)	36	SD 7469
Clapham (W Susx)	11	TQ 0906
Clappers	53	NT 9455
Clappersgate	40	NY 3603
Clapton (Glos.)	17	SP 1617
Clapton (Somer.)	7	ST 4106
Clapton-in-Gordano	16	ST 4774
Clapworthy	6	SS 6724
Clarbeston	14	SN 0421
Clarbeston Road	14	SN 0121
Clarborough	34	SK 7283
Clardon	67	ND 1468
Clare	20	TL 7645
Clarebrand	45	NX 7666
Claremont Park	11	TQ 1363
Clarencefield	45	NY 0968
Clarkston	50	NS 5757
Clashmore	65	NH 7489
Clashnessie	64	NC 0530
Clathy	56	NN 9919
Clatt	61	NJ 5426
Clatter	23	SN 9994
Clattering Brig	57	NO 6678
Clatworthy	7	ST 0530
Claughton (Lancs.)	36	SD 5242
Claughton (Lancs.)	36	SD 5666
Claverdon	25	SP 1964
Claverham	16	ST 4566
Clavering	20	TL 4832
Claverley	24	SO 7993
Claverton	17	ST 7864
Clawdd-newydd	31	SJ 0852
Clawton	4	SX 3599
Claxby (Lincs.)	35	TF 1194
Claxby (Lincs.)	35	TF 4571
Claxton (Norf.)	29	TG 3303
Claxton (N Yorks.)	38	SE 6960
Claybokie	61	NO 0889
Claybrooke Magna	26	SP 4988
Clay Common	29	TM 4781
Clay Coton	26	SP 5977
Clay Cross	33	SK 3963
Claydon (Oxon.)	26	SP 4550
Claydon (Suff.)	21	TM 1350
Claygate	11	TQ 1563
Claygate Cross	12	TQ 6155
Clayhanger (Devon.)	7	ST 0223
Clayhanger (W Mids)	25	SK 0404
Clayhidon	7	ST 1615
Clayock	67	ND 1659
Claypole	34	SK 8449
Clays of Allan	65	NH 8376
Clayton (Staffs.)	33	SJ 8443
Clayton (S Yorks.)	38	SE 4507
Clayton (W Susx)	12	TQ 3014
Clayton (W Yorks.)	37	SE 1131
Clayton-le-Moors	36	SD 7431
Clayton-le-Woods	36	SD 5722
Clayton West	37	SE 2511
Clayworth	34	SK 7288
Cleadale	58	NM 4789
Cleadon	47	NZ 3862
Clearwell	17	SO 5708
Cleasby	42	NZ 2713
Cleat	63	ND 4584
Cleatlam	41	NZ 1118
Cleator	40	NY 0113
Cleator Moor	40	NY 0214
Cleckheaton	37	SE 1825
Cleedownton	24	SO 5880
Cleehill	24	SO 5975
Clee St. Margaret	24	SO 5684
Cleethorpes	39	TA 3008
Cleeton St. Mary	24	SO 6178
Cleeve	16	ST 4566
Cleeve Hill	17	SO 9827
Cleeve Prior	25	SP 0849
Clehonger	24	SO 4637
Cleigh	54	NM 8725
Cleish	56	NT 0998
Cleland	50	NS 7958
Clench Common	17	SU 1765
Clenchwarton	28	TF 5820
Clent	25	SO 9179
Cleobury Mortimer	24	SO 6775
Cleobury North	24	SO 6187
Cleongart	48	NR 6734
Clephanton	60	NH 8450
Clerklands	52	NT 5024
Clestrain	63	HY 3006
Cleuchbrae	45	NY 0673
Clevancy	17	SU 0475
Clevedon	16	ST 4071
Cleveleys	36	SD 3142
Cleverton	17	ST 9785
Clewer	7	ST 4350
Cley next the Sea	29	TG 0444
Cliasamol	63	NB 0706
Cliburn	41	NY 5824
Cliddesden	10	SU 6349
Cliffe (Kent)	12	TQ 7376
Cliffe (N Yorks.)	38	SE 6631
Cliff End	13	TQ 8813
Cliffe Woods	12	TQ 7373
Clifford (Here. and Worc.)	23	SO 2445
Clifford (W Yorks.)	38	SE 4244
Clifford Chambers	25	SP 1952
Clifford's Mesne	17	SO 7023
Cliffsend	13	TR 3464
Clifton (Avon)	17	ST 5673
Clifton (Beds.)	27	TL 1739
Clifton (Central)	55	NN 3230
Clifton (Cumbr.)	40	NY 0429
Clifton (Cumbr.)	40	NY 5326
Clifton (Derby.)	33	SK 1644
Clifton (Here. and Worc.)	25	SO 8446
Clifton (Lancs.)	36	SD 4630
Clifton (Northum.)	47	NZ 2082
Clifton (Notts.)	34	SK 5434
Clifton (Oxon.)	18	SP 4831
Clifton Campville	26	SK 2510
Clifton Hampden	18	SU 5495
Clifton Reynes	27	SP 9051
Clifton upon Dunsmore	26	SP 5276
Clifton upon Teme	24	SO 7161
Climping	11	TQ 0002
Clint	37	SE 2559
Clinterty	62	NJ 8311
Clint Green	29	TG 0210
Clintmains	52	NT 6132
Clippesby	29	TG 4214
Clipsham	34	SK 9616
Clipston (Northants.)	26	SP 7181
Clipston (Notts.)	34	SK 6333
Clipstone	34	SK 6064
Clitheroe	36	SD 7441
Clive	32	SJ 5124
Clivocast	63	HP 6000
Clocaenog	31	SJ 0854
Clochan	61	NJ 4060
Clock Face	32	SJ 5291
Clodock	16	SO 3227
Clola	62	NK 0043
Clophill	19	TL 0838
Clopton	27	TL 0680
Clopton Green	20	TL 7654
Closeburn	45	NX 8992
Close Clark	43	SC 2775
Clothall	19	TL 2732
Clothan	63	HU 4581
Clotton	32	SJ 5263
Clough Foot	37	SD 9123
Cloughton	43	TA 0094
Cloughton Newlands	43	TA 0096
Clousta	63	HU 3157
Clova (Grampn.)	61	NJ 4522
Clova (Tays.)	57	NO 3273
Clovelly	6	SS 2124
Clovenfords	52	NT 4436
Clovenstone	62	NJ 7717
Clovulin	55	NN 0063
Clowne	34	SK 4975
Clows Top	24	SO 7171
Cluer	63	NG 1490
Clun	23	SO 3081
Clunas	60	NH 8846
Clunbury	24	SO 2780
Clunes	59	NN 2088
Clungunford	24	SO 3978
Clunie (Grampn.)	62	NJ 6350
Clunie (Tays.)	56	NO 1043
Clunton	23	SO 3381
Cluny	51	NT 2395
Clutton (Avon)	17	ST 6159
Clutton (Ches.)	32	SJ 4654
Clwt-y-bont	30	SH 5763
Clydach (Gwent)	16	SO 2213
Clydach (W Glam.)	15	SN 6801
Clydach Vale	16	SS 9793
Clydebank	50	NS 5069
Clydey	14	SN 2535
Clyffe Pypard	17	SU 0776
Clynder	49	NS 2484
Clynderwen	14	SN 1219
Clynelish	67	NC 8905
Clynnog-fawr	30	SH 4149
Clyro	23	SO 2143
Clyst Honiton	5	SX 9893
Clyst Hydon	7	ST 0301
Clyst St. George	5	SX 9888
Clyst St. Lawrence	7	ST 0200
Clyst St. Mary	5	SX 9890
Clyth	67	ND 2937
Cnwch Coch	22	SN 7665
Coad's Green	4	SX 2976
Coal Aston	33	SK 3679
Coalbrookdale	24	SJ 6604
Coalburn	50	NS 8034
Coalcleugh	46	NY 8045
Coaley	17	SO 7701
Coalpit Heath	17	ST 6780
Coalport	24	SJ 6902
Coalsnaughton	50	NS 9195
Coaltown of Balgonie	57	NT 2999
Coaltown of Wemyss	51	NT 3295
Coalville	26	SK 4214
Coast	64	NG 9290
Coatbridge	50	NS 7265
Coatdyke	50	NS 7464
Coate (Wilts.)	17	SU 0361
Coate (Wilts.)	17	SU 1782
Coates (Cambs.)	27	TL 3097
Coates (Glos.)	17	SO 9700
Coatham	42	NZ 5925
Coatham Mundeville	42	NZ 2919
Coatsgate	45	NT 0605
Cobbaton	6	SS 6127
Coberley	17	SO 9615
Cobham (Kent)	12	TQ 6768
Cobham (Surrey)	11	TQ 1060
Cobnash	24	SO 4560
Cockayne	42	SE 6298
Cockayne Hatley	27	TL 2549
Cock Bridge	61	NJ 2509
Cockburnspath	53	NT 7770
Cock Clarks	20	TL 8102
Cockenzie and Port Seton	52	NT 4075
Cockerham	36	SD 4651
Cockerington	35	TF 3789
Cockermouth	40	NY 1230
Cockernhoe Green	19	TL 1223
Cockfield (Durham)	42	NZ 1224
Cockfield (Suff.)	21	TL 9054
Cockfosters	19	TQ 2896
Cocking	11	SU 8717
Cockington	5	SX 8964
Cocklake	7	ST 4349
Cockley Cley	28	TF 7904
Cockpole Green	18	SU 7981
Cockshutt	32	SJ 4329
Cockthorpe	29	TF 9842
Cockwood	5	SX 9780
Coddenham	21	TM 1354
Coddington (Ches.)	32	SJ 4455
Coddington (Here. and Worc.)	24	SO 7142
Coddington (Notts.)	34	SK 8354
Codford St. Mary	8	ST 9739
Codford St. Peter	8	ST 9640
Codicote	19	TL 2118
Codnor	33	SK 4149
Codrington	17	ST 7278
Codsall	25	SJ 8603
Codsall Wood	25	SJ 8405
Coedana	30	SH 4381
Coedely	16	ST 0285
Coedkernew	16	ST 2783
Coedpoeth	31	SJ 2850
Coed-y-paen	16	ST 3398
Coelbren	15	SN 8411
Coffinswell	5	SX 8868
Cofton Hackett	25	SP 0075
Cogan	16	ST 1772
Cogenhoe	27	SP 8360
Coggeshall	20	TL 8522
Coillaig	55	NN 0120
Coille Coire Chrannaig	55	NN 4888
Coille Mhorgil	59	NH 1001
Coillore	58	NG 3537
Coity	15	SS 9281
Coker	7	ST 5312
Colaboll	66	NC 5610
Colan	2	SW 8661
Colaton Raleigh	7	SY 0787
Colbost	58	NG 2148
Colby (Cumbr.)	41	NY 6620
Colby (I. of M.)	43	SC 2370
Colby (Norf.)	29	TG 2131
Colchester	21	TM 0025
Cold Ash	10	SU 5169
Cold Ashby	26	SP 6576
Cold Ashton	17	ST 7472
Coldbackie	66	NC 6160
Coldblow	12	TQ 5173
Cold Brayfield	27	SP 9252
Coldean	12	TS 3408
Coldeast	5	SX 8274
Colden Common	9	SU 4822
Coldfair Green	29	TM 4361
Cold Hanworth	35	TF 0383
Coldharbour	11	TQ 1443
Cold Hesledon	47	NZ 4147
Cold Higham	26	SP 6653
Coldingham	53	NT 9065
Cold Kirby	42	SE 5384
Cold Newton	26	SK 7106
Cold Norton	20	TL 8500
Cold Overton	26	SK 8110
Coldrain	56	NO 0700
Coldred	13	TR 2747
Coldridge	5	SS 6907
Coldstream	53	NT 8439
Coldwaltham	11	TQ 0216
Coldwells	62	NK 1039
Coldwells Croft	61	NJ 5622
Cole	8	ST 6633
Colebatch	23	SO 3187
Colebrook	7	ST 0006
Colebrooke	5	SX 7799
Coleby (Humbs.)	39	SE 8919
Coleby (Lincs.)	34	SK 9760
Coleford (Devon.)	5	SS 7701
Coleford (Glos.)	17	SO 5710
Coleford (Somer.)	8	ST 6848
Colehill	8	SU 0300
Coleman's Hatch	12	TQ 4533
Colemere	32	SJ 4232
Colenden	56	NO 1029
Coleorton	33	SK 3917
Colerne	17	ST 8171
Colesbourne	17	SO 9913
Colesden	27	TL 1255
Coleshill (Bucks.)	19	SU 9495
Coleshill (Oxon.)	18	SU 2393
Coleshill (Warw.)	25	SP 1989
Colgate	11	TQ 2332
Colgrain	49	NS 3280
Colinsburgh	57	NO 4703
Colinton	51	NT 2169
Colintraive	49	NS 0374
Colkirk	28	TF 9126
Coll	63	NB 4739
Collace	56	NO 2032
Collafirth (Shetld.)	63	HU 3482
Collafirth (Shetld.)	63	HU 4368
Collaton St, Mary	5	SX 8660
Collessie	57	NO 2813
Collier Row	20	TQ 4991
Collier's End	20	TL 3720
Collier Street	12	TQ 7145
Colliery Row	47	NZ 3449
Collieston	62	NK 0328
Collin	45	NY 0276
Collingbourne Ducis	10	SU 2353
Collingbourne Kingston	10	SU 2355
Collingham (Notts.)	34	SK 8261
Collingham (W Yorks.)	38	SE 3845
Collington	24	SO 6460
Collingtree	26	SP 7555
Colliston	57	NO 6045
Collynie	62	NJ 8436
Collyweston	27	SK 9903
Colmonell	44	NX 1586
Colmworth	27	TL 1058
Colnabaichin	61	NJ 2908
Colnbrook	11	TQ 0277
Colne (Cambs.)	27	TL 2776
Colne (Lancs.)	37	SD 8839
Colne Engaine	20	TL 8530
Colne Valley	20	TL 8529
Colney	29	TG 1808
Colney Heath	19	TL 2005
Colney Street	19	TL 1502
Coln Rogers	17	SP 0809
Coln St. Aldwyns	17	SP 1405
Coln St. Dennis	17	SP 0810
Colp	62	NJ 7448
Colpy	62	NJ 6432
Colsterdale	42	SE 1280
Colsterworth	34	SK 9224
Colston Bassett	34	SK 7033
Coltfield	61	NJ 1163
Coltishall	29	TG 2619
Colton (Cumbr.)	40	SD 3186
Colton (Norf.)	29	TG 1009
Colton (N Yorks.)	38	SE 5444
Colton (Staffs.)	33	SK 0520
Colvister	63	HU 5196
Colwall Green	24	SO 7541
Colwall Stone	24	SO 7542
Colwell	47	NY 9575
Colwich	33	SK 0121
Colwinston	15	SS 9475
Colworth	11	SU 9102
Colwyn Bay	31	SH 8478
Colyford	7	SY 2492
Colyton	7	SY 2493
Combe (Berks.)	10	SU 3760
Combe (Here. and Worc.)	23	SO 3463
Combe (Oxon.)	18	SP 4115
Combe Florey	7	ST 1531
Combe Hay	17	ST 7359
Combeinteignhead	5	SX 9071
Coombe Martin	6	SS 5846
Coombe Moor	24	SO 3663
Coombe Raleigh	7	ST 1502
Comberbach	32	SJ 6477
Comberton	20	TL 3856
Combe St. Nicholas	7	ST 3011
Comb Hill	46	NT 3900
Combrook	26	SP 3051
Coombs (Derby.)	33	SK 0478
Combs (Suff.)	21	TM0456
Coombs Ford	21	TM 0457
Coombwich	7	ST 2542
Comers	62	NJ 6707
Commins Coch	22	SH 8403
Commondale	42	NZ 6610
Common Edge	36	SD 3232
Common Moor	4	SX 2369
Common Side	33	SK 3375
Common, The	9	SU 2432
Compstall	33	SJ 9690
Compton (Berks.)	18	SU 5279
Compton (Devon.)	5	SX 8664
Compton (Hants.)	9	SU 4625
Compton (Surrey)	11	SU 9547
Compton (Wilts.)	17	ST 1352
Compton (W Susx)	10	SU 7714
Compton Abbas	8	ST 8718
Compton Abdale	17	SP 0516
Compton Bassett	17	SU 0372
Compton Beauchamp	18	SU 2887
Compton Bishop	16	ST 3955
Compton Chamberlayne	8	SU 0229
Compton Dando	17	ST 6464
Compton Dundon	7	ST 4933
Compton Martin	16	ST 5456
Compton Pauncefoot	8	ST 6425
Compton Valence	8	SY 5993
Comrie	56	NN 7722
Conchra	49	NS 0288
Concraigie	56	NO 1044
Conderton	25	SO 9637
Condicote	17	SP 1528
Condorrat	50	NS 7373
Condover	24	SJ 4906
Coneyhurst Common	11	TQ 1024
Coneysthorpe	38	SE 7171
Coney Weston	29	TL 9578
Congerstone	26	SK 3706
Congham	28	TF 7123
Congleton	33	SJ 8562
Congresbury	16	ST 4363
Coningsby	35	TF 2258
Conington (Cambs.)	27	TL 1785
Conington (Cambs.)	27	TL 3266
Conisbrough	38	SK 5098
Conisby	48	NR 2661
Conisholme	35	TF 3995
Coniston (Cumbr.)	40	SD 3097
Coniston (Humbs.)	39	TA 1535
Coniston Cold	37	SD 9054
Conistone	37	SD 9867
Connah's Quay	31	SJ 2869
Connel	54	NM 9134
Connel Park	50	NS 6012
Connor Downs	2	SW 5939
Cononbridge	60	NH 5455
Cononley	37	SD 9846
Consall	33	SJ 9748
Consett	47	NZ 1150
Constable Burton	42	SE 1690
Constantine	2	SW 7229
Contin	60	NH 4555
Contlaw	62	NJ 8402
Conway	31	SH 7777
Conyer	13	TQ 9664
Cookbury	4	SS 4005
Cookham	19	SU 8985
Cookham Dean	19	SU 8785
Cookham Rise	19	SU 8884
Cookhill	25	SP 0558
Cookley (Here. and Worc.)	25	SO 8480
Cookley (Suff.)	29	TM 3475
Cookley Green	18	SU 6990
Cookney	62	NO 8793
Cooksbridge	12	TQ 4013
Cooksmill Green	20	TL 6306
Coolham	11	TQ 1222
Cocling	12	TQ 7575
Coombe (Corn.)	4	SS 2011
Coombe (Corn.)	2	SW 9551
Coombe Bissett	8	SU 1026
Coombe Hill	17	SO 8827
Coombe Keynes	8	SY 8484
Coombes	11	TQ 1908
Coopersale Common	20	TL 4702
Copdock	21	TM 1141
Copford Green	21	TL 9222
Copister	63	HU 4778
Cople	27	TL 1048
Copley	41	NZ 0825
Coplow Dale	33	SK 1679
Copmanthorpe	38	SE 5646
Coppathorne	4	SS 2000

Dalavich Dutton

Dalavich 55 NM 9612
Dalbeattie 45 NX 8361
Dalbeg 63 NB 2345
Dalblair 50 NS 6419
Dalbog 57 NO 5871
Dalby 43 SC 2178
Dalcapon 56 NN 9755
Dalchalloch 56 NN 7264
Dalchenna 55 NN 0706
Dalchreichart 59 NH 2912
Dalcross 60 NH 7748
Dalderby 35 TF 2465
Dale (Derby.) 33 SK 4338
Dale (Dyfed) 14 SM 8005
Dale (Shetld.) 63 HU 1852
Dale Head 40 NY 4316
Dalelia 54 NM 7369
Dalgarven 49 NS 2945
Dalginross 56 NN 7721
Dalguise 56 NN 9947
Dalhalvaig 67 NC 8954
Dalham 28 TL 7261
Daliburgh 63 NF 7421
Dalkeith 51 NT 3367
Dall 56 NN 5956
Dallas 61 NJ 1252
Dalleagles 50 NS 5710
Dalle Crucis Abbey (ant.) 32 SJ 2044
Dallinghoo 21 TM 2654
Dallington 12 TQ 6519
Dallmally 55 NN 1527
Dalmary 50 NS 5195
Dalmellington 44 NS 4705
Dalmeny 51 NT 1477
Dalmigavie 60 NH 7419
Dalmore (Highld.) 65 NH 6668
Dalmore (Isle of Lewis) 63 NB 2244
Dalnabreck 54 NM 7069
Dalnavie 65 NH 6473
Dalness 55 NN 1751
Dalnessie 66 NC6315
Dalqueich 56 NO 0704
Dalquharran Castle 44 NS 2702
Dalreavoch 66 NC 7508
Dalry 49 NS 2949
Dalrymple 49 NS 3514
Dalserf 50 NS 7950
Dalston 46 NY 3750
Dalswinton 45 NX 9385
Dalton (Dumf. and Galwy.) 45 NY1173
Dalton (Lancs.) 36 SD 4907
Dalton (Northum.) 47 NY 9158
Dalton (Northum.) 47 NZ 1172
Dalton (N Yorks.) 41 NZ 1108
Dalton (N Yorks.) 42 SE 4376
Dalton (N Yorks.) 34 SK 4593
Dalton in Furness 40 SD 2374
Dalton-le-Dale 47 NZ4047
Dalton-on-Tees 42 NZ 2908
Dalton Piercy 42 NZ 4631
Dalveich 56 NN 6124
Dalwhinnie 56 NN 6384
Dalwood 7 ST 2400
Damerham 8 SU 1015
Damgate 29 TG 3909
Damnaglaur 44 NX 1235
Danbury 20 TL 7805
Danby 43 NZ 7009
Danby Wiske 42 SE 3398
Dandaleith 61 NJ 2845
Danderhall 51 NT 3069
Danebridge 33 SJ 9665
Dane End 20 TL 3321
Danehill 12 TQ 4027
Dane Hills 26 SK 5605
Danskine 52 NT 5667
Daren-felen 16 SO 2212
Darenth 12 TQ 5671
Daresbury 32 SJ 5782
Darfield 38 SE 4104
Dargate 13 TR 0861
Darite 4 SX 2569
Darlaston 25 SO 9796
Darlingscott 26 SP 2342
Darlington 42 NZ 2914
Darliston 32 SJ 5833
Darlochan 48 NR 6723
Darlton 34 SK 7773
Darowen 22 SH 8302
Darras Hall 47 NZ 1571
Darrington 38 SE 4919
Darsham 29 TM 4170
Dartford 12 TQ 5474
Dartington 5 SX 7862
Dartmeet 5 SX 6773
Dartmouth 5 SX 8751
Darton 38 SE 3110
Darvel 50 NS 5637
Darwen 36 SD 6922
Datchet 11 SU 9876
Datchworth 19 TL 2619
Dauntsey 17 ST 9882
Davenham 32 SJ 6570
Daventry 26 SP 5762
Davidstow 4 SX 1587
Davington 46 NT 2302
Daviot (Grampn.) 62 NJ 7528
Daviot (Highld.) 60 NH 7139
Davoch of Grange 61 NJ 4951
Dawley 24 SJ 6807
Dawlish 5 SX 9676
Dawlish Warren 5 SX 9778
Dawn 31 SH 8672
Daws Heath 20 TQ 8188
Dawsmere 35 TF 4430
Daylesford 18 SP 2425
Deadwater 46 NY 6096
Deal 13 TR 3752
Dean (Cumbr.) 40 NY 0725
Dean (Devon.) 5 SX 7364
Dean (Hants.) 9 SU 5619
Dean (Somer.) 8 ST 6743
Deanburnhaugh 51 NT 3911
Deane 10 SU 5450
Deanland 8 ST 9918
Dean Prior 5 SX 7363
Dean Row 33 SJ 8781
Deanscale 40 NY 0926
Deanshanger 26 SP 7639
Deanston 56 NN 7101
Dearham 40 NY 0736
Debach 21 TM 2454
Debden 20 TL 5533
Debden Cross 20 TL 5832
Debenham 29 TM 1763
Dechmont 51 NT 0370
Deddington 18 SP 4631
Dedham 21 TM 0533
Deene 27 SP 9492
Deenethorpe 27 SP 9592
Deepcar 38 SK 2897
Deepcut 11 SU 9057
Deepdale 41 SD 7284
Deeping Gate 27 TF 1509
Deeping St. James 27 TF 1609
Deeping St. Nicholas 35 TF 2115
Deerhurst 17 SO 8729
Defford 25 SO 9143
Defynnog 15 SN 9227
Deganwy 31 SH 7779
Deighton (N Yorks.) 42 NZ 3801
Deighton (N Yorks.) 38 SE 6244
Deiniolen 30 SH 5863
Delabole 4 SX 0683
Delamere 32 SJ 5668
Dell 63 NB 4861
Delliefure 61 NJ 0731
Delph 37 SD 9807
Dembleby 35 TF 0437
Denaby 38 SK 4899
Denbigh 31 SJ 0566
Denbury 5 SX 8268
Denby 33 SK 3946
Denby Dale 37 SE 2208
Denchworth 18 SU 3891
Denend 62 NJ 6038
Denford 27 SP 9976
Dengie 21 TL 9801
Denham (Bucks.) 19 TQ 0386
Denham (Suff.) 28 TL 7561
Denham (Suff.) 29 TM 1974
Denham Green 19 TQ 0388
Denhead (Fife.) 57 NO 4613
Denhead (Grampn.) 62 NJ 9952
Denhead of Gray 57 NO 3431
Denholm 52 NT 5718
Denholme 37 SE 0633
Denmead 9 SU 6511
Dennington 29 TM 2866
Denny 50 NS 8182
Dennyloanhead 50 NS 8180
Denny Lodge 9 SU 3305
Denshaw 37 SD 9710
Denside 62 NO 8095
Densole 13 TR 2141
Denston 20 TL 7652
Denstone 33 SK 0940
Dent 41 SD 7087
Den, The 50 NS 3251
Denton (Cambs.) 27 TL 1487
Denton (Durham) 42 NZ 2118
Denton (E Susx) 12 TQ 502
Denton (Gtr Mches.) 33 SJ 9295
Denton (Kent) 13 TR 2146
Denton (Lincs.) 34 SK 8632
Denton (Norf.) 29 TM 2887
Denton (Northants.) 27 SP 8357
Denton (N Yorks.) 37 SE 1448
Denton (Oxon.) 18 SP 5902
Denver 28 TF 6101
Denwick (Northum.) 53 NU 2014
Deopham 29 TG 0400
Deopham Green 29 TM 0499
Depden Green 20 TL 7756
Deptford (Gtr London) 12 TQ 3676
Deptford (Wilts.) 8 SU 0038
Derby 33 SK 3435
Derbyhaven 43 SC 2867
Deri 16 SO 1202
Derringstone 13 TR 2049
Derrington 33 SJ 8822
Derry Hill 17 ST 9670
Derrythorpe 39 SE 8208
Dersingham 28 TF 6830
Dervaig 54 NM 4351
Derwen 31 SJ 0650
Desborough 26 SP 8083
Desford 26 SK 4703
Detchant 53 NU 0836
Detling 12 TQ 7958
Deuddwr 31 SJ 2317
Devauden 16 ST 4899
Devil's Bridge 22 SN 7477
Devizes 17 SU 0061
Devonport 4 SX 4554
Devonside 50 NS 9296
Devoran 2 SW 7939
Dewlish 8 SY 7798
Dewsall Court 24 SO 4833
Dewsbury 37 SE 2422
Dhoon 43 SC 4586
Dhoor 43 SC 4396
Dhowin 43 NX 4101
Diabaig 64 NG 8060
Dial Post 11 TQ 1519
Dibden 9 SU 3908
Dibden Purlieu 9 SU 4106
Dickleburgh 29 TM 1682
Didbrook 25 SP 0531
Didcot 18 SU 5290
Diddington 27 TL 1965
Diddlebury 24 SO 5085
Didley 24 SO 4432
Didmarton 17 ST 8287
Didsbury 33 SJ 8490
Didworthy 5 SX 6862
Digby 35 TF 0754
Diggle 37 SE 0008
Dihewyd 22 SN 4855
Dilham 29 TG 3325
Dilhorne 33 SJ 9743
Dilston 47 NY 9763
Dilton Marsh 8 ST 8449
Dilwyn 24 SO 4154
Dinas (Dyfed) 14 SN 0139
Dinas (Dyfed) 14 SN 2730
Dinas (Gwyn.) 30 SH 2736
Dinas-Mawddwy 31 SH 8514
Dinas Powis 16 ST 1571
Dinchope 24 SO4583
Dinder 7 ST 5744
Dinedor 24 SO 5336
Dingley 26 SP 7687
Dingwall 60 NH 5458
Dinnet 61 NO 4698
Dinnington (Somer.) 7 ST 4012
Dinnington (S Yorks.) 34 SK 5386
Dinnington (Tyne and Wear) 47 NZ 2073
Dinorwic 30 SH 5961
Dinton 8 SU 0131
Dinwoodie Mains 45 NY 1090
Dinworthy 4 SS 3015
Dippen 49 NR 7937
Dippin 49 NS 0422
Dipple (Grampn.) 61 NJ 3258
Dipple (Strath.) 44 NS 2002
Diptford 5 SX 7256
Dipton 47 NZ 1554
Dirleton 52 NT 5183
Discoed 23 SO 2764
Diseworth 34 SK 4524
Dishes 63 HY 6523
Dishforth 42 SE 3873
Disley 33 SJ 9784
Diss 29 TM 1179
Disserth 23 SO 0458
Distington 40 NY 0023
Ditcheat 8 ST 6236
Ditchingham 29 TM 3391
Ditchling 12 TQ 3215
Dittisham 5 SX 8655
Ditton (Ches.) 32 SJ 4986
Ditton (Kent) 12 TQ 7158
Ditton Green 20 TL 6658
Ditton Priors 24 SO 6089
Dixton (Glos.) 25 SO 9830
Dixton (Gwent) 16 SO 5114
Dobwalls 4 SX 2165
Doccombe 5 SX 7786
Dochgarroch 60 NH 6140
Docking 28 TF 7637
Docklow 24 SO 5657
Dockray 40 NY 3921
Dodburn 52 NT 4707
Doddinghurst 20 TQ 5998
Doddington (Cambs.) 27 TL 4090
Doddington (Kent) 13 TQ 9357
Doddington (Lincs.) 34 SK 8970
Doddington (Northum.) 53 NU 0032
Doddington (Salop) 24 SO 6176
Doddiscombsleigh 5 SX 8586
Dodford (Here. and Worc.) 25 SO 9273
Dodford (Northants.) 26 SP 6160
Dodington (Avon) 17 ST 7579
Dodleston 32 SJ 3661
Dodworth 38 SE 3105
Doe Lea 34 SK 4566
Dogdyke 35 TF 2055
Dogmersfield 10 SU 7852
Dog Village 5 SX 9896
Dolanog 23 SJ 0612
Dolau 23 SO 1367
Dolbenmaen 30 SH 5043
Dolfach 22 SN 9077
Dol-for (Powys) 22 SH 8006
Dolfor (Powys) 23 SO 1087
Dolgarrog 31 SH 7766
Dolgellau 30 SH 7217
Doll 67 NC 8803
Dollar 51 NS 9697
Dolphinholme 36 SD 5153
Dolphinton 51 NT 1046
Dolton 4 SS 5712
Dolwen (Clwyd) 31 SH 8874
Dolwen (Powys) 23 SH 9707
Dolwyddelan 30 SH 7352
Dolyhir 23 SO 2458
Domgay 31 SJ 2819
Doncaster 38 SE 5803
Donhead St. Andrew 8 ST 9124
Donhead St. Mary 8 ST 9024
Donibristle 51 NT 1688
Donington 35 TF 2135
Donington on Bain 35 TF 2382
Donisthorpe 26 SK 3114
Donkey Town 11 SU 9460
Donnington (Berks.) 10 SU 4668
Donnington (Glos.) 17 SP 1928
Donnington (Here. and Worc.) 24 SO 7034
Donnington (Salop) 24 SJ 5807
Donnington (Salop) 24 SJ 7114
Donnington (W Susx) 10 SU 8502
Donyatt 7 ST 3313
Doonfoot 49 NS 3218
Doonholm 49 NS 3317
Dorchester (Dorset) 8 SY 6990
Dorchester (Oxon) 18 SU 5794
Dordon 26 SK 2600
Dore 33 SK 3081
Dores 60 NH 5934
Dorking 11 TQ 1649
Dormans Land 12 TQ 4042
Dormanstown 42 NZ 5823
Dormington 24 SO 5840
Dorney 11 SU 9379
Dornie 59 NG 8826
Dornoch (Highld.) 65 NH 7989
Dornock (Dumf. and Galwy) 46 NY 2366
Dorrery 67 ND 0754
Dorridge 25 SP 1774
Dorrington (Lincs. 35 TF 0752
Dorrington (Salop) 24 SJ 4703
Dorsington 25 SP 1349
Dorstone 23 SO 3142
Dorton 18 SP 6714
Dosthill 26 SP 2199
Doublebois 4 SX 1964
Dougarie 49 NR 8837
Doughton 17 ST 8791
Douglas (I. of M.) 43 SC 3876
Douglas (Strath.) 50 NS 8330
Douglas and Angus 57 NO 4332
Douglas Hill 30 SH 6065
Douglastown 57 NO 4147
Doulting 8 ST 6443
Dounby 63 HY 2920
Doune (Tays.) 56 NN 7201
Douneside 61 NJ 4806
Dounie 65 NH 5590
Dounreay 67 NC 9966
Dousland 4 SX 5368
Dove Holes 33 SK 0778
Dovenby 40 NY 0933
Dover 13 TR 3141
Doverdale 25 SO 8566
Doveridge 33 SK 1134
Dowally 56 NO 0047
Dowdeswell 17 SO 9919
Dowland 4 SS 5610
Dowlish Wake 7 ST 3712
Down Ampney 17 SU 1097
Downderry 4 SX 3153
Downe 12 TQ 4361
Downend (Berks.) 10 SU 4775
Downend (I. of W.) 9 SZ 5387
Downfield 57 NO 3833
Downgate 4 SX 3772
Downham (Cambs.) 28 TL 5284
Downham (Essex) 20 TQ 7395
Downham (Lancs.) 37 SD 7844
Downham (Northum.) 53 NT 8633
Downham Market 28 TF 6003
Down Hatherley 17 SO 8622
Downhead 8 ST 6845
Downhill 2 SW 8669
Downholme 41 SE 1197
Downies 62 NO 9294
Downley 19 SU 8495
Down St. Mary 5 SS 7404
Downton (Hants.) 9 SZ 2693
Downton (Wilts.) 8 SU 1721
Downton on the Rock 24 SO 4273
Dowsby 35 TF 1129
Doxford 53 NU 1823
Doynton 17 ST 7173
Draffan 50 NS 7945
Drakeland Corner 4 SX 5758
Drakemyre 49 NS 2850
Drakes Broughton 25 SO 9248
Draughton (Northants.) 26 SP 7676
Draughton (N Yorks) 37 SE 0352
Drax 38 SE 6726
Draycote 26 SP 4469
Draycott (Derby) 34 SK 4433
Draycott (Glos.) 25 SP 1836
Draycott (Somer.) 7 ST 4750
Draycott in the Clay 33 SK 1528
Draycott in the Moors 33 SJ 9840
Drayton (Hants.) 9 SU 6605
Drayton (Here. and Worc.) 25 SO 9076
Drayton (Leic.) 27 SP 8392
Drayton (Norf.) 29 TG 1713
Drayton (Oxon) 26 SP 4241
Drayton (Oxon) 18 SU 4794
Drayton (Somer.) 7 ST 4024
Drayton Bassett 25 SK 1900
Drayton Parslow 19 SP 8428
Drayton St. Leonard 18 SU 5996
Drefach (Dyfed) 22 SN 3538
Drefach (Dyfed) 22 SN 5045
Drefach (Dyfed) 15 SN 5213
Dreghorn 49 NS 3538
Drem 52 NT 5079
Drewsteignton 5 SX 7391
Driby 35 TF 3874
Driffield 17 SU 0799
Drift 2 SW 4328
Drigg 40 SD 0698
Drighlington 37 SE 2229
Drimnin 54 NM 5553
Drimpton 7 ST 4104
Drinesheader 63 NG 1795
Drinkstone 29 TL 9561
Drinkstone Green 29 TL 9660
Drointon 33 SK 0226
Droitwich 25 SO 8962
Dron 56 NO 1415
Dronfield 33 SK 3578
Dronfield Woodhouse 33 SK 3278
Drongan 50 NS 4418
Dronley 57 NO 3435
Droxford 9 SU 6018
Droylsden 37 SJ 9098
Druid 31 SJ 0343
Druidale 43 SC 3688
Druidston 14 SM 8716
Druimarbin 55 NN 0861
Druimavuic 55 NN 0044
Drum (Grampn.) 62 NJ 8946
Drum (Tays.) 56 NO 0400
Drumbeg 64 NC 1232
Drumblade 61 NJ 5840
Drumbuie (Dumf. and Galwy.) 45 NX 5682
Drumbuie (Highld) 59 NG 7730
Drumburgh 46 NY 2659
Drumchapel 50 NS 5270
Drumchardine 60 NH 5644
Drumclog 50 NS 6339
Drumeldrie 57 NO 4403
Drumelzier 51 NT 1333
Drumfearn 58 NG 6716
Drumgask 60 NN 6193
Drumgley 57 NO 4250
Drumguish 60 NN 7999
Drumhead 62 NO 6092
Drumlassie 62 NJ 6405
Drumlemble 48 NR 6619
Drumlithie 57 NO 7880
Drummore 44 NX 1336
Drumnadrochit 60 NH 5029
Drumnagorrach 61 NJ 5252
Drumrash 45 NX 6871
Drumrunie 66 NC 1605
Drums 62 NJ 9822
Drumsallie 55 NM 9578
Drumshang 49 NS 2513
Drumsturdy 57 NO 4935
Drumuie 58 NG 4546
Drumuillie 60 NH 9420
Drumvaich 56 NN 6803
Drumwhindle 62 NJ 9236
Drunkendub 57 NO 6646
Drury 31 SJ 2964
Drybeck 41 NY 6615
Drybridge (Grampn.) 61 NJ 4362
Drybridge (Strath.) 50 NS 3536
Drybrook 17 SO 6416
Dry Doddington 34 SK 8446
Dry Drayton 27 TL 3862
Dryhope 51 NT 2624
Drymen 50 NS 4788
Drymuir 62 NJ 9146
Drynoch 58 NG 4031
Dubford 62 NJ 7963
Dubton 57 NO 5652
Ducklington 32 SJ 4851
Ducklington 18 SP 3507
Duck's Cross 27 TL 1156
Duddingston 51 NT 2972
Duddington 27 SK 9800
Duddleswell 12 TQ 4628
Duddo 53 NT 9342
Duddon 32 SJ 5164
Duddon Bridge 40 SD 1988
Dudleston Heath 32 SJ 3636
Dudley 25 SO 9390
Duffield 33 SK 3443
Duffryn 15 SS 8495
Dufftown 61 NJ 3240
Duffus 61 NJ 1668
Dufton 41 NY 6925
Duggleby 39 SE 8766
Duirinish 59 NG 7831
Duisdalemore 58 NG 6913
Duisky 55 NN 0176
Dukestown 16 SO 1410
Dukinfield 37 SJ 9497
Dulas (Gwyn.) 30 SH 4789
Dulcote 7 ST 5644
Dulford 7 ST 0606
Dull 56 NN 8049
Dullatur 50 NS 7476
Dullingham 20 TL 6357
Dulnain Bridge 61 NH 9924
Duloe (Beds.) 27 TL 1560
Duloe (Corn.) 4 SX 2358
Dulsie 60 NH 9341
Dulverton 6 SS 9127
Dulwich 12 TQ 3373
Dumbarton 50 NS 4075
Dumbleton 25 SP 0135
Dumfries 45 NX 9775
Dumgoyne 50 NS 5283
Dummer 10 SU 5845
Dun (Tays.) 57 NO 6659
Dunalastair 56 NN 7159
Dunan (Isle of Skye) 58 NG 5828
Dunan (Strath.) 49 NS 1571
Dunans 49 NS 0491
Dunball 7 ST 3140
Dunbar 52 NT 6878
Dunbeath 67 ND 1629
Dunbeg 54 NM 8734
Dunblane 56 NN 7801
Dunbog 57 NO 2817
Duncanston (Grampn.) 61 NJ 5826
Duncanston (Highld.) 60 NH 5956
Dunchurch 26 SP 4871
Duncote 26 SP 6750
Duncow 45 NX 9683
Duncrievie 56 NO 1309
Duncton 11 SU 9516
Dundee 57 NO 4030
Dundon 7 ST 4732
Dundonald 50 NS 3634
Dundonnell 64 NH 0886
Dundraw 46 NY 2149
Dundreggan 59 NH 3114
Dundrennan 45 NX 7447
Dundry 16 ST 5566
Dundurn 56 NN 7023
Dunecht 62 NJ 7509
Dunfermline 51 NT 0987
Dunford Bridge 37 SE 1602
Dunham 34 SK 8174
Dunham-on-the-Hill 32 SJ 4772
Dunhampton 25 SO 8466
Dunhampton 25 SO 8466
Dunham Town 32 SJ 7488
Dunholme 34 TF 0279
Dunino 57 NO 5311
Dunipace 50 NS 8083
Dunkeld 56 NO 0242
Dunkeswell 7 ST 1407
Dunkirk 13 TR 0758
Dunk's Green 12 TQ 6152
Dunlappie 57 NO 5967
Dunley 24 SO 7869
Dunlop 50 NS 4049
Dunmore (Central.) 50 NS 8989
Dunmore (Strath.) 49 NR 7961
Dunnet 67 ND 2171
Dunnichen 57 NO 5048
Dunning 56 NO 0114
Dunnington (Humbs.) 39 TA 1551
Dunnington (N Yorks.) 38 SE 6652
Dunnington (Warw.) 25 SP 0653
Dunnockshaw 37 SD 8127
Dunollie 54 NM 8532
Dunoon 49 NS 1777
Dunragit 44 NX 1557
Duns 53 NT 7853
Dunsby 35 TF 1026
Dunscore 45 NX 8684
Dunscroft 38 SE 6409
Dunsden Green 10 SU 7477
Dunsfold 11 TQ 0036
Dunsford 5 SX 8089
Dunshelt 57 NO 2410
Dunshillock 62 NJ 9848
Dunsley 43 NZ 8511
Dunsmore 19 SP 8605
Dunsop Bridge 36 SD 6549
Dunstable 19 TL 0221
Dunstall 33 SK 1920
Dunstall Green 28 TL 7460
Dunstan 53 NU 2419
Dunster 7 SS 9943
Duns Tew 18 SP 4528
Dunston (Lincs.) 35 TF 0663
Dunston (Norf.) 29 TG 2302
Dunston (Staffs.) 33 SJ 9217
Dunston (Tyne and Wear) 47 NZ 2263
Dunsville 38 SE 6407
Dunswell 39 TA 0735
Dunsyre 51 NT 0748
Dunterton 4 SX 3779
Duntisbourne Abbots 17 SO 9707
Duntisbourne Leer 17 SO 9707
Duntisbourne Rouse 17 SO 9805
Duntish 8 ST 6906
Duntocher 50 NS 4972
Dunton (Beds.) 27 TL 2344
Dunton (Bucks.) 18 SP 8224
Dunton (Norf.) 28 TF 8730
Dunton Bassett 26 SP 5490
Dunton Green 12 TQ 5157
Dunton Wayletts 20 TQ 6590
Duntulm 58 NG 4174
Dunure 49 NS 2515
Dunvant 15 SS 5993
Dunvegan 58 NG 2548
Dunwich 29 TM 4770
Durdar 46 NY 4051
Durham 47 NZ 2742
Durisdeer 45 NS 8903
Durleigh 7 ST 2736
Durley (Hants.) 9 SU 5115
Durley (Wilts.) 10 SU 2364
Durley Street 9 SU 5217
Durnamuck 64 NH 0192
Durness 66 NC 4067
Durno 62 NJ 7128
Durran 67 ND 1863
Durrington (Wilts.) 8 SU 1544
Durrington (W Susx) 11 TQ 1105
Dursley 17 ST 7597
Durston 7 ST 2828
Durweston 8 ST 8508
Dury 63 HU 4560
Duston 26 SP 7261
Duthil 60 NH 9324
Dutlas 23 SO 2077
Duton Hill 20 TL 6026
Dutton 32 SJ 5779

Frizington
Great Gransden

Frizington 40 NY 0316
Frocester 17 SO 7803
Frodesley 24 SJ 5101
Frodsham 32 SJ 5177
Froggatt 33 SK 2476
Froghall 33 SK 0247
Frogmore 10 SU 8360
Frolesworth 26 SP 5090
Frome 8 ST 7747
Frome St. Quintin 8 ST 5902
Fromes Hill 24 SO 6846
Fron (Gwyn.) 30 SH 3539
Fron (Powys) 23 SJ 2203
Fron (Powys) 23 SO 0865
Fron Cysyllte 31 SJ 2741
Fron-goch 31 SH 9039
Frosterley 41 NZ 0237
Froxfield 10 SU 2967
Froxfield Green 10 SU 7025
Fryerning 20 TL 6400
Fryton 42 SE 6875
Fulbeck 34 SK 9450
Fulbourn 20 TL 5256
Fulbrook 18 SP 2513
Fulford (N Yorks.) 38 SE 6149
Fulford (Somer.) 7 ST 2129
Fulford (Staffs.) 33 SJ 9438
Fulham 11 TQ 2576
Fulking 11 TQ 2411
Fuller's Moor 32 SJ 4953
Fuller Street 20 TL 7415
Fullerton 10 SU 3739
Fulletby 35 TF 2973
Full Sutton 38 SE 7455
Fullwood 50 NS 4450
Fulmer 19 SU 9985
Fulmodeston 29 TF 9931
Fulnetby 35 TF 0979
Fulstow 35 TF 3297
Fulwell 47 NZ 3959
Fulwood (Lancs.) 36 SD 5331
Fulwood (S Yorks.) 33 SK 3085
Funtington 10 SU 7908
Funzie 63 HU 6689
Furnace 55 NN 0200
Furneux Pelham 20 TL 4327
Furzehill 6 SS 7245
Fyfett 7 ST 2314
Fyfield (Essex) 20 TL 5707
Fyfield (Glos.) 18 SP 2003
Fyfield (Hants.) 10 SU 2946
Fyfield (Oxon.) 18 SU 4298
Fyfield (Wilts.) 17 SU 1468
Fylingthorpe 43 NZ 9405
Fyvie 62 NJ 7637

Gabroc Hill 50 NS 4551
Gaddesby 26 SK 6813
Gaer 16 SO 1721
Gaerwen 30 SH 4871
Gagingwell 18 SP 4025
Gailey 25 SJ 9110
Gainford 42 NZ 1716
Gainsborough 34 SK 8189
Gainsford End 20 TL 7235
Gairloch 64 NG 8076
Gairlochy 55 NN 1784
Gairney Bank 56 NT 1299
Gaitsgill 46 NY 3946
Galashiels 52 NT 4936
Galby 26 SK 6901
Galgate 36 SD 4855
Galhampton 8 ST 6329
Gall 56 NO 0734
Gallanach (Strath.) 54 NM 8226
Gallatown 51 NT 2994
Galley Common 26 SP 3192
Galleyend 20 TL 7103
Galleywood 20 TL 7002
Gallowfauld 57 NO 4342
Galltair 59 NG 8120
Galmisdale 54 NM 4784
Galmpton (Devon) 5 SX 6940
Galmpton (Devon.) 5 SX 8856
Galphay 37 SE 2572
Galson 63 NB 4358
Galston 50 NS 5036
Galtrigill 58 NG 1854
Gamblesby 41 NY 6039
Gamlingay 27 TL 2452
Gamrie 62 NJ 7962
Gamston (Notts.) 34 SK 6037
Gamston (Notts.) 34 SK 7076
Ganarew 16 SO 5216
Ganavan 54 NM 8632
Ganllwyd 30 SH 7224
Gannachy 57 NO 5970
Ganstead 39 TA 1434
Ganthorpe 38 SE 6870
Ganton 43 SE 9877
Garbhallt 49 NS 0295
Garboldisham 29 TM 0081
Gardenstown 62 NJ 7964
Garderhouse 63 HU 3347
Gare Hill 8 ST 7840
Garelochhead 49 NS 2491
Garford 18 SU 4296
Garforth 38 SE 4033
Gargrave 37 SD 9354
Gargunnock 50 NS 7094
Garinin 63 NB 1944
Garlieston 44 NX 4746
Garlogie 62 NJ 7805
Garmond 62 NJ 8052
Garmouth 61 NJ 3364
Garn 30 SH 2734
Garnant 15 SN 6813
Garn-Dolbenmaen 30 SH 4944
Garnet Bridge 40 SD 5299
Garnkirk 50 NS 6768
Garrabost 63 NB 5133
Garraron 54 NM 8008
Garras 2 SW 7023
Garreg 30 SH 6141
Garreg Bank 23 SJ 2811
Garrick 56 NN 8412
Garrigill 46 NY 7441
Garros 58 NG 4963
Garrow 56 NN 8240
Garrynamonie 63 NF 7416
Garsdale 41 SD 7389
Garsdon 17 ST 9687
Garshall Green 33 SJ 9633
Garsington 18 SP 5802
Garstang 36 SD 4945
Garston 32 SJ 4083
Garswood 36 SJ 5599
Gartcosh 50 NS 6968
Garth (Clwyd) 31 SJ 2542
Garth (I. of M.) 43 SC 3177
Garth (Mid Glam.) 15 SS 8690
Garth (Powys) 23 SN 9549
Garth (Shetld.) 63 HU 2157
Garthbrengy 23 SO 0433
Gartheli 22 SN 5956
Garthmyl 23 SO 1999
Garthorpe (Humbs.) 39 SE 8419
Garthorpe (Leic.) 34 SK 8320
Gartmore 50 NS 5297
Gartness (Central) 50 NS 5086
Gartness (Strath.) 50 NS 7864
Gartocharn 50 NS 4286
Garton 39 TA 2635
Garton-on-the-Wolds 39 SE 9859
Gartymore 67 ND 0114
Garvald 52 NT 5870
Garvan 55 NM 9777
Garvard 48 NR 3691
Garve 65 NH 3961
Garveston 29 TG 0207
Garvock 49 NS 2571
Garway 16 SO 4522
Garynahine 63 NB 2331
Gastard 17 ST 8868
Gasthorpe 29 TL 9780
Gatcombe 9 SZ 4885
Gatebeck 41 SD 5485
Gate Burton 34 SK 8382
Gateforth 38 SE 5528
Gatehead 50 NS 3936
Gate Helmsley 38 SE 6955
Gatehouse 46 NY 7988
Gatehouse of Fleet 45 NX 5956
Gatelawbridge 45 NX 9096
Gateley 29 TF 9624
Gatenby 42 SE 3287
Gateshead 47 NZ 2562
Gatesheath 32 SJ 4760
Gateside (Fife.) 56 NO 1809
Gateside (Strath.) 50 NS 3653
Gateside (Tays.) 57 NO 3749
Gateside (Tays.) 57 NO 4344
Gathurst 36 SD 5307
Gatley 32 SJ 8387
Gattonside 52 NT 5435
Gauldry 57 NO 3723
Gaunt's Common 8 SU 0205
Gautby 35 TF 1772
Gavinton 53 NT 7652
Gawber 38 SE 3207
Gawcott 18 SP 6831
Gawsworth 33 SJ 8869
Gawthrop 41 SD 6987
Gawthwaite 40 SD 2784
Gaydon 26 SP 3654
Gayhurst 27 SP 8446
Gayles 42 NZ 1207
Gay Street 11 TQ 0820
Gayton (Mers) 31 SJ 2680
Gayton (Norf.) 28 TF 7219
Gayton (Northants.) 26 SP 7054
Gayton (Staffs.) 33 SJ 9728
Gayton le Marsh 35 TF 4284
Gayton Thorpe 28 TF 7418
Gaywood 28 TF 6320
Gazeley 28 TL 7264
Geary 58 NG 2661
Gedding 21 TL 9457
Geddington 27 SP 8983
Gedintailor 58 NG 5235
Gedney 35 TF 4024
Gedney Broadgate 35 TF 4022
Gedney Drove End 28 TF 4629
Gedney Dyke 35 TF 4126
Gedney Hill 27 TF 3311
Gee Cross 37 SJ 9593
Geilston 50 NS 3477
Geise 67 ND 1064
Geldeston 29 TM 3891
Gell 31 SH 8569
Gelligaer 16 ST 1397
Gelli Gynan 31 SJ 1854
Gellilydan 30 SH 6839
Gellioedd 31 SH 9344
Gelly 14 SN 0819
Gellyburn 56 NO 0939
Gellywen 14 SN 2723
Gelston 45 NX 7758
Genoch Mains 44 NX 1356
Gentleshaw 25 SK 0511
Geocrab 63 NG 1190
Georgeham 6 SS 4639
George Nympton 6 SS 7023
Georgetown 50 NS 4567
Georgia 2 SW 4836
Georth 63 HY 3625
Germansweek 4 SX 4394
Germoe 2 SW 5829
Gerrans 2 SW 8735
Gerrards Cross 19 TQ 0088
Geshader 63 NB 1131
Gestingthorpe 20 TL 8138
Geuffordd 31 SJ 2114
Gibraltar 35 TF 5558
Gidea Park 20 TQ 5390
Gidleigh 5 SX 6788
Gifford 52 NT 5368
Giggleswick 37 SD 8163
Gilberdyke 39 SE 8329
Gilchriston 52 NT 4865
Gilcrux 40 NY 1138
Gildersome 37 SE 2429
Gildingwells 34 SK 5585
Gileston 16 ST 0167
Gilfach 16 ST 1598
Gilfach Goch 16 SS 9890
Gilfachrheda 22 SN 4058
Gillamoor 42 SE 6890
Gilling East 42 SE 6176
Gillingham (Dorset) 8 ST 8026
Gillingham (Kent) 12 TQ 7768
Gillingham (Norf.) 29 TM 4191
Gilling West 42 NZ 1805
Gillow Heath 33 SJ 8858
Gills 67 ND 3172
Gilmerton (Lothian) 51 NT 2968
Gilmerton (Tays.) 56 NN 8823
Gilmorton 26 SP 5787
Gilsland 46 NY 6366
Gilsland Spa 46 NY 6367
Gilston 52 NT 4456
Gilwern 16 SO 2414
Gimingham 29 TG 2836
Gipping 29 TM 0763
Gipsey Bridge 35 TF 2850
Girlsta 63 HU 4250
Girsby 42 NZ 3508
Girthon 45 NX 6053
Girton (Cambs.) 27 TL 4262
Girton (Notts.) 34 SK 8266
Girvan 44 NX 1897
Gisburn 37 SD 8248
Gisleham 29 TM 5188
Gislingham 29 TM 0771
Gissing 29 TM 1485
Gittisham 7 SY 1398
Glackossian 60 NH 5938
Gladestry 23 SO 2355
Gladsmuir 52 NT 4573
Glais 15 SN 7000
Glaisdale (N Yorks.) 43 NZ 7705
Glamis 57 NO 3846
Glanaber Terrace 30 SH 7547
Glanaman 15 SN 6713
Glan-Conwy 31 SH 8352
Glandford 29 TG 0441
Glandwr (Dyfed) 14 SN 1928
Glandwr (Gwent) 16 SO 2101
Glangrwyne 16 SO 2316
Glan-Mule 23 SO 1690
Glanrhyd 14 SN 1442
Glanton 53 NU 0714
Glanton Pike 53 NU 0514
Glanvilles Wootton 8 ST 6708
Glan-y-don 31 SJ 1679
Glan-yr-afon (Clwyd-Gwyn) 31 SJ 0242
Glan-yr-afon (Gwyn) 31 SH 9141
Glapthorn 27 TL 0290
Glapwell 34 SK 4766
Glasbury 23 SO 1739
Glascote 26 SK 2203
Glascwm 23 SO 1553
Glasdrum 55 NN 0046
Glasfryn 31 SH 9150
Glasgow 50 NS 5865
Glasinfryn 30 SH 5868
Glaspwll 22 SN 7397
Glasserton 44 NX 4238
Glassford 50 NS 7247
Glasshouse Hill 17 SO 7020
Glasshouses 37 SE 1764
Glasslaw 62 NJ 8659
Glasslie 56 NO 2305
Glasson (Cumbr.) 46 NY 2560
Glasson (Lancs.) 36 SD 4455
Glassonby 41 NY 5738
Glasterlaw 57 NO 6051
Glaston 27 SK 8900
Glastonbury 7 ST 4938
Glatton 27 TL 1586
Glazebury 32 SJ 6796
Glazeley 24 SO 7088
Gleadless Townend 33 SK 3883
Gleadsmoss 33 SJ 8469
Gleaston 36 SD 2570
Glemsford 20 TL 8247
Glenalmond (Tays.) 56 NN 9627
Glenancross 58 NM 6691
Glen Auldyn 43 SC 4393
Glenbarr 48 NR 6736
Glen Barry 62 NJ 5554
Glen Bernisdale 58 NG 4048
Glenbervie 57 NO 7680
Glenboig 50 NS 7268
Glenbranter 55 NS 1097
Glen Breackerie 48 NR 6511
Glenbreck 51 NT 0521
Glenbuck 50 NS 7429
Glenburn 50 NS 4761
Glencaple 45 NX 9968
Glencarse 56 NO 1922
Glencloy 49 NS 0036
Glencoe 55 NN 1058
Glencraig 51 NT 1795
Glendaruel 49 NR 9985
Glendevon 56 NN 9804
Glendoick 56 NO 2022
Glenduckie 57 NO 2818
Glenegedale 48 NR 3351
Glenelg 59 NG 8119
Glenfarg 56 NO 1310
Glenfield 26 SK 5306
Glenfinnan 54 NM 9080
Glenfoot 56 NO 1715
Glengarnock 49 NS 3252
Glengrasco 58 NG 4444
Glenkindie 61 NJ 4313
Glenlee 45 NX 6080
Glenlivet 61 NJ 2126
Glenluce 44 NX 1957
Glenmaye 43 SC 2380
Glenmore (Skye) 58 NG 4340
Glenmore (Strath.) 54 NM 8412
Glen Parva 26 SP 5798
Glenridding 40 NY 3817
Glenrothes 57 NO 2600
Glensaugh 57 NO 6778
Glenshee (Tays.) 56 NN 9834
Glensluain 55 NS 0999
Glenstockadale 44 NX 0061
Glenstriven 49 NS 0878
Glentham 34 TF 0090
Glentress 51 NT 2839
Glentrool Village 44 NX 3578
Glentworth 34 SK 9488
Glen Village 50 NS 8878
Glen Vine 43 SC 3378
Glespin 50 NS 8028
Gletness 63 HU 4651
Glewstone 16 SO 5522
Glinton 27 TF 1506
Glooston 26 SP 7596
Glossop 33 SK 0393
Gloster Hill 47 NU 2504
Gloucester 17 SO 8318
Gloup 63 HP 5004
Glusburn 37 SE 0344
Gluss 63 HU 3477
GLympton 18 SP 4221
Glyn 30 SH 7457
Glynarthen 22 SN 3148
Glyn Ceiriog 31 SJ 2038
Glyncorrwg 15 SS 8799
Glyn-Cywarch 30 SH 6034
Glynde 12 TQ 4509
Glyndebourne 12 TQ 4510
Glyn Dyfrdwy 31 SJ 1542
Glyn-Neath 15 SN 8806
Glyntaff 16 ST 0889
Glynteg 14 SN 3637
Glyntrefnant 22 SN 9192
Gnosall 32 SJ 8220
Gnosall Heath 33 SJ 8419
Goadby 26 SP 7598
Goadby Marwood 34 SK 7826
Goatacre 17 SU 0176
Goathill 8 ST 6717
Goathland 43 NZ 8301
Goathurst 7 ST 2534
Gobowen 32 SJ 3033
Godalming 11 SU 9743
Godmanchester 27 TL 2470
Godmanstone 8 SY 6697
Godmersham 13 TR 0650
Godney 7 ST 4842
Godolphin Cross 2 SW 6031
Godre'r-graig 15 SN 7507
Godshill (Hants) 8 SU 1714
Godshill (I. of W.) 9 SZ 5281
Godstone 12 TQ 3551
Goetre 16 SO 3205
Goff's Oak 20 TL 3202
Gogar 51 NT 1672
Goginan 22 SN 6981
Golan 30 SH 5242
Golant 3 SX 1254
Golberdon 4 SX 3271
Golborne 36 SJ 6097
Golcar 37 SE 0915
Goldcliff 16 ST 3683
Golden Cross 12 TQ 5312
Golden Green 12 TQ 6348
Golden Grove 15 SN 5919
Goldenhill 33 SJ 8553
Golden Pot 10 SU 7143
Golden Valley 17 SO 9022
Golders Green 19 TQ 2488
Goldhanger 21 TL 9009
Golding 24 SJ 5403
Goldsborough (N Yorks.) 43 NZ 8314
Goldsborough (N Yorks.) 33 SE 3856
Goldsithney 2 SW 5430
Goldthorpe 38 SE 4604
Gollanfield 60 NH 8052
Golspie 65 NH 8399
Golval 67 NC 8962
Gomersal 37 SE 2026
Gomshall 11 TQ 0847
Gonalston 34 SK 6847
Gonfirth (Shetld.) 63 HU 3661
Good Easter 20 TL 6212
Gooderstone 28 TF 7602
Goodleigh 6 SS 5934
Goodmanham 39 SE 8842
Goodnestone (Kent) 13 TR 0461
Goodnestone (Kent) 13 TR 2554
Goodrich 17 SO 5719
Goodrington 5 SX 8958
Goodwick 14 SM 9438
Goodworth Clatford 10 SU 3642
Goodyers End 26 SP 3385
Goole 38 SE 7423
Goole Fields 38 SE 7519
Goonbell 2 SW 7249
Goonhavern 2 SW 7953
Goseham 4 SS 2316
Goosetrey 32 SJ 7769
Goosey 18 SU 3591
Goosnargh 36 SD 5536
Gordon 52 NT 6443
Gordonbush 67 NC 8409
Gordonstoun 61 NJ 1368
Gordonstown (Grampn.) 61 NJ 5656
Gordonstown (Grampn.) 62 NJ 7138
Gorebridge 51 NT 3461
Gorefield 27 TF 4112
Goring 18 SU 6080
Goring-by-Sea 11 TQ 1102
Gorleston on Sea 29 TG 5203
Gorley 8 SU 1511
Gorrachie 62 NJ 7358
Gorran Haven 3 SX 0141
Gors 22 SN 6277
Gorsedd 31 SJ 1476
Gorseinon 15 SS 5998
Gors-goch 23 SN 9393
Gorslas 15 SN 5713
Gorsley 17 SO 6826
Gorsness 63 HY 4119
Gorstan 65 NH 3862
Gorsty Common 24 SO 4537
Gorton 33 SJ 8996
Gosbeck 21 TM 1555
Gosberton 35 TF 2331
Gosfield 20 TL 7829
Gosforth (Cumbr.) 40 NY 0603
Gosforth (Tyne and Wear) 47 NZ 2467
Gosmore 19 TL 1927
Gosport 9 SZ 6199
Gossabrough 63 HU 5383
Goswick 53 NU 0545
Gotham 34 SK 5330
Gotherington 17 SO 9629
Gott Bay 48 NM 0546
Goudhurst 12 TQ 7337
Goulceby 35 TF 2579
Gourdas 62 NJ 7741
Gourdon 57 NO 8270
Gourock 49 NS 2477
Govan 50 NS 5464
Gowanhill 62 NK 0363
Gowdall 38 SE 6122
Gowerton 15 SS 5896
Gowkhall 51 NT 0589
Goxhill (Humbs.) 39 TA 1021
Goxhill (Humbs.) 39 TA 1844
Graffham (W Susx) 11 SU 9216
Grafham (Cambs.) 27 TL 1669
Grafton (Here. and Worc.) 24 SO 4937
Grafton (Here. and Worc.) 24 SO 5761
Grafton (N Yorks.) 38 SE 4163
Grafton (Oxon.) 18 SP 2600
Grafton Flyford 25 SO 9655
Grafton Regis 26 SP 7546
Grafton Underwood 27 SP 9280
Grafty Green 13 TQ 8748
Graianrhyd 31 SJ 2156
Graig (Clwyd) 31 SJ 0872
Graig (Gwyn.) 31 SH 8071
Graig-fechan 31 SJ 1454
Grain 13 TQ 8876
Grainsby 39 TF 2799
Grainthorpe 35 TF 3896
Graizelound 38 SK 7798
Grampound 2 SW 9348
Grampound Road 2 SW 9150
Gramsdale 63 NF 8255
Granborough 18 SP 7625
Granby 34 SK 7536
Grandborough 26 SP 4866
Grandtully 56 NN 9152
Grange (Cumbr.) 40 NY 2517
Grange (Mers.) 31 SJ 2286
Grange (N Yorks.) 42 SE 5796
Grange (Tays.) 57 NO 2725
Grange Crossroads 61 NJ 4754
Grange Hill 20 TQ 4492
Grange Moor 37 SE 2216
Grangemouth 51 NS 9281
Grange of Lindores 57 NO 2516
Grange-over-Sands 40 SD 4077
Grangepans 51 NT 0282
Grangetown 42 NZ 5420
Grange Villa 47 NZ 2352
Granish 60 NH 8914
Gransmoor 39 TA 1259
Granston 14 SM 8934
Grantchester 20 TL 4355
Grantham 34 SK 9135
Grantley 37 SE 2369
Grantlodge 62 NJ 7017
Granton (Dumf. and Galwy.) 51 NT 0709
Granton (Lothian) 51 NT 2277
Grantown-on-Spey 61 NJ 0327
Grantshouse 53 NT 8065
Grappenhall 32 SJ 6385
Grasby 39 TA 0804
Grasmere 40 NY 3307
Grasscroft 37 SD 9804
Grassendale 32 SJ 3985
Grassholme 41 NY 9221
Grassington 37 SE 0064
Grassmoor 33 SK 4067
Grassthorpe 34 SK 7967
Grateley 10 SU 2741
Gratwich 33 SK 0231
Graveley (Cambs.) 27 TL 2564
Graveley (Herts.) 19 TL 2328
Gravelly Hill 25 SP 1090
Gravels 23 SJ 3300
Graveney 13 TR 0562
Gravesend 12 TQ 6473
Gravir 63 NB 3715
Grayingham 34 SK 9395
Grayrigg 41 SD 5797
Grays 12 TQ 6177
Grayshott 11 SU 8735
Grayswood 11 SU 9234
Grazeley 10 SU 6966
Greasbrough 33 SK 4195
Greasby 31 SJ 2587
Great Abington 20 TL 5348
Great Addington 27 SP 9575
Great Alne 25 SP 1159
Great Altcar 36 SD 3206
Great Amwell 20 TL 3712
Great Asby 41 NY 6813
Great Ashfield 29 TM 0068
Great Ayton 42 NZ 5510
Great Baddow 20 TL 7204
Great Badminton 17 ST 8082
Great Bardfield 20 TL 6730
Great Barford 27 TL 1352
Great Barr 25 SP 0495
Great Barrington 18 SP 2013
Great Barrow 32 SJ 4668
Great Barton 28 TL 8967
Great Barugh 43 SE 7478
Great Bavington 47 NY 9880
Great Bedwyn 10 SU 2764
Great Bentley 21 TM 1121
Great Billing 26 SP 8162
Great Bircham 28 TF 7632
Great Blakenham 21 TM 1150
Great Bolas 32 SJ 6421
Great Bookham 11 TQ 1454
Great Bosullow 2 SW 4133
Great Bourton 26 SP 4545
Great Bowden 26 SP 7488
Great Bradley 20 TL 6753
Great Braxted 21 TL 8614
Great Bricett 21 TM 0350
Great Brickhill 19 SP 9030
Great Bridgeford 33 SJ 8827
Great Brington 26 SP 6665
Great Bromley 21 TM 0826
Great Broughton 42 NZ 5406
Great Budworth 32 SJ 6677
Great Burdon 42 NZ 3116
Great Burstead 20 TQ 6892
Great Busby 42 NZ 5105
Great Canfield 20 TL 5917
Great Carlton 35 TF 4185
Great Casterton 27 TF 0009
Great Chart 13 TQ 9842
Great Chatwell 32 SJ 7914
Great Chesterford 20 TL 5042
Great Cheverell 17 ST 9858
Great Chishill 20 TL 4238
Great Clacton 21 TM 1716
Great Coates 39 TA 2310
Great Comberton 25 SO 9542
Great Corby 46 NY 4754
Great Cornard 21 TL 8840
Great Coxwell 18 SU 2693
Great Cransley 27 SP 8376
Great Cressingham 28 TF 8501
Great Crosby 36 SJ 3199
Great Cubley 33 SK 1637
Great Dalby 34 SK 7414
Great Doddington 27 SP 8864
Great Driffield 39 TA 0257
Great Dunham 28 TF 8714
Great Dunmow 20 TL 6221
Great Durnford 8 SU 1338
Great Easton (Essex) 20 TL 6125
Great Easton (Leic.) 27 SP 8493
Great Eccleston 36 SD 4240
Great Edstone 43 SE 7084
Great Ellingham 29 TM 0196
Great Elm 8 ST 7449
Great Eversden 20 TL 3653
Great Fen 28 TL 5978
Great Finborough 21 TM 0157
Greatford 27 TF 0811
Great Fransham 28 TF 8913
Great Gaddesden 19 TL 0211
Great Gidding 27 TL 1183
Great Givendale 39 SE 8153
Great Glemham 29 TM 3361
Great Glen 26 SP 6597
Great Gonerby 34 SK 8938
Great Gransden 27 TL 2756

Harton Holbrook

Harton (Salop) 24 SO 4888
Harton (Tyne and Wear) 47 NZ 3864
Hartpury 17 SO 7924
Hartshill 26 SP 3293
Hartshorne 33 SK 3221
Hartsop 40 NY 4013
Hartwell 26 SP 7850
Hartwood 50 NS 8459
Harvel 12 TQ 6563
Harvington 25 SP 0548
Harvington Cross 25 SP 0549
Harwell 18 SU 4989
Harwich 21 TM 2431
Harwood (Durham) 41 NY 8133
Harwood (Gtr Mches.) 36 SD 7411
Harwood Dale 43 SE 9595
Harworth 34 SK 6291
Hascombe 11 TQ 0039
Haselbech 26 SP 7177
Haselbury Plucknett 7 ST 4711
Haseley 26 SP 2368
Haselor 25 SP 1257
Hasfield 17 SO 8227
Hasguard 14 SM 8509
Haskayne 36 SD 3507
Hasketon 21 TM 2550
Hasland 33 SK 3969
Haslemere 11 SU 9032
Haslingden 37 SD 7823
Haslingden Grane 37 SD 7523
Haslingfield 20 TL 4052
Haslington 32 SJ 7355
Hassall 32 SJ 7657
Hassall Green 32 SJ 7758
Hassell Street 13 TR 0946
Hassendean 52 NT 5420
Hassingham 29 TG 3605
Hassocks 12 TQ 3015
Hassop 33 SK 2272
Hastigrow 67 ND 2661
Hastingleigh 13 TR 0945
Hastings 12 TQ 8009
Hastingwood 20 TL 4807
Hastoe 19 SP 9209
Haswell 47 NZ 3743
Hatch (Beds.) 27 TL 1547
Hatch (Hants.) 10 SU 6752
Hatch (Wilts.) 8 ST 9228
Hatch Beauchamp 7 ST 3020
Hatch End 19 TQ 1391
Hatching Green 19 TL 1313
Hatchmere 32 SJ 5571
Hatcliffe 39 TA 2100
Hatfield (Here. and Worc.) 24 SO 5859
Hatfield (Herts.) 19 TL 2309
Hatfield (S Yorks.) 38 SE 6609
Hatfield Broad Oak 20 TL 5416
Hatfield Heath 20 TL 5215
Hatfield Peverel 20 TL 7911
Hatfield Woodhouse 38 SE 6708
Hatford 18 SU 3394
Hatherden 10 SU 3450
Hatherleigh 4 SS 5404
Hathern 34 SK 5022
Hatherop 17 SP 1505
Hathersage 33 SK 2381
Hatherton (Ches.) 32 SJ 6847
Hatherton (Staffs.) 25 SJ 9610
Hatley St. George 27 TL 2851
Hattingley 10 SU 6437
Hatton (Ches.) 32 SJ 5982
Hatton (Derby.) 33 SK 2130
Hatton (Grampn.) 62 NK 0537
Hatton (Gtr London) 11 TQ 1075
Hatton (Lincs.) 35 TF 1776
Hatton (Salop) 24 SO 4690
Hatton (Warw.) 26 SP 2367
Hattoncrook 62 NJ 8424
Hatton Heath 32 SJ 4561
Hatton of Fintray 62 NJ 8316
Haugham 35 TF 3381
Haugh Head 53 NU 0026
Haughley 29 TM 0262
Haughley Green 29 TM 0364
Haugh of Urr 45 NX 8066
Haughton (Notts.) 34 SK 6772
Haughton (Salop) 32 SJ 3727
Haughton (Salop) 32 SJ 5516
Haughton (Salop) 24 SO 6795
Haughton (Staffs.) 33 SJ 8620
Haughton Green 33 SJ 9393
Haughton Moss 32 SJ 5756
Haunton 26 SK 2411
Hauxley 47 NU 2703
Hauxton 20 TL 4351
Havant 10 SU 7106
Haven 24 SO 4054
Havenstreet 9 SZ 5690
Haverfordwest 14 SM 9515
Haverhill 20 TL 6745
Haverigg 40 SD 1578
Havering 20 TQ 5587
Havering-atte-Bower 20 TQ 5193
Havering's Grove 20 TQ 6594
Haversham 27 SP 8343
Haverthwaite 40 SD 3483
Hawarden 32 SJ 3165
Hawes 41 SD 8789
Hawford 25 SO 8460
Hawick 52 NT 5014
Hawkchurch 7 ST 3400
Hawkedon 20 TL 7952
Hawkeridge 17 ST 8653
Hawkerland 7 SY 0588
Hawkesbury 17 ST 7687
Hawkesbury Upton 17 ST 7786
Hawkes End 26 SP 2983
Hawkhill 53 NU 2212
Hawkhope 46 NY 7188
Hawkhurst 12 TQ 7630
Hawkinge 13 TR 2139
Hawkley 10 SU 7429
Hawkridge 6 SS 8630
Hawkshead 40 SD 3598
Hawksland 50 NS 8439
Hawkstone 32 SJ 5830
Hawkswick 37 SD 9570
Hawksworth (Notts.) 34 SK 7543
Hawksworth (W Yorks.) 37 SE 1641
Hawkwell 21 TQ 8691
Hawley (Hants.) 10 SU 8558
Hawley (Kent) 12 TQ 5571
Hawling 17 SP 0623
Hawnby 42 SE 5389
Haworth 37 SE 0337
Hawsker 43 NZ 9207
Hawstead 21 TL 8559
Hawthorn Hill 11 SU 8873
Hawton 34 SK 7851
Haxby 38 SE 6057
Haxey 38 SK 7699
Haydock 32 SJ 5696
Haydon 8 ST 6615
Haydon Bridge 47 NY 8464
Haydon Wick 17 SU 1388
Haye 4 SX 3570
Hayes (Gtr London) 19 TQ 0980
Hayes (Gtr London) 12 TQ 4165
Hayfield 33 SK 0386
Hayhillock 57 NO 5242
Hayle 2 SW 5537
Hayling Island 9 SU 7201
Haynes 27 TL 0841
Hay-on-Wye 23 SO 2342
Hayscastle 14 SM 8925
Hayscastle Cross 14 SM 9125
Hayton (Cumbr.) 45 NY 1041
Hayton (Cumbr.) 46 NY 5057
Hayton (Humbs.) 39 SE 8145
Hayton (Notts.) 34 SK 7284
Hayton's Bent 24 SO 5280
Haytor Vale 5 SX 7677
Haywards Heath 12 TQ 3324
Haywood Oaks 34 SK 6055
Hazelbank 50 NS 8344
Hazelbury Bryan 8 ST 7408
Hazeley 10 SU 7459
Hazel Grove 33 SJ 9287
Hazelrigg 53 NU 0533
Hazelslade 25 SK 0212
Hazelton Walls 57 NO 3321
Hazelwood 33 SK 3245
Hazlemere 19 SU 8895
Hazlerigg 47 NZ 2472
Hazleton 17 SP 0718
Heacham 28 TF 6737
Headbourne Worthy 9 SU 4831
Headcorn 12 TQ 8344
Headington 18 SP 5407
Headlam 42 NZ 1818
Headless Cross 25 SP 0365
Headley (Hants.) 10 SU 5162
Headley (Hants.) 10 SU 8236
Headley (Surrey) 11 TQ 2054
Head of Muir 50 NS 8080
Headon 34 SK 7476
Heads Nook 46 NY 4955
Heage 33 SK 3650
Healaugh (N Yorks.) 41 SE 0198
Healaugh (N Yorks.) 38 SE 4947
Heale 6 SS 6446
Healey (Lancs.) 37 SD 8817
Healey (Northum.) 47 NZ 0158
Healey (N Yorks.) 42 SE 1780
Healeyfield 47 NZ 0648
Healing 39 TA 2110
Heamoor 2 SW 4631
Heanish 48 NM 0343
Heanor 33 SK 4346
Heanton Punchardon 6 SS 5035
Heapham 34 SK 8788
Hearthstane 51 NT 1125
Heaste 58 NG 6417
Heath 34 SK4467
Heath and Reach 19 SP 9228
Heathcote 33 SK 1460
Heath End (Hants.) 10 SU 5762
Heath End (Hants.) 11 SU 8550
Heather 26 SK 3910
Heathfield (Devon.) 5 SX 8376
Heathfield (E Susx) 12 TQ 5821
Heathfield (Somer.) 7 ST 1526
Heath Hayes 25 SK 0110
Heath Hill 24 SJ 7614
Heath House 7 ST 4146
Heath, The 21 TL 9043
Heathton 25 SO 8192
Heatley 32 SJ 6988
Heaton (Lancs.) 36 SD 4460
Heaton (Staffs.) 33 SJ 9462
Heaton (Tyne and Wear) 47 NZ 2665
Heaton Moor 37 SJ 8691
Heaverham 12 TQ 5758
Heaviley 33 SJ 9088
Hebburn 47 NZ 3265
Hebden 37 SE 0263
Hebden Bridge 37 SD 9927
Hebden Green 32 SJ 6365
Hebron 47 NZ 1989
Heckfield 10 SU 7260
Heckfield Green 29 TM 1875
Heckington 35 TF 1444
Heckmondwike 37 SE 2123
Heddington 17 ST 9966
Heddle 63 HY 3512
Heddon-on-the-Wall 47 NZ 1366
Hedenham 29 TM 3193
Hedge End 9 SU 4812
Hedgerley 19 SU 9787
Hedging 7 ST 3029
Hedley on the Hill 47 NZ 0759
Hednesford 25 SK 0012
Hedon 39 TA 1828
Hedsor 19 SU 9086
Hegdon Hill 24 SO 5854
Heglibister 63 HU 3952
Heighington (Durham) 42 NZ 2522
Heighington (Lincs.) 34 TF 0269
Heights of Brae 65 NH 5161
Heights of Kinlochewe 64 NH 0764
Heilam 66 NC 4659
Heiton 52 NT 7130
Heldon Hill 61 NJ 1257
Hele (Devon.) 6 SS 5347
Hele (Devon.) 5 SS 9902
Helensburgh 49 NS 2982
Helford 2 SW 7526
Helhoughton 28 TF 8626
Helions Bumpstead 20 TL 6541
Helland 3 SX 0770
Hellesdon 29 TG 1810
Hellidon 26 SP 5158
Hellifield 37 SD 8556
Hellingly 12 TQ 5812
Hellington 29 TG 3103
Hellister 63 HU 3949
Helmdon 26 SP 5843
Helmingham 21 TM 1857
Helmsdale 67 ND 0215
Helmshore 37 SD 7821
Helmsley 42 SE 6183
Helperby 38 SE 4369
Helperthorpe 39 SE 9570
Helpringham 35 TF 1340
Helpston 27 TF 1205
Helsby 32 SJ 4875
Helston 2 SW 6527
Helstone 3 SX 0881
Helton 40 NY 5122
Helwith Bridge 41 SD 8169
Hemblington 29 TG 3411
Hemel Hempstead 19 TL 0506
Hemingbrough 38 SE 6730
Hemingby 35 TF 2374
Hemingford Abbots 27 TL 2870
Hemingford Grey 27 TL 2970
Hemingstone 21 TM 1453
Hemington (Northants.) 27 TL 0985
Hemington (Somer.) 17 ST 7253
Hemley 21 TM 2842
Hempholme 39 TA 0850
Hempnall 29 TM 2494
Hempnall Green 29 TM 2593
Hempriggs 61 NJ 1064
Hempstead (Essex) 20 TL 6338
Hempstead (Norf.) 29 TG 4028
Hempsted (Glos.) 17 SO 8117
Hempsted (Norf.) 29 TG 1037
Hempton (Norf.) 28 TF 9129
Hempton (Oxon.) 18 SP 4431
Hemsby 29 TG 4917
Hemswell 34 SK 9290
Hemsworth 38 SE 4213
Hemyock 7 ST 1313
Henbury (Avon) 16 ST 5478
Henbury (Ches.) 33 SJ 8873
Hendersyde Park 53 NT 7435
Hendon (Gtr London) 19 TQ 2389
Hendon (Tyne and Wear) 47 NZ 4055
Hendy 15 SN 5804
Heneglwys 30 SH 4276
Henfield 11 TQ 2116
Hengoed (Mid Glam.) 16 ST 1495
Hengoed (Powys) 23 SO 2253
Hengoed (Salop) 31 SJ 2833
Hengrave 28 TL 8268
Henham 20 TL 5428
Heniarth 23 SJ 1108
Henley (Salop) 24 SO 5476
Henley (Somer.) 7 ST 4232
Henley (Suff.) 21 TM 1551
Henley (W Susx) 11 SU 8926
Henley-in-Arden 25 SP 1465
Henley on Thames 18 SU 7682
Henley Park 11 SU 9352
Henllan (Clwyd) 31 SJ 0268
Henllan (Dyfed) 22 SN 3540
Henllan Amgoed 14 SN 1820
Henllys 16 ST 2693
Henlow 19 TL 1738
Hennock 5 SX 8380
Henryd 31 SH 7674
Henry's Moat (Castell Hendre) 14 SN 0428
Hensall 38 SE 5923
Henshaw 46 NY 7664
Henstead 29 TM 4986
Henstridge 8 ST 7219
Henstridge Marsh 8 ST 7420
Henton (Oxon.) 18 SP 7602
Henton (Somer.) 7 ST 4845
Henwick 25 SO 8354
Henwood 4 SX 2673
Heogan 63 HU 4743
Heol Senni 15 SN 9223
Heol-y-Cyw 15 SS 9484
Hepburn 53 NU 0724
Hepple 47 NT 9800
Hepscott 47 NZ 2284
Heptonstall 37 SD 9827
Hepworth (Suff.) 29 TL 9874
Hepworth (W Yorks.) 37 SE 1606
Herbrandston 14 SM 8707
Hereford 24 SO 5040
Hergest 23 SO 2655
Heriot 51 NT 3952
Hermitage (Berks.) 10 SU 5072
Hermitage (Borders) 46 NY 5095
Hermitage (Dorset.) 8 ST 6306
Hermitage (Hants.) 10 SU 7505
Hermitage, The 11 TQ 2253
Hermon (Dyfed) 14 SN 2032
Hermon (Dyfed) 14 SN 3630
Hermon (Gwyn.) 30 SH 3868
Herne 13 TR 1866
Herne Bay 13 TR 1768
Herner 6 SS 5926
Hernhill 13 TR 0660
Herodsfoot 4 SX 2160
Herongate 20 TQ 6391
Heronsgate 19 TQ 0294
Herriard 10 SU 6645
Herringfleet 29 TM 4797
Herringswell 28 TL 7170
Herrington 47 NZ 3553
Hersden 13 TR 1961
Hersham 11 TQ 1164
Herstmonceux 12 TQ 6312
Hertford 20 TL 3212
Hertford Heath 20 TL 3510
Hertingfordbury 20 TL 3112
Hesketh Bank 36 SD 4323
Hesketh Lane 36 SD 6141
Hesket Newmarket 40 NY 3438
Heskin Green 36 SD 5315
Hesleden 42 NZ 4438
Hesleyside 46 NY 8183
Heslington 38 SE 6250
Hessay 38 SE 5253
Hessenford 4 SX 3057
Hessett 29 TL 9361
Hessle 39 TA 0326
Hest Bank 36 SD 4566
Heston 11 TQ 1277
Heswall 31 SJ 2682
Hethe 18 SP 5929
Hethersett 29 TG 1505
Hethersgill 46 NY 4767
Hethpool 53 NT 8928
Hett 42 NZ 2836
Hetton 37 SD 9658
Hetton-le-Hole 47 NZ 3548
Heugh 47 NZ 0873
Heugh-Head 61 NJ 3711
Heveningham 29 TM 3372
Hever 12 TQ 4744
Heversham 40 SD 4983
Hevingham 29 TG 2022
Hewelsfield 17 SO 5602
Hewish (Avon) 16 ST 4064
Hewish (Somer.) 7 ST 4108
Hexham 47 NY 9364
Hextable 12 TQ 5170
Hexton 19 TL 1030
Hexworthy 5 SX 6572
Heybridge (Essex) 21 TL 8508
Heybridge (Essex) 20 TQ 6498
Heybridge Basin 21 TL 8707
Heybrook Bay 4 SX 4948
Heydon (Cambs.) 20 TL 4340
Heydon (Norf.) 29 TG 1127
Heydour 34 TF 0039
Heyford 26 SP 6558
Heylipoll 48 NL 9643
Heylor 63 HU 2881
Heysham 36 SD 4161
Heyshott 11 SU 8918
Heytesbury 8 ST 9242
Heythrop 18 SP 3527
Heywood (Gtr Mches.) 37 SD 8510
Heywood (Wilts.) 17 ST 8753
Hibaldstow 39 SE 9702
Hickleton 38 SE 4805
Hickling (Norf.) 29 TG 4124
Hickling (Notts.) 34 SK 6929
Hickling Green 29 TG 4023
Hickling Heath 29 TG 4022
Hidcote Boyce 25 SP 1742
High Ackworth 38 SE 4317
Higham (Derby.) 33 SK 3959
Higham (Kent) 12 TQ 7171
Higham (Lancs.) 37 SD 8036
Higham (Suff.) 28 TL 7465
Higham (Suff.) 21 TM 0335
Higham Dykes 47 NZ 1375
Higham Ferrers 27 SP 9669
Higham Gobion 19 TL 1033
Higham on the Hill 26 SP 3895
Highampton 4 SS 4804
Higham Wood 12 TQ 6048
High Banton 50 NS 7480
High Beach 20 TQ 4097
High Bentham 36 SD 6669
High Bickington 6 SS 5920
High Birkwith 41 SD 8076
High Blantyre 50 NS 6756
High Bonnybridge 50 NS 8378
Highbridge 7 ST 3147
Highbrook 12 TQ 3630
Highburton 37 SE 1813
Highbury 8 ST 6849
High Buston 53 NU 2308
High Callerton 47 NZ 1670
High Catton 38 SE 7153
Highclere 10 SU 4360
Highcliffe 8 SZ 2193
High Cogges 18 SP 3709
High Coniscliffe 42 NZ 2215
High Cross (Hants.) 10 SU 7126
High Cross (Herts.) 20 TL 3618
High Cross Bank 33 SK 3018
High Easter 20 TL 6214
High Ellington 42 SE 1983
Higher Ansty 8 ST 7603
Higher Ballam 36 SD 3630
Higher Ercall 32 SJ 5917
Higher Penwortham 36 SD 5128
Higher Tale 7 ST 0601
Higher Walreddon 4 SX 4771
Higher Walton (Ches.) 32 SJ 5985
Higher Walton (Lancs.) 36 SD 5727
Higher Wych 32 SJ 4943
High Etherley 42 NZ 1628
Highfield (Strath.) 49 NS 3050
Highfield (Tyne and Wear) 47 NZ 1459
Highfields 20 TL 3559
High Garrett 20 TL 7726
High Grange 42 NZ 1731
High Grantley 42 SE 2369
High Green (Here. and Worc.) 25 SO 8745
High Green (Norf.) 29 TG 1305
High Green (S Yorks.) 38 SK 3397
High Halden 13 TQ 9037
High Halstow 12 TQ 7875
High Ham 7 ST 4231
High Hatton 32 SJ 6024
High Hesket 46 NY 4744
High Hoyland 37 SE 2710
High Hunsley 39 SE 9535
High Hurstwood 12 TQ 4926
High Lane 24 SO 6760
High Laver 20 TL 5208
Highleadon 17 SO 7623
High Legh 32 SJ 6984
Highleigh 10 SZ 8498
Highley 24 SO 7483
High Littleton 17 ST 6458
High Lorton 40 NY 1625
High Melton 38 SE 5001
Highmoor Cross 18 SU 7084
Highmoor Hill 16 ST 4689
Highnam 17 SO 7919
High Newton 40 SD 4082
High Newton-by-the-Sea 53 NU 2325
High Offley 32 SJ 7826
High Ongar 20 TL 5603
High Onn 32 SJ 8216
High Roding 20 TL 6017
High Salvington 11 TQ 1206
High Shaw 41 SD 8791
High Spen 47 NZ 1359
Highsted 13 TQ 9161
High Street (Corn.) 2 SW 9753
High Street (Suff.) 21 TM 4355
High Street Green 21 TM 0055
Hightae 45 NY 0979
Hightown (Ches.) 33 SJ 8762
Hightown (Mers.) 36 SD 2903
High Toynton 35 TF 2869
High Trewhitt 47 NU 0105
Highway 17 SU 0474
Highweek 5 SX 8472
Highworth 18 SU 2092
High Wray 40 SD 3799
High Wych 20 TL 4614
High Wycombe 19 SU 8593
Hilborough (Norf.) 28 TF 8200
Hildenborough 12 TQ 5648
Hildersham 20 TL 5448
Hilderstone 33 SJ 9434
Hilderthorpe 39 TA 1765
Hilgay 28 TL 6298
Hill 17 ST 6495
Hillam 38 SE 5028
Hillbeck 41 NY 7915
Hillberry 43 SC 3879
Hillborough (Kent) 13 TR 2168
Hillbrae (Grampn.) 62 NJ 6047
Hillbrae (Grampn.) 62 NJ 7923
Hill Brow 10 SU 7926
Hill Dyke 35 TF 3447
Hill End (Durham) 41 NZ 0135
Hill End (Fife.) 51 NT 0495
Hillend (Fife.) 51 NT 1483
Hillesden 18 SP 6828
Hillesley 17 ST 7689
Hillfarrance 7 ST 1624
Hillhead (Devon.) 5 SX 9053
Hill Head (Hants.) 9 SU 5402
Hillhead (Strath.) 50 NS 4219
Hillhead of Auchentumb 62 NJ 9258
Hillhead of Cocklaw 62 NK 0844
Hilliard's Cross 25 SK 1412
Hilliclay 67 ND 1764
Hillingdon 19 TQ 0882
Hillington 28 TF 7225
Hillmorton 26 SP 5374
Hillockhead 61 NJ 3809
Hill of Beath 51 NT 1690
Hill of Fearn 65 NH 8377
Hill of Maud Crofts 61 NJ 4661
Hill Ridware 33 SK 0718
Hill Row 27 TL 4475
Hillside (Grampn.) 62 NO 9298
Hillside (Shetld) 63 HU 4063
Hillside (Tays.) 57 NO 7061
Hillswick 63 HU 2877
Hill, The 40 SD 1783
Hill Top (Hants.) 9 SU 4002
Hill Top (W Yorks.) 38 SE 3315
Hillwell 63 HU 3714
Hilmarton 17 SU 0175
Hilperton 17 ST 8759
Hilsea 9 SU 6503
Hilton (Cambs.) 27 TL 2966
Hilton (Cleve.) 42 NZ 4611
Hilton (Cumbr.) 41 NY 7320
Hilton (Derby.) 33 SK 2430
Hilton (Dorset) 8 ST 7802
Hilton (Durham) 42 NZ 1621
Hilton (Grampn.) 62 NJ 9434
Hilton (Salop) 24 SO 7795
Hilton of Cadboll 65 NH 8776
Himbleton 25 SO 9458
Himley 25 SO 8891
Hincaster 40 SD 5184
Hinckley 26 SP 4294
Hinderclay 29 TM 0276
Hinderwell 43 NZ 7916
Hindford 32 SJ 3333
Hindhead 11 SU 8736
Hindley 36 SD 6104
Hindley Green 36 SD 6403
Hindlip 25 SO 8758
Hindolveston 29 TG 0329
Hindon 8 ST 9032
Hindringham 29 TF 9836
Hingham 29 TG 0202
Hinstock 32 SJ 6926
Hintlesham 21 TM 0843
Hinton (Avon) 17 ST 7376
Hinton (Hants.) 8 SZ 2095
Hinton (Northants.) 26 SP 5352
Hinton (Salop) 24 SJ 4008
Hinton Ampner 9 SU 5927
Hinton Blewett 17 ST 5956
Hinton Charterhouse 17 ST 7758
Hinton-in-the-Hedges 18 SP 5537
Hinton Marsh 9 SU 5827
Hinton Martell 8 SU 0106
Hinton on the Green 25 SP 0240
Hinton Parva 18 SU 2283
Hinton St. George 7 ST 4212
Hinton St. Mary 8 ST 7816
Hinton Waldrist 18 SU 3799
Hints (Salop) 24 SO 6175
Hints (Staffs.) 25 SK 1503
Hinwick 27 SP 9361
Hinxhill 13 TR 0442
Hinxton 20 TL 4945
Hinxworth 19 TL 2340
Hipperholme 37 SE 1225
Hirn 62 NJ 7300
Hirnant 31 SJ 0423
Hirst 47 NZ 2787
Hirst Courtney 38 SE 6124
Hirwaun 15 SN 9505
Hiscott 6 SS 5426
Histon 27 TL 4363
Hitcham 21 TL 9851
Hitchin 19 TL 1829
Hither Green 12 TQ 3874
Hittisleigh 5 SX 7395
Hixon 33 SK 0026
Hoaden 13 TR 2759
Hoaldalbert 16 SO 3923
Hoar Cross 33 SK 1223
Hoarwithy 16 SO 5429
Hoath 13 TR 2064
Hobarris 23 SO 3078
Hobbister 63 HY 3807
Hobkirk 52 NT 5810
Hobson 47 NZ 1755
Hoby 34 SK 6617
Hockering 29 TG 0713
Hockerton 34 SK 7156
Hockley 20 TQ 8293
Hockley Heath 25 SP 1572
Hockliffe 19 SP 9726
Hockwold cum Wilton 28 TL 7288
Hockworthy 7 ST 0319
Hoddesdon 20 TL 3709
Hoddlesden 36 SD 7122
Hodgeston 14 SS 0399
Hodnet 32 SJ 6128
Hodthorpe 34 SK 5476
Hoe 29 TF 9916
Hoe Gate 9 SU 6213
Hoff 41 NY 6717
Hoggeston 18 SP 8025
Hoghton 36 SD 6125
Hognaston 33 SK 2350
Hogsthorpe 35 TF 5372
Holbeach 35 TF 3625
Holbeach Bank 35 TF 3627
Holbeach Drove 27 TF 3212
Holbeach Hurn 35 TF 3927
Holbeach St. Johns 35 TF 3418
Holbeach St. Marks 35 TF 3731
Holbeach St. Matthew 35 TF 4132
Holbeck 34 SK 5473
Holberrow Green 25 SP 0259
Holbeton 5 SX 6150
Holborn 20 TQ 3181
Holbrook (Derby.) 33 SK 3645

Holbrook
Jamestown

Holbrook (Suff.) 21 TM 1636
Holburn 53 NU 0436
Holbury 9 SU 4303
Holcombe (Devon.) 5 SX 9574
Holcombe (Somer.) 8 ST 6649
Holcombe Rogus 7 ST 0519
Holcot 26 SP 7969
Holden 37 SD 7749
Holdenby 26 SP 6967
Holdgate 24 SO 5589
Holdingham 35 TF 0547
Holestane 45 NX 8799
Holford 7 ST 1541
Holker 40 SD 3577
Holkham 28 TF 8944
Hollacombe 4 SS 3702
Holland (Papa Westray) 63 HY 4851
Holland (Stronsay) 63 HY 6622
Holland Fen 35 TF 2445
Holland-on-Sea 21 TM 2016
Hollandstoun 63 HY 7553
Hollesley 21 TM 3544
Hollingbourne 13 TQ 8455
Hollington (Derby.) 33 SK 2239
Hollington (E Susx) 12 TQ 7911
Hollington (Staffs.) 33 SK 0538
Hollingworth 33 SK 0096
Hollins 37 SD 8108
Hollinsclough 33 SK 0666
Hollins Green 32 SJ 6990
Hollinswood 24 SJ 6909
Hollinwood 32 SJ 5236
Hollocombe 5 SS 6311
Holloway 33 SK 3256
Hollowell 26 SP 6972
Hollybush (Gwent 16 SO 1603
Hollybush (Here. and Worc.) 24 SO 7636
Hollybush (Strath.) 50 NS 3914
Holly End 28 TF 4906
Hollym 39 TA 3425
Holm (Isle of Lewis) 63 NB 4531
Holmbury St. Mary 11 TQ 1144
Holme (Cambs.) 27 TL 1987
Holme (Cumbr.) 40 SD 5278
Holme (Notts.) 34 SK 8059
Holme (W Yorks.) 37 SE 1005
Holme Chapel 37 SD 8728
Holme Hale 28 TF 8807
Holme Lacy 24 SO 5535
Holme Marsh 23 SO 3354
Holme next the Sea 28 TF 7043
Holme on the Wolds 39 SE 9646
Holmer 24 SO 5042
Holmer Green 19 SU 9097
Holmes Chapel 32 SJ 7667
Holmesfield 33 SK 3277
Holmeswood 36 SD 4316
Holme upon Spalding Moor 39 SE 8138
Holmewood 33 SK 4365
Holmfirth 37 SE 1408
Holmhead 50 NS 5620
Holmpton 39 TA 3623
Holmrook 40 SD 0799
Holmsgarth 63 HU 4642
Holne 5 SX 7069
Holnest 8 ST 6509
Holsworthy 4 SS 3403
Holsworthy Beacon 4 SS 3508
Holt (Clwyd) 32 SJ 4053
Holt (Dorset) 8 SU 0203
Holt (Here. and Worc.) 25 SO 8262
Holt (Norf.) 29 TG 0738
Holt (Wilts.) 17 ST 8661
Holtby 38 SE 6754
Holt End 25 SP 0769
Holt Heath 25 SO 8163
Holton (Lincs.) 35 TF 1181
Holton (Oxon.) 18 SP 6006
Holton (Somerset) 8 ST 6826
Holton (Suff.) 29 TM 4077
Holton Heath 8 SY 9491
Holton le Clay 39 TA 2802
Holton le Moor 39 TF 0797
Holton St. Mary 21 TM 0537
Holwell (Herts.) 19 TL 1633
Holwell (Leic.) 34 SK 7323
Holwell (Oxon.) 18 SP 2309
Holwick 41 NY 9026
Holworth 8 SY 7683
Holybourne 10 SU 7341
Holy Cross 25 SO 9279
Holyhead 30 SH 2482
Holymoorside 33 SK 3369
Holyport 11 SU 8977
Holystone 47 NT 9502
Holytown 50 NS 7760
Holywell (Cambs.) 27 TL 3370
Holywell (Clwyd) 31 SJ 1875
Holywell (Corn.) 2 SW 7658
Holywell (Dorset) 8 ST 5904
Holywell Green 37 SE 0918
Holywell Lake 7 ST 1020
Holywell Row 28 TL 7077
Holywood 45 NX 9480
Homer 24 SJ 6101
Homersfield 29 TM 2885
Hom Green 17 SO 5822
Homington 8 SU 1226
Honeyborough 14 SM 9506
Honeybourne 25 SP 1144
Honeychurch 5 SS 6202
Honey Hill 13 TR 1161
Honiley 26 SP 2472
Honing 29 TG 3227
Honingham 29 TG 1011
Honington (Lincs.) 34 SK 9443
Honington (Suff.) 28 TL 9174
Honington (Warw.) 26 SP 2642
Honiton 7 ST 1600
Honley 37 SE 1311
Hoo (Kent) 12 TQ 7872
Hooe (Devon.) 4 SX 5052
Hooe (E Susx) 12 TQ 6809
Hoo Green 21 TM 2559
Hook (Dyfed) 14 SM 9811
Hook (Hants.) 10 SU 7254
Hook (Humbs.) 38 SE 7525
Hook (Surrey) 11 TQ 1764
Hook (Wilts.) 17 SU 0784
Hooke (Dorset) 7 ST 5300
Hookgate 32 SJ 7435
Hook Norton 18 SP 3533
Hookway 5 SX 8598
Hookwood 11 TQ 2643
Hoole 32 SJ 4367
Hooton 32 SJ 3679
Hooton Levitt 34 SK 5291
Hooton Pagnell 38 SE 4808
Hooton Roberts 34 SK 4897
Hope (Clwyd) 32 SJ 3058
Hope (Derby.) 33 SK 1783
Hope (Devon.) 5 SX 6740
Hope (Powys) 23 SJ 2507
Hope (Salop) 23 SJ 3401
Hope Bagot 24 SO 5874
Hope Bowdler 24 SO 4792
Hopeman 61 NJ 1469
Hope Mansell 17 SO 6219
Hopesay 24 SO 3883
Hope under Dinmore 24 SO 5052
Hopton (Norf.) 29 TG 5200
Hopton (Salop) 32 SJ 5926
Hopton (Staffs.) 33 SJ 9426
Hopton (Suff.) 29 TL 9979
Hopton Cangeford 24 SO 5480
Hopton Castle 24 SO 3678
Hopton Wafers 24 SO 6476
Hopwas 25 SK 1705
Hopwood 25 SP 0375
Horam 12 TQ 5717
Horbling 35 TF 1135
Horbury 38 SE 2918
Horden 47 NZ 4441
Horderley 24 SO 4086
Hordle 9 SZ 2795
Hordley 32 SJ 3730
Horeb 22 SN 3942
Horham 29 TM 2172
Horkesley Heath 21 TL 9829
Horkstow 39 SE 9818
Horley (Oxon.) 26 SP 4143
Horley (W Susx) 11 TQ 2843
Hornblotton Green 8 ST 5833
Hornby (Lancs.) 36 SD 5868
Hornby (N yorks) 42 NZ 3605
Horncastle 35 TF 2669
Hornchurch 20 TQ 5487
Horncliffe 53 NT 9249
Horndean 9 SU 7013
Horndon on the Hill 20 TQ 6683
Horne 12 TQ 3344
Horn Hill 19 TQ 0292
Horning 29 TG 3417
Horninghold 26 SP 8097
Horninglow 33 SK 2324
Horningsea 28 TL 4962
Horningsham 8 ST 8241
Horningtoft 29 TF 9323
Hornsby 46 NY 5150
Hornsea 39 TA 2047
Hornsey 20 TQ 3089
Hornton 26 SP 3945
Horrabridge 4 SX 5169
Horringer 28 TL 8261
Horsebridge (E Susx) 12 TQ 5911
Horsebridge (Hants.) 9 SU 3430
Horse Bridge (Staffs.) 33 SJ 9553
Horsebrook 25 SJ 8810
Horsehay 24 SJ 6707
Horseheath 20 TL 6147
Horsehouse 41 SE 0481
Horsell 11 SU 9959
Horseman's Green 32 SJ 4441
Horseway 27 TL 4287
Horsey 29 TG 4523
Horsford 29 TG 1915
Horsforth 37 SE 2337
Horsham (Here. and Worc.) 24 SO 7357
Horsham (W Susx) 11 TQ 1730
Horsham St. Faith 29 TG 2114
Horsington (Lincs.) 35 TF 1868
Horsington (Somer.) 8 ST 7023
Horsley (Derby.) 33 SK 3744
Horsley (Glos.) 17 ST 8398
Horsley (Northum.) 47 NY 8496
Horsley (Northum.) 47 NZ 0966
Horsley Cross 21 TM 1227
Horsleycross Street 21 TM 1228
Horsleyhill 52 NT 5319
Horsley Woodhouse 33 SK 3945
Horsmonden 12 TQ 7040
Horspath 18 SP 5704
Horstead 29 TG 2619
Horsted Keynes 12 TQ 3828
Horton (Avon) 17 ST 7684
Horton (Berks.) 11 TQ 0175
Horton (Bucks.) 19 SP 9219
Horton (Dorset) 8 SU 0307
Horton (Lancs.) 37 SD 8550
Horton (Northants.) 26 SP 8254
Horton (Northum.) 53 NU 0230
Horton (Staffs.) 33 SJ 9457
Horton (W Glam.) 15 SS 4785
Horton (Wilts.) 17 SU 0463
Horton Green 32 SJ 4549
Horton Heath 9 SU 4916
Horton in Ribblesdale 37 SD 8172
Horton Kirby 12 TQ 5668
Horwich 36 SD 6311
Horwood 6 SS 5027
Hose 34 SK 7329
Hosh 56 NN 8523
Hoswick 63 HU 4124
Hotham 39 SE 8934
Hothfield 13 TQ 9644
Hoton 34 SK 5722
Houbie 63 HU 6390
Hough 32 SJ 7151
Hougham 34 SK 8844
Hougharry 63 NF 7071
Hough Green 32 SJ 4885
Hough-on-the-Hill 34 SK 9246
Houghton (Cambs.) 27 TL 2871
Houghton (Cumbr.) 46 NY 4159
Houghton (Dyfed) 14 SM 9807
Houghton (Hants.) 9 SU 3331
Houghton (W Susx) 11 TQ 0111
Houghton Conquest 27 TL 0441
Houghton le Spring 47 NZ 3450
Houghton on the Hill 26 SK 6703
Houghton Regis 19 TL 0224
Houghton St. Giles 29 TF 9235
Houlsyke 43 NZ 7308
Hound Green 10 SU 7259
Houndslow 52 NT 6347
Houndwood 53 NT 8464
Hounslow 11 TQ 1276
Housetter 63 HU 3684
Houston 50 NS 4067
Houstry 67 ND 1534
Hove 11 TQ 2805
Hoveringham 34 SK 6946
Hoveton 29 TG 3018
Hovingham 42 SE 6675
How 46 NY 5056
How Caple 24 SO 6030
Howden 38 SE 7428
Howden-le-Wear 42 NZ 1633
Howe (Cumbr.) 40 SD 4588
Howe (Highld.) 67 ND 3062
Howe (Norf.) 29 TM 2799
Howe Green 20 TL 7403
Howell 35 TF 1346
Howe of Teuchar 62 NJ 7947
Howe Street (Essex) 20 TL 6914
Howe Street (Essex) 20 TL 6934
Howe, The 43 SC 1967
Howey 23 SO 0558
Howgate 51 NT 2457
Howick 53 NU 2517
Howlaws 53 NT 7242
Howle 32 SJ 6823
Howlett End 20 TL 5834
Howmore 63 NF 7636
Hownam 53 NT 7719
Hownam Law 53 NT 7921
Hownam Mains 53 NT 7820
Howsham (Humbs.) 39 TA 0404
Howsham (N Yorks.) 38 SE 7362
Howton 16 SO 4129
Howwood 50 NS 3960
Hoxne 29 TM 1877
Hoylake 31 SJ 2189
Hoyland Nether 38 SE 3600
Hoyland Swaine 37 SE 2604
Hubbert's Bridge 35 TF 2643
Huby 38 SE 5665
Hucclecote 17 SO 8717
Hucking 12 TQ 8358
Hucknall 34 SK 5349
Huddersfield 37 SE 1416
Huddington 25 SO 9457
Hudswell 42 NZ 1400
Huggate 39 SE 8855
Hughenden Valley 19 SU 8695
Hughley 24 SO 5697
Hugh Town 2 SV 9010
Hugmore 32 SJ 3752
Huish (Devon.) 4 SS 5311
Huish (Wilts.) 17 SU 1463
Huish Champflower 7 ST 0429
Huish Episcopi 7 ST 4226
Hulcott 19 SP 8516
Hulland 33 SK 2447
Hullavington 17 ST 8982
Hullbridge 20 TQ 8194
Hulme End 33 SK 1059
Hulme Walfield 33 SJ 8465
Hulne Park 53 NU 1514
Hulver Street 29 TM 4686
Humber Court 24 SO 5356
Humberston 39 TA 3105
Humberstone 26 SK 6206
Humbie 52 NT 4562
Humbleton (Humbs.) 39 TA 2234
Humbleton (Northum.) 53 NT 9728
Hume 52 NT 7041
Humshaugh 47 NY 9171
Huna 67 ND 3573
Huncoat 37 SD 7730
Huncote 26 SP 5197
Hundalee 52 NT 6418
Hunderthwaite 41 NY 9821
Hundleby 35 TF 3966
Hundleton 14 SM 9600
Hundon 20 TL 7348
Hundred Acres 9 SU 5911
Hundred End 36 SD 4122
Hundred, The 24 SO 5264
Hungarton 26 SK 6807
Hungerford (Berks.) 10 SU 3368
Hungerford (Hants.) 8 SU 1612
Hungerford Newtown 10 SU 3571
Hunmanby 43 TA 0977
Hunningham 26 SP 3768
Hunsdon 20 TL 4114
Hunsingore 38 SE 4253
Hunsonby 41 NY 5835
Hunspow 67 ND 2172
Hunstanton 28 TF 6741
Hunstanworth 47 NY 9449
Hunston (Suff.) 29 TL 9768
Hunston (W Susx) 11 SU 8601
Hunstrete 17 ST 6462
Hunt End 25 SP 0364
Hunter's Quay 49 NS 1879
Huntingdon 27 TL 2371
Huntingfield 29 TM 3374
Huntington (Here. and Worc.) 23 SO 2553
Huntingdon (Lothian) 52 NT 4875
Huntingdon (N Yorks.) 38 SE 6156
Huntingdon (Staffs.) 25 SJ 9713
Huntingtower 56 NO 0725
Huntley 17 SO 7219
Huntly 61 NJ 5339
Hunton (Kent) 12 TQ 7149
Hunton (N Yorks.) 42 SE 1892
Hunt's Cross 32 SJ 4385
Huntsham 7 ST 0020
Huntspill 7 ST 3045
Huntworth 7 ST 3134
Hunwick 42 NZ 1832
Hunworth 29 TG 0635
Hurdsfield 33 SJ 9274
Hurley (Berks.) 19 SU 8283
Hurley (Warw.) 26 SP 2495
Hurlford 50 NS 4536
Hurliness 63 ND 2888
Hurn 8 SZ 1296
Hursley 9 SU 4225
Hurst (Berks.) 10 SU 7972
Hurst (Gtr Mches.) 37 SD 9400
Hurst (N Yorks.) 42 NZ 0402
Hurstbourne Priors 10 SU 4346
Hurstbourne Tarrant 10 SU 3853
Hurst Green (E Susx) 12 TQ 7327
Hurst Green (Lancs.) 36 SD 6838
Hurst Green (Surrey) 12 TQ 3951
Hurstpierpoint 11 TQ 2816
Hurtwood Common 11 TQ 0743
Hurworth 42 NZ 3010
Hury 41 NY 9619
Husbands Bosworth 26 SP 6484
Husbourne Crawley 19 SP 9535
Husinish 63 NA 9812
Husthwaite 42 SE 5175
Huthwaite 34 SK 4659
Huttoft 35 TF 5176
Hutton (Avon) 16 ST 3458
Hutton (Borders) 53 NT 9053
Hutton (Cumbr.) 40 NY 4326
Hutton (Essex) 20 TQ 6394
Hutton (Lancs.) 36 SD 4926
Hutton (N Yorks.) 38 SE 7667
Hutton Bonville 42 NZ 3300
Hutton Buscel 43 SE 9784
Hutton Conyers 42 SE 3273
Hutton Cranswick 39 TA 0252
Hutton End 40 NY 4538
Hutton Henry 42 NZ 4236
Hutton-le-Hole 43 SE 7090
Hutton Magna 42 NZ 1212
Hutton Roof (Cumbr.) 40 NY 3734
Hutton Roof (Cumbr.) 41 SD 5777
Hutton Rudby 42 NZ 4606
Hutton Sessay 42 SE 4776
Hutton Wandesley 38 SE 5050
Huxley 32 SJ 5061
Huxter (Shetld.) 63 HU 5662
Huyton 32 SJ 4490
Hycemoor 40 SD 0989
Hyde (Glos.) 17 SO 8801
Hyde (Gtr Mches.) 33 SJ 9294
Hyde Heath 19 SP 9300
Hydestile 11 SU 9740
Hynish 48 NL 9839
Hyssington 23 SO 3194
Hythe (Hants.) 9 SU 4207
Hythe (Kent) 13 TR 1635
Hythe End 11 TQ 0172
Hythie 62 NK 0051

Ibberton 8 ST 7807
Ible 33 SK 2457
Ibsley 8 SU 1509
Ibstock 26 SK 4010
Ibstone 18 SU 7593
Ibthorpe 10 SU 3753
Ibworth 10 SU 5654
Ickburgh 28 TL 8195
Ickenham 19 TQ 0786
Ickford 18 SP 6407
Ickham 13 TR 2258
Ickleford 19 TL 1831
Icklesham 13 TQ 8816
Ickleton 20 TL 4943
Icklingham 28 TL 7772
Ickwell Green 27 TL 1545
Icomb 18 SP 2122
Idbury 18 SP 2320
Iddesleigh 4 SS 5608
Ide 5 SX 8990
Ideford 5 SX 8977
Ide Hill 12 TQ 4851
Iden 13 TQ 9123
Iden Green 12 TQ 8031
Idlicote 26 SP 2844
Idmiston 8 SU 1937
Idridgehay 33 SK 2849
Idrigil 58 NG 3863
Idstone 18 SU 2584
Idvies 57 NO 5347
Ifield (W Susx) 11 TQ 2537
Ifield or Singlewell (Kent) 12 TQ 6471
Ifold 11 TQ 0231
Iford 12 TQ 4007
Ifton Heath 32 SJ 3236
Ightfield 32 SJ 5938
Ightham 12 TQ 5956
Iken 21 TM 4155
Ilam 33 SK 1351
Ilchester 7 ST 5222
Ilderton 53 NU 0121
Ilford 20 TQ 4586
Ilfracombe 6 SS 5147
Ilkeston 34 SK 4642
Ilketshall St. Andrew 29 TM 3887
Ilketshall St. Margaret 29 TM 3485
Ilkley 37 SE 1147
Illey 25 SO 9881
Illingworth 37 SE 0728
Illogan 2 SW 6643
Illston on the Hill 26 SP 7099
Ilmer 18 SP 7605
Ilmington 26 SP 2143
Ilminster 7 ST 3614
Ilsington 5 SX 7876
Ilston 15 SS 5590
Ilton (N Yorks.) 42 SE 1878
Ilton (Somer.) 7 ST 3517
Imachar 49 NR 8640
Imber 8 ST 9648
Immingham 39 TA 1714
Impington 27 TL 4463
Ince 32 SJ 4476
Ince Blundell 36 SD 3203
Ince-in-Makerfield 36 SD 5903
Inchbare 57 NO 6065
Inchberry 61 NJ 3155
Inchinnan 50 NS 4768
Inchlaggan 59 NH 1801
Inchnacardoch 60 NH 3710
Inchnadamph 66 NC 2522
Inchture 57 NO 2728
Inchyra 56 NO 1820
Indian Queens 2 SW 9158
Ingatestone 20 TQ 6499
Ingbirchworth 37 SE 2205
Ingestre 33 SJ 9724
Ingham (Lincs.) 34 SK 9483
Ingham (Norf.) 29 TG 3825
Ingham (Suff.) 28 TL 8570
Ingleby Arncliffe 42 NZ 4400
Ingleby Greenhow 42 NZ 5806
Inglesbatch 17 ST 7061
Inglesham 18 SU 2098
Ingleton (Durham) 42 NZ 1720
Ingleton (N Yorks.) 41 SD 6972
Inglewhite 36 SD 5439
Ingoe 47 NZ 0374
Ingoldisthorpe 28 TF 6832
Ingoldmells 35 TF 5668
Ingoldsby 34 TF 0030
Ingram 53 NU 0116
Ingrave 20 TQ 6292
Ings 40 SD 4498
Ingst 17 ST 5887
Ingworth 29 TG 1929
Inkberrow 25 SP 0157
Inkhorn 62 NJ 9239
Inkpen 10 SU 3564
Inkstack 67 ND 2570
Innellan 49 NS 1469
Innerleithen 51 NT 3336
Innerleven 57 NO 3700
Innermessan 44 NX 0863
Innerwick (Lothian) 52 NT 7273
Innerwick (Tays.) 56 NN 5947
Insch 62 NJ 6327
Insh 60 NH 8101
Inskip 36 SD 4537
Instow 6 SS 4730
Inver (Grampn.) 61 NO 2393
Inver (Highld.) 65 NH 8682
Inver (Tays.) 56 NO 0142
Inverailort 54 NM 7681
Inveralligin 59 NG 8457
Inverallochy 62 NK 0464
Inveramsay 62 NJ 7424
Inveran 65 NH 5797
Inveraray 55 NN 0908
Inverarish 58 NG 5535
Inverarity 57 NO 4444
Inverarnan 55 NN 3118
Inverasdale 64 NG 8286
Inverbervie 57 NO 8372
Invercreran 55 NN 0147
Inverdruie 60 NH 9010
Inverebie 62 NJ 9233
Inveresk 51 NT 3471
Inverey 61 NO 0889
Inverfarigaig 60 NH 5224
Invergarry 59 NH 3101
Invergeldie 56 NN 7427
Invergloy House 59 NN 2288
Invergordon 65 NH 7168
Invergowrie 57 NO 3430
Inverguseran 58 NG 7407
Inverhadden 56 NN 6757
Inverharroch 61 NJ 3831
Inverie 59 NG 7600
Inverinan 55 NM 9917
Inverinate 59 NG 9122
Inverkeilor 57 NO 6649
Inverkeithing 51 NT 1383
Inverkeithny 62 NJ 6246
Inverkip 49 NS 2071
Inverkirkaig 64 NC 0819
Inverlael 64 NH 1885
Inverlochlarig 55 NN 4318
Inver Mallie 55 NN 1388
Invermoriston 60 NH 4117
Invernaver 66 NC 7060
Inverness 60 NH 6645
Invernoaden 55 NS 1197
Inverquharity 57 NO 4057
Inverquhomery 62 NK 0246
Inverroy 55 NN 2581
Inverugie 62 NK 0947
Inveruglas 55 NN 3109
Inverurie 62 NJ 7721
Invervar 56 NN 6648
Inwardleigh 4 SX 5599
Inworth 21 TL 8717
Iping 10 SU 8522
Ipplepen 5 SX 8366
Ipsden 18 SU 6385
Ipstones 33 SK 0249
Ipswich 21 TM 1744
Irby 31 SJ 2584
Irby in the Marsh 35 TF 4763
Irby upon Humber 39 TA 1904
Irchester 27 SP 9265
Ireby (Cumbr.) 40 NY 2338
Ireby (Lancs.) 41 SD 6575
Ireland (Shetld.) 63 HU 3722
Ireleth 40 SD 2277
Ireshopeburn 41 NY 8638
Irlam 32 SJ 7194
Irnham 34 TF 0226
Iron Acton 17 ST 6783
Iron-Bridge 24 SJ 6703
Iron Cross 25 SP 0552
Ironside 62 NJ 8852
Ironville 34 SK 4351
Irstead 29 TG 3620
Irthington 46 NY 4961
Irthlingborough 27 SP 9470
Irton 43 TA 0084
Irvine 49 NS 3239
Isauld 67 NC 9765
Isbister (Shetld.) 63 HU 3791
Isbister (Whalsay) 63 HU 5763
Isfield 12 TQ 4417
Isham 27 SP 8873
Islawr-dref 22 SH 6815
Isle Abbotts 7 ST 3520
Isle Brewers 7 ST 3621
Isleham 28 TL 6474
Isle of Whithorn 44 NX 4736
Isleornsay 58 NG 6912
Islesburgh 63 HU 3369
Isleworth 11 TQ 1675
Isley Walton 33 SK 4225
Islington 20 TQ 3085
Islip (Northants.) 27 SP 9879
Islip (Oxon.) 18 SP 5214
Islivig 63 NA 9927
Istead Rise 12 TQ 6369
Itchen Abbas 9 SU 5332
Itchen Stoke 9 SU 5532
Itchingfield 11 TQ 1328
Itchington 17 ST 6586
Itteringham 29 TG 1430
Itton (Devon.) 5 SX 6898
Itton (Gwent) 16 ST 4896
Ivegill 46 NY 4143
Ivelet 41 SD 9398
Iver 19 TQ 0381
Iver Heath 19 TQ 0283
Iveston 47 NZ 1350
Ivinghoe 19 SP 9416
Ivinghoe Aston 19 SP 9518
Ivington 24 SO 4756
Ivington Green 24 SO 4656
Ivybridge 5 SX 6356
Ivychurch 13 TR 0227
Ivy Hatch 12 TQ 5854
Iwade 13 TQ 9067
Iwerne Courtney or Shroton 8 ST 8512
Iwerne Minster 8 ST 8614
Ixworth 29 TL 9370
Ixworth Thorpe 28 TL 9172

Jack Hill 37 SE 1951
Jackstown 62 NJ 7531
Jackton 50 NS 5953
Jacobstow (Corn.) 4 SX 1995
Jacobstowe (Devon.) 4 SS 5801
Jameston 14 SS 0599
Jamestown (Dumf. and Galwy.) 46 NY 2996

Longslow Melkridge

Longslow 32 SJ 6535
Longstanton 27 TL 3966
Longstock 9 SU 3536
Long Stowe 20 TL 3054
Long Stratton 29 TM 1992
Long Street 26 SP 7947
Long Sutton (Hants.) 10 SU 7347
Long Sutton (Lincs.) 35 TF 4322
Long Sutton (Somer.) 7 ST 4625
Longthorpe 27 TL 1698
Longton (Lancs.) 36 SD 4725
Longton (Staffs.) 33 SJ 9043
Longtown (Cumbr.) 46 NY 3768
Longtown (Here. and Worc.) 16 SO 3228
Longville in the Dale 24 SO 5393
Long Whatton 34 SK 4723
Longwick 18 SP 7805
Long Wittenham 18 SU 5493
Longwitton 47 NZ 0788
Longwood 24 SJ 6007
Longworth 18 SU 3899
Longyester 52 NT 5465
Lonmore 58 NG 2646
Loose 12 TQ 7552
Loosley Row 18 SP 8100
Lootcherbrae 62 NJ 6054
Lopcombe Corner 9 SU 2435
Lopen 7 ST 4214
Loppington 32 SJ 4629
Lorbottle 47 NU 0306
Lornty 56 NO 1746
Loscoe 33 SK 4247
Lossiemouth 61 NJ 2370
Lossit 48 NR 1856
Lostock Gralam 32 SJ 6874
Lostwithiel 3 SX 1059
Lothbeg 67 NC 9410
Lothersdale 37 SD 9545
Lothmore 67 NC 9611
Loudwater 19 SU 8990
Loughborough 34 SK 5319
Loughor 15 SS 5898
Loughton (Bucks.) 19 SP 8337
Loughton (Essex) 20 TQ 4296
Loughton (Salop) 24 SO 6183
Lound (Lincs.) 35 TF 0618
Lound (Notts.) 34 SK 6986
Lound (Suff.) 29 TM 5099
Lount 33 SK 3819
Louth 35 TF 3287
Love Clough 37 SD 8126
Lover 8 SU 2120
Loversall 38 SK 5798
Loves Green 20 TL 6404
Loveston 14 SN 0808
Lovington 8 ST 5931
Low Bradfield 33 SK 2691
Low Bradley 37 SE 0048
Low Braithwaite 46 NY 4242
Low Brunton 47 NY 9269
Low Burnham 38 SE 7702
Lowca 40 NX 9821
Low Catton 38 SE 7053
Low Coniscliffe 42 NZ 2514
Low Crosby 46 NY 4459
Lowdham 34 SK 6646
Low Dinsdale 42 NZ 3411
Low Eggborough 38 SE 5522
Lower Aisholt 7 ST 2035
Lower Assendon 18 SU 7484
Lower Beeding 11 TQ 2227
Lower Benefield 27 SP 9888
Lower Bentham 36 SD 6469
Lower Boddington 26 SP 4752
Lower Bullingham 24 SO 5038
Lower Cam 17 SO 7401
Lower Chapel 23 SO 0235
Lower Chute 10 SU 3153
Lower Cwmtwrch 15 SN 7710
Lower Darwen 36 SD 6824
Lower Down 23 SO 3384
Lower Dunsforth 38 SE 4464
Lower Farringdon 10 SU 7035
Lower Frankton 32 SJ 3732
Lower Froyle 10 SU 7544
Lower Gledfield 65 NH 5990
Lower Green 29 TF 9837
Lower Halstow 13 TQ 8567
Lower Hardres 13 TR 1453
Lower Heyford 18 SP 4824
Lower Higham 12 TQ 7172
Lower Hordley 32 SJ 3929
Lower Killeyan 48 NR 2743
Lower Langford 16 ST 4660
Lower Largo 57 NO 4102
Lower Lemington 18 SP 2134
Lower Lye 24 SO 4067
Lower Maes-coed 23 SO 3431
Lower Mayland 21 TL 9101
Lower Moor 25 SO 9847
Lower Nazeing 20 TL 3906
Lower Penarth 16 ST 1869
Lower Penn 25 SO 8696
Lower Pennington 9 SZ 3193
Lower Peover 32 SJ 7474
Lower Pitcalzean 65 NH 8070
Lower Quinton 25 SP 1847
Lower Shader 63 NB 3854
Lower Shelton 27 SP 9942
Lower Shiplake 10 SU 7779
Lower Shuckburgh 26 SP 4862
Lower Slaughter 17 SP 1622
Lower Stanton St. Quintin 17 ST 9180
Lower Sundon 19 TL 0526
Lower Swanwick 9 SU 4909
Lower Swell 17 SP 1725
Lower Tysoe 26 SP 3445
Lower Upham 9 SU 5219
Lower Vexford 7 ST 1135
Lower Weare 16 ST 4053
Lower Wield 10 SU 6340
Lower Winchendon 18 SP 7312
Lower Woodend 18 SU 8088
Lower Woodford 8 SU 1235
Lowesby 26 SK 7207
Lowestoft 29 TM 5493
Lowestoft End 29 TM 5394
Loweswater 40 NY 1421
Low Gate 47 NY 9064
Lowgill (Cumbr.) 41 SD 6297
Lowgill (Lancs.) 36 SD 6564
Low Ham 7 ST 4329
Low Hartsop 40 NY 4013
Low Hesket 46 NY 4646
Low Hesleyhurst 47 NZ 0997
Lowick (Cumbr.) 40 SD 2985
Lowick (Northants.) 27 SP 9781
Lowick (Northum.) 53 NU 0139
Low Mill 42 SE 6795
Low Moor 36 SD 7241
Lownie Moor 57 NO 4848
Low Redford 41 NZ 0731
Low Row (Cumbr.) 46 NY 5863
Low Row (N Yorks.) 41 SD 9897
Low Santon 39 SE 9312
Lowsonford 25 SP 1867
Low Street 29 TG 3424
Lowthorpe 39 TA 0860
Low Thurlton 29 TM 4299
Lowton 36 SJ 6197
Lowton Common 36 SJ 6397
Low Torry 51 NT 0086
Low Waters 50 NS 7353
Low Worsall 42 NZ 3909
Loxbeare 5 SS 9116
Loxhill 11 TQ 0037
Loxhore 6 SS 6138
Loxley 26 SP 2553
Loxton 16 ST 3755
Loxwood 11 TQ 0431
Lubenham 26 SP 7087
Luccombe 6 SS 9144
Luccombe Village 9 SZ 5880
Lucker 53 NU 1530
Luckett 4 SX 3873
Luckington 17 ST 8383
Lucklawhill 57 NO 4222
Luckwell Bridge 6 SS 9038
Lucton 24 SO 4364
Ludag 63 NF 7714
Ludborough 35 TF 2995
Ludchurch 14 SN 1411
Luddenden 37 SE 0425
Luddesdown 12 TQ 6766
Luddington 39 SE 8216
Ludford (Lincs.) 35 TF 1989
Ludford (Salop) 24 SO 5173
Ludgershall (Bucks.) 18 SP 6617
Ludgershall (Wilts.) 10 SU 2650
Ludgvan 2 SW 5033
Ludham 29 TG 3818
Ludlow 24 SO 5175
Ludwell 8 ST 9122
Ludworth 47 NZ 3641
Luffincott 4 SX 3394
Luffness 52 NT 4780
Lugar 50 NS 5821
Luggiebank 50 NS 7672
Lugton 50 NS 4152
Lugwardine 24 SO 5441
Luib 58 NG 5628
Lulham 24 SO 4041
Lullingstone Castle 12 TQ 5364
Lullington (Derby.) 26 SK 2513
Lullington (Somer.) 17 ST 7851
Lulsgate Bottom 16 ST 5065
Lulsley 24 SO 7455
Lumb 37 SE 0221
Lumby 38 SE 4830
Lumloch 50 NS 6369
Lumphanan 61 NJ 5804
Lumphinnans 51 NT 1692
Lumsdaine 53 NT 8769
Lumsden 61 NJ 4722
Lunan 57 NO 6851
Lunanhead 57 NO 4752
Luncarty 56 NO 0929
Lund (Humbs.) 39 SE 9648
Lund (N Yorks.) 38 SE 6532
Lundie (Tays.) 57 NO 2836
Lundin Links 57 NO 4002
Lunna 63 HU 4869
Lunning 63 HU 5066
Lunsford's Cross 12 TQ 7210
Lunt 36 SD 3401
Luntley 24 SO 3955
Luppitt 7 ST 1606
Lupton 41 SD 5581
Lurgashall 11 SU 9326
Lurgmore 60 NH 5937
Lusby 35 TF 3367
Luskentyre 63 NG 0699
Luss 50 NS 3592
Lusta 58 NG 2756
Lustleigh 5 SX 7881
Luston 24 SO 4863
Luthermuir 57 NO 6568
Luthrie 57 NO 3219
Luton (Beds.) 19 TL 0821
Luton (Devon.) 5 SX 9076
Luton (Kent) 12 TQ 7766
Lutterworth 26 SP 5484
Lutton (Devon.) 4 SX 5959
Lutton (Lincs.) 35 TF 4325
Lutton (Northants.) 27 TL 1187
Luxborough 7 SS 9738
Luxulyan 3 SX 0458
Lybster 67 ND 2435
Lydbury North 23 SO 3486
Lydcott 6 SS 6936
Lydd 13 TR 0421
Lydden 13 TR 2645
Lyddington 27 SP 8797
Lydd-on-Sea 13 TR 0819
Lydeard St. Lawrence 7 ST 1232
Lydford (Devon.) 4 SX 5084
Lydford (Somer.) 7 ST 5731
Lydgate 37 SD 9225
Lydham 23 SO 3391
Lydiard Millicent 17 SU 0986
Lydiate 36 SD 3604
Lydlinch 8 ST 7413
Lydney 17 SO 6203
Lydstep 14 SS 0898
Lye 25 SO 9284
Lye Green 19 SP 9703
Lyford 18 SU 3994
Lymbridge Green 13 TR 1243
Lyme Regis 7 SY 3492
Lyminge 13 TR 1641
Lymington 9 SZ 3295
Lyminster 11 TQ 0204
Lymm 32 SJ 6786
Lymore 9 SZ 2992
Lympne 13 TR 1235
Lympsham 16 ST 3454
Lympstone 5 SX 9984
Lynchat 60 NH 7801
Lyndhurst 9 SU 2907
Lyndon 27 SK 9004
Lyne 11 TQ 0166
Lyneal 32 SJ 4433
Lyneham (Oxon.) 18 SP 2720
Lyneham (Wilts.) 17 SU 0179
Lynemouth 47 NZ 2991
Lyne of Gorthleck 60 NH 5420
Lyne of Skene 62 NJ 7610
Lyness 63 ND 3094
Lyng (Norf.) 29 TG 0617
Lyng (Somer.) 7 ST 3328
Lynmouth 6 SS 7249
Lynsted 13 TQ 9461
Lynton 6 SS 7149
Lyon's Gate 8 ST 6605
Lyonshall 23 SO 3356
Lytchett Matravers 8 SY 9495
Lytchett Minster 8 SY 9593
Lyth 67 ND 2763
Lytham 36 SD 3727
Lytham St. Anne's 36 SD 3427
Lythe 43 NZ 8413
Lythes 63 ND 4589

Maaruig 63 NB 1906
Mabe Burnthouse 2 SW 7634
Mabie 45 NX 9570
Mablethorpe 35 TF 5085
Macclesfield 33 SJ 9173
Macduff 62 NJ 7064
Machany 56 NN 9015
Macharioch 48 NR 7309
Machen 16 ST 2189
Machrihanish 48 NR 6220
Machynlleth 22 SH 7401
Mackworth 33 SK 3137
Macmerry 52 NT 4372
Madderty 56 NN 9522
Maddiston 51 NS 9476
Madehurst 11 SU 9810
Madeley (Salop) 24 SJ 6904
Madeley (Staffs.) 32 SJ 7744
Madingley 27 TL 3960
Madley 24 SO 4138
Madresfield 24 SO 8047
Madron 2 SW 4532
Maenclochog 14 SN 0827
Maendy 16 ST 0176
Maentwrog 30 SH 6640
Maer 32 SJ 7938
Maerdy (Clwyd) 31 SJ 0144
Maerdy (Mid Glam.) 16 SS 9798
Maesbrook 32 SJ 3121
Maesbury Marsh 32 SJ 3125
Maes-glas 16 ST 2985
Maesgwynne 14 SN 2024
Maeshafn 31 SJ 2061
Maesllyn 22 SN 3644
Maesmynis 23 SO 0148
Maesteg 15 SS 8591
Maesybont 15 SN 5616
Maes-y-cwmmer 16 ST 1794
Magdalen Laver 20 TL 5108
Maggieknockater 61 NJ 3145
Magham Down 12 TQ 6111
Maghull 36 SD 3702
Magor 16 ST 4287
Maiden Bradley 8 ST 8038
Maidencombe 5 SX 9268
Maidenhead 19 SU 8881
Maiden Law 47 NZ 1749
Maiden Newton 8 SY 5997
Maidens 49 NS 2107
Maidford 26 SP 6052
Maids' Moreton 18 SP 7035
Maidstone 12 TQ 7656
Maidwell 26 SP 7477
Mail 63 HU 4228
Mains 60 NH 4239
Mains of Ardestie 57 NO 5034
Mains of Balhall 57 NO 5163
Mains of Ballindarg 57 NO 4051
Mains of Dalvey 61 NJ 1132
Mains of Drum 62 NO 8099
Mains of Melgund 57 NO 5456
Mains of Thornton 57 NO 6871
Mains of Throsk 50 NS 8690
Mainstone 23 SO 2687
Maisemore 17 SO 8121
Malborough 5 SX 7039
Malden 11 TQ 2166
Maldon 20 TL 8506
Malham 37 SD 9062
Mallaig 58 NM 6796
Malleny Mills 51 NT 1665
Mallwyd 22 SH 8612
Malmesbury 17 ST 9387
Malpas (Ches.) 32 SJ 4847
Malpas (Cornwall) 2 SW 8442
Maltby (Cleve.) 42 NZ 4613
Maltby (S Yorks.) 34 SK 5392
Maltby le Marsh 35 TF 4681
Malting Green 21 TL 9720
Maltman's Hill 13 TQ 9043
Malton 38 SE 7871
Malvern Link 24 SO 7848
Malvern Wells 24 SO 7742
Mamble 24 SO 6871
Manaccan 2 SW 7625
Manafon 23 SJ 1102
Manaton 5 SX 7481
Manby 35 TF 3986
Mancetter 26 SP 3196
Manchester 37 SJ 8397
Mancot 32 SJ 3267
Mandally 59 NH 2900
Manea 28 TL 4789
Manfield 42 NZ 2213
Mangersta 63 NB 0131
Mangotsfield 17 ST 6676
Manish (Harris) 63 NG 1089
Manish (Isle of Lewis) 63 NA 9513
Mankinholes 37 SD 9523
Manley 32 SJ 5071
Manmoel 16 SO 1703
Mannel 48 NL 9840
Manningford Bohune 17 SU 1357
Manningford Bruce 17 SU 1359
Manning's Heath 11 TQ 2028
Mannington 8 SU 0605
Manningtree 21 TM 1031
Mannofield 62 NJ 9104
Manorbier 14 SS 0698
Manorhill 52 NT 6632
Manorowen 14 SM 9336
Mansell Gamage 24 SO 3944
Mansell Lacy 24 SO 4245
Mansergh 41 SD 6082
Mansfield (Notts.) 34 SK 5361
Mansfield (Strath.) 50 NS 6214
Mansfield Woodhouse 34 SK 5363
Mansriggs 40 SD 2880
Manston 8 ST 8115
Manthorpe 35 TF 0616
Manton (Humbs.) 39 SE 9302
Manton (Leic.) 27 SK 8704
Manton (Wilts.) 17 SU 1768
Manuden 20 TL 4926
Maplebeck 34 SK 7160
Maple Cross 19 TQ 0392
Mapledurham 10 SU 6776
Mapledurwell 10 SU 6851
Maplehurst 11 TQ 1924
Mapleton 33 SK 1648
Mapperley 33 SK 4343
Mapperton 7 SY 5099
Mappleborough Green 25 SP 0866
Mappleton 39 TA 2244
Mappowder 8 ST 7105
Marazion 2 SW 5130
Marbury 32 SJ 5545
March 27 TL 4197
Marcham 18 SU 4596
Marchamley 32 SJ 5929
Marchbankwood 45 NY 0899
Marchington 33 SK 1330
Marchington Woodlands 33 SK 1128
Marchwiel 32 SJ 3547
Marchwood 9 SU 3809
Marcross 15 SS 9269
Marden (Here. and Worc.) 24 SO 5247
Marden (Kent) 12 TQ 7444
Marden (Wilts.) 17 SU 0857
Mardy 16 SO 3016
Marefield 26 SK 7408
Mare Green 7 ST 3326
Mareham le Fen 35 TF 2761
Mareham on the Hill 35 TF 2867
Maresfield 12 TQ 4624
Marfleet 39 TA 1329
Margam 15 SS 7887
Margaret Marsh 8 ST 8218
Margaret Roding 20 TL 5912
Margaretting 20 TL 6601
Margate 13 TR 3670
Margnaheglish 49 NS 0331
Marham 28 TF 7110
Marhamchurch 4 SS 2203
Marholm 27 TF 1402
Marian-glas 30 SH 5084
Mariansleigh 6 SS 7422
Marishader 58 NG 4963
Maristow 4 SX 4764
Mariveg 63 NB 4119
Mark 7 ST 3747
Markbeech 12 TQ 4842
Markby 35 TF 4878
Mark Causeway 7 ST 3547
Mark Cross 12 TQ 5831
Market Bosworth 26 SK 4003
Market Deeping 27 TF 1310
Market Drayton 32 SJ 6734
Market Harborough 26 SP 7387
Markethill 56 NO 2239
Market Lavington 17 SU 0154
Market Overton 34 SK 8816
Market Rasen 35 TF 1089
Market Stainton 35 TF 2279
Market Street 29 TG 2921
Market Weighton 39 SE 8741
Market Weston 29 TL 9877
Markfield 26 SK 4810
Markham 16 SO 1600
Markinch 57 NO 2901
Markington 38 SE 2864
Marksbury 17 ST 6662
Marks Tey 21 TL 9123
Markwell 4 SX 3658
Markyate 19 TL 0616
Marlborough 17 SU 1869
Marlcliff 25 SP 0950
Marldon 5 SX 8663
Marlesford 21 TM 3258
Marley Green 32 SJ 5745
Marlingford 29 TG 1208
Marloes 14 SM 7908
Marlow 19 SU 8587
Marlpit Hill 12 TQ 4447
Marnhull 8 ST 7718
Marnoch 62 NJ 5950
Marple 33 SJ 9588
Marr 38 SE 5105
Marrick 41 SE 0798
Marrister 63 HU 5464
Marros 14 SN 2008
Marsden 37 SE 0411
Marsett 41 SD 9086
Marsh 5 ST 2410
Marshall's Heath 19 TL 1515
Marsham 29 TG 1924
Marshaw 36 SD 5853
Marsh Baldon 18 SU 5699
Marshborough 13 TR 2958
Marshbrook 24 SO 4389
Marshchapel 39 TF 3598
Marshfield (Avon) 17 ST 7773
Marshfield (Gwent) 16 ST 2582
Marshgate 4 SX 1592
Marsh Gibbon 18 SP 6423
Marsh Green (Devon.) 7 SY 0493
Marsh Green (Kent) 12 TQ 4344
Marsh Green (Salop) 24 SJ 6014
Marshside 36 SD 3419
Marsh, The 23 SO 3197
Marshwood 7 SY 3899
Marske 41 NZ 1000
Marske-by-the-Sea 42 NZ 6322
Marston (Ches.) 32 SJ 6474
Marston (Here. and Worc.) 24 SO 3657
Marston (Lincs.) 34 SK 8943
Marston (Oxon.) 18 SP 5208
Marston (Staffs.) 25 SJ 8314
Marston (Staffs.) 33 SJ 9227
Marston (Warw.) 26 SP 2095
Marston (Wilts.) 17 ST 9656
Marston Green 25 SP 1685
Marston Magna 8 ST 5922
Marston Meysey 17 SU 1297
Marston Montgomery 33 SK 1338
Marston Moretaine 27 SP 9941
Marston on Dove 33 SK 2329
Marston St. Lawrence 26 SP 5342
Marston Stannett 24 SO 5655
Marston Trussell 26 SP 6986
Marstow 16 SO 5519
Marsworth 19 SP 9214
Marten 10 SU 2860
Marthall 32 SJ 8076
Martham 29 TG 4518
Martin (Hants.) 8 SU 0719
Martin (Lincs.) 35 TF 1259
Martin Drove End 8 SU 0420
Martinhoe 6 SS 6648
Martin Hussingtree 25 SO 8860
Martinscroft 32 SJ 6589
Martinstown 8 SY 6488
Martlesham 21 TM 2547
Martletwy 14 SN 0310
Martley 24 SO 7559
Martock 7 ST 4619
Marton (Ches.) 33 SJ 8468
Marton (Cleve.) 42 NZ 5115
Marton (Lincs.) 34 SK 8381
Marton (N Yorks.) 38 SE 4162
Marton (N Yorks.) 43 SE 7383
Marton (Salop) 23 SJ 2802
Marton (Warw.) 26 SP 4069
Marwood 6 SS 5437
Marybank 60 NH 4753
Maryburgh 60 NH 5456
Marygold 53 NT 8160
Maryhill 62 NJ 8245
Marykirk 57 NO 6865
Marylebone 36 SD 5807
Marypark 61 NJ 1938
Maryport (Cumbr.) 40 NY 0336
Maryport (Dumf. & Galwy) 44 NX 1434
Marystow 4 SX 4382
Mary Tavy 4 SX 5079
Maryton 57 NO 6856
Marywell (Grampn.) 61 NO 5896
Marywell (Tays.) 57 NO 6544
Masham 42 SE 2280
Mashbury 20 TL 6511
Mason 47 NZ 2073
Mastrick 62 NJ 9007
Matching 20 TL 5212
Matching Green 20 TL 5311
Matching Tye 20 TL 5111
Matfen 47 NZ 0371
Matfield 12 TQ 6541
Mathern 16 ST 5291
Mathon 24 SO 7345
Mathry 14 SM 8832
Matlaske 29 TG 1534
Matlock 33 SK 3060
Matlock Bath 33 SK 2958
Matson 17 SO 8316
Matterdale End 40 NY 3923
Mattersey 34 SK 6889
Mattingley 10 SU 7357
Mattishall 29 TG 0510
Mattishall Burgh 29 TG 0511
Mauchline 50 NS 4927
Maud 62 NJ 9247
Maugersbury 17 SP 1925
Maughold 43 SC 4991
Maulden 19 TL 0538
Maulds Meaburn 41 NY 6216
Maunby 42 SE 3486
Maund Bryan 24 SO 5550
Mautby 29 TG 4712
Mavesyn Ridware 33 SK 0817
Mavis Enderby 35 TF 3666
Mawbray 45 NY 0846
Mawdesley 36 SD 4914
Mawgan 2 SW 7024
Maw Green 25 SP 0197
Mawla 2 SW 6945
Mawnan 2 SW 7827
Mawnan Smith 2 SW 7728
Maxey 27 TF 1208
Maxstoke 26 SP 2386
Maxton 52 NT 6129
Maxwellheugh 53 NT 7333
Maxwellston 48 NS 2600
Maybole 49 NS 3009
Mayfield (E Susx) 12 TQ 5827
Mayfield (Staffs.) 33 SK 1545
Mayford 11 SU 9956
Maypole 16 SO 4716
Maypole Green 29 TM 4195
Maywick 63 HU 3724
Meadle 18 SP 8005
Meadowtown 23 SJ 3101
Meal Bank 41 SD 5495
Mealsgate 46 NY 2141
Mearbeck 37 SD 8160
Meare 7 ST 4541
Mears Ashby 27 SP 8366
Measham 26 SK 3312
Meathop 40 SD 4380
Meaux 39 TA 0939
Meavag 63 NG 1596
Meavy 4 SX 5467
Medbourne 26 SP 7993
Meddon 4 SS 2717
Medmenham 18 SU 8084
Medstead 10 SU 6537
Meerbrook 33 SJ 9860
Meer End 26 SP 2474
Meesden 20 TL 4432
Meeth 4 SS 5408
Meidrim 14 SN 2820
Meifod 23 SJ 1513
Meigle 57 NO 2844
Meikle Earnock 50 NS 7253
Meikleour 56 NO 1539
Meikle Strath 57 NO 6471
Meikle Tarty 62 NJ 9928
Meikle Wartle 62 NJ 7230
Meinciau 15 SN 4610
Meir 33 SJ 9342
Melbost 63 NB 4632
Melbourn (Cambs.) 20 TL 3844
Melbourne (Derby.) 33 SK 3825
Melbourne (Humbs.) 38 SE 7543
Melbury Bubb 8 ST 5906
Melbury Osmond 7 ST 5707
Melbury Sampford 7 ST 5705
Melchbourne 27 TL 0265
Melcombe Bingham 8 ST 7602
Meldon (Devon.) 4 SX 5592
Meldon (Northum.) 47 NZ 1284
Meldreth 20 TL 3746
Melfort 54 NM 8314
Meliden 31 SJ 0580
Melin Court 15 SN 8201
Melin-y-coed 31 SH 8160
Melin-y-ddol 23 SJ 0807
Melin-y-grug 23 SJ 0507
Melin-y-wig 31 SJ 0448
Melkinthorpe 41 NY 5525
Melkridge 46 NY 7363

Melksham

Mustow Green

Melksham 17 ST 9063
Melldalloch 49 NR 9375
Melling (Lancs.) 36 SD 5970
Melling (Mers.) 36 SD 3800
Mellis 29 TM 0974
Mellon Charles 64 NG 8491
Mellon Udrigle 64 NG 8895
Mellor (Gtr Mches.) 33 SJ 9888
Mellor (Lancs.) 36 SD 6530
Mellor Brook 36 SD 6331
Mells 8 ST 7249
Melmerby (Cumbr.) 41 NY 6137
Melmerby (N Yorks.) 41 SE 0785
Melmerby (N Yorks.) 42 SE 3376
Melplash 7 SY 4797
Melrose 52 NT 5433
Melsetter 63 ND 2689
Melsonby 42 NZ 1908
Meltham 37 SE 0910
Melton 21 TM 2850
Meltonby 38 SE 7952
Melton Constable 29 TG 0433
Melton Mowbray 34 SK 7518
Melton Ross 39 TA 0610
Melvaig 64 NG 7486
Melverley 32 SJ 3316
Melvich 67 NC 864
Membury 7 ST 2703
Memsie 62 NJ 9762
Memus 57 NO 4258
Menabilly 3 SX 0951
Menai Bridge 30 SH 5572
Mendham 29 TM 2783
Mendlesham 29 TM 1065
Mendlesham Green 29 TM 0963
Menheniot 4 SX 2862
Mennock 50 NS 8008
Menston 37 SE 1743
Menstrie 50 NS 8596
Mentmore 19 SP 9019
Meole Brace 24 SJ 4811
Meonstoke 9 SU 6119
Meopham 12 TQ 6466
Meopham Station 12 TQ 6467
Mepal 27 TL 4481
Meppershall 19 TL 1336
Merbach 23 SO 3045
Mere (Ches.) 32 SJ 7281
Mere (Wilts.) 8 ST 8132
Mere Brow 36 SD 4118
Mereclough 37 SD 8730
Mere Green 25 SP 1298
Merevale 26 SP 2897
Mereworth 12 TQ 6553
Mergie 62 NO 7988
Meriden 26 SP 2482
Merkadale 58 NG 3831
Merkland 44 NX 2491
Merlin's Bridge 14 SM 9414
Merrington 32 SJ 4621
Merriott 7 ST 4412
Merrivale 4 SX 5475
Merrymeet 4 SX 2766
Mersham 13 TR 0539
Merstham 11 TQ 2953
Merston 11 SU 8903
Merstone 9 SZ 5285
Merther 2 SW 8644
Merthyr 14 SN 3520
Merthyr Cynog 23 SN 9837
Merthyr Dyfan 16 ST 1169
Merthyr Mawr 15 SS 8877
Merthyr Tydfil 16 SO 0406
Merthyr Vale 16 ST 0899
Merton (Devon.) 4 SS 5212
Merton (Gtr London) 11 TQ 2569
Merton (Norf.) 28 TL 9098
Merton (Oxon.) 18 SP 5717
Mervinslaw 52 NT 6713
Meshaw 5 SS 7519
Messing 21 TL 8918
Messingham 39 SE 8904
Metfield 29 TM 2980
Metheringham 35 TF 0661
Methil 57 NT 3699
Methley 38 SE 3826
Methlick 62 NJ 8537
Methven 56 NO 0225
Methwold 28 TL 7394
Methwold Hythe 28 TL 7195
Mettingham 29 TM 3689
Mevagissey 3 SX 0144
Mexborough 38 SK 4799
Mey 67 ND 2872
Meysey Hampton 17 SU 1199
Miavaig 63 NB 0834
Michaelchurch 16 SO 5125
Michaelchurch Escley 23 SO 3134
Michaelchurch-on-Arrow 23 SO 2450
Michaelston-le-Pit 16 ST 1573
Michaelston-y-Fedw 16 ST 2484
Michaelstow 3 SX 0778
Micheldever 10 SU 5138
Michelmersh 9 SU 3426
Mickfield 29 TM 1361
Mickleby 43 NZ 8013
Micklefield 38 SE 4433
Mickleham 11 TQ 1753
Mickleover 33 SK 3034
Mickleton (Durham) 41 NY 9623
Mickleton (Glos.) 25 SP 1543
Mickle Trafford 32 SJ 4469
Mickley 42 SE 2576
Mickley Square 47 NZ 0761
Mid Ardlaw 62 NJ 9464
Midbea 63 HY 4444
Mid Beltie 62 NJ 6200
Mid Cairncross 57 NO 4979
Middle Assendon 18 SU 7385
Middle Aston 18 SP 4726
Middle Barton 18 SP 4326
Middlebie 46 NY 2176
Middle Claydon 18 SP 7125
Middle Drums 57 NO 5957
Middleham 42 SE 1287
Middlehope 24 SO 4988
Middle Littleton 25 SP 0747
Middle Maes-coed 23 SO 3334
Middlemarsh 8 ST 6707
Middle Mill 14 SM 8025
Middle Rasen 35 TF 0889
Middlesbrough 42 NZ 4920
Middlesmoor 41 SE 0974
Middlestone Moor 42 NZ 2532
Middlestown 37 SE 2617
Middleton (Cumbr.) 41 SD 6286
Middleton (Derby.) 33 SK 1963
Middleton (Derby.) 33 SK 2755
Middleton (Essex) 20 TL 8639
Middleton (Grampn.) 62 NJ 8419
Middleton (Gtr Mches.) 37 SD 8606
Middleton (Hants.) 10 SU 4243
Middleton (Here. and Worc.) 24 SO 5469
Middleton (Lancs.) 36 SD 4258
Middleton (Lothian) 51 NT 3657
Middleton (Norf.) 28 TF 6616
Middleton (Northants.) 27 SP 8489
Middleton (Northum.) 53 NU 0024
Middleton (Northum.) 53 NU 1035
Middleton (Northum.) 47 NZ 0585
Middleton (N Yorks.) 43 SE 7885
Middleton (N York. – W Yorks.) 37 SE 1249
Middleton (Salop) 32 SJ 3128
Middleton (Salop) 23 SO 2999
Middleton (Salop) 24 SO 5377
Middleton (Suff.) 29 TM 4267
Middleton (Tays.) 56 NO 1206
Middleton (Tiree) 48 NL 9443
Middleton (Warw.) 25 SP 1798
Middleton (W Yorks.) 38 SE 3027
Middleton Cheney 26 SP 4941
Middleton Green 33 SJ 9935
Middleton Hall 53 NT 9825
Middleton in Teesdale 41 NY 9425
Middleton-on-Sea 11 SU 9800
Middleton on the Hill 24 SO 5464
Middleton-on-the-Wolds 39 SE 9449
Middleton Priors 24 SO 6290
Middleton St. George 42 NZ 3412
Middleton Scriven 24 SO 6787
Middleton Stoney 18 SP 5323
Middleton Tyas 42 NZ 2205
Middletown 23 SJ 3012
Middle Tysoe 26 SP 3344
Middle Wallop 10 SU 2937
Middlewich 32 SJ 7066
Middle Winterslow 9 SU 2432
Middle Witchyburn 62 NJ 6356
Middle Woodford 8 SU 1136
Middlewood Green 29 TM 0961
Middleyard 50 NS 5132
Middlezoy 7 ST 3733
Middridge 42 NZ 2526
Midfield 66 NC 5864
Midge Hall 36 SD 5123
Midgeholme 46 NY 6458
Midgham 10 SU 5567
Midgley 37 SE 0226
Midhopestones 37 SK 2399
Midhurst 11 SU 8821
Midlem 52 NT 5227
Mid Sannox 49 NS 0145
Midsomer Norton 17 ST 6654
Mid Thundergay 49 NR 8846
Midtown 64 NG 8285
Midville 35 TF 3857
Mid Yell 63 HU 4991
Migvie 61 NJ 4306
Milborne Port 8 ST 6718
Milborne St. Andrew 8 SY 7997
Milborne Wick 8 ST 6620
Milbourne 47 NZ 1175
Milburn (Cumbr.) 41 NY 6529
Milbury Heath 17 ST 6690
Milcombe 18 SP 4134
Milden 21 TL 9546
Mildenhall (Suff.) 28 TL 7074
Mildenhall (Wilts.) 10 SU 2069
Milebrook 23 SO 3172
Milebush 12 TQ 7546
Mile Elm 17 ST 9968
Mile End 21 TL 9827
Mileham 28 TF 9119
Milesmark 51 NT 0688
Milfield 53 NT 9333
Milford (Derby.) 33 SK 3445
Milford (Staffs.) 33 SJ 9721
Milford (Surrey) 11 SU 9442
Milford Haven (Dyfed) 14 SM 9006
Milford on Sea 9 SZ 2891
Milkwall 17 SO 5809
Milland 10 SU 8228
Milland Marsh 10 SU 8326
Mill Bank 37 SE 0321
Millbounds 63 HY 5635
Millbreck 62 NK 0045
Millbridge 10 SU 8542
Millbrook (Beds.) 19 TL 0138
Millbrook (Corn.) 4 SX 4252
Millbrook (Hants.) 9 SU 4012
Millburn (Strath.) 50 NS 4429
Millcorner 12 TQ 8223
Milldens 57 NO 5450
Mill End (Bucks.) 18 SU 7885
Mill End (Herts.) 20 TL 3332
Millerhill 51 NT 3269
Miller's Dale 33 SK 1373
Mill Green (Essex) 20 TL 6400
Millgreen (Salop) 32 SJ 6727
Millheugh 50 NS 7551
Mill Hill 19 TQ 2292
Millholme 41 SD 5690
Millhouse 49 NR 9570
Millikenpark 50 NS 4162
Millington 39 SE 8351
Mill Lane 10 SU 7850
Millmeece 32 SJ 8333
Mill of Kingoodie 62 NJ 8425
Millom 40 SD 1780
Millport 49 NS 1655
Mill Street 29 TG 0118
Millthrop 41 SD 6691
Milltimber 62 NJ 8501
Millton of Auchriachan 61 NJ 1718
Millton of Corsindae 62 NJ 6809
Millton of Murtle 62 NJ 8702
Milltown (Derby.) 33 SK 3561
Milltown (Dumf. and Galwy.) 46 NY 3375
Milltown (Grampn.) 61 NJ 4616
Milltown (Grampn.) 61 NJ 5447
Milltown of Aberdalgie 56 NO 0720
Milltown of Auchindown 61 NJ 3540
Milltown of Campfield 62 NJ 6400
Milltown of Craigston 62 NJ 7655
Milltown of Edinvillie 61 NJ 2639
Milltown of Towie 61 NJ 4612
Milnathort 56 NO 1204
Milngavie 50 NS 5574
Milnrow 37 SD 9212
Milnthorpe 40 SD 4981
Milovaig 58 NG 1550
Milson 24 SO 6372
Milstead 13 TQ 9058
Milston 8 SU 1645
Milton (Cambs.) 28 TL 4762
Milton (Central) 55 NN 5001
Milton (Central) 50 NS 4490
Milton (Cumbr.) 46 NY 5560
Milton (Dumf. and Galwy.) 44 NX 2154
Milton (Dumf. and Galwy.) 45 NX 8470
Milton (Grampn.) 61 NJ 5163
Milton (Highld.) 67 ND 3451
Milton (Highld.) 59 NH 3055
Milton (Highld.) 60 NH 4930
Milton (Highld.) 60 NH 5749
Milton (Highld.) 65 NH 7674
Milton (Highld.) 60 NH 9553
Milton (Oxon.) 18 SP 4535
Milton (Oxon.) 18 SU 4892
Milton (Staffs.) 33 SJ 9050
Milton (Strath.) 50 NS 4274
Milton (Tays.) 56 NN 9138
Milton (Tays.) 57 NO 3843
Milton Abbas 8 ST 8001
Milton Abbot 4 SX 4079
Milton Bridge 51 NT 2363
Milton Bryan 19 SP 9730
Milton Clevedon 8 ST 6637
Milton Coldwells 62 NJ 9538
Milton Combe 4 SX 4866
Milton Damerel 4 SS 3810
Miltonduff 61 NJ 1760
Milton Ernest 27 TL 0156
Milton Green 32 SJ 4558
Milton Hill 18 SU 4790
Milton Keynes 27 SP 8939
Milton Lilbourne 17 SU 1860
Milton Malsor 26 SP 7355
Milton Morenish 56 NN 6135
Milton of Auchinhove 61 NJ 5503
Milton of Balgonie 57 NO 3100
Milton of Braicklaich 60 NH 7851
Milton of Campsie 50 NS 6576
Milton of Cushnie 61 NJ 5111
Milton of Lesmore 61 NJ 4628
Milton of Noth 61 NJ 5028
Milton of Potterton 62 NJ 9415
Milton of Tullich 61 NO 3897
Milton on Stour 8 ST 7928
Milton Regis 13 TQ 9064
Milton-under-Wychwood 18 SP 2618
Milverton 7 ST 1225
Milwich 33 SJ 9632
Milwr 31 SJ 1974
Minard 49 NR 9796
Minchinhampton 17 SO 8600
Mindrum 53 NT 8432
Minehead 7 SS 9746
Minera 31 SJ 2651
Minety 17 SU 0290
Minffordd 30 SH 5938
Mingary 63 NF 7426
Miningsby 35 TF 3264
Minions 4 SX 2671
Minishant 49 NS 3314
Minley Manor 10 SU 8157
Minnes 62 NJ 9423
Minnigaff 44 NX 4166
Minskip 38 SE 3864
Minstead 9 SU 2811
Minster (Kent) 13 TQ 9573
Minster (Kent) 13 TR 3164
Minsteracres 47 NZ 0255
Minsterley 24 SJ 3705
Minster Lovell 18 SP 3111
Minsterworth 17 SO 7717
Minterne Magna 8 ST 6504
Minting 35 TF 1873
Mintlaw 62 NK 0048
Minto 52 NT 5620
Minton 24 SO 4290
Minwear 14 SN 0413
Minworth 25 SP 1592
Mirbister 63 HY 3019
Mireland 67 ND 3160
Mirfield 37 SE 2019
Miserden 17 SO 9308
Miskin 16 ST 0481
Misson 34 SK 6895
Misterton (Leic.) 26 SP 5584
Misterton (Notts.) 34 SK 7694
Misterton (Somer.) 7 ST 4508
Mistley 21 TM 1231
Mitcham 11 TQ 2868
Mitcheldean 17 SO 6618
Mitchell 2 SW 8554
Mitchel Troy 16 SO 4910
Mitford 47 NZ 1786
Mithian 2 SW 7450
Mitton 33 SJ 8815
Mixbury 18 SP 6033
Mixon 33 SK 0457
Mobberley 32 SJ 7880
Moccas 24 SO 3542
Mochdre (Clwyd) 31 SH 8278
Mochdre (Powys) 23 SO 0788
Mochrum 44 NX 3446
Mockerkin 40 NY 0823
Modbury 5 SX 6551
Moddershall 33 SJ 9236
Moelfre (Clwyd) 31 SJ 1828
Moelfre (Gwyn.) 30 SH 5186
Moel Tryfan 30 SH 5155
Moffat 45 NT 0805
Mogerhanger 27 TL 1349
Moira 33 SK 3216
Molash 13 TR 0251
Mold 31 SJ 2363
Molehill Green 20 TL 5624
Molescroft 39 TA 0140
Molesworth 27 TL 0775
Molland 6 SS 8028
Mollington (Ches.) 32 SJ 3870
Mollington (Northants.) 26 SP 4347
Mollinsburn 50 NS 7171
Monachty 22 SN 5062
Monboddo 57 NO 7478
Mondynes 57 NO 7879
Monewden 21 TM 2358
Moneydie 56 NO 0629
Moniaive 45 NX 7791
Monifieth 57 NO 4932
Monikie 57 NO 4938
Monimail 57 NO 2914
Monington 14 SN 1344
Monken Hadley 19 TQ 2497
Monk Fryston 38 SE 5029
Monkhopton 24 SO 6293
Monkland 24 SO 4557
Monkleigh 4 SS 4520
Monknash 15 SS 9270
Monkokehampton 4 SS 5805
Monks Eleigh 21 TL 9647
Monks' Heath 33 SJ 8873
Monk Sherborne 10 SU 6056
Monkshill 62 NJ 7941
Monksilver 7 ST 0737
Monks Kirby 26 SP 4683
Monk Soham 29 TM 2165
Monkswood 16 SO 3403
Monkton (Devon.) 7 ST 1803
Monkton (Kent) 13 TR 2865
Monkton (Strath.) 49 NS 3527
Monkton (Tyne and Wear) 47 NZ 3463
Monkton Combe 17 ST 7761
Monkton Deverill 8 ST 8537
Monkton Farleigh 17 ST 8065
Monkton Heathfield 7 ST 2526
Monkton Up Wimborne 8 SU 0113
Monkwood 9 SU 6730
Monmouth 16 SO 5113
Monnington on Wye 24 SO 3743
Monreith 44 NX 3641
Monreith Mains 44 NX 3643
Montacute 7 ST 4916
Montford 32 SJ 4114
Montgarrie 61 NJ 5717
Montgomery 23 SO 2296
Montgreenan 49 NS 3343
Montrave 57 NO 3706
Montrose 57 NO 7157
Monxton 10 SU 3144
Monyash 33 SK 1566
Monymusk 62 NJ 6815
Monzie 56 NN 8725
Moonzie 57 NO 3317
Moorby 35 TF 2964
Moorcot 24 SO 3555
Moor Crichel 8 ST 9908
Moordown 8 SZ 0994
Moore 32 SJ 5584
Moorends 38 SE 6915
Moorhall 33 SK 3175
Moorhampton 24 SO 3846
Moorhouse (Cumbr.) 46 NY 3356
Moorhouse (Notts.) 34 SK 7566
Moorland or Northmoor Green 7 ST 3332
Moorlinch 7 ST 3936
Moor Monkton 38 SE 5056
Moor Nook 36 SD 6537
Moorsholm 43 NZ 6814
Moorside 37 SD 9507
Moor, The 12 TQ 7529
Moortown (I.O.W.) 9 SZ 4283
Moortown (Lincs.) 39 TF 0699
Morar 58 NM 6792
Morborne 27 TL 1391
Morchard Bishop 5 SS 7607
Morcombelake 7 SY 4093
Morcott 27 SK 9200
Morda 31 SJ 2827
Morden (Dorset) 8 SY 9195
Morden (Gtr London) 11 TQ 2567
Mordiford 24 SO 5637
Mordon 42 NZ 3326
More 23 SO 3491
Morebath 5 SS 9525
Morebattle 53 NT 7724
Morecambe 36 SD 4364
Morefield 64 NH 1195
Moreleigh 5 SX 7652
Morenish 56 NN 6035
Moresby 40 NX 9821
Morestead 9 SU 5125
Moreton (Dorset) 8 SY 8089
Moreton (Essex) 20 TL 5307
Moreton (Mers.) 31 SJ 2689
Moreton (Oxon.) 18 SP 6904
Moreton Corbet 32 SJ 5523
Moretonhampstead 5 SX 7586
Moreton-in-Marsh 18 SP 2032
Moreton Jeffries 24 SO 6048
Moreton Morrell 26 SP 3155
Moreton on Lugg 24 SO 5045
Moreton Pinkney 26 SP 5749
Moreton Say 32 SJ 6234
Moreton Valence 17 SO 7809
Morfa Bychan 30 SH 5437
Morfa Glas 15 SN 8606
Morfa Nefyn 30 SH 2840
Morgan's Vale 8 SU 1921
Morland 41 NY 6022
Morley (Derby.) 33 SK 3941
Morley (Durham) 42 NZ 1227
Morley (W Yorks.) 37 SE 2627
Morley Green 32 SJ 8282
Morley St. Botolph 29 TM 0799
Morningside 51 NT 2471
Morningthorpe 29 TM 2192
Morpeth 47 NZ 2085
Morphie 57 NO 7164
Morrey 33 SK 1218
Morriston 15 SS 6698
Morston 29 TG 0043
Mortehoe 6 SS 4545
Mortimer 10 SU 6564
Mortimer's Cross 24 SO 4263
Mortimer West End 10 SU 6363
Mortlake 11 TQ 2075
Morton (Avon) 17 ST 6491
Morton (Derby.) 33 SK 4060
Morton (Lincs.) 34 SK 8091
Morton (Lincs.) 35 TF 0924
Morton (Norf.) 29 TG 1217
Morton (Salop) 31 SJ 2824
Morton Bagot 25 SP 1164
Morton-on-Swale 42 SE 3292
Morvah 2 SW 4035
Morval 4 SX 2556
Morvich 59 NG 9621
Morville 24 SO 6694
Morwenstow 4 SS 2015
Morwick Hall 47 NU 2303
Mosborough 33 SK 4281
Moscow 50 NS 4840
Mosedale 40 NY 3532
Moseley (Here. and Worc.) 25 SO 8159
Moseley (W Mids) 25 SP 0883
Moss (Clwyd) 31 SJ 3052
Moss (Highld.) 54 NM 6868
Moss (S Yorks.) 38 SE 5914
Moss (Tiree) 48 NL 9644
Mossat 61 NJ 4719
Moss Bank (Cumbr.) 36 SJ 5198
Mossbank (Shetld.) 63 HU 4475
Mossburnford 52 NT 6616
Mossdale 45 NX 6571
Mossend 50 NS 7460
Mosside 57 NO 4252
Mossley 37 SD 9702
Moss Nook 32 SJ 8385
Moss of Barmuckity 61 NJ 2461
Moss Side 36 SD 3830
Mosston 57 NO 5444
Mosterton 7 ST 4505
Mostyn 31 SJ 1680
Motcombe 8 ST 8425
Motherwell 50 NS 7557
Mottingham 12 TQ 4272
Mottisfont 9 SU 3226
Mottistone 9 SZ 4083
Mottram in Logdendale 33 SJ 9995
Mouldsworth 32 SJ 5171
Moulin 56 NN 9459
Moulescoomb 12 TQ 3307
Moulsford 18 SU 5984
Moulsoe 27 SP 9041
Moulton (Ches.) 32 SJ 6569
Moulton (Lincs.) 35 TF 3023
Moulton (Northants.) 26 SP 7866
Moulton (N Yorks.) 42 NZ 2303
Moulton (Suff.) 28 TL 6964
Moulton Chapel 35 TF 2918
Moulton Seas End 35 TF 3227
Mount (Corn.) 2 SW 7856
Mount (Corn.) 4 SX 1467
Mountain Ash 16 ST 0498
Mountain Cross 51 NT 1446
Mountain Water 14 SM 9224
Mountbenger 51 NT 3125
Mount Bures 21 TL 9032
Mountfield 12 TQ 7320
Mountgerald 65 NH 5661
Mount Hawke 2 SW 7147
Mountjoy 2 SW 8760
Mountnessing 20 TQ 6297
Mounton 16 ST 5193
Mount Pleasant 29 TM 5077
Mountsorrel 34 SK 5814
Mountstuart (Strath.) 49 NS 1059
Mousehole 2 SW 4626
Mouswald 45 NY 0672
Mow Cop 33 SJ 8557
Mowhaugh 53 NT 8120
Mowsley 26 SP 6489
Mowtie 62 NO 8388
Moy 55 NN 4282
Moy Hall 60 NH 7635
Moy House 61 NJ 0159
Moylgrove 14 SN 1244
Muasdale 48 NR 6840
Muchalls 62 NO 9091
Much Birch 24 SO 5030
Much Cowarne 24 SO 6147
Much Dewchurch 24 SO 4831
Muchelney 7 ST 4224
Much Hadham 20 TL 4319
Much Hoole 36 SD 4723
Muchlarnick 4 SX 2156
Much Marcle 24 SO 6533
Much Wenlock 24 SO 6199
Muckfoot 44 NX 2185
Mucking 20 TQ 6881
Mucklestone 32 SJ 7237
Muckleton 32 SJ 5821
Muckletown 61 NJ 5621
Muckton 35 TF 3781
Muddiford 6 SS 5638
Mudeford 8 SZ 1892
Mudford 7 ST 5719
Mudgley 7 ST 4445
Mugdock Resr 50 NS 5576
Mugeary 58 NG 4438
Mugginton 33 SK 2843
Muggleswick 47 NZ 0450
Muie 66 NC 6704
Muir 61 NO 0689
Muirdrum 57 NO 5637
Muirhead (Fife.) 57 NO 2805
Muirhead (Strath.) 50 NS 3530
Muirhead (Strath.) 50 NS 6869
Muirhead (Tays.) 57 NO 3434
Muirhouses 51 NT 0180
Muirkirk 50 NS 6927
Muir of Fowlis 61 NJ 5612
Muir of Ord 60 NH 5250
Muirshearlich 55 NN 1380
Muirskie 62 NO 8295
Muirtack (Grampn.) 62 NJ 8146
Muirtack (Grampn.) 62 NJ 9937
Muirton 65 NH 7463
Muirton of Ardblair 56 NO 1743
Muirton of Ballochy 57 NO 6462
Muirtown 56 NN 9211
Muiryfold 62 NJ 7651
Muker 41 SD 9198
Mulbarton 29 TG 1901
Mulben 61 NJ 3450
Mulgrave Castle 43 NZ 8412
Mulindry 48 NR 3659
Mullion 2 SW 6719
Mumbles, The 15 SS 6287
Mumby 35 TF 5174
Muncaster Castle 40 SD 1096
Munderfield Row 24 SO 6451
Munderfield Stocks 24 SO 6550
Mundesley 29 TG 3136
Mundford 28 TL 8093
Mundham (Norf.) 29 TM 3298
Mundham (W. Susx) 11 SU 8701
Mundon Hill 21 TL 8702
Mundurno 62 NJ 9413
Munerigie 59 NH 2602
Mungrisdale 40 NY 3630
Munlochy 60 NH 6453
Munsley 24 SO 6640
Munslow 24 SO 5187
Munslow Aston 24 SO 5086
Murcott 18 SP 5815
Murkle 67 ND 1668
Murlaggan (Highld.) 55 NN 3181
Murrow 27 TF 3707
Mursley 18 SP 8128
Murthill 57 NO 4657
Murthly 56 NO 0938
Murton (Cumbr.) 41 NY 7221
Murton (Durham) 47 NZ 3947
Murton (Northum.) 53 NT 9748
Murton (N Yorks.) 38 SE 6452
Musbury 7 SY 2794
Muscoates 42 SE 6880
Musselburgh 51 NT 3472
Muston (Leic.) 34 SK 8237
Muston (N Yorks.) 43 TA 0979
Mustow Green 25 SO 8774

Mutford North Pickenham

Mutford 29 TM 4888
Muthill 56 NN 8616
Mutterton 7 ST 0304
Mybster 67 ND 1652
Myddfai 15 SN 7730
Myddle 32 SJ 4623
Mydroilyn 22 SN 4555
Mylor Bridge 2 SW 8036
Mynachlog-ddu 14 SN 1430
Myndtown 24 SO 3889
Mynytho 30 SH 3031
Myrebird 62 NO 7498
Mytchett 11 SU 8855
Mytholm 37 SD 9827
Mytholmroyd 37 SE 0125
Myton-on-Swale 38 SE 4366

Naburn 38 SE 5945
Nackington 13 TR 1554
Nacton 21 TM 2240
Nafferton 39 TA 0559
Naisea 16 ST 4670
Nailstone 26 SK 4107
Nailsworth 17 ST 8499
Nairn 60 NH 8756
Nancegollan 2 SW 6632
Nanhoron 30 SH 2831
Nannau 30 SH 7420
Nannerch 31 SJ 1669
Nanpantan 34 SK 5017
Nanpean 2 SW 9556
Nant-ddu 16 SO 0015
Nanternis 22 SN 3756
Nantgaredig 15 SN 4921
Nantgarw 16 ST 1285
Nant-glas 23 SN 9965
Nantglyn 31 SJ 0061
Nantlle 30 SH 5053
Nantmawr 31 SJ 2424
Nantmel 23 SO 0366
Nantmor 30 SH 6046
Nantwich 32 SJ 6552
Nant-y-derry 16 SO 3306
Nantyffyllon 15 SS 8492
Nantyglo 16 SO 1911
Nant-y-moel 15 SS 9393
Naphill 19 SU 8496
Nappa 37 SD 8553
Napton on the Hill 26 SP 4661
Narberth 14 SN 1114
Narborough (Leic.) 26 SP 5497
Narborough (Norf.) 28 TF 7413
Nasareth 30 SH 4749
Naseby 26 SP 6878
Nash (Bucks.) 18 SP 7734
Nash (Gwent) 16 ST 3483
Nash (Here. and Worc.) 23 SO 3062
Nash (Salop) 24 SO 6071
Nash Lee 19 SP 8408
Nassington 27 TL 0696
Nasty 20 TL 3624
Nateby (Cumbr.) 41 NY 7706
Nateby (Lancs.) 36 SD 4644
Natland 40 SD 5289
Naughton 21 TM 0249
Naunton (Glos.) 17 SP 1123
Naunton (Here. and Worc.) 25 SO 8739
Naunton Beauchamp 25 SO 9652
Naust 64 NG 8283
Navenby 34 SK 9857
Navestock 20 TQ 5397
Navestock Side 20 TQ 5697
Nawton 42 SE 6584
Nayland 21 TL 9734
Nazeing 20 TL 4106
Neacroft 8 SZ 1897
Neal's Green 26 SP 3384
Neap 63 HU 5060
Near Cotton 33 SK 0646
Neasham 42 NZ 3210
Neath 15 SS 7597
Neatishead 29 TG 3421
Nebo (Dyfed) 22 SN 5465
Nebo (Gwyn.) 30 SH 4750
Nebo (Gwyn.) 31 SH 8356
Necton 28 TF 8709
Nedd 64 NC 1332
Nedging Tye 21 TM 0149
Needham 29 TM 2281
Needham Market 21 TM 0855
Needingworth 27 TL 3472
Neen Savage 24 SO 6777
Neen Sollars 24 SO 6572
Neenton 24 SO 6487
Nefyn 30 SH 3040
Neilston 50 NS 4657
Nelson (Lancs.) 37 SD 8737
Nelson (Mid Glam.) 16 ST 1195
Nelson Village 47 NZ 2577
Nemphlar 50 NS 8544
Nempnett Thrubwell 16 ST 5360
Nenthead 46 NY 7743
Nenthorn 52 NT 6837
Nercwys 31 SJ 2260
Nereabolls 48 NR 2255
Nerston 50 NS 6457
Nesbit 53 NT 9833
Ness (Ches.) 32 SJ 3075
Ness (N Yorks.) 43 SE 6878
Nesscliffe 32 SJ 3819
Neston (Ches.) 31 SJ 2877
Neston (Wilts.) 17 ST 8667
Nether Alderley 33 SJ 8476
Netheravon 8 SU 1448
Nether Blainslie 52 NT 5443
Netherbrae 62 NJ 7959
Nether Broughton 34 SK 6925
Netherburn 50 NS 7947
Nether Burrow 41 SD 6174
Netherbury 7 SY 4799
Netherby 46 NY 3971
Nether Cerne 8 SY 6698
Nether Compton 8 ST 5907
Nether Crimond 62 NJ 8222
Nether Dallachy 61 NJ 3663
Netherend 17 SO 5900
Nether Exe 5 SS 9300
Netherfield 12 TQ 7018
Netherhampton 8 SU 1029
Nether Handwick 57 NO 3641
Nether Haugh 33 SK 4196
Nether Howecleuch 51 NT 0312
Nether Kellet 36 SD 5067
Nether Kinmundy 62 NK 0444
Nether Kirkton 50 NS 4757
Nether Langwith 34 SK 5371
Netherlaw 45 NX 7445
Netherley 62 NO 8593
Nethermill 45 NY 0487
Nethermuir 62 NJ 9143
Nether Padley 33 SK 2478
Netherplace 50 NS 5155
Nether Poppleton 38 SE 5654
Netherseal 26 SK 2813
Nether Silton 42 SE 4592
Nether Stowey 7 ST 1939
Netherstreet 17 ST 9764
Netherthird 50 NS 5818
Netherthong 37 SE 1309
Netherton (Central) 50 NS 5579
Netherton (Devon.) 5 SX 8971
Netherton (Here. and Worc.) 25 SO 9941
Netherton (Mers.) 36 SD 3500
Netherton (Northum.) 53 NT 9907
Netherton (Tays.) 56 NO 1452
Netherton (Tays.) 57 NO 5457
Netherton (W Yorks.) 38 SE 2716
Nethertown (Cumbr.) 40 NX 9807
Nethertown (Island of Stroma) 67 ND 3578
Nether Wallop 9 SU 3036
Nether Whitacre 26 SP 2393
Netherwitton 47 NZ 1090
Nether Worton 18 SP 4230
Nethy Bridge 61 NJ 0020
Netley 9 SU 4508
Netley Marsh 9 SU 3312
Nettlebed 18 SU 7086
Nettlebridge 8 ST 6448
Nettlecombe 7 SY 5195
Nettleden 19 TL 0210
Nettleham 34 TF 0075
Nettlestead 12 TQ 6852
Nettlestead Green 12 TQ 6850
Nettlestone 9 SZ 6290
Nettleton (Lincs.) 39 TA 1000
Nettleton (Wilts.) 17 ST 8178
Neuk, The 62 NO 7397
Nevendon 20 TQ 7390
Nevern 14 SN 0840
New Abbey 45 NX 9665
New Aberdour 62 NJ 8863
New Addington 12 TQ 3863
New Alresford 9 SU 5832
New Alyth 57 NO 2447
New Annesley 34 SK 5153
Newark (Cambs.) 27 TF 2100
Newark (Sanday) 63 HY 7242
Newart-on-Trent 34 SK 7953
Newarthill 50 NS 7859
Newbald 39 SE 9136
New Bewick 53 NU 0620
Newbiggin (Cumbr.) 46 NY 5649
Newbiggin (Cumbr.) 41 NY 6228
Newbiggin (Cumbr.) 36 SD 2669
Newbiggin (Durham) 41 NY 9127
Newbiggin (N Yorks.) 41 SD 9591
Newbiggin (N Yorks.) 41 SD 9985
Newbiggin Common 41 NY 9131
Newbiggin-by-the-Sea 47 NZ 3187
Newbigging (Strath.) 51 NT 0145
Newbigging (Tays.) 57 NO 2841
Newbigging (Tays.) 57 NO 4237
Newbigging (Tays.) 57 NO 4936
Newbiggin on Lune 41 NY 7005
Newbold (Derby.) 33 SK 3773
Newbold (Leic.) 33 SK 4018
Newbold on Avon 26 SP 4877
Newbold on Stour 26 SP 2446
Newbold Pacey 26 SP 2957
Newbold Verdon 26 SK 4403
New Bolingbroke 35 TF 3058
Newborough (Gwyn.) 30 SH 4265
Newborough (Cambs.) 27 TF 2006
Newborough (Staffs.) 33 SK 1325
Newbottle 18 SP 5236
Newbourn 21 TM 2743
Newbridge (Clwyd) 31 SJ 2841
Newbridge (Corn.) 2 SW 4231
Newbridge (Gwent) 16 ST 2197
Newbridge (Hants.) 9 SU 2915
Newbridge (I. of W.) 9 SZ 4187
Newbridge (Lothian) 51 NT 1272
Newbridge-on-Usk 16 ST 3894
Newbridge on Wye 23 SO 0158
New Brighton 31 SJ 3093
New Brinsley 34 SK 4550
Newbrough 47 NY 8767
New Buckenham 29 TM 0890
Newburgh (Fife) 56 NO 2318
Newburgh (Grampn.) 62 NJ 9925
Newburgh (Lancs.) 36 SD 4810
Newburn 47 NZ 1765
Newbury 10 SU 4666
Newby (Cumbr.) 41 NY 5921
Newby (N Yorks.) 42 NZ 5012
Newby (N Yorks.) 36 SD 7269
Newby Bridge 40 SD 3686
Newby East 46 NY 4758
New Byth 62 NJ 8254
Newby West 46 NY 3653
Newby Wiske 42 SE 3687
Newcastle (Gwent) 16 SO 4417
Newcastle (Salop) 23 SO 2482
Newcastle Emlyn 22 SN 3040
Newcastleton 46 NY 4887
Newcastle-under-Lyme 33 SJ 8445
Newcastle upon Tyne 47 NZ 2464
Newchapel (Dyfed) 14 SN 2239
Newchapel (Staffs.) 33 SJ 8654
Newchapel (Surrey) 12 TQ 3642
Newchurch (Dyfed) 15 SN 3724
Newchurch (Gwent) 16 ST 4597
Newchurch (I. of W.) 9 SZ 5585
Newchurch (Kent) 13 TR 0531
Newchurch (Powys) 23 SO 2150
Newchurch in Pendle 37 SD 8239
New Clipstone 34 SK 5863
New Costessey 29 TG 1710
Newcott 7 ST 2309
New Cross 22 SN 6376
New Cumnock 50 NS 6113
New Deer 62 NJ 8846
Newdigate 11 TQ 2042
New Duston 26 SP 7162
New Earswick 38 SE 6155
New Edlington 38 SK 5399
New Ellerby 39 TA 1639
Newell Green 11 SU 8771
New Eltham 12 TQ 4573
New End 25 SP 0560
Newenden 12 TQ 8327
Newent 17 SO 7226
New Farnley 37 SE 2431
New Ferry 32 SJ 3385
Newfield (Durham) 42 NZ 2033
Newfield (Highld.) 65 NH 7877
New Fryston 38 SE 4526
Newgale 14 SM 8422
New Galloway 45 NX 6377
Newgate 29 TG 0443
Newgate Street 20 TL 3005
New Gilston 57 NO 4207
Newgord 63 HP 5706
Newgrounds 17 SO 7204
Newhall (Ches.) 32 SJ 6045
Newhall (Derby.) 33 SK 2821
Newham (Gtr London) 20 TQ 4082
Newham (Northum.) 53 NU 1728
Newham Hall 53 NU 1729
New Hartley 47 NZ 3076
Newhaven 12 TQ 4401
New Hedges 14 SN 1302
New Hey 37 SD 9311
New Holland 39 TA 0724
Newholm 43 NZ 8610
New Houghton (Derby.) 34 SK 4965
New Houghton (Norf.) 28 TF 7827
Newhouse 50 NS 7961
New Houses 41 SD 8073
New Hutton 41 SD 5691
New Hythe 12 TQ 7159
Newick 12 TQ 4121
Newington (Kent) 13 TQ 8665
Newington (Kent) 13 TR 1737
Newington (Oxon.) 18 SU 6196
New Inn (Gwent) 16 SO 4800
New Inn (Gwent) 16 ST 3099
New Inn (N Yorks.) 37 SD 8072
New Invention 23 SO 2976
New Kelso 59 NG 9442
New Lanark 50 NS 8742
Newland (Glos.) 16 SO 5509
Newland (Here. and Worc.) 24 SO 7948
Newland (N Yorks.) 38 SE 6824
Newlandrig 51 NT 3662
Newlands (Grampn.) 61 NJ 3051
Newlands (Northum.) 47 NZ 0955
Newlands of Geise 67 ND 0865
New Lane 36 SD 4212
New Leake 35 TF 4057
New Leeds 62 NJ 9954
New Longton 36 SD 5125
New Luce 44 NX 1764
Newlyn 2 SW 4628
Newlyn East 2 SW 8256
Newmachar 62 NJ 8819
Newmains 50 NS 8256
New Mains of Ury 62 NO 8787
Newmarket (Isle of Lewis) 63 NB 4235
Newmarket (Suff.) 28 TL 6463
New Marske 42 NZ 6221
New Marton 32 SJ 3334
Newmill (Borders) 52 NT 4510
New Mill (Corn.) 2 SW 4534
Newmill (Grampn.) 61 NJ 4352
New Mill (Herts.) 19 SP 9212
New Mill (W Yorks.) 37 SE 1608
Newmill of Inshewan 57 NO 4260
New Mills (Corn.) 2 SW 8952
New Mills (Derby.) 33 SK 0085
New Mills (Gwent) 16 SO 5107
Newmills (Lothian) 51 NT 1667
New Mills (Powys) 23 SJ 0901
Newmiln 56 NO 1230
Newmilns 50 NS 5337
New Milton 9 SZ 2495
New Moat 14 SN 0625
Newnham (Glos.) 17 SO 6911
Newnham (Hants.) 10 SU 7054
Newnham (Herts.) 19 TL 2437
Newnham (Kent) 13 TQ 9557
Newnham (Northants.) 26 SP 5859
Newnham Bridge 24 SO 6469
New Park 9 SU 2904
New Pitsligo 62 NJ 8855
New Polzeath 2 SW 9379
Newport (Devon) 6 SS 5631
Newport (Dyfed) 14 SN 0639
Newport (Essex) 20 TL 5234
Newport (Glos.) 17 ST 7097
Newport (Gwent) 16 ST 3187
Newport (Highld.) 67 ND 1224
Newport (Humbs.) 39 SE 8530
Newport (I. of W.) 9 SZ 4989
Newport (Norf.) 29 TG 5017
Newport (Salop) 32 SJ 7419
Newport-on-Tay 57 NO 4228
Newport Pagnell 27 SP 8743
Newpound Common 11 TQ 0627
New Prestwick 49 NS 3424
Newquay (Corn.) 2 SW 8161
New Quay (Dyfed) 22 SN 3859
New Rackheath 29 TG 2812
New Radnor 23 SO 2161
New Rent 40 NY 4536
New Romney 13 TR 0624
New Rossington 38 SK 6198
New Sauchie 50 NS 8993
New Scone 56 NO 1325
Newseat (Grampn.) 62 NJ 7033
Newseat (Grampn.) 62 NK 0749
Newsham (Northum.) 47 NZ 3079
Newsham (N Yorks.) 41 NZ 1010
Newsholme (Humbs.) 38 SE 7229
Newsholme (Lancs.) 37 SD 8451
New Silksworth 47 NZ 3853
Newstead (Borders) 52 NT 5634
Newstead (Northum.) 53 NU 1526
Newstead (Notts.) 34 SK 5252
New Stevenston 50 NS 7659
Newthorpe 38 SE 4632
Newtimber Place 11 TQ 2613
New Tolsta 63 NB 5348
Newton (Borders) 52 NT 6020
Newton (Cambs.) 35 TF 4314
Newton (Cambs.) 20 TL 4349
Newton (Ches.) 32 SJ 5059
Newton (Ches.) 32 SJ 5274
Newton (Cumbr.) 36 SD 2371
Newton (Dumf. and Galwy.) 45 NY 1194
Newton (Grampn.) 61 NJ 1663
Newton (Here. and Worc.) 23 SO 3433
Newton (Here. and Worc.) 24 SO 5054
Newton (Highld.) 66 NC 2331
Newton (Highld.) 67 ND 3449
Newton (Highld.) 60 NH 7448
Newton (Highld.) 65 NH 7866
Newton (Lancs.) 41 SD 5974
Newton (Lancs.) 36 SD 6950
Newton (Lincs.) 35 TF 0436
Newton (Lothian) 51 NT 0877
Newton (Mid Glam.) 15 SS 8377
Newton (Norf.) 28 TF 8315
Newton (Northants.) 27 SP 8883
Newton (North Uist) 63 NF 8977
Newton (Northum.) 47 NZ 0364
Newton (Notts.) 34 SK 6841
Newton (Staffs.) 33 SK 0325
Newton (Strath.) 55 NS 0498
Newton (Strath.) 50 NS 6560
Newton (Strath.) 51 NS 9331
Newton (Suff.) 21 TL 9140
Newton (Warw.) 26 SP 5378
Newton (W Glam.) 15 SS 6088
Newton (W Yorks.) 38 SE 4427
Newton (Wilts.) 9 SU 2322
Newton Abbot 5 SX 8671
Newton Arlosh 45 NY 1955
Newton Aycliffe 42 NZ 2824
Newton Bewley 42 NZ 4626
Newton Blossomville 27 SP 9251
Newton Bromswold 27 SP 9966
Newton Burgoland 26 SK 3609
Newton by Toft 35 TF 0487
Newton Ferrers 4 SX 5447
Newton Flotman 29 TM 2198
Newtongarry Croft 61 NJ 5735
Newtongrange 51 NT 3364
Newton Harcourt 26 SP 6397
Newtonill 62 NO 9193
Newton Kyme 38 SE 4644
Newton-le-Willows (Mers.) 32 SJ 5894
Newton-le-Willows (N Yorks.) 42 SE 2189
Newton Longville 19 SP 8431
Newton Mearns 50 NS 5456
Newtonmill 57 NO 6064
Newtonmore 60 NN 7199
Newton Mountain 14 SM 9807
Newton of Balcanquhal 56 NO 1510
Newton-on-Ouse 38 SE 5059
Newton-on-Rawcliffe 43 SE 8090
Newton-on-the-Moor 47 NU 1605
Newton on Trent 34 SK 8374
Newton Poppleford 7 SY 0889
Newton Purcell 18 SP 6230
Newton Regis 26 SK 2707
Newton Reigny 40 NY 4731
Newton St. Cyres 5 SX 8797
Newton St. Faith 29 TG 2117
Newton St. Loe 17 ST 7064
Newton St. Petrock 4 SS 4112
Newton Solney 33 SK 2825
Newton Stacey 10 SU 4040
Newton Stewart 44 NX 4165
Newton Toney 10 SU 2140
Newton Tracey 6 SS 5226
Newton under Roseberry 42 NZ 5613
Newton upon Derwent 38 SE 7149
Newton Valence 10 SU 7232
Newtown (Ches.) 32 SJ 6247
Newtown (Ches.) 33 SJ 9784
Newtown (Corn.) 2 SW 7323
Newtown (Cumbr.) 46 NY 5062
Newtown (Dorset) 8 SZ 0393
Newtown (Hants.) 9 SU 2710
Newtown (Hants.) 9 SU 3023
Newtown (Hants.) 10 SU 4763
Newtown (Hants.) 9 SU 6013
Newtown (Here. and Worc.) 24 SO 6145
Newtown (Highld.) 59 NH 3504
Newtown (I. of M.) 43 SC 3273
Newtown (I. of W.) 9 SZ 4290
New Town (Lothian) 52 NT 4470
Newtown (Northum.) 53 NT 9731
Newtown (Northum.) 47 NU 0300
Newtown (Northum.) 53 NU 0425
Newtown (Powys) 23 SO 1091
Newtown (Salop) 32 SJ 4831
Newtown (Staffs.) 33 SJ 9060
Newtown (Wilts.) 8 ST 9128
Newton Linford 26 SK 5110
Newtown St. Boswells 52 NT 5731
New Tredegar 16 SO 1403
New Tupton 33 SK 3966
Newtyle 57 NO 2941
New Ulva 48 NR 7080
New Walsoken 28 TF 4709
New Waltham 39 TA 2804
New Wimpole 20 TL 3450
New Winton 52 NT 4271
New Yatt 18 SP 3713
New York (Lincs.) 35 TF 2455
New York (Tyne and Wear) 47 NZ 3270
Neyland 14 SM 9605
Nibley 17 ST 6882
Nicholashayne 7 ST 1015
Nicholaston 15 SS 5188
Nidd 42 SE 3060
Nigg (Grampn.) 62 NJ 9402
Nigg (Highld.) 65 NH 8071
Nightcott 6 SS 8925
Nine Ashes 20 TL 5902
Ninebanks 46 NY 7853
Ninfield 12 TQ 7012
Ningwood 9 SZ 3989
Nisbet 52 NT 6725
Niton 9 SZ 5076
Nitshill 50 NS 5160
Noak Hill 20 TQ 5493
Nobottle 26 SP 6763
Nocton 35 TF 0564
Noke 18 SP 5413
Nolton 14 SM 8718
No Man's Heath (Ches.) 32 SJ 5148
No Man's Heath (Warw.) 26 SK 2709
Nomansland (Devon) 5 SS 8313
Nomansland (Wilts.) 9 SU 2517
Noneley 32 SJ 4727
Nonington 13 TR 2552
Nook 46 NY 4679
Noran Water 57 NO 4860
Norbury (Ches.) 32 SJ 5547
Norbury (Derby.) 33 SK 1242
Norbury (Salop) 24 SO 3693
Norbury (Staffs.) 32 SJ 7823
Nordelph 28 TF 5501
Norden (Dorset) 8 SY 9483
Norden (Gtr Mches) 37 SD 8514
Nordley 24 SO 6998
Norham 53 NT 9047
Norley 32 SJ 5672
Norleywood 9 SZ 3597
Normanby (Humbs.) 39 SE 8716
Normanby (Lincs.) 34 SK 9988
Normanby (N Yorks.) 43 SE 7381
Normanby le Wold 35 TF 1294
Norman Cross 27 TL 1691
Normandy 11 SU 9251
Norman's Green 7 ST 0503
Normanton (Derby.) 33 SK 3433
Normanton (Lincs.) 34 SK 9446
Normanton (Notts.) 34 SK 7054
Normanton (W Yorks.) 38 SE 3822
Normanton le Heath 26 SK 3712
Normanton on Soar 34 SK 5123
Normanton on the Wolds 34 SK 6232
Normanton on Trent 34 SK 7868
Normoss 36 SD 3437
Norrington Common 17 ST 8864
Norris Hill 33 SK 3216
Northallerton 42 SE 3793
Northam (Devon.) 6 SS 4429
Northam (Hants.) 9 SU 4312
Northampton 26 SP 7561
North Aston 18 SP 4728
North Ashton 36 SD 5401
Northaw 19 TL 2802
North Baddesley 9 SU 3920
North Ballachulish 55 NN 0560
North Barrow 8 ST 6029
North Barsham 28 TF 9135
North Benfleet 20 TQ 7590
North Berwick 52 NT 5485
North Boarhunt 9 SU 6010
Northborough 27 TF 1508
Northbourne 13 TR 3352
North Bovey 5 SX 7483
North Bradley 17 ST 8554
North Brentor 4 SX 4781
North Buckland 6 SS 4740
North Burlingham 29 TG 3610
North Cadbury 8 ST 6327
North Cairn 44 NW 9770
North Carlton 34 SK 9477
North Cave 39 SE 8832
North Cerney 17 SP 0208
Northchapel 11 SU 9529
North Charford 8 SU 1919
North Charlton 53 NU 1622
Northchurch 19 SP 9708
North Cliffe 39 SE 8737
North Clifton 34 SK 8272
North Cotes 39 TA 3400
Northcott 4 SX 3392
North Cove 29 TM 4689
North Cowton 42 NZ 2803
North Crawley 27 SP 9244
North Cray 12 TQ 4972
North Creake 28 TF 8538
North Curry 7 ST 3125
North Dalton 39 SE 9352
North Dawn 63 HY 4803
North Deighton 38 SE 3851
North Duffield 38 SE 6837
North Elkington 35 TF 2890
North Elmham 29 TF 9820
North End (Avon) 16 ST 4167
Northend (Avon) 17 ST 7867
North End (Berks.) 10 SU 4063
Northend (Bucks.) 18 SU 7392
North End (Hants.) 9 SU 6502
Northend (Warw.) 26 SP 3852
North End (W Susx) 11 TQ 1209
North Erradale 64 NG 7481
North Fearns 58 NG 5835
North Ferriby 39 SE 9826
Northfield (Borders) 53 NT 9167
Northfield (Grampn.) 62 NJ 9008
Northfield (W Mids.) 25 SP 0179
Northfleet 12 TQ 6274
North Frodingham 39 TA 1053
North Green 29 TM 2288
North Grimston 39 SE 8467
North Haven (Grampn.) 62 NK 1138
North Hayling 10 SU 7203
North Heasley 6 SS 7333
North Heath 11 TQ 0621
North Hill 4 SX 2776
North Hinksey 18 SP 4806
North Holmwood 11 TQ 1646
North Huish 5 SX 7156
North Hykeham 34 SK 9465
Northiam 12 TQ 8324
Northill 27 TL 1446
Northington 10 SU 5637
North Kelsey 39 TA 0401
North Kessock 60 NH 6548
North Kilvington 42 SE 4285
North Kilworth 26 SP 6183
North Kingennie 57 NO 4736
North Kyme 35 TF 1452
North Lancing 11 TQ 1805
Northlands 35 TF 3453
Northleach 17 SP 1114
North Lee (Bucks.) 19 SP 8309
Northleigh (Devon.) 7 SY 1995
North Leigh (Oxon.) 18 SP 3813
North Leverton with Habblesthorpe 34 SK 7882
Northlew 4 SX 5099
North Littleton 25 SP 0847
North Lopham 29 TM 0383
North Luffenham 27 SK 9303
North Marden 10 SU 8015
North Marston 18 SP 7722
North Middleton 51 NT 3559
North Molton 6 SS 7329
Northmoor 18 SP 4202
Northmoor Green or Moorland 7 ST 3332
North Moreton 18 SU 5689
Northmuir 57 NO 3855
North Muskham 34 SK 7958
North Newbald 39 SE 9136
North Newington 18 SP 4139
North Newnton 17 SU 1257
North Newton 7 ST 2931
North Nibley 17 ST 7396
North Oakley 10 SU 5354
North Ockendon 20 TQ 5984
Northolt 19 TQ 1285
Northop 31 SJ 2468
Northop Hall 31 SJ 2767
North Ormsby 35 TF 2893
Northorpe (Lincs.) 34 SK 8996
Northorpe (LIncs.) 35 TF 0917
North Otterington 42 SE 3589
Northover 7 ST 5223
North Owersby 35 TF 0594
Northowram 37 SE 1127
North Perrott 7 ST 4709
North Petherton 7 ST 2832
North Petherwin 4 SX 2889
North Pickenham 28 TF 8606

Purfleet Rowanburn

Purfleet 12 TQ 5578
Puriton 7 ST 3241
Purleigh 20 TL 8301
Purley (Berks.) 10 SU 6676
Purley (Gtr London) 12 TQ 3161
Purlogue 23 SO 2877
Purls Bridge 28 TL 4787
Purse Caundle 8 ST 6917
Purslow 24 SO 3680
Purston Jaglin 38 SE 4319
Purton (Glos.) 17 SO 6605
Purton (Glos.) 17 SO 6904
Purton (Wilts.) 17 SU 0887
Purton Stoke 17 SU 0890
Pury End 26 SP 7045
Pusey 18 SU 3596
Putley 24 SO 6437
Putney 11 TQ 2274
Puttenham (Herts.) 19 SP 8814
Puttenham (Surrey) 11 SU 9347
Puxton 16 ST 4063
Pwll 15 SN 4801
Pwllcrochan 14 SM 9202
Pwlldefaid 30 SH 1526
Pwllheli 30 SH 3735
Pwllmeyric 16 ST 5192
Pwll-y-glaw 15 SS 7993
Pyecombe 11 TQ 2912
Pye Corner 16 ST 3485
Pyle (I. of W.) 9 SZ 4879
Pyle (Mid Glam.) 15 SS 8282
Pylle 8 ST 6038
Pymore 28 TL 4986
Pyrford 11 TQ 0458
Pyrton 18 SU 6895
Pytchley 27 SP 8574
Pyworthy 4 SS 3102

Quabbs 23 SO 2080
Quadring 35 TF 2233
Quainton 18 SP 7419
Quanter Ness 63 HY 4114
Quarff 63 HU 4235
Quarley 10 SU 2743
Quarndon 33 SK 3340
Quarrier's Homes 50 NS 3666
Quarrington 35 TF 0544
Quarrington Hill 42 NZ 3337
Quarrybank (Ches.) 32 SJ 5465
Quarry Bank (W Mids.) 25 SO 9386
Quarryhill 65 NH 7281
Quarry, The 17 ST 7399
Quarrywood 61 NJ 1864
Quarter 50 NS 7251
Quatford 24 SO 7390
Quatt 24 SO 7588
Quebec 47 NZ 1743
Quedgeley 17 SO 8114
Queen Adelaide 28 TL 5681
Queenborough 13 TQ 9471
Queenborough in Sheppey 13 TQ 9174
Queen Camel 8 ST 5924
Queen Charlton 17 ST 6366
Queensbury 37 SE 1030
Queensferry (Clwyd) 32 SJ 3168
Queensferry (Lothian) 51 NT 1278
Queenzieburn 50 NS 6977
Quendale 63 HU 3713
Quendon 20 TL 5130
Queniborough 26 SK 6412
Quenington 17 SP 1404
Quernmore 36 SD 5160
Quethiock 4 SX 3164
Quidenham 29 TM 0287
Quidhampton (Hants.) 10 SU 5150
Quidhampton (Wilts.) 8 SU 1030
Quilquox 62 NJ 9038
Quindry 63 ND 4392
Quinton 26 SP 7754
Quoditch 4 SX 4097
Quoig 56 NN 8222
Quorndon 34 SK 5616
Quothquan 51 NS 9939
Quoyloo 63 HY 2420
Quoys 63 HP 6112

Raby 32 SJ 3179
Rachub 30 SH 6268
Rackenford 5 SS 8418
Rackham 11 TQ 0514
Rackheath 29 TG 2814
Racks 45 NY 0374
Rackwick (Hoy) 63 ND 1999
Rackwick (Westray) 63 HY 4449
Radcliffe (Gtr Mches) 37 SD 7806
Radcliffe (Northum.) 47 NU 2602
Radcliffe on Trent 34 SK 6439
Radclive 18 SP 6734
Radcot 18 SU 2899
Radernie 57 NO 4609
Radford Semele 26 SP 3464
Radlett 19 TL 1600
Radley 18 SU 5398
Radnage 18 SU 7897
Radstock 17 ST 6854
Radstone 26 SP 5840
Radway 26 SP 3648
Radway Green 32 SJ 7754
Radwell 19 TL 2335
Radwinter 20 TL 6037
Radyr 16 ST 1380
Raerinish 63 NB 4024
Rafford 61 NJ 0656
Ragdale 34 SK 6619
Raglan 16 SO 4107
Ragnall 34 SK 8073
Rahane 49 NS 2386
Rainford 36 SD 4700
Rainham (Gtr London) 20 TQ 5282
Rainham (Kent) 12 TQ 8165
Rainhill 32 SJ 4990
Rainhill Stoops 32 SJ 5090
Rainigadale 63 NB 2201
Rainow 33 SJ 9575
Rainton 42 SE 3775
Rainworth 34 SK 5958
Raisbeck 41 NY 6407
Rait 56 NO 2226
Raithby (Lincs.) 35 TF 3084
Raithby (Lincs.) 35 TF 3767
Rake 10 SU 8027
Ramasaig 58 NG 1644
Rame (Corn.) 2 SW 7233
Rame (Corn.) 4 SX 4249
Ram Lane 13 TQ 9646
Rampisham 7 ST 5502
Rampside 36 SD 2366
Rampton (Cambs.) 27 TL 4268
Rampton (Notts.) 34 SK 7978
Ramsbottom 37 SD 7916
Ramsbury 10 SU 2771
Ramscraigs 67 ND 1427
Ramsdean 10 SU 7021
Ramsdell 10 SU 5957
Ramsden 18 SP 3515
Ramsden Bellhouse 20 TQ 7194
Ramsden Heath 20 TQ 7195
Ramsey (Cambs.) 27 TL 2885
Ramsey (Essex) 21 TM 2130
Ramsey (I. of M.) 43 SC 4594
Ramsey Forty Foot 27 TL 3187
Ramsey Hollow 27 TL 3186
Ramsey Mereside 27 TL 2889
Ramsey St. Mary's 27 TL 2588
Ramsgate 13 TR 3865
Ramsgate Street 29 TG 0933
Ramsgill 37 SE 1170
Ramshorn 33 SK 0845
Ranby 34 SK 6480
Rand 35 TF 1078
Randwick 17 SO 8206
Ranfurly 50 NS 3865
Rangemore 33 SK 1822
Rangeworthy 17 ST 6886
Rankinston 50 NS 4514
Ranskill 34 SK 6587
Ranton 33 SJ 8524
Ranworth 29 TG 3514
Rascarrel 45 NX 7948
Raskelf 38 SE 4971
Rassau 16 SO 1411
Rastrick 37 SE 1321
Ratagan 59 NG 9220
Ratby 26 SK 5105
Ratcliffe Culey 26 SP 3299
Ratcliffe on the Wreake 34 SK 6314
Rathen 62 NK 0060
Rathillet 57 NO 3620
Rathmell 37 SD 8059
Ratho 51 NT 1370
Rathven 61 NJ 4465
Ratley 26 SP 3847
Ratlinghope 24 SO 4096
Rattar 67 ND 2672
Ratten Row 36 SD 4241
Rattery 5 SX 7361
Rattlesden 21 TL 9758
Rattray 56 NO 1745
Rauceby 34 TF 0146
Raughton Head 46 NY 3745
Raunds 27 SP 9972
Ravenfield 34 SK 4895
Ravenglass 40 SD 0896
Raveningham 29 TM 3996
Ravenscar 43 NZ 9801
Ravensdale 43 SC 3592
Ravensden 27 TL 0754
Ravenshead 34 SK 5654
Ravensmoor 32 SJ 6250
Ravensthorpe (Northants.) 26 SP 6670
Ravensthorpe (W Yorks.) 37 SE 2220
Ravenstone (Bucks.) 27 SP 8450
Ravenstone (Leic.) 26 SK 4013
Ravenstonedale 41 NY 7203
Ravenstruther 50 NS 9245
Ravensworth 42 NZ 1407
Raw 43 NZ 9305
Rawcliffe (Humbs.) 38 SE 6822
Rawcliffe (N Yorks.) 38 SE 5855
Rawcliffe Bridge 38 SE 6921
Rawmarsh 38 SK 4396
Rawreth 20 TQ 7793
Rawridge 7 ST 2006
Rawtenstall 37 SD 8122
Raydon 21 TM 0438
Raylees 47 NY 9291
Rayleigh 20 TQ 8090
Rayne 20 TL 7222
Reach 28 TL 5666
Read 37 SD 7634
Reading 10 SU 7272
Reading Street 13 TQ 9230
Reagill 41 NY 6017
Rearquhar 65 NH 7492
Rearsby 34 SK 6514
Rease Heath 32 SJ 6454
Reaster 67 ND 2565
Reawick 63 HU 3244
Reay 67 NC 9664
Reculver 13 TR 2269
Redberth 14 SN 0804
Redbourn 19 TL 1012
Redbourne 39 SK 9699
Redbridge 20 TQ 4389
Redbrook 16 SO 5310
Redbrook Street 13 TQ 9336
Redburn (Highld.) 65 NH 5767
Redburn (Highld.) 60 NH 9447
Redcar 42 NZ 6024
Redcastle (Highld.) 60 NH 5849
Redcastle (Tays.) 57 NO 6850
Redcliff Bay 16 ST 4475
Red Dial 46 NY 2545
Redding 50 NS 9178
Reddingmuirhead 50 NS 9177
Reddish 33 SJ 8993
Redditch 25 SP 0468
Rede 20 TL 8055
Redenhall 29 TM 2684
Redesmouth 47 NY 8681
Redford 57 NO 5644
Redgrave 29 TM 0478
Redheugh 57 NO 4463
Redhill (Avon) 16 ST 4962
Redhill (Grampn.) 62 NJ 6837
Redhill (Grampn.) 62 NJ 7704
Redhill (Surrey) 11 TQ 2850
Redisham 29 TM 4084
Redland (Avon) 17 ST 5875
Redland (Orkney) 63 HY 3724
Redlingfield 29 TM 1871
Redlynch (Somer.) 8 ST 6933
Redlynch (Wilts.) 8 SU 2020
Redmarley D'Abitot 24 SO 7531
Redmarshall 42 NZ 3821
Redmile 34 SK 7935
Redmire 41 SE 0491
Redmoor 3 SX 0761
Rednal 32 SJ 3628
Redpath 52 NT 5835
Redpoint (Highld.) 64 NG 7368
Red Rock 36 SD 5809
Red Roses 14 SN 2012
Red Row 47 NZ 2599
Redruth 2 SW 6941
Red Street 32 SJ 8251
Red Wharf Bay (Gwyn.) 30 SH 5281
Redwick (Avon) 16 ST 5485
Redwick (Gwent) 16 ST 4184
Redworth 42 NZ 2423
Reed 20 TL 3636
Reedham 29 TG 4201
Reedness 38 SE 7922
Reef 63 NB 1134
Reepham (Lincs.) 35 TF 0373
Reepham (Norf.) 29 TG 1023
Reeth 41 SE 0499
Regaby 43 SC 4397
Reiff 64 NB 9614
Reigate 11 TQ 2550
Reighton 43 TA 1275
Reiss 67 ND 3354
Rejerrah 2 SW 8055
Relubbus 2 SW 5632
Relugas 61 NH 9948
Remenham 18 SU 7784
Remenham Hill 18 SU 7883
Rempstone 34 SK 5724
Rendcomb 17 SP 0109
Rendham 29 TM 3564
Renfrew 50 NS 4967
Renhold 27 TL 0953
Renishaw 34 SK 4477
Rennington 53 NU 2118
Renton 50 NS 3878
Renwick 46 NY 5943
Repps 29 TG 4116
Repton 33 SK 3026
Rescobie 57 NO 5152
Resipole 54 NM 7264
Resolis 65 NH 6765
Resolven 15 SN 8202
Reston 53 NT 8861
Reswallie 57 NO 5051
Retew 2 SW 9256
Rettendon 20 TQ 7698
Revesby 35 TF 2961
Rewe 5 SX 9499
Reydon 29 TM 4977
Reymerston 29 TG 0206
Reynalton 14 SN 0909
Reynoldston 15 SS 4890
Rhandirmwyn 22 SN 7843
Rhayader 23 SN 9668
Rhedyn 30 SH 3032
Rheindown 60 NH 5147
Rhemore 54 NM 5750
Rhes-y-cae 31 SJ 1870
Rhewl (Clwyd) 31 SJ 1060
Rhewl (Clwyd) 31 SJ 1744
Rhiconich 66 NC 2552
Rhicullen 65 NH 6971
Rhigos 15 SN 9205
Rhilochan 66 NC 7407
Rhiroy 64 NH 1589
Rhiwbryfdir 30 SH 6946
Rhiwderyn 16 ST 2587
Rhiwlas (Clwyd) 31 SJ 1931
Rhiwlas (Gwyn.) 30 SH 5765
Rhiwlas (Gwyn.) 31 SH 9237
Rhodesia 34 SK 5680
Rhodes Minnis 13 TR 1542
Rhondda 16 SS 9696
Rhonehouse or Kelton Hill 45 NX 7459
Rhoose 16 ST 0666
Rhos (Dyfed) 15 SN 3835
Rhos (W Glam.) 15 SN 7303
Rhoscolyn 30 SH 2675
Rhoscrowther 14 SM 9002
Rhosesmor 31 SJ 2168
Rhos-fawr 30 SH 3838
Rhosgadfan 30 SH 5057
Rhosgoch (Gwyn.) 30 SH 4189
Rhosgoch (Powys) 23 SO 1847
Rhoslan 30 SH 4841
Rhoslefain 22 SH 5705
Rhosllanerchrugog 31 SJ 2946
Rhosmeirch 30 SH 4677
Rhosneigr 30 SH 3172
Rhosnesni 32 SJ 3451
Rhos-on-Sea 31 SH 8480
Rhossili 15 SS 4188
Rhosson 14 SM 7225
Rhostryfan 30 SH 4958
Rhostyllen 32 SJ 3148
Rhosybol 30 SH 4288
Rhos-y-gwaliau 31 SH 9434
Rhos-y-llan 30 SH 2337
Rhu (Strath.) 49 NS 2783
Rhuallt 31 SJ 0774
Rhuban 63 NF 7811
Rhuddlan 31 SJ 0277
Rhue 64 NH 0997
Rhulen 23 SO 1350
Rhunahaorine 48 NR 7048
Rhyd (Gwyn.) 30 SH 6341
Rhydargaeau 15 SN 4326
Rhydcymerau 22 SN 5738
Rhydd 25 SO 8345
Rhyd-Ddu 30 SH 5652
Rhydding 15 SS 7498
Rhydlewis 22 SN 3447
Rhydlios 30 SH 1830
Rhyd-lydan 31 SH 8950
Rhydowen 22 SN 4445
Rhydrosser 22 SN 5667
Rhydtalog 31 SJ 2354
Rhyd-y-clafdy 30 SH 3235
Rhydycroesau 31 SJ 2330
Rhydyfelin (Dyfed) 22 SN 5979
Rhydyfelin (Mid Glam.) 16 ST 0988
Rhydyfro 15 SN 7105
Rhydymain 31 SH 7922
Rhyd-y-meirch 16 SO 3107
Rhydymwyn 31 SJ 2066
Rhyd-yr-onnen 22 SH 6102
Rhyl 31 SJ 0181
Rhymney 16 SO 1107
Rhyn 32 SJ 3136
Rhynd 56 NO 1520
Rhynie (Grampn.) 61 NJ 4927
Rhynie (Highld.) 65 NH 8578
Ribbesford 24 SO 7874
Ribblesdale 37 SD 8059
Ribbleton 36 SD 5630
Ribchester 36 SD 6435
Ribigill 66 NC 5854
Riby 39 TA 1807
Riccall 38 SE 6237
Riccarton 50 NS 4235
Richards Castle 24 SO 4969
Richmond 42 NZ 1701
Richmond upon Thames 11 TQ 1874
Rickarton 62 NO 8188
Rickinghall Inferior 29 TM 0475
Rickinghall Superior 29 TM 0475
Rickling 20 TL 4931
Rickmansworth 19 TQ 0594
Riddell 52 NT 5124
Riddings 46 NY 4075
Riddlecombe 5 SS 6013
Riddlesden 37 SE 0742
Ridge (Dorset) 8 SY 9386
Ridge (Herts.) 19 TL 2100
Ridge (Wilts.) 8 ST 9531
Ridgehill (Avon) 16 ST 5362
Ridge Hill (Here. and Worc.) 24 SO 5035
Ridge Lane 26 SP 2994
Ridgeway Cross 24 SO 7147
Ridgewell 20 TL 7340
Ridgewood 12 TQ 4719
Ridgmont 19 SP 9736
Riding Mill 47 NZ 0161
Ridlington (Leic.) 27 SK 8402
Ridlington (Norf.) 29 TG 3430
Ridsdale 47 NY 9084
Riechip 56 NO 0647
Rievaulx 42 SE 5785
Rigg 46 NY 2966
Riggend 50 NS 7670
Righoul 60 NH 8851
Rigside 50 NS 8734
Rileyhill 33 SK 1115
Rilla Mill 4 SX 2973
Rillington 43 SE 8574
Rimington 37 SD 8045
Rimpton 8 ST 6021
Rimswell 39 TA 3128
Rinaston 14 SM 9825
Ringford 45 NX 6857
Ringland 29 TG 1313
Ringmer 12 TQ 4412
Ringmore 5 SX 6545
Ringorm 61 NJ 2644
Ring's End 27 TF 3902
Ringsfield 29 TM 4088
Ringsfield Corner 29 TM 4187
Ringshall (Bucks.) 19 SP 9814
Ringshall (Suff.) 21 TM 0452
Ringshall Stocks 21 TM 0551
Ringstead (Norf.) 28 TF 7040
Ringstead (Northants.) 27 SP 9875
Ringwood 8 SU 1405
Ringwould 13 TR 3648
Rinnigill 63 ND 3193
Rinsey 2 SW 5927
Ripe 12 TQ 5010
Ripley (Derby.) 33 SK 3950
Ripley (Hants.) 8 SZ 1698
Ripley (N Yorks.) 38 SE 2860
Ripley (Surrey) 11 TQ 0556
Riplingham 39 SE 9631
Ripon 38 SE 3171
Rippingale 35 TF 0927
Ripple (Here. and Worcs.) 25 SO 8737
Ripple (Kent) 13 TR 3550
Ripponden 37 SE 0319
Rireavach 64 NH 0396
Risabus 48 NR 3143
Risbury 24 SO 5455
Risby (Humbs.) 39 SE 9214
Risby (Suff.) 28 TL 7966
Risca 16 ST 2391
Rise 39 TA 1541
Risegate 35 TF 2029
Riseley (Beds.) 27 TL 0463
Riseley (Berks.) 10 SU 7263
Rishangles 29 TM 1568
Rishton 36 SD 7229
Rishworth 37 SE 0317
Risley 34 SK 4635
Risplith 37 SE 2467
Rispond 66 NC 4565
Rivar 10 SU 3161
Rivenhall End 20 TL 8316
River Bank 28 TL 5368
Riverhead 12 TQ 5156
Rivington 36 SD 6214
Roade 26 SP 7551
Roadmeetings 50 NS 8649
Roadside 67 ND 1560
Roadside of Kinneff 57 NO 8476
Roadwater 7 ST 0238
Roag 58 NG 2744
Roa Island 36 SD 2364
Roath 16 ST 1978
Roberton (Borders) 52 NT 4314
Roberton (Strath.) 51 NS 9428
Robertsbridge 12 TQ 7323
Roberttown 37 SE 1922
Robeston Cross 14 SM 8809
Robeston Wathen 14 SN 0815
Robin Hood's Bay 43 NZ 9505
Roborough 4 SS 5717
Roby 32 SJ 4291
Roby Mill 36 SD 5106
Rocester 33 SK 1039
Roch 14 SM 8821
Rochdale 37 SD 8913
Roche 3 SW 9860
Rochester (Kent) 12 TQ 7467
Rochester (Northum.) 47 NY 8397
Rochford (Essex) 21 TQ 8790
Rochford (Here. and Worc.) 24 SO 6268
Rock (Corn.) 2 SW 9475
Rock (Here. and Worc.) 24 SO 7371
Rock (Northum.) 53 NU 2020
Rockbeare 7 SY 0195
Rockbourne 8 SU 1118
Rockcliffe (Cumbr.) 46 NY 3561
Rockcliffe (Dumf. and Galwy.) 45 NX 8553
Rock Ferry 32 SJ 3386
Rockfield (Gwent) 16 SO 4814
Rockfield (Highld.) 65 NH 9282
Rockhampton 17 ST 6593
Rockingham 27 SP 8691
Rockland All Saints 29 TL 9896
Rockland St. Mary 29 TG 3104
Rockland St. Peter 29 TL 9897
Rockley 17 SU 1571
Rockwell End 18 SU 7988
Rodbourne 17 ST 9383
Rodd 23 SO 3162
Roddam 53 NU 0220
Rodden 8 SY 6184
Rode 17 ST 8053
Rode Heath (Ches.) 32 SJ 8056
Rodeheath (Ches.) 33 SJ 8766
Rodel 63 NG 0483
Roden 32 SJ 5716
Rodhuish 7 ST 0139
Rodington 32 SJ 5814
Rodley 17 SO 7411
Rodmarton 17 ST 9397
Rodmell 12 TQ 4106
Rodmersham 13 TQ 9261
Rodney Stoke 7 ST 4849
Rodsley 33 SK 2040
Roecliffe 38 SE 3765
Roehampton 11 TQ 2373
Roesound 63 HU 3365
Roewen 30 SH 7571
Roffey 11 TQ 1931
Rogart 66 NC 7303
Rogate 10 SU 8023
Rogerstone 16 ST 2688
Rogerton 50 NS 6256
Rogiet 16 ST 4587
Roker 47 NZ 4059
Rollesby 29 TG 4415
Rolleston (Leic.) 26 SK 7300
Rolleston (Notts.) 34 SK 7452
Rolleston (Staffs.) 33 SK 2327
Rolston 39 TA 2145
Rolvenden 13 TQ 8431
Rolvenden Layne 13 TQ 8530
Romaldkirk 41 NY 9921
Romanby 42 SE 3693
Romannobridge 51 NT 1547
Romansleigh 6 SS 7220
Romford 20 TQ 5188
Romiley 33 SJ 9390
Romsey 9 SU 3521
Romsley (Here. and Worc.) 25 SO 9679
Romsley (Salop) 24 SO 7883
Ronague 43 SC 2472
Rookhope 47 NY 9342
Rookley 9 SZ 5084
Rooks Bridge 16 ST 3752
Roos 39 TA 2830
Rootpark 51 NS 9554
Ropley 9 SU 6431
Ropley Dean 9 SU 6331
Ropsley 34 SK 9834
Rora 62 NK 0650
Rorrington 23 SJ 3000
Rose 2 SW 7754
Roseacre 36 SD 4336
Rose Ash 6 SS 7821
Rosebank 50 NS 8049
Rosebrough 53 NU 1326
Rosedale 43 SE 7295
Rosedale Abbey 43 SE 7296
Roseden 53 NU 0321
Rosehearty 62 NJ 9367
Rosehill 32 SJ 6630
Roseisle 61 NJ 1367
Rosemarket 14 SM 9508
Rosemarkie 60 NH 7357
Rosemary Lane 7 ST 1514
Rosemount (Strath.) 50 NS 3729
Rosemount (Tays.) 56 NO 2043
Rosewell 51 NT 2862
Roseworthy 2 SW 6139
Rosgill 40 NY 5316
Roshven 54 NM 7078
Roskhill 58 NG 2745
Rosley 46 NY 3245
Roslin 51 NT 2663
Rosliston 33 SK 2416
Rosneath 49 NS 2583
Ross (Dumf. and Galwy.) 45 NX 6444
Ross (Northum.) 53 NU 1336
Ross (Tays.) 56 NN 7621
Rossett 32 SJ 3657
Rossington 38 SK 6298
Rosskeen 65 NH 6869
Rossland 50 NS 4370
Ross-on-Wye 17 SO 6024
Roster 67 ND 2639
Rostherne 32 SJ 7483
Rosthwaite 40 NY 2514
Roston 33 SK 1241
Rosyth 51 NT 1183
Rothbury 47 NU 0601
Rotherby 34 SK 6716
Rotherfield 12 TQ 5529
Rotherfield Greys 18 SU 7282
Rotherfield Peppard 18 SU 7081
Rotherham 34 SK 4492
Rothersthorpe 26 SP 7156
Rotherwick 10 SU 7156
Rothes 61 NJ 2749
Rothesay 49 NS 0864
Rothiebrisbane 62 NJ 7437
Rothiemurchus 60 NH 9206
Rothienorman 62 NJ 7235
Rothiesholm 63 HY 6123
Rothley 26 SK 5812
Rothmaise 62 NJ 6832
Rothwell (Lincs.) 39 TF 1599
Rothwell (Northants.) 26 SP 8181
Rothwell (W Yorks.) 38 SE 3428
Rotsea 39 TA 0651
Rottal 57 NO 3769
Rottingdean 12 TQ 3702
Rottington 40 NX 9613
Roud 9 SZ 5280
Rougham 28 TF 8320
Rougham Green 28 TL 9061
Roughburn 55 NN 3781
Rough Close 33 SJ 9239
Rough Common 13 TR 1359
Roughlee 37 SD 8440
Roughley 25 SP 1399
Roughsike 46 NY 5275
Roughton (Lincs.) 35 TF 2364
Roughton (Norf.) 29 TG 2136
Roughton (Salop) 24 SO 7594
Roundhay 38 SE 3235
Roundstreet Common 11 TQ 0528
Roundway 17 SU 0163
Rounton 42 NZ 4103
Rousdon 7 SY 2990
Rous Lench 25 SP 0153
Routenburn 49 NS 1961
Routh 39 TA 0842
Row (Corn.) 3 SX 0976
Row (Cumbr.) 40 SD 4589
Rowanburn 46 NY 4177

Rowde

Semington

Rowde	17	ST 9762
Rowfoot	46	NY 6860
Rowhedge	21	TM 0221
Rowhook	11	TQ 1234
Rowington	26	SP 2069
Rowland	33	SK 2072
Rowland's Castle	10	SU 7310
Rowland's Gill	47	NZ 1658
Rowledge	10	SU 8243
Rowley (Devon.)	6	SS 7219
Rowley (Humbs.)	39	SE 9732
Rowley (Salop)	23	SJ 3006
Rowley Regis	25	SO 9787
Rowlstone	16	SO 3727
Rowly	11	TQ 0441
Rowney Green	25	SP 0471
Rownhams	9	SU 3816
Rowsham	19	SP 8518
Rowsley	33	SK 2566
Rowston	35	TF 0856
Rowton (Ches.)	32	SJ 4464
Rowton (Salop)	32	SJ 6119
Roxburgh	52	NT 6930
Roxby (Humbs.)	39	SE 9217
Roxby (N Yorks.)	43	NZ 7616
Roxton	27	TL 1554
Roxwell	20	TL 6408
Royal Leamington Spa	26	SP 3166
Royal Tunbridge Wells	12	TQ 5839
Roybridge	55	NN 2781
Roydon (Essex)	20	TL 4009
Roydon (Norf.)	28	TF 7022
Roydon (Norf.)	29	TM 0980
Royston (Herts.)	20	TL 3541
Royston (S Yorks.)	38	SE 3611
Royton	37	SD 9207
Ruabon	32	SJ 3043
Ruaig	48	NM 0647
Ruan Lanihorne	2	SW 8942
Ruan Minor	2	SW 7115
Ruardean	17	SO 6117
Ruardean Woodside	17	SO 6216
Rubery	25	SO 9777
Ruckcroft	46	NY 5344
Ruckinge	13	TR 0233
Ruckland	35	TF 3378
Ruckley	24	SJ 5300
Ruddington	34	SK 5733
Rudge	17	ST 8252
Rudgeway	17	ST 6286
Rudgwick	11	TQ 0934
Rudhall	17	SO 6225
Rudry	16	ST 1986
Rudston	39	TA 0967
Rudyard	33	SJ 9557
Rufford	36	SD 4515
Rufforth	38	SE 5251
Rugby	26	SP 5075
Rugeley	33	SK 0418
Ruilick	60	NH 5046
Ruishton	7	ST 2624
Ruislip	19	TQ 0987
Ruislip Common	19	TQ 0789
Rumbling Bridge	56	NT 0199
Rumburgh	29	TM 3581
Rumford	2	SW 8970
Rumney	16	ST 2179
Runcorn	32	SJ 5182
Runcton	11	SU 8802
Runcton Holme	28	TF 6109
Runfold	11	SU 8747
Runhall	29	TG 0507
Runham	29	TG 4610
Runnington	7	ST 1121
Runswick	43	NZ 8016
Runtaleave	57	NO 2867
Runwell	20	TQ 7494
Rushall (Here. and Worc.)	24	SO 6434
Rushall (Norf.)	29	TM 1982
Rushall (Wilts.)	17	SU 1255
Rushall (W Mids.)	25	SK 0201
Rushbrooke	28	TL 8961
Rushbury	24	SO 5191
Rushden (Herts.)	20	TL 3031
Rushden (Northants.)	27	SP 9566
Rushford	29	TL 9281
Rush Green	20	TQ 5187
Rushlake Green	12	TQ 6218
Rushmere	29	TM 4987
Rushmere St. Andrew	21	TM 2046
Rushmoor	11	SU 8740
Rushock	25	SO 8871
Rusholme	33	SJ 8494
Rushton (Ches.)	32	SJ 5863
Rushton (Northants.)	27	SP 8483
Rushton (Salop)	24	SJ 6008
Rushton Spencer	33	SJ 9363
Rushwick	25	SO 8353
Rushyford	42	NZ 2828
Ruskie	56	NN 6200
Ruskington	35	TF 0850
Rusland	40	SD 3488
Rusper	11	TQ 2037
Ruspidge	17	SO 6512
Russell's Water	18	SU 7089
Rustington	11	TQ 0502
Ruston Parva	39	TA 0661
Ruswarp	43	NZ 8809
Rutherford	52	NT 6530
Rutherglen	50	NS 6161
Ruthernbridge	3	SX 0166
Ruthin	31	SJ 1257
Ruthrieston	62	NJ 9204
Ruthven (Grampn.)	61	NJ 5046
Ruthven (Highld.)	60	NH 8133
Ruthven (Tays.)	57	NO 2848
Ruthvoes	2	SW 9360
Ruthwell	45	NY 1067
Ruyton-XI-Towns	32	SJ 3922
Ryal	47	NZ 0174
Ryal Fold	36	SD 6621
Ryall	7	SY 4094
Ryarsh	12	TQ 6659
Rydal	40	NY 3606
Ryde	9	SZ 5992
Rye	13	TQ 9220
Rye Foreign	13	TQ 8822
Rye Harbour	13	TQ 9419
Ryhall	27	TF 0311
Ryhill	38	SE 3814
Ryhope	47	NZ 4152
Ryknild Street (Warw.) (ant.)	25	SP 0762
Rylstone	37	SD 9758
Ryme Intrinseca	7	ST 5810
Ryther	38	SE 5539
Ryton (Glos.)	24	SO 7232
Ryton (N Yorks.)	43	SE 7975
Ryton (Salop)	24	SJ 7502
Ryton (Tyne and Wear)	47	NZ 1564
Ryton-on-Dunsmore	26	SP 3874
Sabden	37	SD 7737
Sacombe	20	TL 3419
Sacriston	47	NZ 2447
Sadberge	42	NZ 3416
Saddell	49	NR 7832
Saddington	26	SP 6591
Saddle Bow	28	TF 6015
Saffron Walden	20	TL 5438
Saham Toney	28	TF 9002
Saighton	32	SJ 4462
St. Abbs	53	NT 9167
St. Agnes	2	SW 7150
St. Albans	19	TL 1507
St. Allen	2	SW 8250
St. Andrews	57	NO 5016
St. Andrews Major	16	ST 1471
St. Anne's (Lancs.)	36	SD 3129
St. Ann's (Dumf. and Galwy.)	45	NY 0793
St. Ann's Chapel	4	SX 4170
St. Anthony	2	SW 7725
St. Arvans	16	ST 5196
St. Asaph	31	SJ 0374
St. Athan	16	ST 0168
St. Austell	3	SX 0152
St. Bees	40	NX 9611
St. Blazey	3	SX 0654
St. Boswells	52	NT 5930
St. Breock	2	SW 9771
St. Breward	3	SX 0977
St. Briavels	16	SO 5504
St. Brides	14	SM 8010
St. Bride's Major	15	SS 8974
St. Brides Netherwent	16	ST 4289
St. Brides-super-Ely	16	ST 1078
St. Bride's Wentlooge	16	ST 2982
St. Budeaux	4	SX 4558
St. Buryan	2	SW 4025
St. Catherines	55	NN 1207
St. Clears	14	SN 2716
St. Cleer	4	SX 2468
St. Clement	2	SW 8443
St. Clether	4	SX 2084
St. Colmac	49	NS 0467
St. Columb Major	2	SW 9163
St. Columb Minor	2	SW 8362
St. Columb Road	2	SW 9059
St. Combs	62	NK 0563
St. Cross South Elmham	29	TM 2984
St. Cyrus	57	NO 7464
St. David's (Dyfed)	14	SM 7525
St. Davids (Fife.)	51	NT 1582
St. David's (Tays.)	56	NN 9420
St. Day	2	SW 7242
St. Dennis	2	SW 9558
St. Devereux	24	SO 4431
St. Dogmaels	14	SN 1646
St. Dogwells	14	SM 9728
St. Dominick	4	SX 3967
St. Donats	15	SS 9368
St. Edith's Marsh	17	ST 9764
St. Endellion	3	SW 9978
St. Enoder	2	SW 8956
St. Erme	2	SW 8449
St. Erth	2	SW 5435
St. Erth Praze	2	SW 5735
St. Ervan	2	SW 8870
St. Ewe	2	SW 9745
St. Fagans	16	ST 1177
St. Fergus	62	NK 0951
St. Fillans	56	NN 6924
St. Florence	14	SN 0801
St. Gennys	4	SX 1497
St. George (Clwyd)	31	SH 9775
St. George's (S Glam.)	16	ST 0976
St. Germans	4	SX 3557
St. Giles in the Wood	4	SS 5318
St. Giles-on-the-Heath	4	SX 3590
St. Harmon	23	SN 9872
St. Helena	29	TG 1816
St. Helen Auckland	42	NZ 1826
St. Helens (I. of W.)	9	SZ 6288
St. Helens (Mers.)	32	SJ 5095
St. Hilary (Corn.)	2	SW 5531
St. Hilary (S Glam.)	16	ST 0173
St. Illtyd	16	SO 2102
St. Ishmael's	14	SM 8307
St. Issey	2	SW 9271
St. Ive (Corn.)	4	SX 3167
St. Ives (Cambs.)	27	TL 3171
St. Ives (Corn.)	2	SW 5140
St. Ives (Dorset)	8	SU 1203
St. James South Elmham	29	TM 3281
St. John (Corn.)	4	SX 4053
St. Johns (Here. and Worc.)	25	SO 8453
St. John's (Durham)	41	NZ 0734
St. John's (I. of M.)	43	SC 2781
St. John's Chapel	41	NY 8837
St. John's Fen End	28	TF 5311
St. John's Highway	28	TF 5314
St. John's Town of Dalry	45	NX 6281
St. Jude's	43	SC 3996
St. Just (Corn.)	2	SW 3631
St. Just (Corn.)	2	SW 8435
St. Katherines	62	NJ 7834
St. Keverne	2	SW 7821
St. Kew	3	SX 0276
St. Kew Highway	3	SX 0375
St. Keyne	4	SX 2460
St. Lawrence (Corn.)	3	SX 0466
St. Lawrence (Essex)	21	TL 9604
St. Lawrence (I. of W.)	9	SZ 5476
St. Leonards (Bucks.)	19	SP 9006
St. Leonards (Dorset)	8	SU 1002
St. Leonards (E Susx)	12	TQ 8009
St. Levan	2	SW 3722
St. Lythans	16	ST 1073
St. Mabyn	3	SX 0373
St. Margarets	24	SO 3534
St. Margaret's at Cliffe	13	TR 3644
St. Margaret's Bay	13	TR 3744
St. Margaret's Hope (Fife.)	51	NT 1181
St. Margaret's Hope (S. Ronaldsay)	63	ND 4493
St. Margaret South Elmham	29	TM 3183
St. Mark's	43	SC 2974
St. Martin (Corn.)	4	SX 2555
St. Martin's (Is. of Sc.)	2	SV 9215
St. Martin's (Salop)	32	SJ 3236
St. Martins (Tays.)	56	NO 1530
St. Martin's Green	2	SW 7324
St. Mary Bourne	10	SU 4250
St. Mary Church	16	ST 0071
St. Mary Cray	12	TQ 4767
St. Mary Hill	15	SS 9678
St. Mary in the Marsh	13	TR 0628
St. Marylebone	19	TQ 2881
St. Mary's (Orkney)	63	HY 4701
St. Mary's Bay	13	TR 0927
St. Mary's Grove	16	ST 4769
St. Mary's Hoo	12	TQ 8076
St. Mary's Isle	45	NX 6749
St. Mawes	2	SW 8433
St. Mawgan	2	SW 8765
St. Mellion	4	SX 3865
St. Mellons	16	ST 2281
St. Merryn	2	SW 8874
St. Mewan	3	SW 9951
St. Michael Caerhays	2	SW 9642
St. Michael Penkevil	2	SW 8542
St. Michaels (Here. and Worc.)	24	SO 5765
St. Michaels (Kent)	13	TQ 8835
St. Michael's Mount	2	SW 5130
St. Michael's on Wyre	36	SD 4640
St. Michael South Elmham	29	TM 3483
St. Minver	2	SW 9677
St. Monans	57	NO 5201
St. Neot (Corn.)	4	SX 1867
St. Neots (Cambs.)	27	TL 1860
St. Nicholas (Dyfed)	14	SM 9035
St. Nicholas (S Glam.)	16	ST 0874
St. Nicholas at Wade	13	TR 2666
St. Ninians	50	NS 7991
St. Osyth	21	TM 1215
St. Owen's Cross	16	SO 5324
St. Pauls Cray	12	TQ 4768
St. Paul's Walden	19	TL 1922
St. Peter's	13	TR 3668
St. Petrox	14	SR 9797
St. Pinnock	4	SX 2063
St. Quivox	50	NS 3723
St. Stephen (Corn.)	2	SW 9453
St. Stephens (Corn.)	4	SX 3285
St. Stephen's (Corn.)	4	SX 4158
St. Teath	3	SX 0680
St. Tudy	3	SX 0676
St. Twynnells	14	SR 9597
St. Vigeans	57	NO 6443
St. Wenn	2	SW 9664
St. Weonards	16	SO 4924
Saintbury	25	SP 1139
Saint Hill	12	TQ 3835
Salcombe	5	SX 7338
Salcombe Regis	7	SY 1488
Salcott	21	TL 9413
Sale	32	SJ 7990
Saleby	35	TF 4578
Sale Green	25	SO 9358
Salehurst	12	TQ 7424
Salem (Dyfed)	15	SN 6226
Salem (Dyfed)	22	SN 6684
Salem (Gwyn.)	30	SH 5456
Salen (Highld.)	54	NM 6864
Salen (Island of Mull)	54	NM 5743
Salesbury	36	SD 6732
Sales Point	21	TM 0209
Salford (Beds.)	27	SP 9339
Salford (Gtr Mches.)	32	SJ 7796
Salford (Oxon.)	18	SP 2828
Salford Priors	25	SP 0751
Salfords	11	TQ 2846
Salhouse	29	TG 3114
Saline	51	NT 0292
Salisbury	8	SU 1429
Sall	29	TG 1024
Sallachy (Highld.)	66	NC 5408
Sallachy (Highld.)	59	NG 9130
Salmonby	35	TF 3273
Salmond's Muir	57	NO 5837
Salperton	17	SP 0720
Salph End	27	TL 0752
Salsburgh	50	NS 8262
Salt	33	SJ 9527
Saltash	4	SX 4259
Saltburn	65	NH 7269
Saltburn-by-the-Sea	42	NZ 6621
Saltby	34	SK 8426
Saltcoats	49	NS 2441
Saltdean	12	TQ 3802
Salter	36	SD 6073
Salterforth	37	SD 8845
Saltergate	43	SE 8594
Salterswall	32	SJ 6267
Saltfleet	35	TF 4593
Saltfleetby All Saints	35	TF 4590
Saltfleetby St. Clements	35	TF 4591
Saltfleetby St. Peter	35	TF 4389
Saltford	17	ST 6867
Salthouse	29	TG 0743
Saltmarshe	38	SE 7824
Saltney	32	SJ 3864
Salton	43	SE 7180
Saltwick	47	NZ 1780
Saltwood	13	TR 1536
Salwarpe	25	SO 8762
Salwayash	7	SY 4596
Samala	63	NF 7962
Sambourne	25	SP 0561
Sambrook	32	SJ 7124
Samlesbury	36	SD 5829
Samlesbury Bottoms	36	SD 6229
Sampford Arundel	7	ST 1018
Sampford Brett	7	ST 0940
Sampford Courtenay	5	SS 6301
Sampford Peverell	7	ST 0214
Sampford Spiney	4	SX 5372
Samuelston	52	NT 4870
Sanaigmore	48	NR 2370
Sancreed	2	SW 4029
Sancton	39	SE 8939
Sand	63	HU 3447
Sandaig	58	NG 7102
Sandbach	32	SJ 7560
Sandbank	49	NS 1580
Sandbanks	8	SZ 0487
Sandend	61	NJ 5566
Sanderstead	12	TQ 3461
Sandford (Avon)	16	ST 4159
Sandford (Cumbr.)	41	NY 7216
Sandford (Devon.)	5	SS 8202
Sandford (Dorset)	8	SY 9289
Sandford (Strath.)	50	NS 7143
Sandfordhill	62	NK 1141
Sandford-on-Thames	18	SP 5301
Sandford Orcas	8	ST 6220
Sandford St. Martin	18	SP 4226
Sandgarth	63	HY 5215
Sandgate	13	TR 2035
Sandgreen	45	NX 5752
Sandhaven	62	NJ 9667
Sandhead	44	NX 0949
Sandhoe	47	NY 9766
Sandholme (Humbs.)	39	SE 8230
Sandholme (Lincs.)	35	TF 3337
Sandhurst (Berks.)	10	SU 8361
Sandhurst (Glos.)	17	SO 8223
Sandhurst (Kent)	12	TQ 8028
Sandhutton (N Yorks.)	42	SE 3881
Sand Hutton (N Yorks.)	38	SE 6958
Sandiacre	34	SK 4736
Sandilands	35	TF 5280
Sandiway	32	SJ 6070
Sandleheath	8	SO 1214
Sandleigh	18	SP 4501
Sandling	12	TQ 7558
Sandness	63	HU 1956
Sandon (Essex)	20	TL 7404
Sandon (Herts.)	20	TL 3234
Sandon (Staffs.)	33	SJ 9429
Sandown	9	SZ 5984
Sandplace	4	SX 2457
Sandridge (Herts.)	19	TL 1710
Sandridge (Wilts.)	17	ST 9465
Sandringham	28	TF 6928
Sandsend	43	NZ 8512
Sand Side	40	SD 2282
Sandsound	63	HU 3548
Sandtoft	38	SE 7408
Sandwich	13	TR 3358
Sandwick (Cumbr.)	40	NY 4219
Sandwick (Isle of Lewis)	63	NB 4432
Sandwick (Shetld.)	63	HU 4323
Sandwick (S. Ronaldsay)	63	ND 4389
Sandy	27	TL 1649
Sandycroft	32	SJ 3366
Sandygate	43	SC 3797
Sandy Lane	17	ST 9668
Sangobeg	66	NC 4266
Sanna	54	NM 4469
Sanquhar	50	NS 7809
Santon Bridge	40	NY 1001
Santon Downham	28	TL 8187
Sapcote	26	SP 4893
Sapey Common	24	SO 7064
Sapiston	28	TL 9175
Sapperton (Glos.)	17	SO 9403
Sapperton (Lincs.)	34	TF 0133
Saracen's Head	35	TF 3427
Sarclet	67	ND 3443
Sarisbury	9	SU 5008
Sarn (Mid Glam.)	15	SS 9083
Sarn (Powys)	23	SO 2090
Sarnau (Dyfed)	22	SN 3151
Sarnau (Dyfed)	14	SN 3318
Sarnau (Gwyn.)	31	SH 9739
Sarnau (Powys)	31	SJ 2315
Sarn-bach	30	SH 3026
Sarnesfield	24	SO 3750
Sarn Meyllteyrn	30	SH 2432
Saron (Dyfed)	15	SN 3738
Saron (Dyfed)	15	SN 6012
Sarratt	19	TQ 0499
Sarre	13	TR 2565
Sarsden	18	SP 2822
Satley	47	NZ 1143
Satterleigh	6	SS 6622
Satterthwaite	40	SD 3392
Sauchen	62	NJ 7010
Saucher	56	NO 1933
Sauchieburn	57	NO 6669
Sauchrie	49	NS 3014
Saughall	32	SJ 3669
Saughtree	46	NY 5696
Saul	17	SO 7409
Saundby	34	SK 7888
Saundersfoot	14	SN 1304
Saunderton	18	SP 7901
Saunton	6	SS 4537
Sausthorpe	35	TF 3869
Savalmore	66	NC 5908
Sawbridgeworth	20	TL 4814
Sawdon	43	SE 9485
Sawley (Derby.)	33	SK 4731
Sawley (Lancs.)	37	SD 7746
Sawley (N Yorks.)	37	SE 2467
Sawrey	40	SD 3695
Sawston	20	TL 4849
Sawtry	27	TL 1683
Saxby (Leic.)	34	SK 8220
Saxby (Lincs.)	34	TF 0086
Saxby All Saints	39	SE 9816
Saxelbye	34	SK 6921
Saxilby	34	SK 8875
Saxlingham	29	TG 0239
Saxlingham Nethergate	29	TM 2397
Saxmundham	29	TM 3863
Saxondale	34	SK 6839
Saxon Street	20	TL 6859
Saxtead	29	TM 2665
Saxtead Green	29	TM 2564
Saxthorpe	29	TG 1130
Saxton	38	SE 4736
Sayers Common	11	TQ 2618
Scackleton	42	SE 6472
Scadabay	63	NG 1792
Scaftworth	34	SK 6691
Scagglethorpe	39	SE 8372
Scalasaig	48	NR 3894
Scalby	43	TA 0090
Scaldwell	26	SP 7672
Scaleby	46	NY 4563
Scalebyhill	46	NY 4363
Scale Houses	46	NY 5845
Scales (Cumbr.)	40	NY 3426
Scales (Cumbr.)	36	SD 2772
Scalford	34	SK 7724
Scaling	43	NZ 7413
Scalloway	63	HU 4039
Scalpay (Harris)	63	NG 2395
Scalpay (Island of Skye)	58	NG 6030
Scamblesby	35	TF 2778
Scamodale	54	NM 8473
Scampston	43	SE 8575
Scampton	34	SK 9479
Scapa	63	HY 4309
Scar	63	HY 6745
Scarastavore	63	NG 0092
Scarborough	43	TA 0388
Scarcliffe	34	SK 4968
Scarcroft	38	SE 3540
Scardroy	59	NH 2151
Scarff	63	HU 2479
Scarfskerry	67	ND 2673
Scargill	41	NZ 0510
Scarinish	48	NM 0444
Scarisbrick	36	SD 3713
Scarning	29	TF 9512
Scarrington	34	SK 7341
Scarth Hill	36	SD 4206
Scartho	39	TA 2606
Scatsta	63	HU 3872
Scaur of Kippford	45	NX 8355
Scawby	39	SE 9605
Scawton	42	SE 5483
Scayne's Hill	12	TQ 3723
Scethrog	16	SO 1025
Scholar Green	32	SJ 8357
Scholes (W Yorks.)	37	SE 1507
Scholes (W Yorks.)	38	SE 3736
Scleddau	14	SM 9434
Scole	29	TM 1579
Scolton	14	SM 9922
Sconser	58	NG 5232
Scoor	54	NM 4119
Scopwick	35	TF 0658
Scoraig	64	NH 0096
Scorborough	39	TA 0145
Scorrier	2	SW 7244
Scorton (Lancs.)	36	SD 5048
Scorton (N Yorks.)	42	NZ 2400
Sco Ruston	29	TG 2821
Scotby	46	NY 4454
Scotforth	36	SD 4759
Scothern	35	TF 0377
Scotland Gate	47	NZ 2584
Scotlandwell	56	NO 1801
Scotney Castle	12	TQ 6835
Scotsburn	65	NH 7275
Scotscraig	57	NO 4428
Scots' Gap	47	NZ 0486
Scotstown	54	NM 8263
Scotter	39	SE 8800
Scotterthorpe	39	SE 8701
Scotton (Lincs.)	39	SK 8899
Scotton (N Yorks.)	42	SE 1895
Scotton (N Yorks.)	38	SE 3259
Scottow	29	TG 2623
Scoughall	52	NT 6183
Scoulton	29	TF 9800
Scourie	66	NC 1544
Scousburgh	63	HU 3717
Scrabster	67	ND 0970
Scrainwood	53	NT 9909
Scrane End	35	TF 3841
Scraptoft	26	SK 6405
Scratby	29	TG 5115
Scrayingham	38	SE 7360
Scredington	35	TF 0940
Scremby	35	TF 4467
Scremerston	53	NU 0049
Screveton	34	SK 7343
Scriven	38	SE 3458
Scrooby	34	SK 6590
Scropton	33	SK 1930
Scrub Hill	35	TF 2355
Scruton	42	SE 2992
Sculthorpe	28	TF 8931
Scunthorpe	39	SE 8910
Seaborough	7	ST 4205
Seacombe	32	SJ 3190
Seacroft	35	TF 5660
Seafield	51	NT 0066
Seaford	12	TV 4899
Seaforth	32	SJ 3297
Seagrave	34	SK 6117
Seaham	47	NZ 4149
Seahouses	53	NU 2132
Seal	12	TQ 5556
Sealand	32	SJ 3268
Seamer (N Yorks.)	42	NZ 4910
Seamer (N Yorks.)	43	TA 0183
Seamill	49	NS 2047
Sea Palling	29	TG 4327
Searby	39	TA 0605
Seasalter	13	TR 0864
Seathwaite (Cumbr.)	40	NY 2312
Seathwaite (Cumbr.)	40	SD 2296
Seaton (Corn.)	4	SX 3054
Seaton (Cumbr.)	40	NY 0130
Seaton (Devon.)	7	SY 2490
Seaton (Durham)	47	NZ 4049
Seaton (Humbs.)	39	TA 1646
Seaton (Leic.)	27	SP 9098
Seaton (Northum.)	47	NZ 3276
Seaton Carew	42	NZ 5229
Seaton Delaval	47	NZ 3075
Seaton Ross	38	SE 7741
Seaton Sluice	47	NZ 3376
Seave Green	42	NZ 5600
Seaview	9	SZ 6291
Seavington St. Mary	7	ST 3914
Seavington St. Michael	7	ST 4015
Sebergham	46	NY 3541
Seckington	26	SK 2607
Sedbergh	41	SD 6592
Sedbusk	41	SD 8891
Sedgeberrow	25	SP 0238
Sedgebrook	34	SK 8537
Sedgefield	42	NZ 3528
Sedgeford	28	TF 7136
Sedgehill	8	ST 8627
Sedgley	25	SO 9193
Sedgwick	40	SD 5186
Sedlescombe	12	TQ 7818
Seend	17	ST 9460
Seend Cleeve	17	ST 9260
Seer Green	19	SU 9691
Seething	29	TM 3197
Sefton	36	SD 3500
Seghill	47	NZ 2874
Seighford	33	SJ 8725
Seilebost	63	NG 0696
Seisdon	25	SO 8394
Selattyn	31	SJ 2633
Selborne	10	SU 7433
Selby	38	SE 6132
Selham	11	SU 9320
Selkirk	52	NT 4728
Sellack	17	SO 5627
Sellafirth	63	HU 5198
Sellindge	13	TR 0938
Selling	13	TR 0356
Sells Green	17	ST 9462
Selly Oak	25	SP 0482
Selmeston	12	TQ 5007
Selsdon	12	TQ 3562
Selsey	11	SZ 8593
Selsfield Common	12	TQ 3434
Selston	34	SK 4553
Selworthy	6	SS 9146
Semblister	63	HU 3350
Semer	21	TL 9946
Semington	17	ST 8960

South Raynham Sturry

South Raynham 28 TF 8723
Southrepps 29 TG 2536
South Reston 35 TF 4082
Southrey 35 TF 1366
Southrop 17 SP 1903
Southrope 10 SU 6744
South Runcton 28 TF 6308
South Scarle 34 SK 8463
Southsea 9 SZ 6498
South Shian 54 NM 9042
South Shields 47 NZ 3667
South Shore 36 SD 3033
South Skirlaugh 39 TA 1439
South Somercotes 35 TF 4193
South Stainley 38 SE 3063
South Stoke (Avon) 17 ST 7461
South Stoke (Oxon.) 18 SU 6083
South Stoke (W Susx) 11 TQ 0210
South Street 12 TQ 3918
South Tawton 5 SX 6594
South Thoresby 35 TF 4077
South Tidworth 10 SU 2347
South Town (Hants.) 9 SU 6536
Southwaite 46 NY 4445
South Walsham 29 TG 3613
Southwark 12 TQ 3278
South Warnborough 10 SU 7247
Southwater 11 TQ 1526
Southway 7 ST 5142
South Weald 20 TQ 5793
Southwell (Dorset) 8 SY 6870
Southwell (Notts.) 34 SK 7053
South Weston 18 SU 7098
South Wheatley 4 SX 2492
Southwick (Hants.) 9 SU 6208
Southwick (Northants.) 27 TL 0192
Southwick (Tyne and Wear) 47 NZ 3758
Southwick (Wilts.) 17 ST 8354
Southwick (W Susx) 11 TQ 2405
South Widcombe 17 ST 5756
South Wigston 26 SP 5898
South Willingham 35 TF 1983
South Wingfield 33 SK 3755
South Witham 34 SK 9219
Southwold 29 TM 5076
South Wonston 9 SU 4635
Southwood (Norf.) 29 TG 3905
Southwood (Somer.) 7 ST 5533
South Woodham Ferrers 20 TQ 8097
South Wootton 28 TF 6422
South Wraxall 17 ST 8364
South Zeal 5 SX 6593
Soutra Mains 52 NT 4559
Sowerby (N Yorks.) 42 SE 4381
Sowerby (W Yorks.) 37 SE 0423
Sowerby Bridge 37 SE 0523
Sowerby Row 46 NY 3940
Sowton 5 SX 9792
Spa Common 29 TG 2930
Spalding 35 TF 2422
Spaldington 38 SE 7533
Spaldwick 27 TL 1272
Spalford 34 SK 8369
Sparham 29 TG 0619
Spark Bridge 40 SD 3084
Sparkford 8 ST 6026
Sparkwell 4 SX 5757
Sparrowpit 33 SK 0980
Sparsholt (Hants.) 9 SU 4331
Sparsholt (Oxon.) 18 SU 3487
Spaunton 43 SE 7289
Spaxton 7 ST 2236
Spean Bridge 55 NN 2281
Speen (Berks.) 10 SU 4568
Speen (Bucks.) 19 SU 8499
Speeton 43 TA 1574
Speke 32 SJ 4383
Speldhurst 12 TQ 5541
Spellbrook 20 TL 4817
Spelsbury 18 SP 3421
Spencers Wood 10 SU 7166
Spennithorne 42 SE 1489
Spennymoor 42 NZ 2533
Spetchley 25 SO 8953
Spettisbury 8 ST 9002
Spexhall 29 TM 3780
Spey Bay 61 NJ 3866
Spilsby 35 TF 4066
Spindlestone 53 NU 1533
Spinningdale 65 NH 6789
Spirthill 17 ST 9975
Spital 67 ND 1654
Spithurst 12 TQ 4217
Spittal (Dyfed) 14 SM 9723
Spittal (Lothian) 52 NT 4677
Spittal (Northum.) 53 NU 0051
Spittalfield 56 NO 1040
Spittal of Glenmuick 57 NO 3184
Spittal of Glenshee 56 NO 1070
Spixworth 29 TG 2415
Spofforth 38 SE 3650
Spondon 33 SK 3935
Spooner Row 29 TM 0997
Sporle 28 TF 8411
Spott 52 NT 6775
Spratton 26 SP 7170
Spreakley 10 SU 8341
Spreyton 5 SX 6996
Spridlington 34 TF 0084
Springburn 50 NS 5968
Springfield (Fife.) 57 NO 3411
Springfield (Grampn.) 61 NJ 0559
Springfield (W Mids.) 25 SP 1082
Springholm 45 NX 8070
Springside 50 NS 3639
Springthorpe 34 SK 8789
Sproatley 39 TA 1934
Sproston Green 32 SJ 7367
Sprotbrough 38 SE 5302
Sproughton 21 TM 1244
Sprouston 53 NT 7535
Sprowston 29 TG 2412
Sproxton (Leic.) 34 SK 8524
Sproxton (N Yorks.) 42 SE 6181
Spurstow 32 SJ 5556
Stackhouse 37 SD 8165
Stacksteads 37 SD 8421
Staddiscombe 4 SX 5151
Staddlethorpe 39 SE 8428
Stadhampton 18 SU 6098
Staffield 46 NY 5442
Staffin 58 NG 4967
Stafford 33 SJ 9223
Stagsden 27 SP 9849
Stainburn 37 SE 2448
Stainby 34 SK 9022
Staincross 38 SE 3210
Staindrop 41 NZ 1220
Staines 11 TQ 0471
Stainfield (Lincs.) 35 TF 0724
Stainfield (Lincs.) 35 TF 1173
Stainforth (N Yorks.) 37 SD 8267
Stainforth (S Yorks.) 38 SE 6411
Staining 36 SD 3435
Stainland 37 SE 0719
Stainsacre 43 NZ 9108
Stainton (Cleve.) 42 NZ 4714
Stainton (Cumbr.) 40 NY 4827
Stainton (Cumbr.) 40 SD 5285
Stainton (Durham) 41 NZ 0718
Stainton (N Yorks.) 41 SE 1096
Stainton (S Yorks.) 34 SK 5593
Stainton by Langworth 35 TF 0577
Staintondale 43 SE 9898
Stainton le Vale 35 TF 1794
Stainton with Adgarley 36 SD 2472
Stair (Cumbr.) 40 NY 2321
Stair (Strath.) 50 NS 4323
Staithes 43 NZ 7818
Stakeford 47 NZ 2785
Stake Pool 36 SD 4148
Stalbridge 8 ST 7317
Stalbridge Weston 8 ST 7216
Stalham 29 TG 3725
Stalham Green 29 TG 3824
Stalisfield Green 13 TQ 9652
Stallingborough 39 TA 2011
Stalling Busk 41 SD 9185
Stalmine 36 SD 3745
Stalybridge 37 SJ 9698
Stambourne 20 TL 7238
Stamford 27 TF 0207
Stamford Bridge 38 SE 7155
Stamfordham 47 NZ 0772
Stanborough 19 TL 2210
Stanbridge (Beds.) 19 SP 9623
Stanbridge (Dorset) 8 SU 0003
Stand 50 NS 7668
Standburn 51 NS 9274
Standeford 25 SJ 9107
Standen 13 TQ 8539
Standford 10 SU 8134
Standish 36 SD 5609
Standlake 18 SP 3902
Standon (Hants.) 9 SU 4227
Standon (Herts.) 20 TL 3922
Standon (Staffs.) 32 SJ 8134
Stane 50 NS 8859
Stanfield 29 TF 9320
Stanford (Beds.) 27 TL 1641
Stanford (Kent) 13 TR 1238
Stanford Bishop 24 SO 6851
Stanford Bridge 24 SO 7165
Stanford Dingley 10 SU 5771
Stanford in the Vale 18 SU 3493
Stanford le Hope 20 TQ 6882
Stanford on Avon 26 SP 5878
Stanford on Soar 34 SK 5422
Stanford on Teme 24 SO 7065
Stanford Rivers 20 TL 5301
Stanghow 42 NZ 6715
Stanhoe 28 TF 8036
Stanhope 41 NY 9939
Stanion 27 SP 9187
Stanley (Derby.) 33 SK 4140
Stanley (Durham) 47 NZ 1953
Stanley (Staffs.) 33 SJ 9252
Stanley (Tays.) 56 NO 1033
Stanley (W Yorks.) 38 SE 3422
Stanmer 12 TQ 3309
Stanmore (Berks.) 10 SU 4778
Stanmore (Gtr London) 19 TQ 1692
Stannington (Northum.) 47 NZ 2179
Stannington (S Yorks.) 33 SK 2988
Stansbatch 23 SO 3461
Stansfield 20 TL 7852
Stanstead 20 TL 8449
Stanstead Abbots 20 TL 3811
Stansted 12 TQ 6062
Stansted Mountfitchet 20 TL 5124
Stanton (Glos.) 25 SP 0634
Stanton (Northum.) 47 NZ 1390
Stanton (Staffs.) 33 SK 1246
Stanton (Suff.) 29 TL 9673
Stanton by Bridge 33 SK 3627
Stanton by Dale 34 SK 4637
Stanton Drew 17 ST 5963
Stanton Fitzwarren 17 SU 1790
Stanton Harcourt 18 SP 4105
Stanton Hill 34 SK 4860
Stanton in Peak 33 SK 2464
Stanton Lacy 24 SO 4978
Stanton Long 24 SO 5690
Stanton on the Wolds 34 SK 6330
Stanton Prior 17 ST 0962
Stanton St. Bernard 17 SU 0962
Stanton St. John 18 SP 5709
Stanton St. Quintin 17 ST 9079
Stanton Street 29 TL 9566
Stanton under Bardon 26 SK 4610
Stanton upon Hine Heath 32 SJ 5624
Stanton Wick 17 ST 6162
Stanwardine in the Fields 32 SJ 4124
Stanway (Essex) 21 TL 9324
Stanway (Glos.) 25 SP 0532
Stanwell 11 TQ 0574
Stanwell Moor 11 TQ 0474
Stanwick 27 SP 9871
Stanydale 63 HU 2850
Stape 43 SE 7993
Stapehill 8 SU 0500
Stapeley 32 SJ 6749
Staple 13 TR 2756
Staple Cross 12 TQ 7822
Staplefield 11 TQ 2728
Staple Fitzpaine 7 ST 2618
Stapleford (Cambs.) 20 TL 4751
Stapleford (Herts.) 20 TL 3117
Stapleford (Leic.) 34 SK 8018
Stapleford (Lincs.) 34 SK 8757
Stapleford (Notts.) 34 SK 4837
Stapleford (Wilts.) 8 SU 0637
Stapleford Abbots 20 TQ 5096
Stapleford Tawney 20 TQ 5098
Staplegrove 7 ST 2126
Staple Hill 7 ST 2416
Staplehurst 12 TQ 7843
Staplers 9 SZ 5189
Stapleton (Avon) 17 ST 6175
Stapleton (Cumbr.) 46 NY 5071
Stapleton (Here. and Worc.) 23 SO 3265
Stapleton (Leic.) 26 SP 4398
Stapleton (N Yorks.) 42 NZ 2612
Stapleton (Salop) 24 SJ 4604
Stapleton (Somer.) 7 ST 4621
Stapley 7 ST 1813
Staploe 27 TL 1460
Star (Dyfed) 14 SN 2435
Star (Fife.) 57 NO 3103
Star (Somer.) 16 ST 4358
Starbotton 41 SD 9574
Starcross 5 SX 9781
Starston 29 TM 2384
Startforth 41 NZ 0416
Startley 17 ST 9482
Stathe 7 ST 3728
Stathern 34 SK 7731
Station Town 42 NZ 4036
Staughton Highway 27 TL 1364
Staunton (Glos.) 16 SO 5412
Staunton (Glos.) 17 SO 7929
Staunton on Arrow 24 SO 3660
Staunton on Wye 24 SO 3645
Staveley (Cumbr.) 40 SD 3786
Staveley (Cumbr.) 40 SD 4698
Staveley (Derby.) 33 SK 4374
Staveley (N Yorks.) 38 SE 3662
Staverton (Devon.) 5 SX 7964
Staverton (Glos.) 17 SO 8923
Staverton (Northants.) 26 SP 5461
Staverton (Wilts.) 17 ST 8560
Stawell 7 ST 3638
Staxigoe 67 ND 3852
Staxton 43 TA 0179
Staylittle 22 SN 8892
Staythorpe 34 SK 7554
Stean 41 SE 0873
Stearsby 38 SE 6171
Steart 7 ST 2745
Stebbing 20 TL 6624
Stedham 11 SU 8622
Steele Road 46 NY 5292
Steen's Bridge 24 SO 5457
Steep 10 SU 7525
Steeple (Dorset) 8 SY 9080
Steeple (Essex) 21 TL 9303
Steeple Ashton 17 ST 9056
Steeple Aston 18 SP 4725
Steeple Barton 18 SP 4424
Steeple Bumpstead 20 TL 6741
Steeple Claydon 18 SP 7027
Steeple Gidding 27 TL 1381
Steeple Langford 8 SU 0337
Steeple Morden 27 TL 2842
Steeton 37 SE 0344
Steinmanhill 62 NJ 7642
Stelling Minnis 13 TR 1446
Stemster 67 ND 1862
Stenalees 3 SX 0157
Stenhousemuir 50 NS 8682
Stenness 63 HU 2176
Stenton 52 NT 6274
Steppingley 19 TL 0135
Stepps 50 NS 6668
Sternfield 21 TM 3861
Stert 17 SU 0259
Stetchworth 20 TL 6458
Stevenage 19 TL 2325
Stevenston 49 NS 2642
Steventon (Hants.) 10 SU 5547
Steventon (Oxon.) 18 SU 4691
Stevington 27 SP 9853
Stewartby 27 TL 0242
Stewarton 50 NS 4246
Stewkley 19 SP 8525
Stewton 35 TF 3687
Steyning 11 TQ 1711
Steynton 14 SM 9108
Stibb 4 SS 2210
Stibbard 29 TF 9828
Stibb Cross 4 SS 4314
Stibb Green 10 SU 2262
Stibbington 27 TL 0898
Stichill 52 NT 7138
Sticker 2 SW 9750
Stickford 35 TF 3560
Sticklepath 5 SX 6394
Stickney 35 TF 3456
Stiffkey 29 TF 9743
Stifford's Bridge 24 SO 7348
Stilligarry 63 NF 7638
Stillingfleet 38 SE 5940
Stillington (Cleve. Durham) 42 NZ 3723
Stillington (N Yorks.) 38 SE 5867
Stilton 27 TL 1689
Stinchcombe 17 ST 7298
Stinsford 8 SY 7191
St Ippollitts 19 TL 1927
Stirchley 24 SJ 6906
Stirling 50 NS 7993
Stisted 20 TL 8024
Stithians 2 SW 7336
Stivichall 26 SP 3376
Stixwould 35 TF 1765
Stoak 32 SJ 4273
Stobieside 50 NS 6239
Stobo 51 NT 1837
Stoborough 8 SY 9286
Stoborough Green 8 SY 9184
Stock 20 TQ 6998
Stockbridge 9 SU 3535
Stockbriggs 50 NS 7936
Stockbury 13 TQ 8461
Stockcross 10 SU 4368
Stockdalewath 46 NY 3845
Stockerston 27 SP 8397
Stock Green 25 SO 9859
Stockingford 26 SP 3391
Stocking Pelham 20 TL 4529
Stockinish 63 NG 1391
Stockland 7 ST 2404
Stockland Bristol 7 ST 2443
Stockleigh English 5 SS 8406
Stockleigh Pomeroy 5 SS 8703
Stockley 17 SU 0067
Stockport 33 SJ 8989
Stocksbridge 37 SK 2798
Stocksfield 47 NZ 0561
Stockton (Here. and Worc.) 24 SO 5161
Stockton (Norf.) 29 TM 3894
Stockton (Salop) 24 SO 7299
Stockton (Warw.) 26 SP 4363
Stockton (Wilts.) 8 ST 9738
Stockton Heath 32 SJ 6185
Stockton-on-Tees 42 NZ 4419
Stockton on Teme 24 SO 7167
Stockton on the Forest 38 SE 6556
Stockwith 34 SK 7994
Stock Wood 25 SP 0058
Stodmarsh 13 TR 2160
Stody 29 TG 0535
Stoer 64 NC 0428
Stoford (Somer.) 7 ST 5613
Stoford (Wilts.) 8 SU 0835
Stogumber 7 ST 0937
Stogursey 7 ST 2042
Stoke (Devon.) 4 SS 2324
Stoke (Hants.) 10 SU 4051
Stoke (Hants.) 10 SU 7202
Stoke (Kent) 12 TQ 8275
Stoke Abbott 7 ST 4500
Stoke Albany 26 SP 8088
Stoke Ash 29 TM 1170
Stoke Bardolph 34 SK 6441
Stoke Bliss 24 SO 6562
Stoke Bruerne 26 SP 7450
Stoke by Clare 20 TL 7443
Stoke-by-Nayland 21 TL 9836
Stoke Canon 5 SX 9397
Stoke Charity 10 SU 4839
Stoke Climsland 4 SX 3574
Stoke D'Abernon 11 TQ 1259
Stoke Doyle 27 TL 0286
Stoke Dry 27 SP 8597
Stoke Ferry 28 TF 7000
Stoke Fleming 5 SX 8648
Stokeford 8 SY 8787
Stoke Gabriel 5 SX 8457
Stoke Gifford 17 ST 6280
Stoke Golding 26 SP 3997
Stoke Goldington 27 SP 8348
Stokeham 34 SK 7876
Stoke Hammond 19 SP 8829
Stoke Holy Cross 29 TG 2301
Stokeinteignhead 5 SX 9170
Stoke Lacy 24 SO 6149
Stoke Lyne 18 SP 5628
Stoke Mandeville 19 SP 8310
Stokenchurch 18 SU 7596
Stoke Newington 20 TQ 3286
Stokenham 5 SX 8042
Stoke-on-Trent 33 SJ 8745
Stoke Orchard 17 SO 9128
Stoke Poges 19 SU 9884
Stoke Prior (Here. and Worc.) 24 SO 5256
Stoke Prior (Here. and Worc.) 25 SO 9467
Stoke Rivers 6 SS 6335
Stoke Rochford 34 SK 9127
Stoke Row 18 SU 6883
Stoke St. Gregory 7 ST 3426
Stoke St. Mary 7 ST 2622
Stoke St. Michael 8 ST 6646
Stoke St. Milborough 24 SO 5682
Stokesay 24 SO 4381
Stokes Bay 9 SZ 5897
Stokesby 29 TG 4310
Stokesley 42 NZ 5208
Stoke sub Hamdon 7 ST 4717
Stoke Talmage 18 SU 6799
Stoke Trister 8 ST 7328
Stoke upon Tern 32 SJ 6327
Stolford 7 ST 2245
Stondon Massey 20 TL 5800
Stone (Bucks.) 18 SP 7812
Stone (Glos.) 17 ST 6895
Stone (Here. and Worc.) 25 SO 8675
Stone (Kent) 12 TQ 5774
Stone (Kent) 13 TQ 9427
Stone (Staffs.) 33 SJ 9034
Stone Allerton 7 ST 3950
Ston Easton 17 ST 6253
Stonebroom 33 SK 4159
Stone Cross 12 TQ 6104
Stonefield 50 NS 6957
Stonegate 12 TQ 6628
Stonegate Crofts 62 NK 0339
Stonegrave 42 SE 6577
Stonehaugh 46 NY 7976
Stonehaven 57 NO 8685
Stone House (Cumbr.) 41 SD 7785
Stonehouse (Glos.) 17 SO 8005
Stonehouse (Northum.) 46 NY 6958
Stonehouse (Strath.) 50 NS 7546
Stoneleigh 26 SP 3272
Stonely 27 TL 1067
Stonesby 34 SK 8224
Stonesfield 18 SP 3917
Stones Green 21 TM 1626
Stoneybridge 63 NF 7433
Stoneyburn 51 NS 9762
Stoney Cross 9 SU 2511
Stoneygate 26 SK 6102
Stoneyhills 21 TQ 9497
Stoneykirk 44 NX 0853
Stoney Middleton 33 SK 2275
Stoney Stanton 26 SP 4894
Stoney Stratton 7 ST 6539
Stoney Stretton 24 SJ 3809
Stoneywood 62 NJ 8910
Stonganess 63 HP 5402
Stonham Aspal 21 TM 1359
Stonnall 25 SK 0603
Stonor 18 SU 7388
Stonton Wyville 26 SP 7395
Stonybreck 63 HU 2071
Stony Stratford 26 SP 7840
Stoodleigh 5 SS 9218
Stopham 11 TQ 0219
Stopsley 19 TL 1023
Storeton 32 SJ 3084
Stornoway 63 NB 4333
Storridge 24 SO 7448
Storrington 11 TQ 0814
Storth 40 SD 4780
Stotfold 19 TL 2136
Stottesdon 24 SO 6782
Stoughton (Leic.) 26 SK 6402
Stoughton (Surrey) 11 SU 9851
Stoughton (W Susx) 10 SU 8011
Stoul 58 NM 7594
Stoulton 25 SO 9049
Stourbridge 25 SO 8984
Stourhead 8 ST 7734
Stourpaine 8 ST 8509
Stourport-on-Severn 25 SO 8171
Stour Provost 8 ST 7921
Stour Row 8 ST 8220
Stourton (Here. and Worc.) 25 SO 8585
Stourton (Warw.) 18 SP 2936
Stourton (Wilts.) 8 ST 7733
Stourton Caundle 8 ST 7114
Stove 63 HY 6036
Stoven 29 TM 4481
Stow (Borders) 52 NT 4644
Stow (Lincs.) 34 SK 8781
Stow Bardolph 28 TF 6205
Stow Bedon 29 TL 9596
Stowbridge 28 TF 6007
Stow cum Quy 28 TL 5260
Stowe (Salop) 23 SO 3173
Stowe (Staffs.) 33 SK 0027
Stowell 8 ST 6822
Stowford 4 SX 4386
Stowlangtoft 29 TL 9568
Stow Longa 27 TL 1171
Stow Maries 20 TQ 8399
Stowmarket 21 TM 0458
Stow-on-the-Wold 17 SP 1925
Stowting 13 TR 1241
Stowupland 29 TM 0659
Straad 49 NS 0462
Strachan 62 NO 6792
Strachur 55 NN 0901
Stradbroke 29 TM 2373
Stradishall 20 TL 7452
Stradsett 28 TF 6605
Stragglethorpe 34 SK 9152
Straiton (Lothian) 51 NT 2766
Straiton (Strath.) 44 NS 3804
Straloch (Grampn.) 62 NJ 8621
Straloch (Tays.) 56 NO 0463
Stramshall 33 SK 0735
Strands 40 NY 1204
Stranraer 44 NX 0660
Strata Florida 22 SN 7465
Stratfield Mortimer 10 SU 6764
Stratfield Saye 10 SU 6961
Stratfield Turgis 10 SU 6959
Stratford St. Andrew 29 TM 3560
Stratford St. Mary 21 TM 0434
Stratford Tony 8 SU 0926
Stratford-upon-Avon 26 SP 2055
Strathan (Highld.) 64 NC 0821
Strathan (Highld.) 59 NM 9891
Strathaven 50 NS 7044
Strathblane 50 NS 5679
Strathcarron 59 NG 9442
Strathconon 60 NH 4055
Strathdon 61 NJ 3513
Strath Fleet 66 NC 7016
Strath Gairloch 64 NG 7977
Strathkanaird 66 Nc 1501
Strathkinness 57 NO 4516
Strathmiglo 56 NO 2109
Strathpeffer 60 NH 4858
Strathwhillan 49 NS 0235
Strathy 67 NC 8465
Strathyre 55 NN 5617
Stratton (Corn.) 4 SS 2306
Stratton (Dorset) 8 SY 6593
Stratton (Glos.) 17 SP 0103
Stratton Audley 18 SP 6026
Stratton-on-the-Fosse 8 ST 6550
Stratton St. Margaret 17 SU 1787
Stratton St. Michael 29 TM 2093
Stratton Strawless 29 TG 2220
Stravithie 57 NO 5311
Streat 12 TQ 3515
Streatham 11 TQ 2972
Streatley (Beds.) 19 TL 0728
Streatley (Berks.) 18 SU 5980
Street (Lancs.) 36 SD 5252
Street (N Yorks.) 43 NZ 7304
Street (Somer.) 7 ST 4836
Street End 10 SZ 8599
Streethay 25 SK 1410
Streetly 25 SP 0898
Strefford 24 SO 4485
Strensall 38 SE 6360
Strensham 25 SO 9040
Stretcholt 7 ST 2943
Strete 5 SX 8447
Stretford 32 SJ 7894
Stretford Court 24 SO 4455
Strethall 20 TL 4939
Stretham 28 TL 5174
Strettington 11 SU 8807
Stretton (Ches.) 32 SJ 4452
Stretton (Ches.) 32 SJ 6182
Stretton (Derby.) 33 SK 3961
Stretton (Leic.) 34 SK 9415
Stretton (Staffs.) 25 SJ 8811
Stretton (Staffs.) 33 SK 2526
Stretton en le Field 26 SK 3012
Stretton Grandison 24 SO 6344
Stretton Heath 24 SJ 3610
Stretton-on-Dunsmore 26 SP 4072
Stretton on Fosse 18 SP 2238
Stretton under Fosse 26 SP 4581
Stretton Westwood 24 SO 5998
Strichen 62 NJ 9455
Stringston 7 ST 1742
Strixton 27 SP 9061
Stroat 17 ST 5798
Stromeferry 59 NG 8634
Stromemore 59 NG 8635
Stromness 63 HY 2509
Stronachlachar 55 NN 4010
Stronchrubie 66 NC 2419
Strond 63 NG 0384
Strone (Highld.) 60 NH 5228
Strone (Strath.) 49 NS 1980
Stronenaba 55 NN 2084
Stronmilchan 55 NN 1528
Strontian 54 NM 8161
Strood 12 TQ 7369
Stroud (Glos.) 17 SO 8504
Stroud (Hants.) 10 SU 7223
Struan 58 NG 3438
Struan Station 56 NN 8065
Strubby 35 TF 4582
Strumpshaw 29 TG 3507
Strutherhill 50 NS 7650
Struy 60 NH 4039
Stuartfield 62 NJ 9745
Stubbington 9 SU 5503
Stubbins 37 SD 7918
Stubhampton 8 ST 9113
Stubton 34 SK 8748
Stuckgowan 55 NN 3202
Stuckton 8 SU 1613
Studham 19 TL 0215
Studland 8 SZ 0382
Studley (Oxon.) 18 SP 5912
Studley (Warw.) 25 SP 0763
Studley (Wilts.) 17 ST 9671
Studley Roger 38 SE 2970
Stump Cross 20 TL 5044
Stuntney 28 TL 5578
Sturbridge 32 SJ 8330
Sturmer 20 TL 6944
Sturminster Common 8 ST 7812
Sturminster Marshall 8 SY 9499
Sturminster Newton 8 ST 7813
Sturry 13 TR 1760

Tidenham

Upper Gravenhurst

Tidenham 16 ST 5596
Tideswell 33 SK 1575
Tidmarsh 10 SU 6374
Tidmington 18 SP 2538
Tidpit 8 SU 0718
Tiers Cross 14 SM 9010
Tiffield 26 SP 6951
Tifty 62 NJ 7740
Tigerton 57 NO 5364
Tigharry 63 NF 7171
Tighnabruaich 49 NR 9772
Tighnafiline 64 NG 8789
Tigley 5 SX 7560
Tilbrook 27 TL 0769
Tilbury 12 TQ 6376
Tile Cross 25 SP 1687
Tile Hill 26 SP 2777
Tilehurst 10 SU 6673
Tilford 11 SU 8743
Tillathrowie 61 NJ 4634
Tillicoultry 50 NS 9197
Tillingham 21 TL 9903
Tillington (Here. and Worc.) 24 SO 4645
Tillington (W Susx) 11 SU 9621
Tillington Common 24 SO 4546
Tillyarblet 57 NO 5267
Tillycorthie 62 NJ 9123
Tillyfourie 62 NJ 6412
Tillygarmond 62 NO 6393
Tillygreig 62 NJ 8823
Tilmanstone 13 TR 3051
Tilney All Saints 28 TF 5618
Tilney High End 28 TF 5617
Tilney St. Lawrence 28 TF 5414
Tilshead 8 SU 0347
Tilstock 32 SJ 5337
Tilston 32 SJ 4551
Tilstone Fearnall 32 SJ 5660
Tilsworth 19 SP 9724
Tilton on the Hill 26 SK 7405
Timberland 35 TF 1158
Timbersbrook 33 SJ 8962
Timberscombe 6 SS 9542
Timble 37 SE 1752
Timperley 32 SJ 7988
Timsbury (Avon) 17 ST 6658
Timsbury (Hants.) 9 SU 3424
Timworth Green 28 TL 8669
Tincleton 8 SY 7691
Tindale 46 NY 6159
Tingewick 18 SP 6533
Tingley 38 SE 2826
Tingrith 19 TL 0032
Tinhay 4 SX 4085
Tinshill 37 SE 2540
Tinsley 33 SK 3990
Tintagel 3 SX 0588
Tintern Parva 16 SO 5200
Tintinhull 7 ST 5019
Tintwistle 37 SK 0297
Tinwald 45 NY 0081
Tinwell 27 TF 0006
Tipperty 62 NJ 9627
Tipton 25 SO 9592
Tipton St. John 7 SY 0991
Tiptree 21 TL 8916
Tirabad 22 SN 8741
Tirley 17 SO 8328
Tirphil 16 SO 1303
Tirril 40 NY 5026
Tir y mynach 23 SH 9302
Tisbury 8 ST 9429
Tissington 33 SK 1752
Titchberry 4 SS 2427
Titchfield 9 SU 5305
Titchmarsh 27 TL 0279
Titchwell 28 TF 7543
Tithby 34 SK 6936
Titley 23 SO 3260
Titlington 53 NU 1015
Tittensor 33 SJ 8738
Tittleshall 28 TF 8920
Tiverton (Ches.) 32 SJ 5560
Tiverton (Devon.) 5 SS 9512
Tivetshall St. Margaret 29 TM 1787
Tivetshall St. Mary 29 TM 1686
Tixall 33 SJ 9722
Tixover 27 SK 9700
Toab 63 HU 3811
Tobermory 54 NM 5055
Toberonochy 54 NM 7408
Tobson 63 NB 1438
Tocher 62 NJ 6932
Tockenham 17 SU 0379
Tockenham Wick 17 SU 0381
Tockholes 36 SD 6623
Tockington 17 ST 6186
Tockwith 38 SE 4652
Todber 8 ST 7919
Toddington (Beds.) 19 TL 0129
Toddington (Glos.) 25 SP 0432
Todenham 18 SP 2436
Todhills 46 NY 3663
Todmorden 37 SD 9324
Todwick 34 SK 4984
Toft (Cambs.) 20 TL 3655
Toft (Ches.) 32 SJ 7676
Toft (Lincs.) 35 TF 0617
Toft Monks 29 TM 4295
Toft next Newton 35 TF 0488
Toftrees 28 TF 8927
Toftwood 29 TF 9811
Togston 47 NU 2401
Tokavaig 58 NG 6012
Tokers Green 10 SU 7077
Tolland 7 ST 1032
Tollard Royal 8 ST 9417
Toller Fratrum 7 SY 5797
Toller Porcorum 7 SY 5697
Tollerton (Notts.) 34 SK 6134
Tollerton (N Yorks.) 38 SE 5164
Tollesbury 21 TL 9510
Tolleshunt D'Arcy 21 TL 9312
Tolleshunt Major 21 TL 9011
Toll of Birness 62 NK 0034
Tolob 63 HU 3811
Tolpuddle 8 SY 7994
Tolstachaolais 63 NB 1938
Tolworth 11 TQ 1965
Tomatin 60 NH 8028
Tombreck 60 NH 6934
Tomdoun 59 NH 1501
Tomich (Highld.) 59 NH 3127
Tomich (Highld.) 60 NH 5348
Tomich (Highld.) 65 NH 7071
Tomintoul (Grampn.) 61 NJ 1618
Tomintoul (Grampn.) 61 NO 1490
Tomnavoulin 61 NJ 2026
Ton 16 SO 3301
Tonbridge 12 TQ 5845
Tondu 15 SS 8984
Tong (Lewis) 63 NB 4436
Tong (Salop) 24 SJ 7907
Tonge 33 SK 4123
Tongham 11 SU 8848
Tongland 45 NX 6953
Tongue 66 NC 5957
Tongwynlais 16 ST 1581
Tonna 15 SS 7798
Tonwell 20 TL 3317
Tonypandy 16 SS 9992
Tonyrefail 16 ST 0188
Toot Baldon 18 SP 5600
Toot Hill (Essex) 20 TL 5102
Toot Hill (Hants.) 9 SU 3718
Topcliffe 42 SE 3976
Topcroft 29 TM 2693
Topcroft Street 29 TM 2692
Toppesfield 20 TL 7337
Toppings 36 SD 7213
Topsham 5 SX 9788
Torbay 5 SX 8962
Torbeg 49 NR 8929
Torbryan 5 SX 8266
Torcastle 55 NN 1378
Torcross 5 SX 8242
Tore 60 NH 6052
Torhousemuir 44 NX 3957
Torksey 34 SK 8378
Torlum (Benbecula) 63 NF 7850
Torlundy 55 NN 1477
Tormarton 17 ST 7678
Tormitchell 44 NX 2394
Tormore 49 NR 8932
Tormsdale 67 ND 1350
Tornagrain 60 NH 7649
Tornahaish 61 NJ 2908
Tornaveen 62 NJ 6106
Torness 60 NH 5727
Torpenhow 40 NY 2039
Torphichen 51 NS 9672
Torphins 62 NJ 6202
Torpoint 4 SX 4355
Torquay 5 SX 9164
Torquhan 52 NT 4447
Torran (Raasay) 58 NG 5949
Torran (Strath.) 54 NM 8704
Torrance 50 NS 6174
Torridon 59 NG 9055
Torrin 58 NG 5720
Torrisdale 66 NC 6761
Torrish 67 NC 9718
Torrisholme 36 SD 4464
Torroble 66 NC 5904
Torry (Grampn.) 61 NJ 4339
Torry (Grampn.) 62 NJ 9404
Torryburn 51 NT 0286
Torrylin 49 NR 9621
Torterston 62 NK 0747
Torthorwald 45 NY 0378
Tortington 11 TQ 0005
Tortworth 17 ST 6992
Torvaig 58 NG 4944
Torver 40 SD 2894
Torwood 50 NS 8484
Torworth 34 SK 6586
Toscaig 58 NG 7138
Toseland 27 TL 2362
Tosside 37 SD 7655
Tostock 29 TL 9563
Totaig 58 NG 2050
Tote 58 NG 4149
Totegan 67 NC 8268
Totland 9 SZ 3286
Totley 33 SK 3179
Totnes 5 SX 8060
Toton 34 SK 5034
Totscore 58 NG 3866
Tottenham 20 TQ 3491
Tottenhill 28 TF 6310
Totteridge 19 TQ 2494
Totternhoe 19 SP 9921
Tottington 37 SD 7712
Totton 9 SU 3513
Tournaig 64 NG 8783
Toux (Grampn.) 61 NJ 5458
Toux (Grampn.) 61 NJ 9850
Tovil 12 TQ 7554
Toward 49 NS 1368
Towcester 26 SP 6948
Towednack 2 SW 4838
Tower Hamlets 20 TQ 3582
Towersey 18 SP 7305
Towie 61 NJ 4412
Towiemore 61 NJ 3945
Tow Law 41 NZ 1139
Town End (Cambs.) 27 TL 4195
Town End (Cumbr.) 40 SD 4483
Townend (Strath.) 50 NS 4076
Townhead 45 NX 6946
Townhead of Greenlaw 45 NX 7465
Townhill 51 NT 1089
Townshend 2 SW 5932
Town Street 28 TL 7786
Town Yetholm 53 NT 8228
Towthorpe 38 SE 6258
Towton 38 SE 4839
Towyn (Clwyd) 31 SH 9779
Towyn (Gwyn.) 22 SH 5800
Toynton All Saints 35 TF 3964
Toynton Fen Side 35 TF 3961
Toynton St. Peter 35 TF 4063
Toy's Hill 12 TQ 4751
Trabboch 50 NS 4321
Trabbochburn 50 NS 4621
Traboe 2 SW 7421
Tradespark (Highld.) 60 NH 8656
Tradespark (Orkney) 63 HY 4408
Trafford Park 37 SJ 7996
Trallong 15 SN 9629
Tranent 52 NT 4072
Trantlemore 67 NC 8853
Tranwell 47 NZ 1883
Trapp 15 SN 6519
Traprain 52 NT 5975
Traquair 51 NT 3334
Trawden 37 SD 9138
Trawsfynydd 30 SH 7035
Trealaw 16 SS 9992
Treales 36 SD 4432
Trearddur Bay 30 SH 2478
Treaslane 58 NG 3953
Trebartha 4 SX 2677
Trebarwith 3 SX 0585
Trebetherick 2 SW 9377
Treborough 7 ST 0036
Trebudannon 2 SW 8961
Treburley 4 SX 3477
Trecastle 15 SN 8729
Trecwn 14 SM 9632
Trecynon 16 SN 9903
Tredavoe 2 SW 4528
Tre-ddiog 14 SM 8928
Tredegar 16 SO 1409
Tredington 26 SP 2543
Tredinnick 2 SW 9270
Tredomen 23 SO 1231
Tredunnock 16 ST 3795
Treen 2 SW 3923
Treeton 34 SK 4387
Trefdraeth 30 SH 4070
Trefecca 23 SO 1431
Trefeglwys 23 SN 9690
Trefenter 22 SN 6068
Treffgarne 14 SM 9523
Treffynnon 14 SM 8428
Trefil 16 SO 1212
Trefilan 22 SN 5457
Trefnannau 31 SJ 2015
Trefnant 31 SJ 0570
Trefonen 31 SJ 2526
Trefor 30 SH 3779
Trefriw 31 SH 7763
Tregadillett 4 SX 2983
Tregaian 30 SH 4579
Tregare 16 SO 4110
Tregaron 22 SN 6759
Tregarth 30 SH 6067
Tregeare 4 SX 2486
Tregeiriog 31 SJ 1733
Tregele 30 SH 3592
Tregidden 2 SW 7523
Treglemais 14 SM 8229
Tregole 4 SX 1998
Tregonetha 2 SW 9563
Tregony 2 SW 9244
Tregoyd 23 SO 1937
Tre-groes 22 SN 4044
Tregurrian 2 SW 8465
Tregynon 23 SO 0999
Trehafod 16 ST 0491
Treharris 16 ST 1097
Treherbert 15 SS 9398
Trelawnyd 31 SJ 0879
Trelech 14 SN 2830
Trelech a'r Betws 14 SN 3026
Treleddyd-fawr 14 SM 7528
Trelewis 16 ST 1197
Trelights 3 SW 9879
Trelill 3 SX 0477
Trelleck 16 SO 5005
Trelleck Grange 16 SO 4901
Trelogan 31 SJ 1180
Trelystan 23 SJ 2603
Tremadog 30 SH 5640
Tremail 4 SX 1686
Tremain 14 SN 2348
Tremaine 4 SX 2388
Tremar 4 SX 2568
Trematon 4 SX 3959
Tremeirchion 31 SJ 0773
Trenance 2 SW 8567
Trenarren 3 SX 0348
Trench 24 SJ 6913
Treneglos 4 SX 2088
Trenewan 4 SX 1753
Trent 8 ST 5918
Trentham 33 SJ 8640
Trentishoe 6 SS 6448
Treoes 15 SS 9478
Treorchy 15 SS 9596
Tre'r-ddol 22 SN 6592
Tresaith 14 SN 2751
Trescott 25 SO 8497
Trescowe 2 SW 5731
Tresham 17 ST 7991
Tresillian 2 SW 8646
Tresinwen 14 SM 9040
Tresmeer 4 SX 2387
Tressait 56 NN 8160
Tresta (Fetlar) 63 HU 6190
Tresta (Shetld.) 63 HU 3650
Treswell 34 SK 7779
Trethurgy 3 SX 0355
Tretio 14 SM 7829
Tretire 16 SO 5124
Tretower 16 SO 1821
Treuddyn 31 SJ 2458
Trevalga 3 SX 0889
Trevanson 2 SW 9772
Trevarren 2 SW 9160
Trevarrick 2 SW 9843
Trevellas 2 SW 7452
Treverva 2 SW 7631
Trevethin 16 SO 2802
Trevigro 4 SX 3369
Trevine 14 SM 8432
Treviscoe 2 SW 9455
Trevone 2 SW 8975
Trevor 30 SH 3746
Trewarmett 3 SX 0686
Trewarthenick 2 SW 9044
Trewassa 4 SX 1486
Trewellard 2 SW 3733
Trewen 4 SX 2583
Trewidland 4 SX 2560
Trewint 4 SX 1897
Trewithian 2 SW 8737
Trewoon 3 SW 9952
Treyford 10 SU 8218
Trickett's Cross 8 SU 0801
Trimdon 42 NZ 3634
Trimdon Colliery 42 NZ 3835
Trimdon Grange 42 NZ 3735
Trimingham 29 TG 2738
Trimley 21 TM 2736
Trimley St. Mary 21 TM 2737
Trimpley 24 SO 7978
Trimsaran 15 SN 4504
Trimstone 6 SS 5043
Trinant 16 SO 2000
Tring 19 SP 9211
Trinity 57 NO 6061
Trislaig 55 NN 0874
Trispen 2 SW 8450
Tritlington 47 NZ 2092
Trochrie 56 NN 9740
Troedyraur 22 SN 3245
Troedyrhiw 16 SO 0702
Trofarth 31 SH 8571
Troon (Corn.) 2 SW 6638
Troon (Strath.) 49 NS 3230
Troston 28 TL 8972
Trottiscliffe 12 TQ 6460
Trotton 10 SU 8322
Troutbeck 40 NY 4103
Troutbeck Bridge 40 NY 4000
Trowbridge 17 ST 8557
Trow Green 17 SO 5706
Trowle Common 17 ST 8358
Trows 52 NT 6932
Trowse Newton 29 TG 2406
Trudoxhill 8 ST 7443
Trull 7 ST 2122
Trumisgarry 63 NF 8674
Trumpan 58 NG 2261
Trumpet 24 SO 6539
Trumpington 20 TL 4455
Trunch 29 TG 2834
Truro 2 SW 8244
Trusham 5 SX 8582
Trusley 33 SK 2535
Trusthorpe 35 TF 5183
Trysull 25 SO 8494
Tubney 18 SU 4498
Tuckenhay 5 SX 8156
Tuddenham (Suff.) 28 TL 7371
Tuddenham (Suff.) 21 TM 1948
Tudeley 12 TQ 6245
Tudhoe 42 NZ 2635
Tudweiloig 30 SH 2336
Tuffley 17 SO 8315
Tugby 26 SK 7601
Tugford 24 SO 5587
Tullibody 50 NS 8595
Tullich (Highld.) 65 NH 8576
Tullich (Strath.) 55 NN 0815
Tullich Muir 65 NH 7373
Tulliemet 56 NN 9952
Tulloch (Grampn.) 57 NO 7671
Tulloch (Highld.) 65 NH 6192
Tullochgorm 49 NR 9695
Tulloes 57 NO 5145
Tullybannocher 56 NN 7521
Tullyfergus 56 NO 2149
Tullynessle 61 NJ 5519
Tumble 15 SN 5411
Tumby 35 TF 2359
Tumby Woodside 35 TF 2657
Tummel Bridge 56 NN 7659
Tunstall (Humbs.) 39 TA 3032
Tunstall (Kent) 13 TQ 8961
Tunstall (Lancs.) 41 SD 6073
Tunstall (Norf.) 29 TG 4107
Tunstall (N Yorks.) 42 SE 2195
Tunstall (Staffs.) 33 SJ 8551
Tunstall (Suff.) 21 TM 3655
Tunstead 29 TG 3022
Tunworth 10 SU 6748
Tupsley 24 SO 5340
Turgis Green 10 SU 6959
Turin 57 NO 5352
Turkdean 17 SP 1017
Tur Langton 26 SP 7194
Turnastone 24 SO 3536
Turnberry 44 NS 2005
Turnditch 33 SK 2946
Turner's Hill 12 TQ 3435
Turners Puddle 8 SY 8293
Turnworth 8 ST 8107
Turriff 62 NJ 7249
Turton Bottoms 36 SD 7315
Turvey 27 SP 9452
Turville 18 SU 7691
Turville Heath 18 SU 7391
Turweston 18 SP 6037
Tushingham cum Grindley 32 SJ 5246
Tutbury 33 SK 2129
Tutnall 25 SO 9870
Tutshill 16 ST 5394
Tuttington 29 TG 2227
Tuxford 34 SK 7370
Twatt (Orkney) 63 HY 2624
Twatt (Shetld.) 63 HU 3252
Twechar 50 NS 6975
Tweedmouth 53 NT 9952
Tweedsmuir 51 NT 1024
Twelveheads 2 SW 7642
Twenty 35 TF 1520
Twerton 17 ST 7263
Twickenham 11 TQ 1473
Twigworth 17 SO 8421
Twineham 11 TQ 2519
Twinhoe 17 ST 7359
Twinstead 21 TL 8637
Twiss Green 32 SJ 6595
Twitchen (Devon) 6 SS 7830
Twitchen (Salop) 24 SO 3679
Two Bridges 5 SX 6075
Two Dales 33 SK 2762
Two Gates 26 SK 2101
Twycross 26 SK 3305
Twyford (Berks.) 10 SU 7975
Twyford (Bucks.) 18 SP 6626
Twyford (Hants.) 9 SU 4724
Twyford (Leic.) 26 SK 7210
Twyford (Norf.) 29 TG 0124
Twyford Common 24 SO 5135
Twynholm 45 NX 6654
Twyning 25 SO 8936
Twyning Green 25 SO 9037
Twynllanan 15 SN 7524
Twyn-y-Sheriff 16 SO 4005
Twywell 27 SP 9578
Tyberton 24 SO 3739
Tyburn 25 SP 1490
Tycroes 15 SN 6010
Tycrwyn 31 SJ 1018
Tydd Gote 35 TF 4518
Tydd St. Giles 35 TF 4216
Tydd St. Mary 35 TF 4418
Ty-hen 30 SH 1731
Tyldesley 36 SD 6902
Tyler Hill 13 TR 1460
Tylers Green 19 SU 9094
Tylorstown 16 ST 0195
Tylwch 23 SN 9780
Ty-mawr 31 SH 9047
Ty-nant (Clwyd) 31 SH 9944
Ty-nant (Gwyn.) 31 SH 9026
Tyndrum 55 NN 3330
Ty'n-dwr 31 SJ 2342
Tyneham 8 SY 8880
Tynehead 51 NT 3959
Tynemouth (Tyne and Wear) 47 NZ 3468
Tynewydd 15 SS 9399
Tyninghame 52 NT 6179
Tynribbie 55 NM 9446
Tynron 45 NX 8093
Tyn-y-ffridd 31 SJ 1230
Tyn-y-graig 23 SO 0149
Ty'n-y-groes 31 SH 7771
Tyringham 27 SP 8547
Tythegston 15 SS 8578
Tytherington (Avon) 17 ST 6788
Tytherington (Ches.) 33 SJ 9175
Tytherington (Somer.) 8 ST 7744
Tytherington (Wilts.) 8 ST 9140
Tytherleigh 7 ST 3203
Tywardreath 3 SX 0854
Tywyn 31 SH 7878
Tywyn Trewan 30 SH 3175

Uachdar 63 NF 7955
Ubbeston Green 29 TM 3271
Ubley 16 ST 5257
Uckerby 42 NZ 2402
Uckfield 12 TQ 4721
Uckington 17 SO 9224
Uddingston 50 NS 6960
Uddington 50 NS 8633
Udimore 13 TQ 8718
Udny Green 62 NJ 8726
Udstonhead 50 NS 7047
Uffcot 17 SU 1277
Uffculme 7 ST 0612
Uffington (Lincs.) 27 TF 0608
Uffington (Oxon.) 18 SU 3089
Uffington (Salop) 24 SJ 5313
Ufford (Northants.) 27 TF 0904
Ufford (Suff.) 21 TM 2953
Ufton 26 SP 3762
Ufton Nervet 10 SU 6367
Ugborough 5 SX 6755
Uggeshall 29 TM 4580
Ugglebarnby 43 NZ 8707
Ugley 20 TL 5128
Ugley Green 20 TL 5227
Ugthorpe 43 NZ 7911
Uig (Lewis) 63 NB 0534
Uig (Skye) 58 NG 1952
Uig (Skye) 58 NG 3963
Uigshader 58 NG 4246
Uisken 54 NM 3819
Ulbster 67 ND 3241
Ulceby (Humbs.) 39 TA 1014
Ulceby (Lincs.) 35 TF 4272
Ulcombe 13 TQ 8449
Uldale 40 NY 2536
Uley 17 ST 7898
Ulgham 47 NZ 2392
Ullapool 64 NH 1294
Ullenhall 25 SP 1267
Ullenwood 17 SO 9416
Ulleskelf 38 SE 5140
Ullesthorpe 26 SP 5087
Ulley 34 SK 4687
Ullingswick 24 SO 5950
Ullinish 58 NG 3237
Ullock 40 NY 0724
Ulpha 40 SD 1993
Ulrome 39 TA 1656
Ulsta 63 HU 4680
Ulverston 40 SD 2878
Ulzieside 50 NS 7708
Umberleigh 6 SS 6023
Unapool 66 NC 2333
Underbarrow 40 SD 4692
Underhoull 63 HP 5704
Under River 12 TQ 5552
Underwood 34 SK 4750
Undy 16 ST 4386
Unifirth 63 HU 2856
Union Cottage 62 NO 8290
Union Mills 43 SC 3578
Unstone 33 SK 3777
Upavon 17 SU 1354
Up Cerne 8 ST 6502
Upchurch 13 TQ 8467
Upcott 23 SO 3250
Upend 20 TL 7058
Up Exe 5 SS 9302
Uphall 51 NT 0571
Upham (Devon.) 5 SS 8808
Upham (Hants.) 9 SU 5320
Up Hatherley 17 SO 9120
Uphill (Avon) 16 ST 3158
Up Hill (Kent) 13 TR 2140
Up Holland 36 SD 5105
Uplawmoor 50 NS 4355
Upleadon 17 SO 7527
Upleatham 42 NZ 6319
Uplees 13 TQ 9964
Uplowman 7 ST 0115
Uplyme 7 SY 3293
Upminster 20 TQ 5686
Up Nately 10 SU 6951
Upnor 12 TQ 7470
Upottery 7 ST 2007
Uppark 10 SU 7717
Upper Affcot 24 SO 4486
Upper Ardchronie 65 NH 6188
Upper Arley 24 SO 7680
Upper Astrop 18 SP 5137
Upper Basildon 10 SU 5976
Upper Beeding 11 TQ 1910
Upper Benefield 27 SP 9789
Upper Boddington 26 SP 4853
Upper Borth 22 SN 6088
Upper Breinton 24 SO 4640
Upper Broughton 34 SK 6826
Upper Brow Top 36 SD 5258
Upper Bucklebury 10 SU 5368
Upper Caldecote 27 TL 1645
Upper Chapel 23 SO 0040
Upper Chute 10 SU 2953
Upper Clatford 10 SU 3543
Upper Clynnog 30 SH 4746
Upper Cokeham 11 TQ 1605
Upper Coll 63 NB 4539
Upper Cwmtwrch 15 SN 7611
Upper Dallachy 61 NJ 3662
Upper Dean 27 TL 0467
Upper Denby 37 SE 2207
Upper Derraid 61 NJ 0233
Upper Dicker 12 TQ 5510
Upper Elkstone 33 SK 0559
Upper End 33 SK 0876
Upper Ethie 65 NH 7663
Upper Farringdon 10 SU 7135
Upper Framilode 17 SO 7510
Upper Froyle 10 SU 7542
Upper Gravenhurst 19 TL 1136

Upper Green West Farleigh

Upper Green 10 SU 3663
Upper Hackney 33 SK 2961
Upper Hale 10 SU 8448
Upper Hambleton 27 SK 8907
Upper Hardres Court 13 TR 1550
Upper Hartfield 12 TQ 4634
Upper Heath 24 SO 5685
Upper Helmsley 38 SE 6956
Upper Heyford 18 SP 4926
Upper Hill 24 SO 4753
Upper Hopton 37 SE 1918
Upper Hulme 33 SK 0160
Upper Inglesham 18 SU 2096
Upper Killay 15 SS 5892
Upper Knockando 61 NJ 1843
Upper Lambourn 18 SU 3180
Upper Langwith 34 SK 5169
Upper Lochton 62 NO 6997
Upper Longdon 33 SK 0614
Upper Lybrook 17 SO 6015
Upper Maes-coed 23 SO 3335
Uppermill 37 SD 9906
Upper Minety 17 SU 0091
Upper North Dean 19 SU 8598
Upper Poppleton 38 SE 5554
Upper Quinton 25 SP 1746
Upper Sanday 63 HY 5303
Upper Sapey 24 SO 6863
Upper Scoulag 49 NS 1059
Upper Seagry 17 ST 9580
Upper Shelton 27 SP 9943
Upper Sheringham 29 TG 1441
Upper Skelmorlie 49 NS 1968
Upper Slaughter 17 SP 1523
Upper Soudley 17 SO 6610
Upper Stondon 19 TL 1535
Upper Stowe 26 SP 6456
Upper Street (Hants.) 8 SU 1418
Upper Street (Norf.) 29 TG 3516
Upper Sundon 19 TL 0527
Upper Swell 17 SP 1726
Upper Tasburgh 29 TM 2095
Upper Tean 33 SK 0139
Upperthong 37 SE 1208
Upper Tillyrie 56 NO 1006
Upperton 11 SU 9522
Upper Tooting 11 TQ 2772
Upper Town (Avon) 16 ST 5265
Uppertown (Stroma) 67 ND 3576
Upper Tysoe 26 SP 3343
Upper Upham 10 SU 2277
Upper Wardington 26 SP 4946
Upper Weald 18 SP 8037
Upper Weedon 26 SP 6258
Upper Wield 10 SU 6238
Upper Winchendon 18 SP 7414
Upper Woodford 8 SU 1237
Uppingham 27 SP 8699
Uppington 24 SJ 5909
Upsall 42 SE 4587
Upshire 20 TL 4100
Up Somborne 9 SU 3932
Upstreet 13 TR 2262
Up Sydling 8 ST 6201
Upton (Berks.) 11 SU 9879
Upton (Bucks.) 18 SP 7711
Upton (Cambs.) 27 TL 1778
Upton (Cambs.) 27 TF 1000
Upton (Ches.) 32 SJ 4069
Upton (Dorset) 8 SY 9893
Upton (Hants.) 10 SU 3555
Upton (Hants.) 9 SU 3716
Upton (Lincs.) 34 SK 8686
Upton (Mers.) 31 SJ 2687
Upton (Norf.) 29 TG 3912
Upton (Northants.) 26 SP 7160
Upton (Notts.) 34 SK 7354
Upton (Notts.) 34 SK 7476
Upton (Oxon.) 18 SU 5186
Upton (Somer.) 7 SS 9928
Upton (W Yorks.) 38 SE 4713
Upton Bishop 17 SO 6427
Upton Cheyney 17 ST 6969
Upton Cressett 24 SO 6592
Upton Cross 4 SX 2872
Upton Grey 10 SU 6948
Upton Hellions 5 SS 8303
Upton Lovell 8 ST 9440
Upton Magna 24 SJ 5512
Upton Noble 8 ST 7139
Upton Pyne 5 SX 9197
Upton St. Leonards 17 SO 8615
Upton Scudamore 8 ST 8647
Upton Snodsbury 25 SO 9454
Upton upon Severn 25 SO 8540
Upton Warren 25 SO 9267
Upwaltham 11 SU 9413
Upware 28 TL 5370
Upwell 28 TF 5002
Upwey 8 SY 6684
Upwood 27 TL 2582
Uradale 63 HU 4137
Urafirth (Shetld.) 63 HU 3078
Urchal 60 NH 7544
Urchany 60 NH 8849
Urchfont 17 SU 0356
Urdimarsh 24 SO 5249
Ure 63 HU 2180
Urgha 63 NG 1799
Urishay Common 23 SO 3137
Urlay Nook 42 NZ 4014
Urmston 32 SJ 7695
Urquhart 61 NJ 2863
Urra 42 NZ 5702
Urray 60 NH 5053
Urswick 40 SD 2674
Ushaw Moor 47 NZ 2342
Usk 16 SO 3701
Usselby 35 TF 0993
Utley 37 SE 0542
Uton 5 SX 8298
Utterby 35 TF 3093
Uttoxeter 33 SK 0933
Uwchmynydd (Gwyn.) 30 SH 1425
Uwch-mynydd (Gwyn.) 30 SH 6419
Uxbridge 19 TQ 0583
Uyeasound (Unst) 63 HP 5901
Uzmaston 14 SM 9714

Valley 30 SH 2979
Valleyfield 51 NT 0086
Valsgarth 63 HP 6413
Valtos (Skye) 58 NG 5163
Valtos (Lewis) 63 NB 0936
Vange 20 TQ 7287
Vardre 15 SN 6902
Varteg 16 SO 2506
Vatten 58 NG 2843
Vaul 48 NM 0448
Vauld, The 24 SO 5349
Vaynol Hall 30 SH 5369
Vaynor 16 SO 0410
Veensgarth 63 HU 4244
Velindre (Dyfed) 14 SN 1039
Velindre (Dyfed) 22 SN 3538
Velindre (Powys) 23 SO 1836
Veness (Eday) 63 HY 5729
Vennington 23 SJ 3309
Venn Ottery 7 SY 0791
Ventnor 9 SZ 5677
Vernham Dean 10 SU 3356
Vernham Street 10 SU 3457
Vernolds Common 24 SO 4780
Verwig 14 SN 1849
Verwood 8 SU 0908
Veryan 2 SW 9139
Vicarage 7 SY 2088
Vickerstown 36 SD 1868
Victoria 3 SW 9961
Vidlin 63 HU 4765
Viewpark 50 NS 7161
Villavin 4 SS 5816
Vinehall Street 12 TQ 7520
Vine's Cross 12 TQ 5917
Virginia Water 11 SU 9967
Virginstow 4 SX 3792
Vobster 8 ST 7048
Voe (Shetld.) 63 HU 4062
Vowchurch 24 SO 3636
Voxter 63 HU 3769
Voy 63 HY 2515

Wackerfield 42 NZ 1522
Wacton 29 TM 1891
Wadborough 25 SO 8947
Waddesdon 18 SP 7416
Waddingham 34 SK 9896
Waddington (Lancs.) 36 SD 7243
Waddington (Lincs.) 34 SK 9764
Wadebridge 3 SW 9972
Wadeford 7 ST 3110
Wadenhoe 27 TL 0083
Wadesmill 20 TL 3517
Wadhurst 12 TQ 6431
Wadshelf 33 SK 3171
Wadworth 34 SK 5697
Waen Fach 31 SJ 2017
Wainfleet All Saints 35 TF 4959
Wainfleet Bank 35 TF 4759
Wainhouse Corner 4 SX 1895
Wainscott 12 TQ 7471
Wainstalls 37 SE 0428
Waitby 41 NY 7507
Wakefield 38 SE 3320
Wakerley 27 SP 9599
Wakes Colne 21 TL 8928
Walberswick 29 TM 4974
Walberton 11 SU 9705
Walcot (Lincs.) 35 TF 0535
Walcot (Lincs.) 35 TF 1256
Walcot (Salop) 24 SJ 5912
Walcot (Salop) 23 SO 3485
Walcott (Warw.) 25 SP 1258
Walcote 26 SP 5683
Walcott (Norf.) 29 TG 3632
Walden 41 SE 0082
Walden Head 41 SD 9880
Walden Stubbs 38 SE 5516
Walderslade 12 TQ 7563
Walderton 10 SU 7910
Walditch 7 SY 4892
Waldridge 47 NZ 2549
Waldringfield 21 TM 2744
Waldron 12 TQ 5419
Wales 34 SK 4782
Walesby (Lincs.) 35 TF 1392
Walesby (Notts.) 34 SK 6870
Walford (Here. and Worc.) 24 SO 3872
Walford (Here. and Worc.) 17 SO 5820
Walford (Salop) 32 SJ 4320
Walgherton 32 SJ 6948
Walgrave 26 SP 8071
Walkden 36 SD 7303
Walker 47 NZ 2864
Walkerburn 51 NT 3637
Walker Ford 36 SD 6742
Walkeringham 34 SK 7692
Walkerith 34 SK 7892
Walkern 19 TL 2926
Walker's Green 24 SO 5248
Walkerton 56 NO 2301
Walkhampton 4 SX 5369
Walkington 39 SE 9936
Walk Mill 37 SD 8629
Wall (Northum.) 47 NY 9168
Wall (Staffs.) 25 SK 0906
Wallacetown 49 NS 3422
Wallasey 31 SJ 2992
Wall Bank 24 SO 5092
Wallend 13 TQ 8775
Walling Fen 39 SE 8829
Wallingford 18 SU 6089
Wallington (Gtr London) 11 TQ 2863
Wallington (Hants.) 9 SU 5806
Wallington (Herts.) 19 TL 2933
Wallis 14 SN 0125
Walliswood 11 TQ 1138
Walls 63 HU 2449
Wallsend 47 NZ 2766
Wallyford 51 NT 3671
Walmer 13 TR 3750
Walmer Bridge 36 SD 4724
Walmersley 37 SD 8013
Walmley 25 SP 1393
Walpole 29 TM 3674
Walpole Highway 28 TF 5113
Walpole St. Andrew 28 TF 5017
Walpole St. Peter 28 TF 5016
Walsall 25 SP 0198
Walsall Wood 25 SK 0403
Walsden 37 SD 9322
Walsgrave on Sowe 26 SP 3781
Walsham le Willows 29 TM 0071
Walsoken 28 TF 4710
Walston 51 NT 0545
Walterstone 16 SO 3425
Waltham (Humbs.) 39 TA 2503
Waltham (Kent) 13 TR 1148
Waltham Abbey 20 TL 3800
Waltham Chase 9 SU 5614
Waltham on the Wolds 34 SK 8025
Waltham St. Lawrence 10 SU 8276
Walthamstow 20 TQ 3788
Walton (Bucks.) 27 SP 8936
Walton (Cumbr.) 46 NY 5264
Walton (Derby.) 33 SK 3569
Walton (Leic.) 26 SP 5987
Walton (Powys) 23 SO 2559
Walton (Salop) 32 SJ 5818
Walton (Somer.) 7 ST 4636
Walton (Suff.) 21 TM 2935
Walton (Warw.) 26 SP 2853
Walton (W Yorks.) 38 SE 3516
Walton (W Yorks.) 38 SE 4447
Walton Cardiff 25 SO 9032
Walton East 14 SN 0123
Walton-in-Gordano 16 ST 4273
Walton-le-Dale 36 SD 5627
Walton-on-Thames 11 TQ 1066
Walton-on-the-Hill (Staffs.) 33 SJ 9520
Walton on the Hill (Surrey) 11 TQ 2255
Walton on the Naze 21 TM 2521
Walton on the Wolds 34 SK 5919
Walton-on-Trent 33 SK 2118
Walton West 14 SM 8713
Walworth 42 NZ 2218
Walwyn's Castle 14 SM 8711
Wambrook 7 ST 2907
Wanborough 18 SU 2082
Wandsworth 11 TQ 2673
Wangford 29 TM 4679
Wanlip 26 SK 5910
Wanlockhead 50 NS 8712
Wansford (Cambs.) 27 TL 0799
Wansford (Humbs.) 39 TA 0656
Wanstead 20 TQ 4087
Wanstow 8 ST 7141
Wanswell 17 SO 6801
Wantage 18 SU 4087
Wapley 17 ST 7179
Wappenbury 26 SP 3769
Wappenham 26 SP 6245
Warbleton 12 TQ 6018
Warborough 18 SU 6093
Warboys 27 TL 3080
Warbstow 4 SX 2090
Warburton 32 SJ 7089
Warcop 41 NY 7415
Warden 13 TR 0271
Ward Green 29 TM 0564
Wardington 26 SP 4946
Wardlaw Hill 50 NS 6822
Wardle (Ches.) 32 SJ 6057
Wardle (Gtr Mches.) 37 SD 9116
Wardley 27 SK 8300
Wardlow 33 SK 1874
Wardy Hill 28 TL 4782
Ware 20 TL 3614
Wareham 8 SY 9287
Warehorne 13 TQ 9832
Warenford 53 NU 1328
Waren Mill 53 NU 1534
Warenton 53 NU 1030
Wareside 20 TL 3915
Waresley 27 TL 2454
Warfield 11 SU 8872
Wargrave 10 SU 7878
Warham All Saints 29 TF 9441
Warham St. Mary 29 TF 9441
Wark (Northum.) 53 NT 8238
Wark (Northum.) 47 NY 8576
Warkleigh 6 SS 6422
Warkton 27 SP 8980
Warkworth 47 NU 2406
Warlaby 42 SE 3591
Warland 37 SD 9419
Warleggan 4 SX 1569
Warley 25 SP 0086
Warlingham 12 TQ 3658
Warmfield 38 SE 3720
Warmingham 32 SJ 7161
Warmington (Northants.) 27 TL 0791
Warmington (Warw.) 26 SP 4147
Warminster 8 ST 8644
Warmsworth 38 SE 5400
Warmwell 8 SY 7585
Warndon 25 SO 8856
Warnford 9 SU 6223
Warnham 11 TQ 1633
Warninglid 11 TQ 2526
Warren (Ches.) 33 SJ 8870
Warren (Dyfed) 14 SR 9397
Warren Row 18 SU 8180
Warren Street 13 TQ 9253
Warrington (Bucks.) 27 SP 8954
Warrington (Ches.) 32 SJ 6088
Warsash 9 SU 4905
Warslow 33 SK 0858
Warsop 34 SK 5667
Warter 39 SE 8750
Warthill 38 SE 6755
Wartling 12 TQ 6509
Wartnaby 34 SK 7123
Warton (Lancs.) 36 SD 4028
Warton (Lancs.) 40 SD 4972
Warton (Northum.) 47 NU 0002
Warton (Warw.) 26 SK 2803
Warwick (Cumbr.) 46 NY 4656
Warwick (Warw.) 26 SP 2865
Warwick Bridge 46 NY 4756
Wasbister 63 HY 3932
Washaway 3 SX 0369
Washbourne 5 SX 7954
Washfield 5 SS 9315
Washfold 41 NZ 0502
Washford 7 ST 0441
Washford Pyne 5 SS 8111
Washingborough 34 TF 0170
Washington (Tyne and Wear) 47 NZ 3356
Washington (W Susx) 11 TQ 1212
Wasing 10 SU 5764
Waskerley 47 NZ 0545
Wasperton 26 SP 2659
Wass 42 SE 5579
Watchet 7 ST 0743
Watchfield (Oxon.) 18 SU 2490
Watchfield (Somer.) 7 ST 3446
Watchgate 40 SD 5399
Water 37 SD 8425
Waterbeach 28 TL 4965
Waterbeck 46 NY 2477
Waterden 28 TF 8835
Water End (Herts.) 19 TL 0310
Water End (Herts.) 19 TL 2304
Waterfall 33 SK 0851
Waterfoot (Lancs.) 37 SD 8321
Waterfoot (Strath.) 50 NS 5654
Waterford 20 TL 3114
Waterhead (Cumbr.) 40 NY 3703
Waterhead (Strath.) 50 NS 5411
Waterheads 51 NT 2451
Waterhouses (Durham) 47 NZ 1841
Waterhouses (Staffs.) 33 SK 0850
Wateringbury 12 TQ 6853
Wateringhouse 63 ND 3090
Waterloo (Dorset) 8 SZ 0194
Waterloo (Mers.) 36 SJ 3297
Waterloo (Norf.) 29 TG 2219
Waterloo (Strath.) 50 NS 8153
Waterloo (Tays.) 56 NO 0636
Waterlooville 9 SU 6809
Water Meetings 51 NS 9513
Watermillock 40 NY 4322
Water Newton 27 TL 1097
Water Orton 25 SP 1791
Waterperry 18 SP 6206
Waterrow 7 ST 0525
Watersfield 11 TQ 0115
Waterside (Strath.) 50 NS 4308
Waterside (Strath.) 50 NS 4843
Waterside (Strath.) 50 NS 5160
Waterside (Strath.) 50 NS 6773
Waterstock 18 SP 6305
Waterston 14 SM 9306
Water Stratford 18 SP 6534
Waters Upton 32 SJ 6319
Water Yeat 40 SD 2889
Watford (Herts.) 19 TQ 1196
Watford (Northants.) 26 SP 6069
Wath (N Yorks.) 37 SE 1467
Wath (N Yorks.) 42 SE 3277
Wath Upon Dearne 38 SE 4300
Watlington (Norf.) 28 TF 6211
Watlington (Oxon.) 18 SU 6994
Watnall Chaworth 34 SK 4946
Watten 67 ND 2454
Wattisfield 29 TM 0174
Wattisham 21 TM 0151
Watton (Humbs.) 39 TA 0150
Watton (Norf.) 28 TF 9100
Watton-at-Stone 20 TL 3019
Wattston 50 NS 7770
Wattstown 15 ST 0194
Waunarlwydd 15 SS 6095
Waunfawr 30 SH 5259
Wavendon 19 SP 9137
Waverton (Ches.) 32 SJ 4663
Waverton (Cumbr.) 46 NY 2247
Wawne 39 TA 0836
Waxham 29 TG 4326
Waxholme 39 TA 3229
Wayford 7 ST 4006
Way Village 5 SS 8810
Wealdstone 19 TQ 1689
Weare 16 ST 4152
Weare Giffard 6 SS 4721
Weasenham All Saints 28 TF 8421
Weasenham St. Peter 28 TF 8522
Weaverham 32 SJ 6173
Weaverthorpe 39 SE 9670
Webheath 25 SP 0266
Weddington 26 SP 3693
Wedhampton 17 SU 0557
Wedmore 7 ST 4347
Wednesbury 25 SP 0095
Wednesfield 25 SJ 9400
Weedon 18 SP 8118
Weedon Bec 26 SP 6259
Weedon Lois 26 SP 6047
Weeford 25 SK 1404
Week 5 SS 7316
Weekley 27 SP 8880
Week St. Mary 4 SX 2397
Weeley 21 TM 1422
Weeley Heath 21 TM 1520
Weem 56 NN 8449
Weeping Cross 33 SJ 9421
Weeting 28 TL 7788
Weeton (Lancs.) 36 SD 3834
Weeton (W Yorks.) 38 SE 2846
Weir 37 SD 8724
Welbeck Colliery Village 34 SK 5869
Welborne 29 TG 0610
Welbourn 34 SK 9654
Welburn 38 SE 7168
Welbury 42 NZ 3902
Welby 34 SK 9738
Welches Dam 28 TL 4786
Welcombe 4 SS 2218
Weldon 27 SP 9289
Welford (Berks.) 10 SU 4073
Welford (Northants.) 26 SP 6480
Welford-on-Avon 25 SP 1552
Welham 26 SP 7692
Welham Green 19 TL 2305
Well (Hants.) 10 SU 7646
Well (Lincs.) 35 TF 4473
Well (N Yorks.) 42 SE 2682
Welland 24 SO 7940
Wellesbourne Hastings 26 SP 2856
Wellesbourne Mountford 26 SP 2756
Well Hill (Kent) 12 TQ 4963
Welling 12 TQ 4575
Wellingborough 27 SP 8968
Wellingham 28 TF 8722
Wellingore 34 SK 9856
Wellington (Here. and Worc.) 24 SO 4948
Wellington (Salop) 24 SJ 6411
Wellington (Somer.) 7 ST 1320
Wellington Heath 24 SO 7140
Wellow (Avon) 17 ST 7358
Wellow (I. of W.) 9 SZ 3887
Wellow (Notts.) 34 SK 6666
Wells 7 ST 5445
Wellsborough 26 SK 3602
Wells-Next-The-Sea 28 TF 9143
Wells of Ythan 62 NJ 6338
Wellwood 51 NT 0888
Welney 28 TL 5294
Welshampton 32 SJ 4334
Welsh Bicknor 17 SO 5917
Welsh End 32 SJ 5035
Welsh Frankton 32 SJ 3633
Welsh Hook 14 SM 9327
Welsh Newton 16 SO 4918
Welshpool (Trallwng) 23 SJ 2207
Welsh St. Donats 16 ST 0276
Welton (Cumbr.) 46 NY 3544
Welton (Humbs.) 39 SE 9527
Welton (Lincs.) 34 TF 0079
Welton (Northants.) 26 SP 5865
Welton le Marsh 35 TF 4768
Welton le Wold 35 TF 2787
Welwick 39 TA 3421
Welwyn 19 TL 2316
Welwyn Garden City 19 TL 2412
Wem 32 SJ 5129
Wembdon 7 ST 2837
Wembley 19 TQ 1985
Wembury 4 SX 5148
Wembworthy 5 SS 6609
Wemyss Bay 49 NS 1869
Wenallt 31 SH 9842
Wendens Ambo 20 TL 5136
Wendlebury 18 SP 5519
Wendling 29 TF 9213
Wendover 19 SP 8708
Wendron 2 SW 6731
Wendy 20 TL 3247
Wenhaston 29 TM 4275
Wennington (Cambs.) 27 TL 2379
Wennington (Essex) 20 TQ 5381
Wennington (Lancs.) 36 SD 6169
Wensley (Derby.) 33 SK 2661
Wensley (N Yorks.) 41 SE 0989
Wentbridge 38 SE 4817
Wentnor 24 SO 3892
Wentworth (Cambs.) 28 TL 4878
Wentworth (S Yorks.) 38 SK 3898
Wenvoe 16 ST 1272
Weobley 24 SO 4051
Weobley Marsh 24 SO 4151
Wereham 28 TF 6801
Wergs 25 SJ 8601
Wernrheolydd 16 SO 3913
Werrington (Cambs.) 27 TF 1703
Werrington (Devon) 4 SX 3287
Werrington (Staffs.) 33 SJ 9647
Wervin 32 SJ 4171
Wesham 36 SD 4132
Wessington 33 SK 3757
West Acre 28 TF 7715
West Allerdean 53 NT 9646
West Alvington 5 SX 7243
West Anstey 6 SS 8527
West Ashby 35 TF 2672
West Ashling 10 SU 8007
West Ashton 17 ST 8755
West Auckland 42 NZ 1826
West Bagborough 7 ST 1633
West Barns 52 NT 6578
West Barsham 28 TF 9033
West Bay (Dorset) 7 SY 4690
West Beckham 29 TG 1339
Westbere 13 TR 1961
West Bergholt 21 TL 9527
West Bexington 7 SY 5386
West Bilney 28 TF 7115
West Blatchington 11 TQ 2706
Westbourne (Dorset) 8 SZ 0690
Westbourne (W Susx) 10 SU 7507
West Bradenham 29 TF 9209
West Bradford 36 SD 7444
West Bradley 7 ST 5536
West Bretton 38 SE 2813
West Bridgford 34 SK 5837
West Bromwich 25 SP 0091
West Buckland (Devon.) 6 SS 6510
West Buckland (Somer.) 7 ST 1720
West Burrafirth 63 HU 2557
West Burton (N Yorks.) 41 SE 0186
West Burton (W Susx) 11 TQ 0014
Westbury (Bucks.) 18 SP 6235
Westbury (Salop) 24 SJ 3509
Westbury (Wilts.) 8 ST 8751
Westbury Leigh 8 ST 8649
Westbury-on-Severn 17 SO 7114
Westbury-sub-Mendip 7 ST 5049
Westby 36 SD 3731
West Caister 29 TG 5011
West Calder 51 NT 0163
West Camel 7 ST 5724
West Challow 18 SU 3688
West Charleton 5 SX 7542
West Chelborough 7 ST 5405
West Chevington 47 NZ 2297
West Chiltington 11 TQ 0918
West Clandon 11 TQ 0452
West Cliffe 13 TR 3445
Westcliff-on-Sea 21 TQ 8685
West Coker 7 ST 5113
Westcombe 8 ST 6739
West Compton (Dorset) 7 SY 5694
West Compton (Somer.) 8 ST 5942
Westcote 18 SP 2120
Westcott (Bucks.) 18 SP 7117
Westcott (Devon.) 7 ST 0104
Westcott (Surrey) 11 TQ 1348
Westcott Barton 18 SP 4224
West Cross 15 SS 6189
West Curry 4 SX 2893
West Curthwaite 46 NY 3248
Westdean (E Susx) 12 TV 5299
West Dean (Wilts.) 9 SU 2526
West Dean (W Susx) 10 SU 8512
West Deeping 27 TF 1009
West Derby 32 SJ 3993
West Dereham 28 TF 6500
West Ditchburn 53 NU 1320
West Down (Devon.) 6 SS 5142
West Down (Wilts.) 8 SU 0548
West Drayton (Gtr London) 11 TQ 0679
West Drayton (Notts.) 34 SK 7074
West End (Avon) 16 ST 4469
West End (Beds.) 27 SP 9853
West End (Hants.) 9 SU 4614
West End (Herts.) 20 TL 3306
West End (Norf.) 29 TG 4911
West End (N Yorks.) 37 SE 1457
West End (Oxon.) 18 SP 4204
West End (Surrey) 11 SU 9461
West End Green 10 SU 6661
Wester Clynekirton 67 NC 8906
Wester Culbeuchly Crofts 62 NJ 6562
Westerdale (Highld.) 67 ND 1251
Westerdale (N Yorks.) 42 NZ 6605
Westerdale Moor 42 NZ 6502
Wester Denoon 57 NO 3543
Westerfield (Shetld.) 63 HU 3551
Westerfield (Suff.) 21 TM 1747
Wester Fintray 62 NJ 8116
Westergate 11 SU 9305
Wester Gruinards 65 NH 5292
Westerham 12 TQ 4454
Westerleigh 17 ST 6979
Wester Lonvine 65 NH 7172
Wester Skeld 63 HU 2943
Wester Teaninich 65 NH 6267
Westerton 57 NO 6654
Wester Wick 63 HU 2842
West Farleigh 12 TQ 7152